THE BRONX

THE COLUMBIA HISTORY OF URBAN LIFE

THE COLUMBIA HISTORY OF URBAN LIFE

Kenneth T. Jackson, General Editor

Deborah Dash Moore, *At Home in America: Second Generation New York Jews* 1981

Edward K. Spann, *The New Metropolis: New York City, 1840–1857* 1981

Matthew Edel, Elliott D. Sclar, and Daniel Luria, *Shaky Palaces: Homeownership and Social Mobility in Boston's Suburbanization* 1984

Steven J. Ross, *Workers on the Edge: Work, Leisure, and Politics in Industrializing Cincinnati, 1788–1890* 1985

Andrew Lees, *Cities Perceived: Urban Society in European and American Thought, 1820–1940* 1985

R. J. R. Kirkby, *Urbanization in China: Town and Country in a Developing Economy, 1949–2000 A.D.* 1985

Judith Ann Trolander, *Professionalism and Social Change: From the Settlement House Movement to Neighborhood Centers, 1886 to the Present* 1987

Marc A. Weiss, *The Rise of the Community Builders: The American Real Estate Industry and Urban Land Planning* 1987

Jacqueline Leavitt and Susan Saegert, *From Abandonment to Hope: Community-Households in Harlem* 1990

Richard Plunz, *A History of Housing in New York City: Dwelling Type and Social Change in the American Metropolis* 1990

David Hamer, *New Towns in the New World: Images and Perceptions of the Nineteenth-Century Urban Frontier* 1990

Andrew Heinze, *Adapting to Abundance: Jewish Immigrants, Mass Consumption, and the Search for American Identity* 1990

Chris McNickle, *To Be Mayor of New York: Ethnic Politics in the City* 1993

Clay McShane, *Down the Asphalt Path: The Automobile and the American City* 1994

Clarence Taylor, *The Black Churches of Brooklyn* 1994

Frederick Binder and David Reimers, *"All the Nations Under Heaven": A Racial and Ethnic History of New York City* 1995

Clarence Taylor, *Knocking at Our Own Door: Milton A. Galamison and the Struggle to Integrate New York City Schools* 1997

Andrew S. Dolkart, *Morningside Heights: A History of Its Architecture and Development* 1998

Craig Steven Wilder, *A Covenant with Color: Race and Social Power in Brooklyn* 2000

A. Scott Henderson, *Housing and the Democratic Ideal* 2000

François Weil, *History of New York* 2004

THE
BRONX

EVELYN GONZALEZ

COLUMBIA UNIVERSITY PRESS
NEW YORK

COLUMBIA UNIVERSITY PRESS

Publishers Since 1893

New York   Chichester, West Sussex

Copyright © 2004 Columbia University Press

All rights reserved

Library of Congress Cataloging-in-Publication Data

Gonzalez, Evelyn Diaz.

   The Bronx / Evelyn Gonzalez.

     p. cm.

   Includes bibliographical references (p.) and index.

   ISBN 0–231–12114–8 (cloth)

    1. Bronx (New York, N.Y.)—History. 2. Bronx (New York, N.Y.)—Social conditions. 3. New York (N.Y.)—History. 4. New York (N.Y.)—Social conditions. 5. City and town life—New York (State)—New York—History. 6. Social problems—New York (State)—New York—History. I. Title. II. Series.

F128.68.B8G66   2004

974.7'275—dc21

                                      2003055206

Columbia University Press books are printed on permanent and durable acid-free paper.

Printed in the United States of America

c 10 9 8 7 6 5 4 3 2 1

Designed by Lisa Hamm

To Pedro and Douglas

CONTENTS

LIST OF MAPS

LIST OF TABLES

ACKNOWLEDGMENTS

*This work would not have been possible without
my mentor, Dr. Kenneth T. Jackson. It was he
who suggested I write a dissertation on the Bronx
and made sure I finished it. Years afterward, he
urged me to enlarge the scope of the study and
again pushed me to complete the manuscript. I
am grateful beyond words. I also want to thank
Dr. Michael Ebner, who introduced me to urban
history, and Dr. Joel Schwartz, whose dissertation on Morrisania paved the way for my research. Two others deserve special mention:
Leonora Gidlund, deputy director of the New
York City Municipal Archives and a close friend,
was always there with encouragement and cheer;
and Dr. Isabel Tirado, dean of the College of
Humanities and Social Sciences at William Pa-
terson University of New Jersey and also a
friend, drove me on constantly. I also want to ac-
knowledge the help of countless archivists and li-
brarians, from my friend Director Kenneth Cobb
of the New York City Municipal Archives to
Laura Tosi and Peter Derrick of the Bronx
County Historical Society.*

THE BRONX

THE BRONX AND
ITS NEIGHBORHOODS

INTRODUCTION

The home of the Yankees, the Bronx Zoo, and the Cross-Bronx Express-way, the Bronx is New York City's northernmost borough (see map 1.1). It was once known for Fort Apache—the police precinct immortalized on film—and Charlotte Street—the place where Presidents Carter and Reagan saw what urban decay really was. During the 1960s and 1970s, the Bronx became a national symbol of urban deterioration. Neighborhoods that had held generations of Bronx families disappeared under waves of arson, crime, and housing abandonment, with solid blocks of brick apartment buildings turning into rubble-filled empty acres. The Bronx is also known for racial change and white flight. The South Bronx, in particular, went from being two-thirds white in 1950 to two-thirds African American and Hispanic by 1960. Forty years later, by 2000, the entire borough was almost all of black and Spanish-speaking ancestry.[1]

While the image of poverty and decay still lingers, the borough has undergone an "astonishing recovery" and a "tremendous community revival." In recognition, the National Civic League gave the Bronx its "All-America City" award in 1997. Getting this award "is literally man bites dog," said Bronx Borough President Fernando Ferrer. "Over a decade ago, the Bronx was everybody's idea of urban failure. Now it's a national example of what you can do to revive cities."[2]

There is more to the Bronx than just its decline and resurgence. The borough has a long history of urban development, neighborhood change, and population movements, all key elements in the devastation and subsequent revival that occurred. This study contends that the very process of urban growth and community creation, within which space and structures were commodities for sale and profit as well as accommodations for waves of different ethnic and racial groups and classes, engendered the conditions

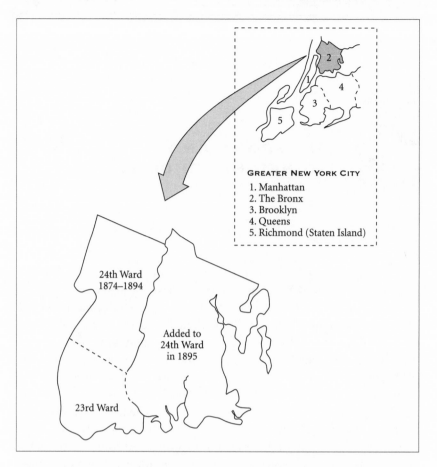

GREATER NEW YORK CITY
1. Manhattan
2. The Bronx
3. Brooklyn
4. Queens
5. Richmond (Staten Island)

24th Ward 1874–1894

Added to 24th Ward in 1895

23rd Ward

MAP 1.1 The Borough of the Bronx with Former Ward Boundaries, 1874–1897

that resulted in the extreme neighborhood deterioration of the borough. The urban crisis of the Bronx was not just a race and crime problem as it was usually portrayed in the media; nor was it just the discrimination and residential segregation of a racist society; nor was it even the result of postwar liberalism and big government.[3] Instead, the devastation of the Bronx was influenced by the economic transactions, political decisions, and human choices that created the city and its ethnic and racial neighborhoods in the first place and then continuously re-created them. Different forces were at the fore in each particular time, of course, but these are better understood when examined against the backdrop of the ever-changing city—what Roy Lubove called "the process of city-building over time."[4]

The following chapters outline and analyze this urbanization from the 1840s to the present. The first chapter provides an overview of the Bronx and its early history, along with an explanation of urban growth and neighborhood change. Subsequent chapters alternate between those covering the development of the whole borough and those dealing with the growth of the South Bronx neighborhoods from which the entire Bronx eventually grew. The last two chapters overlap chronologically for purposes of clarity. Chapter 7 covers from the late 1940s to the early 1980s and discusses the decline of the South Bronx and the spread of its decay and its name to other parts of the borough. Chapter 8 examines the revitalization efforts from the 1970s until the present and contains a summary and evaluation of the whole book.

A note on sources is in order. I have read everything I could find on the Bronx. But for each stage of the borough's history, I have gathered local information by scrutinizing one particular source. Chapters 1 and 2 benefited greatly from the information and sources found in Joel Schwartz's Ph.D. dissertation on early Morrisania, the village from which the Bronx developed. Chapters 3, 4, and 5, on the other hand, were based on the weekly *Real Estate Record and Builders' Guide* from 1872 to 1916, which detailed how the urban infrastructure of the Bronx was created. Similarly, for chapters 4 and 5, I scanned the weekly issues of the *Bronx Home News* from 1907 until 1915 when it became a daily newspaper. Its columns on politics and community events showed that new streets and apartments had indeed become neighborhoods. Gaps in chapters 4, 5, and 6 were filled with information from the Community Service Society Papers and the Lillian Wald Papers. Both collections contain folders and clipping files on tenements, communities, and social conditions in the city and the borough from 1900 to the early 1930s. For the postwar years in chapter 7, I relied heavily on the papers of Mayor Robert F. Wagner, who was in city government from the late 1940s and mayor from 1954 to 1965. His records have voluminous files on housing, urban renewal, juvenile delinquency, integration efforts, and Puerto Ricans. Finally, *The New York Times* was especially helpful for chapters 7 and 8. A thorough reading of its index from 1960 to 1980 revealed the beginning and spread of poverty, crime, arson, and abandonment long before these problems were noticed or even addressed by city officials.

THE BRONX

The Bronx is separated from Manhattan Island by the Harlem River, and divided by the Bronx River. When it began to be settled in the 1840s, the Bronx was part of Westchester County. The portion west of the Bronx River—the towns of Morrisania, West Farms, and Kingsbridge—was annexed in 1874 and became the Twenty-third and Twenty-fourth wards of New York City. In 1895, the portion east of the Bronx River—the town of Westchester and parts of the towns of Eastchester and Pelham, the rest of what is now the Bronx—was added to the Twenty-fourth Ward. Both halves became the Borough of the Bronx when Queens, Brooklyn, and Staten Island were consolidated into Greater New York City in 1898. In 1914, after having been part of New York County for forty years, the Bronx became a separate county, on a par with the other boroughs.[5]

The southern part was a manor known as Morrisania. In 1790, Lewis Morris—a signer of the Declaration of Independence and the owner of

TABLE 1.1 Population of the Bronx, 1890–2000

Year	Population	Percent of Population West of Bronx River
1890	88,908[a]	—
1900	200,507	89%
1905	271,630	89
1910	430,980	89
1915	615,600	91
1920	732,016	91
1925	872,168	87
1930	1,265,258	79
1940	1,394,711	77
1950	1,451,277	73
1960	1,424,815	70
1970	1,471,701	67
1980	1,168,972	58
1990	1,203,789	60
2000	1,332,650	60

[a] Includes only the population west of the Bronx River.

Source: Walter Laidlaw, *Population of The City of New York, 1890–1930*, 51, 54–56; U.S. Bureau of the Census, *Census Tract Data on Population and Housing, New York City: 1940* (New York City, September 1942), 5; Ira Rosenwaike, *Population History of New York City* (Syracuse, NY: Syracuse University Press, 1972), 133; U.S.Bureau of the Census, *United States Census of the Population: 1950, New York, New York* (Washington, DC, 1952); U.S. Bureau of the Census, *U.S. Census of Population and Housing: 1960* (Washington, DC, 1962); U.S. Bureau of the Census, *1970 Census of Population and Housing, New York* (Washington, DC, 1971); U.S. Bureau of the Census, *1980 Census of Population and Housing, New York, N.Y.* (Washington, DC, August 1983); New York City Department of City Planning, *1990 Census* (New York, March 25, 1991); New York City Department of City Planning, *Citywide and Borough Population, 1990 & 2000*; New York City government Web site, www.nyc.gov/html/dcp.

Morrisania—proposed his property as the site of the future capital of the United States.[6] A year later, Morrisania remained the agricultural hinterland for the still small city of New York just eight miles to the south, as the Morris family continued growing vegetables on the open fields away from the manor house until the 1840s when suburban villages began to develop. The area retained its bucolic image until the late nineteenth century. Indeed, as late as 1905, Borough President Louis F. Haffen could describe the borough as "only on the frontier of a Greater Bronx when our population will be counted by millions, and when the seat of municipal power and wealth will be located north of the Harlem River." Haffen concluded that the Bronx was to be "the most contented and the most progressive borough of the greatest city in the world."[7]

After 1890, the Bronx became a haven for tens of thousands of second-generation immigrants seeking to leave the crowded tenements of East Harlem and the Lower East Side. Connected to Manhattan by inexpensive rapid transit, its population rose to well over a million people by 1930 (see table 1.1). Between 1880 and 1930, it was one of the fastest growing urban areas in the world.[8] Its civic and political leaders boosted the Bronx as the "banner home ward of the city" and the "Wonder Borough" of homes, parks, and universities, and denied there were any slums.[9] The Bronx became famous for its stable ethnic neighborhoods and housing units that on average were better than those of Brooklyn and Manhattan. Indeed, Bronx apartment buildings typically epitomized the latest in modern urban living, and often featured elevators, sunken living rooms, and liveried doormen.[10]

This positive view of the Bronx eroded by 1960. Population shifts, racial change, housing deterioration, and residents' search for better housing were exacerbated by housing shortages, suburbanization, erection of public housing and Mitchell-Lama co-ops, and a changing economy. In addition, federal highway construction and urban renewal programs coincided with an outbreak of drug-related street crime, leading to abandoned and burned buildings and white flight.[11] Most assessments of the devastation of the 1960s and 1970s emphasize race, crime, poverty, the Cross-Bronx Expressway, and Co-op City and ignore a century of urban growth in the Bronx.[12] Yet it is this ongoing urbanization and neighborhood change that helps explain the devastation and consequent revival that occurred.

One factor in the post–World War II decline of the area was the density of the population. Beginning as a suburban retreat, the Bronx soon reached residential density levels that approached Manhattan's. Throughout the twentieth century, in fact, the Bronx had the highest population densities of any predominantly residential area in the United States, with street plans, transit lines, construction patterns, and buildings that allowed for indiscriminate crowding.[13] As late as 1930, 80 percent of its residents lived west of the Bronx River (see table 1.1). Ten years later, this area still held three quarters of the population as "closely built 5 and 6 story walk-ups and newer elevator apartments . . . line[d] many miles of the Bronx streets."[14]

The Bronx soon had the most multifamily dwellings and the fewest owner-occupied homes of any city or county in America, except Manhattan. The result was a collection of crowded, contiguous ethnic neighborhoods that allowed for an intense street life—memories of which accounted for much nostalgia, but which discouraged residents from remaining when they earned more.[15] By 1940, the oldest and most concentrated Bronx communities were no longer adequate in quality for middle-class families. By the late 1940s, therefore, the Bronx was the only place in which the city's latest wave of migrants could settle.

Neighborhoods

The Bronx is a collection of neighborhoods. Formed by the interrelation between social and physical factors, neighborhoods are physically delimited social areas in which residents can associate with each other in a neighborly way.[16] The image or reputation of a neighborhood influences movement into or out of the area and thus stimulates or detracts from the area's viability. Hence, a neighborhood can go quickly from desirable to unattractive.[17] A neighborhood also interacts with the larger urban area to which it belongs. Since the second quarter of the nineteenth century, cities have been spreading outward because of population pressure, economic growth, and the separation of home and work. Typically, land values rose as competition for space in accessible sections increased. As commercial enterprises expanded, the space available for homes decreased and caused overcrowding. Meanwhile, transportation innovations allowed better-off residents to move to newer neighborhoods on the periphery. This stimulated capital investment—as people speculated in property, built housing, and provided goods and services to investors and new residents alike—and led to "a constant movement of people, jobs, and capital."[18]

The resulting spatial rearrangement is usually explained with models of widening concentric rings and outward-spreading wedges, having enclosed clusters or sectors. What emerges is a pattern of class-segregated neighborhoods predicated on the interplay between land values and the individual's ability to pay and complicated by locational preferences or restrictions based on age, family, race, and ethnicity. Those with young children predominate in the outer, less dense zones; older people remain in the inner, more convenient sections; and certain racial and ethnic groups cluster together irrespective of class or life cycle stage. All, however, try to get the best housing they can afford.[19]

This process is often called neighborhood succession. As cities grow, their physical extent and internal configurations change. Within this model, neighborhoods pass through distinct stages, evolving from vacant land to buildings to obsolescence to, perhaps, urban renewal or gentrification.[20] Residential mobility occurs because of stage in life cycle, status improvement, population invasion and succession, and encroaching business or industrial land use. As residents move on to other areas, the same housing stock is utilized by subsequent waves of newcomers, usually of lower socioeconomic status. When demand slackens, buildings are abandoned or demolished and the neighborhood ceases to be viable. This neighborhood transition is not inevitable and can be altered by residents, property owners, investors, or public officials. But in the past, it has been engendered and reinforced by rapid city growth and population pressure, real estate practices and new neighborhood construction, ethnic and racial preferences or segregation, status and mobility concerns, and a rising standard of living.[21]

The neighborhoods from which the Bronx originally grew were Mott Haven, Melrose, Morrisania, Claremont, Hunts Point, and Crotona Park East (see map 1.2), all north and west of the Harlem and Bronx rivers in that portion annexed in 1874, specifically in the former towns of Morrisania and West Farms. These neighborhoods were nearest to midtown Manhattan and the first to receive rapid transit connections. Old and densely settled, they were the first sections of the borough to become blighted. By the 1930s Melrose and the southeastern parts of Morrisania were occasionally lumped together with Mott Haven as the South or Lower Bronx.[22] During the twenties and thirties, as the new, higher-rent areas that arose near the Grand Concourse came to be called the "West Bronx," the rest of the neighborhoods—Morrisania, Claremont, Crotona Park East, and Hunts Point— were often collectively referred to as the "East Bronx," though the real East Bronx was east of the Bronx River. Distinctions disappeared by the 1970s, when the tide of destruction enveloped the old "South," "East," and "West" Bronx sections, reaching up to Fordham Road, the current northern border of the South Bronx.[23]

Neighborhood boundaries were often imprecise. Mott Haven and Melrose had clearly defined geographic and historical borders, but those of Morrisania, Claremont, and Hunts Point were fuzzy, sometimes encompassing adjacent subareas, at times shrinking away from newer neighbor-

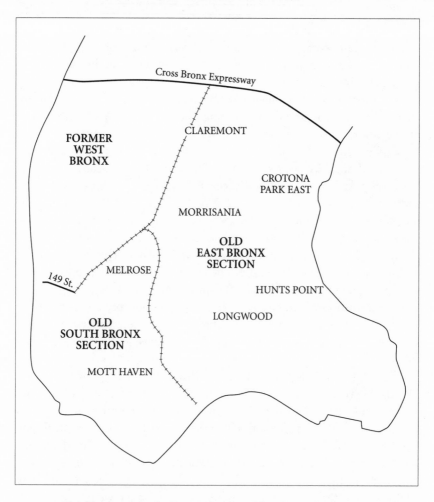

MAP 1.2 Neighborhoods in the Former South and East Bronx Sections, 1950

hoods. The streets east of Prospect Avenue were alternately ascribed to Morrisania, Hunts Point, Crotona Park East, and, during the early period of development, West Farms. Some of this confusion was due to topography and transit connections, but residents and realtors often worsened matters. While the old village names remained in property owners' associations, churches, and social clubs, residents referred to their localities by street names or as just "the Bronx."[24] One lived on Fox Street or Claremont Parkway, near St. Mary's or Crotona parks, or in the Bronx. Occasionally, builders labeled new subdivisions with the name of the developer, the former landowner, or again a nearby street, making designations such as "the

A-RE-CO district" or "the Longwood section" commonplace. In the 1960s city agencies muddied the issue further by arbitrarily outlining city planning areas and Community Districts. The one name that spread along with its borders was the "South Bronx."[25]

The Early Bronx

Until 1846, the region across the Harlem River contained the four towns of Westchester, Yonkers, Eastchester, and Pelham, the first completely within the borders of the present-day Bronx, the others stretching into Westchester County proper (see map 1.3). At the time, the future Bronx area had fewer than 9,000 residents (see table 1.2). Most of Yonkers never joined New York City and neither did much of Eastchester and Pelham. Meanwhile, lower Westchester County was dotted with farms, manor houses, and estates, with one or two hamlets strung along the roads connecting the city to Albany and Boston. The only industrial sites were the small mill village of West Farms on the Bronx River and the newly installed Mott Iron Works at the county's southern tip.[26]

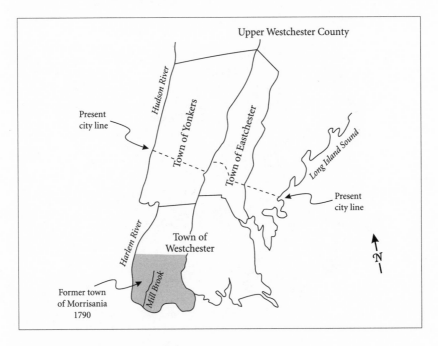

MAP 1.3 Towns in Lower Westchester County, 1840

TABLE 1.2 Population of Southern Westchester, 1840

Town	Population
Westchester	4,154
Yonkers	2,968
Eastchester	1,502
Pelham	789

Source: New York State, Census for 1865, xl–xli.

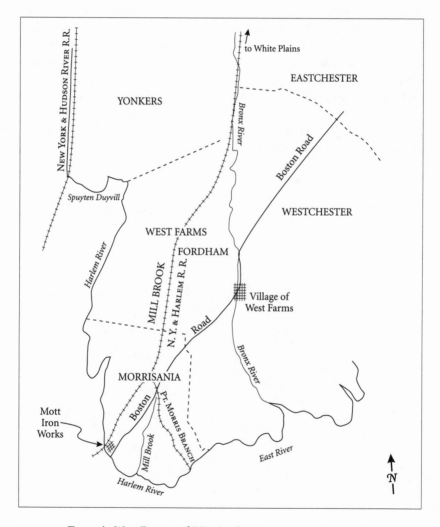

MAP 1.4 Towns in West Farms and Morrisania, 1855

In 1841, the region's first railroad, the New York and Harlem, bridged the Harlem River a bit west of Boston Road (later Third Avenue), passed through the manor lands of the Morris family, and continued to the county seat via the Mill Brook and Bronx River valleys, reaching Fordham in October 1841 and White Plains in late 1844 (see map 1.4). In 1852, the Harlem line completed its new branch to Port Morris, by then a much promoted, would-be entrepôt north of the Harlem River.[27]

The railroad had an immediate impact. In 1846, the town of West Farms was carved out of the larger Westchester Township. The new town lay west of the Bronx River and reflected lower Westchester's reorientation toward the railroad. A continued rise in the number of inhabitants led to the establishment of yet another town in 1855, Morrisania, taken from West Farms itself and occupying the lands of old Morrisania manor. In 1860, the combined population of West Farms and Morrisania passed 16,000, far exceeding the number of people living east of the river in the town of Westchester (see table 1.3). Population growth had indeed followed the railroad.[28]

The new towns and their "numerous small villages" were products of the many subdivisions that occurred around mid-century (see map 1.5). From the late 1840s on, lower Westchester was opened up to individual holders, as much farm land was sold off by lot rather than by acre. These promotions were part of a larger suburban real estate boom. Speculators offered lots for every taste or budget, subdividing at least twenty-nine areas between 1847

TABLE 1.3 Population of Southern Westchester, 1840–1870

Year	Towns			
	Westchester	West Farms[a]	Morrisania[b]	Morrisania & West Farms[c]
1840	4,154			
1845	5,052			
1850	2,492	4,436		
1855	3,464	12,436		
1860	4,250	7,098	9,245	16,343
1865	3,926	7,333	11,691	19,024
1870	6,015	9,372	19,610	28,982

[a] West Farms created in 1846.
[b] Morrisania created in 1855.
[c] Population of Morrisania and West Farms (excludes Lower Yonkers—the future town of Kingsbridge).

Source: New York State, Census for 1865, xl–xli; New York State, Census for 1875 (Albany, NY, 1877).

and 1857, largely adjacent to or nearby the rail line in Morrisania and West Farms (see table 1.4). Rail access and an upswing in the economy allowed the more prosperous clerks, merchants, "mechanics and working men doing business in the city" to own cottages in the lower Westchester towns and "go back and forth daily on the lines of railroad."[29] In the early 1860s, investors began new subdivisions. These new plats ranged from one at the county's southern tip—North New York—to one just below the city line—Woodlawn Heights.[30]

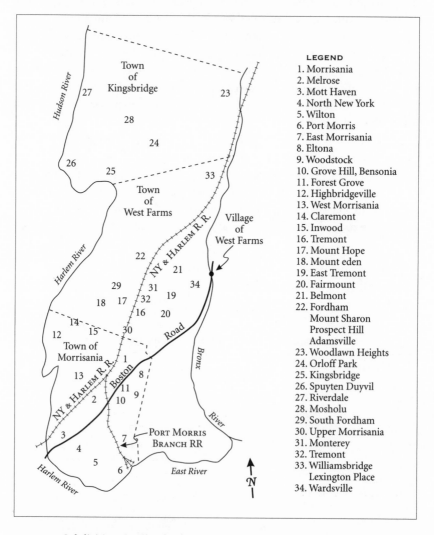

LEGEND
1. Morrisania
2. Melrose
3. Mott Haven
4. North New York
5. Wilton
6. Port Morris
7. East Morrisania
8. Eltona
9. Woodstock
10. Grove Hill, Bensonia
11. Forest Grove
12. Highbridgeville
13. West Morrisania
14. Claremont
15. Inwood
16. Tremont
17. Mount Hope
18. Mount eden
19. East Tremont
20. Fairmount
21. Belmont
22. Fordham
    Mount Sharon
    Prospect Hill
    Adamsville
23. Woodlawn Heights
24. Orloff Park
25. Kingsbridge
26. Spuyten Duyvil
27. Riverdale
28. Mosholu
29. South Fordham
30. Upper Morrisania
31. Monterey
32. Tremont
33. Williamsbridge
    Lexington Place
34. Wardsville

MAP 1.5 Subdivisions in Kingsbridge, West Farms, and Morrisania, 1847–1873

TABLE 1.4 Subdivisions in Lower Westchester Towns, 1847–1873

1847–1857

Morrisania	West Farms	Kingsbridge
Morrisania	Fairmount	Kingsbridge
West Morrisania	Monterey	Spuyten Duyvil (upper)
East Morrisania	Belmont	Spuyten Duyvil (lower)
Melrose	Mount Hope	Hudson Park
South Melrose	Mount Sharon	Riverdale
East Melrose	Prospect Hill	The Park (Riverdale)
North Melrose	Upper Morrisania (South Fordham)	
Mott Haven	Central Morrisania	
Highbridgeville	South Belmont	
Claremont	Mount Eden	
Port Morris	Wardsville	
Woodstock	Adamsville	
Grove Hill	Lexington Place	
Eltona		
Bensonia		
Wilton		

1862–1873

Morrisania	West Farms	Kingsbridge
North New York (3 parcels)	Inwood	Orloff Park
Forest Grove	East Tremont	Woodlawn
	Tremont	

Source: John A. Henry, ed., *Henry's Directory of Morrisania and Vicinity for 1853–4* (Morrisania, NY: Sprat-ley's Westchester Gazette Print, 1853), 5; M. Dripps, *Map of the Southern Part of Westchester County, 1853*; "As-sessment Roll of the Town of West Farms for the Year 1857," MS, New York Historical Society; J. H. French, *Gazetteer of the State of New York* (Port Washington, NJ, 1860, reprinted 1969), 701–707; F. W. Beers, *Map of the Town of Morrisania, Westchester Co., N.Y.*; F. W. Beers, *Atlas of New York and Vicinity, 1868*; Thomas H. Edsall, *History of the Town of Kings Bridge: Now part of the 24th Ward, New York City* (New York: the author, 1887), 52–61; Joel Schwartz, "Community Building on the Bronx Frontier: Morrisania, 1848–1875" (Ph.D. diss., University of Chicago, 1972), 325.

Throughout this period, former manor owners and new investors hawked lower Westchester as a rural retreat, "combined with frequent and convenient access at all hours to the city." After selling the parcels where the first villages arose, the Morris family began to subdivide their own land. Astoundingly, the price of lower Westchester lots rose fivefold between 1848 and 1853.[31] By then, Morrisania's Reverend Clark marveled at how "The unbroken soil and solitude of nature are suddenly transformed into city-sites, whose homes dot the landscape as far as the eye can extend." Some town building schemes remained more hope than fact, but they demonstrated that "Corner lots" had replaced pastures as the main concern of landowners.[32]

The many subdivisions were influenced by the "suburban ideal." By the 1860s, Andrew Jackson Downing's popular writings on gardens, landscaping, and parks had helped transform the nation's traditional agrarian heritage into a suburban setting. While mainly addressed to the well-to-do, his widely read articles propounded the aesthetic and moral superiority of rural life.[33] Morrisania's Reverend Clark expressed similar sentiments when he insisted that "thousands, once cribbed in the city, many of whom still do business there, have airy homes and beautiful gardens [instead of] . . . the incessant roar of the metropolis." The suburban ideal influenced how the lots were advertised to the public and inspired many to come to lower Westchester.[34]

In the area across from the Harlem River, however, something more was at work. Downing-style suburbs were beyond the financial reach of artisans and tradesmen. To answer this need, voluntary building associations mushroomed around mid-century and were instrumental in founding and settling various lower Westchester communities—the village of Morrisania being the most notable example. Building associations pooled members' funds and provided mortgage money. When subdivisions were made with expectations of higher land values, as was common, aspiring homeowners flocked all the more to building associations, regardless of the members' ability to sustain payments or of the soundness of the associations themselves.[35] But neither the suburban ideal nor the dream of a cottage home deterred capitalists from planning for added profits or the new residents from trying to get urban amenities in their "rural" suburbs.

The lower Westchester communities had able political, civic, and business leaders who guided the region, while minding their own personal benefit. To enhance the prospects of the area, and so of their projects, Morrisanians, West Farmers, and a few from Kingsbridge often approached the state legislature and their own taxpayers with proposals for streets, transit, bridges, and dredging the Harlem River.[36] Lower Westchesterites, meanwhile, cashed in on their rural assets. Newspaper ads continually reminded New Yorkers that "Westchester County is exempt from the restriction" on Sunday liquor sales. One could have "Pleasant and Inviting Excursions" to the "Morrisania Pleasure Gardens" and enjoy "Home Brewed Lager and Pure Rhine Wines . . . under the shade of forest trees Hundreds of Years Old."[37]

Visions of growth relied heavily on New York City. Between 1820 and 1860, the city's population expanded at decennial rates that never dropped

TABLE 1.5 Population of New York City[a], 1790–1880

Year	Population	Percentage of Increase
1790	33,131	
1800	60,515	
1810	96,373	
1820	123,706	
1830	202,589	64%
1840	312,710	54
1850	515,547	64
1860	813,669	58
1870	942,292	
1880	1,164,643	

[a]Manhattan only.

Source: Laidlaw, *Population of New York City, 1890–1930*, 51.

below 54 percent (see table 1.5). Manhattan's built-up district swelled from 200,000 people in 1830 to more than 800,000 residents in 1860. Congestion increased as "the demands of commerce" pushed people out of the lower wards. An 1850 population density of 135.6 people per acre in the "fully settled area" of the city worsened by 1860 to more than 300 per acre in parts of the Sixth, Eleventh, and Thirteenth wards.[38] Such concentration led to chronic housing shortages and unhealthy conditions. At the same time, enhanced land values encouraged real estate speculation and propelled Gotham uptown. This growth forced the city to develop water, fire-fighting, police, and transit systems. Lower Westchesterites hoped transportation improvements would "set the Public mind northward" and "hasten the period of the city's 'Manifest Destiny' . . . [of] a dense population to the shores of its northern boundary."[39]

New Yorkers looked to the north as the metropolis grew. During the 1860s, half of the population lived in crowded tenements and much of the rest was in cramped row houses. Condemning the tenements as dangerous to health and morals, medical and social reformers secured the beginnings of tenement house reform in the late 1860s. While a portent for the future, the tentative early housing laws could not reduce congestion or provide adequate shelter, as the number of city dwellers soared to 900,000 in 1870 and to a million five years later.[40] The suburbs seemed the only answer. New Yorkers had been migrating outward for years, moving uptown or ferrying across the rivers toward Brooklyn or New Jersey. Though farther away, lower Westchester compared favorably with those suburbs.

Whether one believed that it would "be given over to charming residences for our wealthier citizens" or that it was "the natural outlet for our pent-up thousands," lower Westchester was directly in the line of New York City's expansion.[41]

The region across the Harlem River meant different things to different New Yorkers. To Democratic Party leader and Tammany Hall Boss William M. Tweed, lower Westchester was a fertile field for "improvements" and pay-offs, and he ultimately planned "to gobble up" seven Westchester towns. Tweed's attempt was too blatant to gain support from most of those who favored annexation. In contrast, avowed reformer Andrew Haswell Green was an equally ardent booster of New York's expansion. As one of the Central Park Commissioners, Green was intimately involved in planning roads and bridges in Westchester and upper Manhattan. He saw lower Westchester as an inevitable part of a greatly enlarged future New York City. However one viewed the county, annexation seemed assured.[42]

From the 1850s on, the press discussed how Gotham would eventually encompass all contiguous areas, including "a considerable portion of Westchester County beyond Harlem River." Politicians incessantly pointed out that the city lost thousands of taxpayers every year, some, no doubt, to the lower Westchester towns.[43] When in 1869, the state legislature empowered the Central Park Commissioners to coordinate street plans on both sides of the Harlem, both New Yorkers and Westchester residents approved.[44] The western half of the lower county was prepared for annexation by 1870, but held back because it was linked to Tweed corruption. Once the Tweed connection was eliminated, the towns themselves initiated the process that resulted in their becoming the city's upper wards.[45]

The population of southern Westchester grew steadily. Morrisania and West Farms had almost 29,000 inhabitants by 1870. A new town was added in 1872 when the former lower Yonkers became the town of Kingsbridge (see maps 1.1 and 1.5). In 1875, the three former towns had 36,000 people, who would have constituted a fourth of Westchester County's population had annexation not occurred a year earlier (see table 1.6). There was, furthermore, a "considerable amount of manufactures." In addition to the long-established mills at West Farms, the Bronx had extensive foundries, gas works, breweries, piano factories, and numerous smaller establishments, supplemented by railroads, ferries, and a horsecar line.[46] By 1875, the city's new wards contained more than 5,000 dwellings, most of which were substantial cottages and villas, in an area where decades before there had been one small village and a few scattered farms and manor houses.[47]

Annexation came about after twenty-five years of steady growth in Morrisania, West Farms, and Kingsbridge. And it came because for all their

TABLE 1.6 Population of 23rd and 24th Wards,
New York City, 1875

Ward	Population[a]
23rd	24,320
24th	11,874
Total	36,194

[a] These figures differ slightly from a corrected tabulation done by
election districts a year later.
Source: New York State, *Census for 1875*, 258.

progress and their high-flown rhetoric, the towns lacked the resources to fully implement necessary improvements. By 1870, the region's most populated sections suffered from inadequate police and fire protection, poor sanitation, and a scarcity of water, services New York City was providing its citizens and would extend to newer wards. Moreover, the district "intended by nature as the territory upon which New York can overflow" would be able to receive extensions of the city's elevated transit system. Owners, meanwhile, would "appreciate the importance" of bringing their property "into a market where financial institutions—now by law restricted in advancing money to city property only—can then also pay attention to the real estate of Westchester." Everybody benefited if the towns joined the city.[48]

The towns of Morrisania, West Farms, and Kingsbridge became the Twenty-third and Twenty-fourth wards on January 1, 1874 (see map 1.1).[49] The original annexation bill was amended because of opposition from the governor and the city's new, post–Tweed era administration. The compromise proposal left the annexation decision to the voters of New York City and the concerned towns, rather than to the legislature, and consigned the new area to Parks Department jurisdiction to forestall any charges of corruption regarding public improvements. In early November, both the city and the three towns voted for annexation.[50] After years of community building, lower Westchesterites had placed themselves firmly in the city. Influential landowners and local politicians, organized as the joint Citizens' Committee on Annexation, predicted that in a few years, "Westchester wards will be so thickly populated that the Harlem River, instead of being . . . [north] of the city, will be the centre of its commerce." Despite such high expectations, the new wards were thereafter referred to as the "Annexed District," though residents preferred the name of the "North Side." The newly coined appellation, however, aptly revealed that

New Yorkers viewed the upper wards as only an appendage of a Greater New York.[51]

The contrast between the early years of the future Bronx and the latter-day borough transcends a simple village-city dichotomy. The area developed within New York City's orbit, dependent upon its economy, population, and transit. The subsequent boosting and installation of city services in a small-town setting enhanced the rural yet urban image of lower Westchester and served to further entice Gotham's populace. But to continue to receive Manhattan's overflow, lower Westchester needed transportation and sanitary innovations. Unsurprisingly, landowners, from the Morris family to the latest village investor, linked profits with rapid transit and public improvements. Since the "proposed route of the Underground Railroad is along Central [Jerome] Avenue," declared Lewis G. Morris as he advertised his Jerome Avenue lots in 1869, "the speculator . . . who desires to invest profitably, and the men who see only a rural retreat, have all alike an interest in securing now, therefore, the building sites which are offered to them."[52] From the first, the Bronx was a speculative suburb, a source of profit predicated on New York City's growth.[53]

2 EARLY BEGINNINGS

By the time of annexation, lower Westchester contained the communities from which the Bronx would grow. In the town of Morrisania, the core villages of Mott Haven, Melrose, and Morrisania would expand into larger neighborhoods. But in 1865, they were the ideal place for "the erection of small dwellings in the suburbs, where each family could have a house to itself, and thus realize something of the comforts and decencies of home." The town of West Farms, meanwhile, "had the appearance of an unimproved farming district" but would later provide the vacant land for the future neighborhoods of Hunts Point–Crotona Park East. With neither villages nor neighborhoods, the Hunts Point–West Farms tract was a far cry from the "socially depressed and physically blighted" South Bronx of the 1960s and 1970s or even the resurgent area of the late 1990s.[1]

MOTT HAVEN

Only seven miles from City Hall, Mott Haven is the southern tip of the Bronx, bounded on the north by 149th Street and on the south by the Harlem and East rivers. Currently part of Community District 1, Mott Haven has had suburban villas and run-down tenements, elegant townhouses and modest cottages, and businesses of all kinds. It has been the home of notable New Yorkers from Gouverneur Morris, member of the federal Constitutional Convention, American Minister to France, and member of the 1807 New York Commission, to Dutch Schultz, bootlegger and gangster of the 1920s and '30s.[2] Throughout, Mott Haven has sheltered different waves of native-born and immigrant Americans, sometimes providing a refuge from the city's ills and sometimes contributing to them.

Mott Haven grew from four suburban subdivisions that developed after commuter rail service began in the 1840s (see map 2.1). These became part

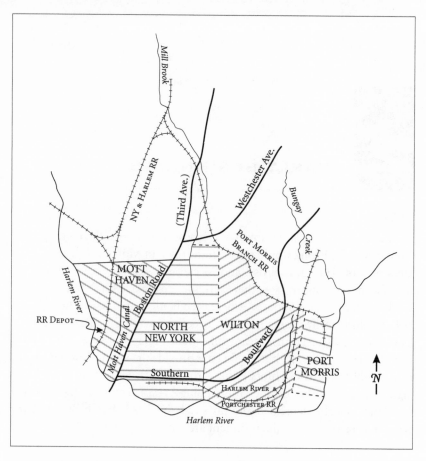

MAP 2.1 Mott Haven and Its Early Villages, 1870

of Morrisania Township in 1855 and its first ward in 1864. The land where the villages would stand belonged to the Morris family: Gouverneur Morris's son and namesake owned the property east of the Mill Brook and his cousin Lewis Morris owned that west of it. After Lewis Morris sold the right of way to the New York and Harlem Railroad in 1840, the cousins began to capitalize on their holdings, selling some outright while improving others for future sale.[3]

Jordan L. Mott founded Mott Haven village in 1849. Eight years earlier, when the railroad had crossed the Harlem River, Mott had moved his home and iron foundry to the southwestern tip of Westchester County. In the late 1840s and early 1850s, Mott was director and trustee of various land associations and building societies that helped workers to own homes. He collaborated with others interested in Westchester lands to found the village of Morrisania in 1848 and began his own village a year later.[4]

During 1848 and 1849, Mott bought from Lewis Morris more than a hundred acres directly north of his foundry on the Harlem River and Boston Road. Mott platted the area into a grid of more than 400 lots and in 1850 advertised it as the future "downtown of Westchester County." His village had a residential "uptown" section, an industrial "downtown" area, and its own railroad depot. The northern residential part had 50 x 100-foot lots and required buyers to build "a neat dwelling House" valued at $500 and set back from the sidewalk that could not be used for anything "pernicious to health or noxious or offensive to the neighborhood." The southern half had no setbacks and smaller, 25 x 100-foot lots, and by the mid-1850s offered industrial sites along a 3,000-foot canal that had been dug east of the railroad.[5] Glue works, slaughterhouses, and breweries were not welcomed, the first two being exceptionally obnoxious, the latter in keeping with Mott's temperance leanings.[6]

Mott chose the site well. The village lay across the two travel arteries between the city and Westchester County, within commuting distance via the Harlem Railroad and its new Mott Haven depot. Throughout the 1850s and 1860s, Mott speculated in Mott Haven real estate, increased his holdings by filling in his Harlem River shoreline, and boosted land north of the Harlem.[7] His cottage plots and industrial sites offered alternatives to the congestion of New York City. But such minute subdivision also greatly enhanced the value of his property and created the setting for many profitable transactions.

Port Morris, on the extreme eastern shore, was a 100-acre, marshy headland called Stony Island that bordered a deep part of the East River. During the 1850s and 1860s, owner Gouverneur Morris harbored visions of a deep-water seaport served by docking facilities and railroads. Morris filled in the marsh and platted the newly named Port Morris with a grid to accommodate factories and warehouses. In 1852 the Port Morris Branch Railroad arrived, via the Harlem Railroad up to Melrose village and a newly laid southeasterly track to the East River. Promoters touted the Port Morris Branch line as a commuter service. But for Morris and subsequent investors, the railroad added to heady expectations of industrial and commercial development.[8]

Wilton lay between Mott Haven and Port Morris. In 1857, Robert H. Elton, a New York City bookseller, publisher, and developer of other subdivisions, divided a 325-acre tract into 35 large plots. Elton promoted Wilton as a suburb for well-to-do New Yorkers, boasting that the "Splendid Villa sites" had "charming" harbor views and were near the Manhattan horsecar lines. The former owner, Gouverneur Morris, added to the bucolic setting by opening up 138th Street as a 100-foot-wide, tree-shaded thoroughfare connecting Wilton to Mott Haven and Port Morris.[9]

North New York, the last section to make up Mott Haven, was developed in 1860, when Robert Campbell and Edward Willis purchased 80 acres bounded by Boston Road, Brook Avenue, and 138th Street for more than $204,000. The property, at first called South Morrisania, was subdivided into a grid of 1,000, 25 x 100-foot lots and put up for sale in 1862. Costing from $200 to $1,000, the building sites were on tree-shaded, gas-lit, curbed streets. Campbell leveled hills and filled in hollows to make his "Model Town," thus obliterating the original landscape in the search for urban efficiency and maximum profits. Campbell and his partners also invested in real estate, gas works, and streetcar lines.[10]

Two large adjoining parcels remained off the market until the later 1860s. Lewis Morris's heirs sold 1,500 lots directly south of North New York to Clarence S. Brown in November 1865. Gouverneur Morris sold the adjacent area, more than 300 lots south of Wilton along with all of Port Morris, to the Port Morris Land and Improvement Company in 1868. Both tracts continued the pattern of North New York, with narrow lots, a rectilinear street plan, and disregard for the natural terrain. With these sales, all of future Mott Haven was available for real estate development and subsequent population growth.[11]

Mott Haven village grew quickly. By 1860 there were more than 100 frame dwellings near the Mott works, providing living quarters for the foundry's 110 employees and for the workers of several brass and machine shops in the village. This part of Mott Haven had two-story, wooden row houses with no front yards, along with 26 liquor stores and lager saloons straddling Boston Road. North of 138th Street, middle-class families lived in comfortable wooden cottages worth $1,000 or more. By 1868, Mott Haven had more dwelling houses than Wilton, North New York, and Port Morris combined. Though smaller, the village was the most developed and densely populated part of Mott Haven throughout the 1860s.[12] Wilton remained the seat of fine homes on spacious grounds, while Port Morris continued to base its hopes on industry rather than residences. By 1865, Port Morris held the freight yards and wharves of the Branch Railroad, the iron works of the Columbian Foundry, and the gas works of the Westchester Gas Light Company. This was more industry than existed in Mott Haven village but a mere fraction of what had been envisioned for the section.[13]

North New York followed a different course. Lot sales quickened a bit after the 1863 New York City Draft Riots, when Campbell's newspaper ads stressed how far North New York was from the city's ills: "Those who wish to secure a quiet home sufficiently remote from the city . . . within a convenient business distance, should at once secure a fine building-site at North New York." Now augmented by the newly available land south of 138th Street, North New York was the largest area of latter-day Mott Haven, yet the least developed. Real estate investors still looked toward the future. The proximity of Manhattan, the opening of a horsecar line on Boston Road in 1864, the planning of a new boulevard from Harlem Bridge to West Farms village in 1867, and the possibility of annexation to the city made North New York a speculator's haven despite its slow start.[14]

During the 1850s, some Mott Havenites may have been among the hundreds of Harlem, Melrose, and Morrisania town residents who commuted. By 1871 the Harlem Road carried "a mixed class of passengers" into the city, its four morning trains averaging 1,300 commuting "mechanics," "laborers," "clerks and salesmen." In that same year, only 175 residents of Mott Haven villages, or roughly 3 percent of the population, had New York City business addresses in the *Morrisania Directory*. The 1871 *Directory* also listed many small establishments in Mott Haven and the larger township that were providing more business and job opportunities. The area by then had acquired a native population, apart from elite landowners and outside promoters, that was intimately tied to real estate interests and concerned with perpetuating its growth.[15]

The population of the villages more than tripled between 1865 and 1875, reaching 2,000 in Mott Haven and almost 7,000 in the area as a whole (see table 2.1). Most residents lived near the Boston Road (later Third Avenue),

TABLE 2.1 Estimated Population of Mott Haven, 1850–1875

Village	1855	1865–66[a]	1875[b]
Mott Haven	843	1,403	2,336
Wilton		234	
Port Morris		117	4,542
North New York		468	
Total	843	2,222	6,878

[a] Derived by correlating each village's 1866 percentage of the total dwelling in the township with the 1865 population of the Town of Morrisania, which was 11,691.

[b] Mott Haven village population estimated from a corrected tabulation of the 1875 state census showing numeration by election districts. Population derived by method described in note a, using the number of dwellings in each district as per G. W. Bromley & Co., *Atlas of the Entire City of New York, 1879* (New York: Geo. W. Bromley & E. Robinson, 1879).

Source: New York State, *Census for 1865*, xlix–lxi, 15; "Communication From the Secretary of State Showing the Population in Each Election District of the City of New York," in New York State, *Assembly Documents, 1876*, vol. 6, no. 55, p. 14.

TABLE 2.2 Churches in Mott Haven Region, 1841–1873

Name and Address	Date Founded
St. Ann's Episcopal Church, 295 St. Ann's Avenue	1841[a]
Mott Haven Dutch Reformed Church, 348 East 146th Street	1851[b]
St. Mary's Episcopal Church, 338 Alexander Avenue	1857[c]
North New York Methodist Mission, 141st Street and Willis Avenue	1865[d]
St. Jerome's Roman Catholic Church, 138th Street and Alexander Avenue	1869[d]
First Baptist Church of North New York, 141st Street and Alexander Avenue	1872[d]
First Presbyterian Church of North New York, 420 East 137th Street	1873[d]

[a] Coincided with entrance of Mott's Foundry.
[b] Coincides with settlement of Mott Haven village.
[c] Reflects growth of Mott Haven village and the new villas in Wilton.
[d] Demonstrates the stages of population increase in North New York.

Source: Works Projects Administration Historical Records Survey, *Guide to Vital Statistics in the City of New York, Borough of The Bronx, Churches* (New York: Works Projects Administration, 1942), 1–10.

in Mott Haven village and upper North New York. Ninety percent of the residents were native-born or naturalized American citizens, of northern and western European origin—specifically old-stock Americans, Irish Catholics, and Germans, a fact underscored by the six Protestant churches founded from 1841 on (see table 2.2). The only Catholic church, St. Jerome's, was not founded until 1869, when there were enough Irish residents in the area to start a parish that would be identified with the Irish for generations.[16] At the time, Germans were too few to found their own institutions, but the Lutheran and German Catholic churches of Melrose village were nearby.[17]

Protestant and middle-class residents associated in churches, volunteer fire companies, baseball teams, and reform organizations. Volunteer fire companies, a necessity because of the predominance of wooden structures, provided a camaraderie that was enhanced by the similar ethnic and occupational background of each unit.[18] Baseball, on the other hand, emphasized team play, discipline, good sportsmanship, and abstinence from liquor—the last in sharp contrast to the firemen, whose "keg of lager [was] the most indispensable equipment"—and appealed to Protestants and upper middle-class residents who supported temperance and Bible crusades, more schools, lower commuting fares, greater police protection, and well-lit, cleaner streets.[19]

For the Irish, ethnic ties were stronger than class. Since participation in fire companies and baseball teams required time and money and some reform efforts were counter to their interests, most Irish residents enjoyed the convivial atmosphere of boarding houses and saloons, many of which served as hiring halls for the labor contractors upon which Irish workers depended. By the late 1860s, two of Mott Haven's volunteer fire companies were predominantly Irish Catholic. The Irish socialized and found friends and marriage partners among their own. Sharing little with the wider community—their institutional contacts were the church, the saloon, and the court—the Irish-born remained the lowest on Mott Haven's social scale throughout the community-building period.[20]

After the 1860s, Louis B. Brown, Benjamin A. Willis, Thomas Ray, and Herman Stursberg replaced the original town planners of North New York, Edward Willis and Robert Campbell. Jordan L. Mott Jr. continued the family tradition of nurturing Mott Haven village, but sold the canal and hundreds of adjoining lots to William Rider and Theodore Conkling.[21] The Port Morris Land and Improvement Company took over from Gouverneur Morris and became one of the largest property owners in lower Westchester. Like the early developers, new investors concerned themselves with sewer, water, and rapid transit systems, matters they felt needed the knowledge and resources of New York City, and thus called for annexation.[22]

Except for Wilton, a uniform grid prevailed everywhere.[23] The town planners took their cue from Manhattan—right-angle streets could accommodate more lots, houses, and people, and ultimately produce more profits. In the early 1870s, a Morrisania street commission extended the grid across Wilton's villa sites. "Based in great measure on the divisions already made by property-owners," reported engineer and Wilton resident George S. Greene, the Morrisania plan was "the real estate dealer's idea of making the most of a tract." And so, Mott Haven streets would eventually be solidly lined with narrow tenements and row houses. But in the 1870s, only the lack of better transit kept the empty village avenues from becoming replicas of Manhattan's Lower East Side.[24]

After 1870, the separation of factories and homes slowly disappeared. The Port Morris Land and Improvement Company merged its holdings with its North New York lots, setting the scene for the indiscriminate mixing of factories and dwellings. The lengthening of the Mott Haven Canal in 1868 brought industrial sites closer to the village's residential section. And in 1872 the Harlem River and Portchester Railroad skirted the southern rim of North New York. Leased almost immediately by the New Haven Line, the tracks and freight yards of the Portchester Road made the adjoining blocks less suitable for homes and impeded public access to the shoreline.[25] Owners of waterfront property requested the dredging of the Harlem River and the Hell Gate channel. Hoping that Gotham's economy, like its population, would expand northward, they relegated the riverfront to industrial purposes.[26]

On the eve of the 1874 annexation, the Mott Haven region remained a collection of villages dependent upon the railroad.[27] The communities were created by those who put their money and effort into lower Westchester, usually out of self-interest, most times in pursuit of profits, occasionally for ideals, and often for comfort and peace of mind. Before 1841, society in what was to be the Mott Haven section consisted of a few related families and their servants. By 1873 Mott Havenites had created a varied social life, where each class or nationality group lived and associated with its own kind, concerned with disparate activities yet interacting in many significant ways.

MELROSE

Melrose is centered in the South Bronx, directly north of Mott Haven, its larger neighbor. Its boundaries are 149th Street on the south, Park Avenue on the west, and Brook Avenue on the north and east (see map 1.2). Currently part of Community District 1, it lies astride Conrail's Harlem Division and Port Morris Branch, routes that were the first railroads into then lower Westchester County and allowed for its initial settlement. In the 1840s, North Melrose, Melrose, and South Melrose were separate tracts of vacant land owned by four Morris cousins (see map 2.2). A century later, Melrose was a densely built urban neighborhood, flanked by freight yards and a commercial area known as the Hub and delimited on all sides by rail transit lines. Now it has public housing, high-rise co-ops covering the rail lines, many new rows of owner-occupied townhouses, and the still thriving business and commercial Hub.

The transition of Melrose from rural to urban began in the 1850s under the aegis of Robert H. Elton and Samuel Denman. A subsequent investor in other villages, Elton bought the seven acres that comprised North Melrose from Gouverneur Morris in December 1849. Months later, Brooklynite and professional realtor Denman purchased 120 acres of South Melrose from Gerard and Henry Morris. Together, Elton and Denman marketed their holdings along with those of William H. Morris, the owner of Melrose, platting right-angle streets and dividing the three tracts into more than 1,000, 50 x 100-foot lots.[28]

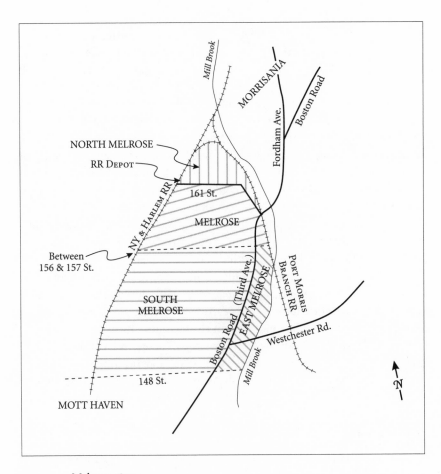

MAP 2.2 Melrose, 1850s

The promoters emphasized Melrose's rural location adjacent to the railroad, but imposed no restrictions against nuisances and no setback or building requirements. In South Melrose, most buyers did not build the "good and substantial" dwelling that the deeds required. In 1851, a visitor described Melrose in less than idyllic terms: "the majority of the dwellings are small cottages of no great value; and as but a few of them are painted, the village, especially near the station, presents rather a mean appearance." Advertising South Melrose lots as "A Morris title and no onerous building restrictions," as Elton proudly did in that same year, did not ensure the creation of a model village.[29]

Members of building societies purchased Melrose and South Melrose lots and subsequently steered fellow members and craftsmen to the locality. Among these were John Roeber and Herman Ludwig, a woodworker and piano maker, respectively, who were also officers in the German Building Association-Concordia, and John Dunham, a piano manufacturer and trustee of the St. Nicholas Building Association who later established a four-story piano factory on his South Melrose lots.[30] Melrose and South Melrose lots were bought up by artisans, craftsmen, and small shopkeepers, largely of German origin. In contrast, North Melrose lots went to Irish and old-stock Americans.[31] Melrose residents came from the ranks of native-born and immigrant New Yorkers seeking a healthy country life within commuting distance who could not afford costlier houses or preferred the company of fellow workers and compatriots.

Up to annexation, the population of Melrose was predominantly German. There was, however, a sprinkling of native-born, old-stock American and Irish residents and the merest indication of a black presence.[32] The village's volunteer fire companies, militia units, singing societies, social clubs, saloons, parochial schools, and most of its churches shared a common Teutonic heritage (see table 2.3). As early as 1853, a German Catholic newspaper remarked that "the new German church of the Immaculate Conception in Melrose . . . will supply an urgent need," since "many Catholic German families have in recent times settled in that beautiful and healthy region." The main street, Courtlandt Avenue, would eventually be dubbed

TABLE 2.3 Churches in Melrose Region, 1852–1872

Name and Address	Date Founded
German Methodist Church (Elton Avenue Methodist), Elton Avenue at 158th Street	1852
Immaculate Conception Roman Catholic Church (German), East 150th Street between Melrose and Courtlandt avenues	1853
Melrose Reformed Church in America (German), 157th Street and Elton Avenue	1854
St. Matthew's Lutheran Church (German), 376 East 156th Street	1862
First Baptist Church of Melrose (Ascension Baptist Church), 290 East 161st Street	1864
St. Paul's African Methodist Episcopal Church (African American), 158th Street between Washington and Courtlandt avenues	1868
Second Congregational Church (African American), Washington Avenue and 158th Street	ca. 1871

Source: WPA Historical Records Survey, Bronx Churches, 3–11; Frisbee and Coles, Morrisania and Tremont Directory, xxvi, 134; John M. Weyer to C. Smith, no date, Chauncey Smith Papers, NYHS.

"Dutch Broadway."[33] The post–Civil War spurt of immigration intensified the village's already Germanic tone. Though not yet a part of New York City, Melrose had become an extension of Manhattan's German quarter.[34]

Melrose took on the character of its new population. Tailors and piano makers lined entire streets. Grocers, milk dealers, and shopkeepers occupied corner lots along Courtlandt Avenue, while saloons and backyard breweries were everywhere. By 1860, North Melrose had a small colony of Bohemian cigar rollers as well as a few boarding houses filled with Irish carpenters, masons, and laborers. The German and Irish newcomers kept chickens, goats, and pigs and borrowed indiscriminately from fellow residents, to the dismay of their native-born American neighbors, who complained loudly of, in the words of Elton, the "character of a portion of the surrounding population." Melrose harbored few of the professional or upper classes, but provided many artisans and tradesmen with lots suited for multipurpose use, one lot often the setting for dwelling, workshop, store, kitchen garden, and barnyard combined. By the 1870s, the district was still the locus of shopkeepers and craftsmen, although it had acquired a contingent of unskilled laborers, peddlers, and junk dealers living in numerous boarding houses and tenements on the main north/south thoroughfares.[35]

Melrose was densely built. Its number of dwelling houses more than doubled in twelve years, rising from almost 400 in 1856 to over 800 by 1868. Its population increased as well, going from more than 4,000 residents in 1865 to 8,000 inhabitants ten years later (see table 2.4). More people and houses meant less vacant land for future speculation and development.

TABLE 2.4 Estimated Population of Melrose, 1865–1875

Village	1865–66a	1875b
South Melrose	2,455	5,121
Melrose	1,052	1,789
East Melrose	584	705
North Melrose	350	411
TOTAL	4,441	8,026

a Derived by correlating each subdivision's 1866 percentage of the total dwellings in the township with the 1865 population of Morrisania, which was 11,691.

b Melrose's population obtained from the corrected 1875 state census. Population derived by method described in note a, using the number of dwellings in each district as per G. W. Bromley & Co., *Atlas of the Entire City of New York, 1879.*

Source: New York State, *Census for 1865*, 15; "Communication From the Secretary of State Showing the Population in Each District of the City of New York, 1876," 14.

Melrose would enter the postannexation years with few of the vast tracts of land possessed by other communities in lower Westchester.[36]

Ethnic and occupational commonality gave Melrose a seemingly more cohesive community structure. The different German churches accommodated the disparate faiths of the populace and also provided a setting for social activities in the new suburb. Volunteer fire units also became centers of companionship and neighborhood pride. But it was the gymnastic and singing societies—the *Vereine*—and the saloon that highlighted Melrose's Teutonic character.[37] The neighborhood had its own "Lieder-Tafel" singing society and local *Turnvereins* engaging in elaborate musical and gymnastic festivals. The saloons served as headquarters for many of these groups and were family-oriented establishments, a few intimately located amid the homes of German residents. They were at once social centers and hiring halls, their owners acting as friends, employers, and intermediaries between Melrose's Germans and the wider town.[38]

Throughout the preannexation period, Melrose was an economically viable locality. It began as a commuter suburb—with 91 residents using the Harlem Railroad daily—and turned into a center for home industries, the building trades, and small shops. Melrose held few large business establishments; its industry arose from individual initiative, not from a concerted effort as existed elsewhere. Commuters, however, were still critical to the economy, for much of the industry that existed fed on or began with the commuting population.[39]

In the 1870s, the community was dotted with butchers, bakers, blacksmiths, grocers, milkmen, furniture makers, saloons, and liquor dealers. Taken collectively, laborers, carpenters, masons, and painters were the largest occupational group and depended on the continued development of Melrose and the surrounding villages. Piano makers pursued their craft in the two piano factories; shoemakers, tailors, dressmakers, and cigar makers labored for merchant entrepreneurs at home or in small shops; and moulders worked in the Mott Works or the Janes and Kirtland Foundry in East Morrisania. Because of the railroad line on the west and, after 1864, a horsecar line on the east, Melrose was convenient to both the town and the city. These transit connections extended New York's economic opportunities northward and provided jobs for Melrose workers who did not wish to commute.[40]

Melrose profited from urban services brought about by reformers and entrepreneurs based outside of Melrose proper. The road schemes by which so many of the propertied in Morrisania and West Farms enhanced their land holdings did not on the surface seem to favor Melrose since the town's elite did not come from there. But roads, like transit lines, provided jobs, opened up more land to developers and settlement, and thus laid the groundwork for the greater economic opportunities Melrose residents hoped for. When the Morrisania Commissioners drew up the street plan in the early 1870s, Melrose's right-angle streets were adopted in toto. Even without large realtors, landowners, or boosters nurturing the community's interests, Melrose nevertheless shared in the grandiose expections held by the town.[41]

MORRISANIA AND HUNTS POINT– WEST FARMS DISTRICT

Morrisania lies just northeast of Melrose, a mile and a half from the Harlem River. It extends east to west from Webster and Brook to Prospect avenues, and north to south from the Cross-Bronx Expressway and Crotona Park South to 149th Street. In the 1850s, these confines held the village plats of Morrisania, Eltona, Woodstock, East Morrisania, and Central Morrisania (see map 2.3).[42] As it was the name of the former manor, and after 1855 the new township, "Morrisania" became a blanket term describing the town, the other subdivisions, and the original village itself. Its borders encompass Morrisania proper and Claremont, both currently in Community District 3. For a century after its village beginnings, Morrisania was a residential neighborhood, with manufacturing and commercial establishments here and there. Between the 1960s and the 1980s, its blocks were filled with either abandoned hulks or acres of public housing. An area that was once an aspiring suburb and later a thriving residential community had become the home of a poor, minority population and, because of its many vacant tracts, a site to which the city tried to attract industry. Morrisania has been rebuilt since then, but it is still poor.[43]

Morrisania was the first commuter village of lower Westchester County. Originally founded in September 1848 as the "New Village," it was rechristened Morrisania in July 1850. The village was a collaboration between utopian yet capitalist entrepreneurs and a group of New York City artisans in the woodworking trades. The entrepreneurs were Jordan L. Mott, of later Mott Haven fame, and Nicholas McGraw, a New York–based furniture workshop owner. Both men were involved in building associations and were staunch supporters of total abstinence. Under their guidance, a village site was purchased and surveyed into right-angle streets with 170 one-acre lots, three of which were set aside for a square, a school, and a depot. Less than an hour's ride from New York City, the 200-acre site was acquired from Gouverneur Morris for $34,622 (approximately $173 per acre) and lay

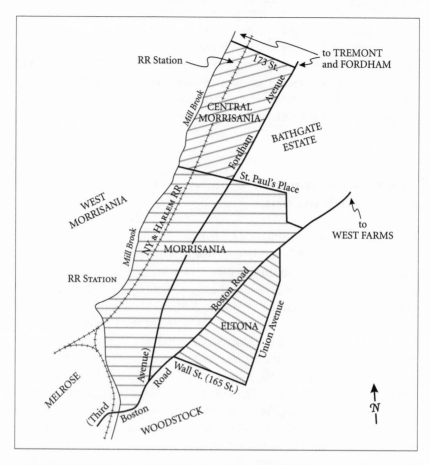

MAP 2.3 Morrisania, Central Morrisania, and Eltona, 1850s

astride the Boston Road and the New York and Harlem Railroad. Under the express condition of the seller, "no intoxicating drinks" could be manufactured, bought, or sold on the premises.[44]

The village was advertised by word of mouth and at numerous outings that McGraw organized and at which the village was planned. Lot buyers were often neighbors or of similar occupations. The new owners were young—half were in their thirties—and many were subscribers to the American Benefit Association, an earlier venture sponsored by Mott and McGraw.[45] The planned village combined a measure of reform with a practical appraisal of property rights, land values, and housing needs. Mott and McGraw were well versed in the city's housing problem: artisans—even those with skills and higher wages—could not aspire to more than high rents and cramped living quarters. And though the temperance clause was removed in July 1849 because it might impede sales of land, Morrisania continued to provide clean, countrylike surroundings, far from the disorderly aspects of the downtown wards but close enough to the city for commuters.[46]

Though they called themselves "humble mechanics," the new Morrisanians were securely above that. The deeds reveal more than 80 trades and professions, among which were cabinet makers, carpenters, piano makers, ship joiners, machinists, silversmiths, painters, and doctors, but no laborers or workingmen. Annual commutation fares ranged from $30 to $37.50. The lots, furthermore, were not cheap. While more than half sold for $150, some ran as high as $900 and others hovered around $550. Only a few went for as low as $40 to $75 and one for a rock-bottom price of $18.75. Yet no one failed to pay. Moreover, most of the 48 residents who had settled in time for the 1850 census held other property. By September 1851 (the village's third anniversary), all but two of the lots had dwellings valued in excess of the $300 deed requirement. The new inhabitants of old Morrisania manor were comfortable enough to live in their own homes in a newly laid-out village while commuting to work in New York City.[47]

Two other subdivisions would become part of the future neighborhood. Developed in 1851 by Melrose village developer Robert H. Elton, Eltona was east of Morrisania, on the other side of the high ground through which Boston Road ascended, and stretched east and south to Union Avenue and 165th Street (see map 2.3). Elton subdivided 50 acres into more than 70 lots, each 75 by 100 feet. With large residential plots, Eltona soon became a higher-status area of Morrisania.[48] Central Morrisania, on the other hand, was too close to the main arteries of travel to prohibit future commercial or manufacturing use. As part of the Bathgate Farm, Central Morrisania extended northerly from Morrisania between the Harlem Railroad and Fordham Avenue (the upper part of Third Avenue).[49] From 1851 on, the Bathgate brothers joined other lower Westchester proprietors in marketing their land, but without the systematic planning in which Elton, Mott, or McGraw had engaged.[50]

The former Woodstock–East Morrisania area is just south of Morrisania. Both communities were originally in the estate of Gouverneur Morris and both were subdivided immediately after the establishment of Morrisania, Mott Haven, and Melrose. The success of the earlier villages induced Morris to try his hand at real estate promotion. Woodstock at first encompassed lands east of the Mill Brook and Boston Road and north of Westchester Avenue; East Morrisania lay south of these roads and north of the Harlem Railroad's Port Morris Branch. Now they are both firmly ensconced in the South Bronx—partly covered by low-income public housing and new owner-occupied row houses, and rarely referred to by their old village titles.[51]

After 1849, other developers invested in Woodstock and East Morrisania (see map 2.4). Samuel Denman (also of Melrose village) and Robert Elton continued Morris's Woodstock endeavor; Elton and Benjamin Benson platted the area east of the Mill Brook into Bensonia; R. Henwood and John Shaw subdivided Grove Hill in 1853. By then, D. Winton was advertising East Morrisania's 371 lots as "beautiful, . . . in full view of the East River, and in the immediate vicinity of residences of several of the most wealthy and respectable citizens of Westchester County." In the 1860s, two large estates between Grove Hill and Eltona became the Forest Grove subdivision.[52]

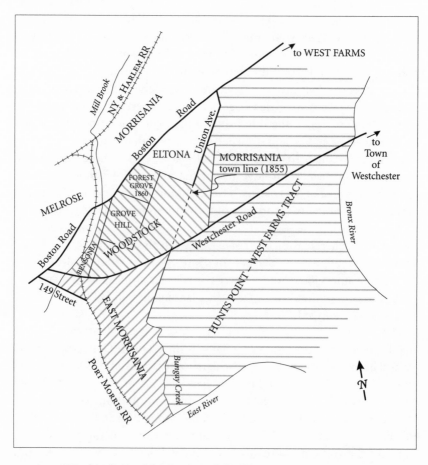

MAP 2.4 Woodstock, East Morrisania, and the Hunts Point–West Farms Tract, 1850s

The "wealthy" homes referred to were east of the Morris land in the Hunts Point–West Farms tract. In 1851, N. Parker Willis noted that "once away from the rail-track, in Westchester, you find yourself in a region of 'county-seats'—no poor people's abodes, or other humble belongings, anywhere visible." Over a century later, Hunts Point would be "one of the most deteriorated communities in the city." But in the 1850s, the estates ranged from 40 to 120 acres and belonged to William W. Fox, W. J. Beck, Edward G. Faile, E. A. Tiffany, Charles Dennison, Paul Spofford, and Philip Dater, among others. These large holdings would later be major news items in real estate circles as they were subdivided and put on the market, but for now they remained "private grounds" with "trim hedges and well-placed shrubberies, fine houses and large stables, neat gravel-walks and nobody on them."[53]

The early settlers of Eltona and Woodstock resembled those in Morrisania village. Almost half of the forty occupations listed in *Henry's Directory* were artisanal; there were carpenters, machinists, printers, tailors, and shoemakers, plus an assortment of craftsmen. But there was also a publisher, a banker, three merchants, a real estate agent (Elton himself), a minister, a druggist, an engineer, an actor, a physician, and a number of white-collar workers and laborers. Except for banker Charles Dennison and merchants Henry and Philip Dater, who lived east of the new subdivision, most of the better-off businessmen and professionals resided in Eltona, where larger plots excluded all but the most prosperous of artisans. Woodstock lots, in comparison, housed those in more modest circumstances—including seventeen laborers, twelve of whom roomed on Forest Avenue.[54]

With its lots fully sold, Morrisania quickly became the political and economic center of the lower Westchester communities. By 1866, Morrisania had more than twice the number of homes than the other subdivisions combined and an estimated population of over 3,000 (see table 2.5).[55] By 1875, its population had grown to almost 6,000. Although Central Morrisania, Bensonia, Grove Hill, and East Morrisania had less development and the Hunts Point–West Farms tract remained an area of well-to-do "elegant mansions" on "ample grounds," their large tracts would serve for later subdivisions. By 1875, the entire Morrisania–Hunts Point region had an estimated population of almost 9,000 residents. This was slightly more than either Mott Haven or the more densely settled Melrose, but much lower than one would have thought after the heady expectations of the 1850s.[56]

On the eve of annexation, the Morrisania–Hunts Point region had all the occupations necessary for a viable area, from grocers, butchers, and bakers to lawyers, realtors, physicians, dentists, and policemen. But except for sizable

TABLE 2.5 Estimated Population of Morrisania–Hunts Point Region, 1849–1875

Village	1849	1850	1855	1865–66[a]		1875[b]	
Morrisania	441	961	2,587	3,157			
					3,391	5,640	
Eltona				234			
							6,351
Central Morrisania						711	
Woodstock				351			
Grove Hill				117			
					1,170		
East Morrisania				585			2,644
Bensonia				117		117	
Forest Grove							
Total	441	961	2,587	4,561		8,995	

[a] Population estimated by correlating each subdivision's 1866 percentage of total dwellings in the township with the 1865 population of Morrisania, which was 11,691.

[b] Estimated from the corrected 1875 state census showing the population by election district. Population was estimated via method described in note a, using Bromley, *Atlas of the City of New York, 1879*, for number of dwellings in each district.

Source: New York Tribune, 12 September 1850; New York State, *Census for 1865*, xlix–lvi, 15–16; "Communication From the Secretary of State Showing the Population in Each Election District of the City of New York, 1876," 14.

contingents of cigar makers, tailors, and brewery workers, primarily in the village of Morrisania, the most represented occupational groups were in the building trades. Carpenters, masons, and painters headed the list of skilled workers; laborers—the largest cohort by far—topped that of the unskilled. Employed by eight contractors and twenty-one builders, they depended for their livelihood upon continued community building in lower Westchester.[57] There were others just as concerned. This segment of the population included lawyers, real estate dealers, surveyors, civil engineers, and anyone who owned property, from the Morris family and the early village developers to owners of homes and single lots.[58]

In the 1870s, the population of the Morrisania region was native-born American and northern European.[59] Two of the seven Protestant churches—German Bethel and St. John's Lutheran—held services solely in German, and the one Catholic church—St. Augustine's—served both German and Irish Catholics; the rest attended to old-stock and British-born Amer-

TABLE 2.6 Churches in Morrisania–Hunts Point Region, 1847–1868

Name and Address	Date Founded
Centenary Methodist Church, Washington Avenue and 166th Street	1847
Morrisania Presbyterian Church (Potts Memorial), 1205 Washington Avenue	1849
St. Augustine's Roman Catholic Church, 167th Street between Fulton and Franklin avenues	1849
Forest Avenue Congregational Church (First of Morrisania), 166th Street and Forest Avenue	1851
St. Paul's Morrisania Protestant Episcopal Church, Washington Avenue and 170th Street	1853
Fulton Avenue Baptist Church (German Bethel of Morrisania), 1127 Fulton Avenue	1857
St. John's Lutheran Church (German), 1343 Fulton Avenue	1860
Trinity Morrisania Protestant Episcopal Church, 698 East 166th Street	1868

Source: WPA Historical Records Survey, *Bronx Churches*, 1–10.

icans (see table 2.6).[60] Germans settled throughout the Morrisania–Hunts Point section but predominated in the "downtown" area of Morrisania village, directly north of the Teutonic Melroses. For the most part, the Irish lived in boarding houses in Woodstock, East Morrisania, and nearby the Harlem Railroad in Morrisania village. Native-born Americans and those of British stock resided in all areas, but they were in the majority in the higher-priced, healthier, exclusively residential sections where larger lots still prevailed.[61]

These broad settlement patterns reflected differences in class, occupation, and national background, for although there were well-to-do in all ethnic groups, old-stock Americans and the British filled the upper income levels; the Germans and Irish, the middle and bottom ranks. As the lowest strata, the Germans and Irish lived closer to their fellow craftsmen and to their place of work, in areas that had either more clustered housing or more inhabitants per house—the Germans near the breweries and shops of master tailors, cigar makers, and carpenters in Melrose and lower Morrisania village; the Irish close by factories in East Morrisania and Port Morris and the estates that employed servant labor. By the early 1870s, the Morrisania area provided less congested surroundings than the city, but its various localities split along class and ethnic lines.[62]

Community building involved institutional development and sociocultural activities as well. The ready-made population of Morrisania village led the way in founding churches, schools, social clubs, and ad hoc societies, each segment forming associational ties suited to its needs and proclivities.[63] In keeping with their nativist tendencies and their growing personal attachment to their community, Protestant Americans fervently engaged in reforming the social and physical environment via Bible societies, temperance organizations, charities, and law enforcement leagues, endeavors that, while based in Morrisania village, drew recruits from the entire town. Old-stock American Morrisanians shared an affinity for baseball with their Mott Haven counterparts. The sport was more than just recreation, for it exemplified their mores and concerns for a clean, orderly, sober suburban society, which seemed threatened by the rise of liquor stores, breweries, and unlicensed saloons once the temperance restriction had been removed.[64] To the German and Irish residents of Morrisania and environs, however, the saloons and the beer gardens were centers for employment, fellowship, and good times. The Germans especially, like those in Melrose, often based their gymnastic and singing societies and rifle clubs in local saloons.[65] Fire crews were an important part of the social scene in Morrisania and East Morrisania, the composition of which revealed the ethnic divisions within the sections.[66] During the community-building period, the Irish and, to a lesser extent, the Germans mingled with their own irrespective of class instead of with the wider American society. Morrisania's three distinct groups had evolved dissimilar community styles.[67]

Party politics and town government arose and grew along with the villages. Aided by lower Westchester resident Jordan L. Mott and manor squire Gouverneur Morris, the ready-made, politically savvy population of Morrisania village adjusted easily to suburban living and the town politics of West Farms. Firmly dividing themselves from the "sleepy West Farmers," the new village dwellers of Morrisania manor campaigned successfully for their own town status in 1855. During the Civil War, the town government raised bounties, found substitutes for the draft, supported soldiers' families, and contended with the spillover from the city's draft riots. The extra responsibilities led to the incorporation of the town in 1864.[68]

Besides the Civil War, the prime impetus for enhanced town government was the need and demand for sanitation, police, fire, and public improvements. Against this background, both parties grew apace—the nativist, reforming section of the town backing Republican fortunes; Mott and later Mott Jr. joining those more willing to use town government to enhance individual holdings in the Democratic fold. By 1870, Morrisania's own William Cauldwell and West Farms's John B. Haskin were their towns' respective Democratic Party bosses, leading a party system based in local saloons, fire companies, and police precincts. The Republicans differed only in their local club settings. Despite political differences, there was a remarkable consensus of opinion on matters concerning street layout, town growth, real estate expectations, and annexation to New York City. Though different interests argued over where public improvements should be made or the amount of taxes to be raised, Mott Havenites, Melrose dwellers, and all Morrisanians agreed that their town would one day be "one of the densely populated wards of the city."[69]

The different village promoters acted within the prevailing ethos of private property and private enterprise. They had subdivided for profit—in Morrisania's case, with a touch of idealism—and in the end supplied affordable home sites for crowded city dwellers. But all the investors, from Mott and McGraw on down, fully accepted that narrow streets, cramped lots, unfettered real estate activity, and indiscriminate mixing of homes and businesses were normal and unavoidable aspects of urban growth. What distinguished the localities of the Morrisania–Hunts Point region from lower Manhattan was their lack of closely built, multistoried brick buildings. And this was more a function of the area's sparsity of population than of dedication to continued suburban status. Though there were sections of wider lots and estates, it was never doubted that these would be narrowed whenever population and economics warranted.[70]

The lower Westchester suburbs had problems. Unprotected train crossings caused many deaths and injuries. Burglaries were commonplace and on weekends, the numerous saloons lining Boston Road added to the disorder caused by brawling fire crews, militia units, and local gangs. The Mott Haven Canal was a fetid cesspool by 1865, while the Mill Brook had become the "natural sewer" of the entire town. Speaking to suburban sanitary officers in September 1869, Dr. Elisha Harris of the Metropolitan

TABLE 2.7 Estimated Population of Mott Haven, Melrose, and the Morrisania–Hunts Point Region, 1865–1875

Neighborhood	1865–1866[a]	1875
Mott Haven	2,222	6,878
Melrose	4,441	8,026
Morrisania–Hunts Point	4,561	8,995
Estimated Total	11,224	23,641

[a] Population estimated by correlating each subdivision's 1866 percentage of total dwellings in the township with the 1865 population of Morrisania, which was 11,691.

Source: New York State, Census for 1865, 15; "Communication From the Secretary of State Showing the Population in Each Election District of the City of New York, 1876," 14.

TABLE 2.8 Population of the Town of Morrisania and the 23rd and
24th Wards, 1865–1875

Area	1865	Area	1875
Town of Morrisania	11,691	23rd Ward	24,331
		24th Ward	11,875
Total	11,691[a]		36,206

[a] This figure differs slightly from the estimated total of table 2.7, which was 11,224 (see note a, table 2.7).

Source: New York State, *Census for 1865*, 15; "Communication From the Secretary of State Showing the Population in Each Election District of the City of New York, 1876," 14.

Board of Health warned that traveling by way of 138th and St. Ann's
Church "must emperil health and even life" because of "the concentrated
malaria." The inadequate water supply caused wells to be built close to
privy vaults and polluted watercourses, and increased the danger of fire for
the tightly clustered frame houses.[71]

In 1875, Mott Haven, Melrose, and the Morrisania–Hunts Point region
were the most populated communities of the city's newest territory (see tables 2.7 and 2.8). They accounted for 97 percent of the population of the
Twenty-third Ward and 65 percent of that in both wards. With its smaller
acreage, Melrose was the most densely settled of the three distinct sections,
though the Morrisania–Hunts Point area had more inhabitants. Every in-
cipient neighborhood had a mixture of old-stock Americans, British, Germans, and Irish Catholics in varying proportions. Yet only in Melrose were
there African American institutions.[72] The lower Westchester villages thus
contained separate sociocultural and racial enclaves that could serve as
beacons to downtown compatriots.

THE CHANGING LANDSCAPE

The development of the Bronx depended upon the nature and timing of public improvements. To compete with suburbs in New Jersey and Brooklyn, the new wards needed streets, schools, parks, mass transit, and other urban services. If planned well, these amenities enhanced land values and generated positive growth. If not, they burdened neighborhoods with inadequate installations for years. In either case, local promoters expected to profit from New York City's growth and did all they could to establish urban services in the newly annexed wards. This bias is markedly revealed in the struggle for street plans, parks, and rapid transit, features that abetted and reinforced the urban landscape of the future Bronx borough. In the end, Bronx boosters laid the foundation for a city rather than a suburb.

STREET PLANS AND PUBLIC IMPROVEMENTS

Initially, street plans, road construction, and other public improvements were put in the hands of the Central Park Commissioners and their successor, the Department of Public Parks. The former Westchester towns received little from the department at first. With no coherent street plan or procedures for street openings during the tenure of the Parks Department, the new wards had few roads, sewers, and bridges and scant repairs on those that existed. These conditions changed radically after 1890 when the wards took charge of improvements and street layouts. The pace of public improvements quickened, helping to impart to the Bronx an image of progress and modernity that lasted well into the twentieth century.[1]

The Parks Department controlled the western Bronx between 1869 and 1890. An early advocate of New York City's expansion, Parks Commissioner Andrew Haswell Green believed one agency could better plan the street layout of both upper Manhattan and the district north of the Harlem River because lower Westchester was "so intimately connected with and dependent upon the City of New York." In 1869, the Parks Department was allowed to plan bridges, streets, "proper sewerage and drainage," the "supply of pure and wholesome water," and the improvement of navigation on the Harlem River.[2] Considering it the best agency for the job, *The New York Times* lauded the 1873 annexation act for "very properly" keeping the Department of Parks in charge of improvements since "their engineers and surveyors are presumably best qualified to carry their own work to its natural termination."[3]

Lack of funds and jurisdictional disputes checked the department's initial progress, since the towns failed to pay their full share for the surveys and often had conflicting road commissions. By 1872, Parks Department president Henry G. Stebbins explained they had "tried to get around this by doing piece meal plans where the need was greatest." With annexation in 1874, the work continued "under municipal laws and at the general expense of the city."[4]

The most important project was a comprehensive street layout for the western Bronx. Residents and property owners "expressed a strong desire for the early completion of the plans."[5] But in 1875, the Park Board's new president, William R. Martin, insisted that the Bronx be redrawn by Frederick Law Olmsted, the department's landscape architect and the designer of Central Park. Olmsted worked on maps for three years, submitting, revising, and designing anew in the face of objections from property owners and parks commissioners alike.[6] With time, however, the department's commitment to a comprehensive Bronx layout waned. Those who had favored overall planning, commissioners Martin and Stebbins, were replaced by political hacks who neither knew nor cared about urban planning or parks. The new Board of Park Commissioners discharged Olmsted in early 1878 and abolished his Bureau of Design and Superintendence. The Olmsted layouts remained, but between 1879 and 1890 the designs were reworked and revised so often that it was as if no overall plan had been done. As Mayor Hugh L. Grant noted in 1889, the only "comprehensive plan" for the annexed district was "the whim of the adjoining property-owners."[7]

Commissioner Martin opposed the early layouts because they provided for improvements "on such a scale of expense as in themselves to be barriers to progress." As a former president of the West Side Association, an amalgam of uptown real estate interests, Martin wanted to encourage development without imposing high costs. While the city paid for layouts out of general taxes, landowners in the new wards would be taxed for the street openings and improvements the plans designated. Martin thus argued for temporary and inexpensive public improvements that would quickly prepare the region for "its profitable and productive ultimate occupation." Once it was populated, increasing land values and profits would allow for more costly permanent public works.[8]

Olmsted had set out "distinct sections" of business, suburbs, and compact housing, interlaced with parks, connecting parkways, and local steam transit routes. In a series of maps and reports done with John James Robertson Croes, Olmsted argued against applying New York City's rigid grid layout to the Bronx's rugged terrain. In their view, the grid encouraged speculation, perpetuated small lot sizes and cramped houses, and ignored "different topographical conditions." It thus fostered commerce and industry but not communities, a fault Olmsted and Croes tried to ameliorate by planning on a neighborhood scale. Their designs projected functionally discrete neighborhoods that, in the absence of zoning, were buffered from one another and from through traffic by a system of irregular streets, parkways, and transit lines. This did not encourage construction of more compact housing in outlying suburbs and towns if the central business district spread into residential areas. Olmsted's visionary plans played down the view that the city was the locus for and the result of economic transactions, what most entrepreneurs regarded as New York City's *raison d'être*.[9]

As Olmsted well knew, the gridiron plan was basic to New York City's economic and physical growth. Along with the 25 x 100-foot lot, the grid layout allowed for continuous or sporadic development, for the sale and resale of undeveloped lots, and for the most efficient use of property under all conditions and for any purpose. It was simpler to survey, buy, sell, and improve property on right-angle streets. In a city where nothing was permanently fixed, many believed that rectilinear streets offered the most rational, modern use of space. Thus the grid advanced commerce and reinforced the city's continuous rebuilding process. But it could also foster a monotonous urban landscape, devoid of natural features and open spaces, the very same aspects Olmsted decried and wished to avoid in the plans for the Bronx.[10]

Commissioner Stebbins objected to the Olmsted/Croes designs. Finding no fault with the grid system, he agreed with engineer George S. Greene's earlier observation that "small subdivisions attract population, and large ones repel it." Greene had defended the 25' x 100' lot, not because it was good, but because it was what the property owners wanted. To attempt any "fanciful shapes," Stebbins warned, would lead to "great confusion in readjusting boundaries" and "depreciation of the property" because of its unsuitability for further subdivision. Stebbins wanted to allow for the possibility that today's suburb would be tomorrow's central business district. Olmsted thought of his suburb as a "Permanent Suburban Quarter."[11]

Without finalized plans and the ensuing street openings, no improvements could be made, and the greater part of the newly annexed area would remain inaccessible and undervalued. Not surprisingly, property owners clamored incessantly for "the proper improvement and development of the territory" and in 1880 asserted Olmsted's plans were "a necessary preliminary to the occupation of these wards with population, and should be completed as speedily as possible, for the tendency of population to settle in these wards if the streets and avenues are made ready is very decided."[12]

The district north of the Harlem River became part of the city at the onset of the 1873 depression, during a retrenchment in municipal spending. Convinced that property owners should assume the costs of opening and improving streets, Comptroller Andrew Green believed local improvements should not be done to stimulate development of vacant areas to the north while downtown streets remained impassable.[13] Appropriations for the Parks Department were cut back repeatedly, retarding the development of the city's newest wards.[14] As late as 1889, a state legislative committee found "nearly sixty miles of public highways in a wretched and deplorable condition, and in the more thickly populated sections almost impassable; . . . and almost a total absence of drainage, in the midst of a population of nearly ninety-thousand people."[15]

The situation became intolerable after the elevated trains entered the Bronx in 1886. The rapid transit link to Manhattan quickened construction activity and in turn "rendered the opening of many streets imperatively necessary." In response, several local taxpayers' groups petitioned the state legislature in 1889 for "a special Commissioner of street improvements."[16] The requested legislation became law in June 1890. Thereafter the Commissioner of Street Improvements took over from the Department of Public Parks in a form of local self-government not enjoyed by any other part of the city. The bill passed despite the combined initial opposition of both political parties, the Parks Department, and the city authorities, all of whom preferred to keep the annexed wards under centralized control and thus in Tammany's hands.[17]

The local taxpayers' groups were composed primarily of the "respectable" element from the "thickly settled parts." The groups' members were dissatisfied with their local political leaders, for neither Tammany leader Henry D. Purroy nor the Republican's North Side and Suburban clubs had alleviated matters. Consequently, residents and property owners of both political stripes called for a new independent agency and commissioner.[18] Naming themselves the Citizens' Local Improvement Party, the coalition chose Louis J. Heintz, a German American brewer, as its candidate. Tammany Hall's choice, Louis F. Haffen, was also of German ancestry, but disgust with prevailing conditions doomed his chances. After a bitter campaign in which Heintz was denigrated as only fit to draw beer, Bronx voters overwhelmingly elected Heintz Commissioner of Street Improvements, temporarily breaking Tammany's hold on the western Bronx area.[19]

Commissioner Heintz had to finalize the street layout begun years earlier by the Parks Department. Long before, the town of Morrisania had adopted a grid pattern that Olmsted had found irredeemable.[20] But in the intervening years, the lack of public improvements and the ongoing suburban plans of Olmsted coupled with few public improvements kept the Bronx "a sort of rural-residence district," with large villa sites for the well-to-do. By 1890, with the exception of Mott Haven, Melrose, and Morrisania, most of the street system existed only on paper and was still based on the assumption that the Bronx would be a suburb. By then, however, as the elevated trains made the lower Bronx more accessible, the demand for substantial plots had become "exceedingly limited," while that for smaller parcels suited for townhouses had risen. Not able to efficiently subdivide land on the irregularly shaped streets, property owners besieged Commissioner Heintz "on nearly every side" to remap the future Bronx on the "checkerboard plan." In response, the commissioner decided to replot the entire district along straight lines and "not to suit the whims of a few villa-owners," but "to establish lines and grades of streets and avenues with a view to the requirements of the vast population which in the near future must inevitably flow into these wards."[21]

As soon as the el bridged the Harlem River, suburban property became city lots. The resulting higher land prices forced property owners and builders to use land more efficiently, which meant greater reliance on attached row and tenement housing, a form of urban construction that fit well with a gridiron street plan. Bronx promoters now assumed that the region north of the Harlem River would receive Gotham's excess populace, irrespective of class, not just the upper middle-class suburbanites for whom they had earlier been aiming. A street system to make that possible, Louis A. Risse declared in 1891, would advance the "important future [the borough seemed] destined to fill."[22]

The whole discussion was about the fate of the Bronx. Should it be a suburb? Or should it be a city with right-angle streets to facilitate speculation, commercial interests, and urban growth? While the outcome was important to the entire metropolis, it was not discussed by municipal authorities outside Heintz's department and hardly touched upon by the press. The earlier schism between Commissioner Stebbins and Landscape Architect Olmsted had drawn little attention. This time only two journals referred to the matter. *The New York Times* deplored the extension of the gridiron, while the weekly *Real Estate Record and Builders Guide* asked Bronx property owners to "consider whether they will not lose more than they gain by the adoption of a checker-board plan . . . [because New York] is one of the worst planned cities in the world." "If the North Side is to be made as ugly," continued the *Record and Guide,* they "ought to be very certain that the conditions which partially justify the uniformity south of the Harlem are going to prevail north of that river." The *Record and Guide* doubted whether the "pressure of population on space" would be as great in the Twenty-third and Twenty-fourth Wards as in the lower city. These editorials, however, evoked no public debate on the changeover from what *The New York Times* called "a new and good system" to "an old and bad one."[23]

In its first year, the Department of Street Improvements built streets and sewers "in all directions," astonishing "the natives who were accustomed to the slow methods of the Parks Department." The "exceedingly lively" pace of improvements continued under Louis Haffen, the commissioner appointed upon Heintz's death in 1893, and extended in 1895 to the newly annexed towns east of the Bronx River.[24] Haffen pursued Heintz's pet project, the Grand Boulevard and Concourse, and in 1895, after completing the street plan along the lines set by his predecessor, boasted that property valuations had doubled since his department began operations. In 1897, just before the commissioner's office was absorbed into the borough presidency, prominent realtor J. Clarence Davies described Haffen's surveys and maps as "the foremost factor in the recent rapid growth of the north side." The *Evening Post* conceded as much, but noted that "real improvement" meant altering the landscape "to such an extent that the face of nature has been entirely changed, and is recognizable now only in the parks and in the upper sections which have thus far escaped the flood of population." The Bronx was "being constructed . . . to meet the requirements of the future and greater city." As Haffen put it in 1893, remapping was simply "the conversion of this great area from farm land into city property."[25]

The Bronx, then, was to be urban. For more than twenty years, the Parks Department and Bronx interests tussled over the development of their area. During that time, the metropolis to the south grew by leaps and bounds, its seemingly insurmountable problems of health, safety, and transportation solved by engineering and technology, and in ways that allowed for extra entrepreneurial opportunities. Convinced that the urban was good and their own borough's urbanization even better, Bronx promoters looked southward and opted for a cityscape of concrete, curb, and pavement on right-angle streets—in essence, continuing Manhattan across the Harlem River. If that meant effacing the natural terrain, well, that was progress. Indeed, with so much growth and innovation, the urban setting of the late nineteenth century seemed an improvement over nature.[26]

PARKS AND PARKWAYS

A city, however, must also have parks. Except for a few neglected public squares, the only "parks" within the Bronx before 1884 were the outdoor picnic grounds of saloons and beer gardens. Afterward, the uptown wards

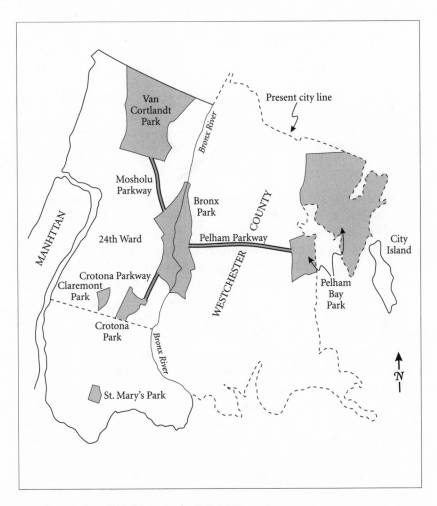

MAP 3.1 Parks and Parkways in the Bronx, 1884

TABLE 3.1 Parks and Parkways on the North Side, 1884

Parks[a]	Acres
Van Cortlandt—part of Van Cortlandt Estate	1,070
Bronx—parts of the Lydig, Lorillard, and Neale Estates	653
Pelham Bay—estates and farms of many families, including the	
Bartow, Iselin, Morris, and Hurst estates	1,740
Crotona—former Bathgate Estate	135
Claremont—Zborowski Estate and Farm	39
St. Mary's—former Janes Estate	25

Parkways	
Mosholu	80
Pelham	91
Crotona	12

[a] Parts of Bronx, Crotona, and St. Mary's parks had been used as parkland by early Bronx residents long before the park movement began.

Source: Report to the New York Legislature of the Commission to Select and Locate Lands for Public Parks in the Twenty-third and Twenty-fourth Wards of the City of New York, and in the Vicinity Thereof (New York: Martin B. Brown, 1884), 87–122; John Mullaly, *New Parks Beyond the Harlem* (New York: Real Estate Record and Builders Guide, 1887), 50; *Record and Guide*, 13 October 1988.

contained six large parks and connecting parkways (see map 3.1 and table 3.1). The pleasure grounds lent a countrified, suburban air to the Bronx, yet they were hailed and ultimately sold to the public as places for the "denizens of the tenement house district." They would be "what Central [Park] has never been—the playgrounds of the people."[27]

The idea for the park system began when the parks commissioners and Frederick Law Olmsted suggested and designed parade grounds, parks, and parkways. When annexation was first broached, New York City had been urged to "do it right" and buy land for public needs while property was still cheap.[28] After annexation, Bronx residents generally asked for pleasure grounds in areas previously used for picnics, while municipal officials designated lands not yet subdivided or with steep or rugged terrain.[29] Owners of proposed park sites (who could not sell, lease, or build upon their land yet still had to pay taxes on it) clamored for speedy acquisition. But the city insisted that neighboring property owners pay for the land with special assessment taxes, since the value of their parcels would undoubtedly increase because of the parks. These owners vigorously objected. Moreover, the same political infighting and insufficient funding that hampered public improvements in the western Bronx helped keep parks in the planning stage.[30]

A new parks movement began in 1881 with a series of *New York Herald* articles that depicted parks as a panacea for urban crowding.[31] Editor John Mullaly asserted that New York would need more parks to take its rightful place among the cities of the world. And there were "good spots" for these in the upper wards, both east and west of the city line, that "will rival in beauty those of London or Paris." Fearing that the city fathers would "allow New York to rush on from street to street in a pell-mell, hurried way . . . [and thus] the new parts of the city will be no better than the old," Mullaly stressed the need for open public space. A "grand system" of "great rural parks" will prevent a "repetition of the dense and swarming sections of the lower island." If Gotham had parks, Mullaly argued, there would "be no packing into close, narrow, pest-breeding apartments." Hence, the city needed the open spaces north of the Harlem River that, because they were "natural parks," would not require costly "artificial conceptions"; would provide sites for a parade ground, a zoo, or a world's fair; and would be made accessible by rapid transit. These parks, in turn, would raise land values and taxes as Manhattan's Central Park had done years before and ultimately pay for themselves.[32]

Mullaly's campaign led to the formation of the New York Park Association in November 1881. The association was headed by substantial, civic-minded citizens and included many Bronx promoters.[33] To overcome mayoral opposition, the New York Park Association bypassed the city administration and appealed to the state legislature in 1882. The group published pamphlets, held public meetings, and drafted bills to secure parks for the city's "large and rapidly increasing population." The combination of downtown leaders and uptown support overcame the obstacles that had hindered progress on the issue.[34]

Mullaly had touted part of the Van Cortlandt estate in the western Bronx and a site on Long Island Sound, in the Town of Pelham, as potential parks. The first had always been seen as a public space; the second compensated for New York's lack of a recreational shore and presented a further problem because it was outside the city line. The Park Association overcame this by proposing annexation of the area east of the Bronx River and by citing the pre-1874 duties that the Parks Department had had in lower Westchester County. Remembering the "Wonderful Effect" Central Park had had on real estate values, the Park Association believed that this "backward and much neglected part of the country would be inspired with new life, and new villages would spring up along its lines of rapid transit." While being "Lungs for the Metropolis," these open spaces would also increase population and real estate development.[35]

Two and a half years after its founding, the New York Park Association secured legislation for six separate recreational areas and three connecting parkways in the future Bronx (see map 3.1). By then, the elevated railroad had bridged the Harlem, imparting "unwonted activity to building operations" and necessitating "a chain of small parks in easy reach of the populace."[36] These public pleasure grounds, furthermore, would not be like "the rich man's [Central] park." Bronxite Fordham Morris asserted their terrain would "be without much artificial adornment, left in its natural state, where the military could parade and where the poor man could take his family on a picnic." The meadows would be for children instead of sheep and would be the breathing places for the millions who would move uptown.[37] The new bill was held up until 1887 because of repeated court challenges and repeal attempts. But with a nonpartisan, reform stance and the active help of the press, the parks measure overcame all opposition.[38]

The new parks were an instant success. In the 1890s, Bronx Park became the location of the zoo and botanical gardens; St. Mary's green acres gave relief from the ever denser new urban environment of the lower Bronx; and Pelham Bay Park and Parkway helped in the movement to annex the other portion of lower Westchester County. At the same time, Crotona Park became the weekend spot of Manhattan's lower East Side and abetted a small building boom in the neighboring Claremont area. The natural terrain of Van Cortlandt and Claremont parks, meanwhile, made nearby lots even more potentially valuable.[39]

Ideally, parks would enhance the health, beauty, and greatness of New York City and prevent the middle class from moving to the suburbs. But if parks increased land values in the Bronx, would this not help to create the same densely built environment as in the lower city, as lot sizes remained narrow and population grew? To be sure, as he wrote more and more, Mullaly's argument became more subtle, linking parks and rapid transit, one to attract people and the other to allow access. Mullaly dreamed of rows of "neat, commodious cottages at moderate rents . . . free from that moral and physical contamination which is the curse of overcrowded cities," but as long as Gotham's populace increased and real estate practices remained unfettered, there was always the danger the tenement house system would spread northward. Long before Heintz and Haffen spoke of preparing their area for the masses, it seems, Mullaly and his backers knew that the upper wards would be given up to a dense population, and that only by setting some land apart could this be alleviated. In the final analysis, parks were not to keep the people away.[40]

The park movement, the ultimate public improvement, occurred during the struggle for street plans, rapid transit, and other public works. Between the selection of the first two sites in 1882 and the actual passage of the 1884 bill, Bronx legislators added parkways and extra parks to the measure. Bronxites viewed pleasure grounds as a way to raise property values, create an attractive home environment, and utilize land not quite right for subdivision. Every square foot, other than the sites eventually chosen, could be built upon, thereby accelerating the coming of transit and facilitating the eventual change from a suburban Bronx to a more compact, urban one.[41]

RAPID TRANSIT

Rapid transit was the next essential ingredient. The new wards were just across the river from northern Manhattan but still too far away from the central business district. In the mid-1870s, however, the existing commuter transportation did not foster the further development of either the settled or the vacant areas of the western Bronx. The railroads were too expensive or inaccessible because of the physical terrain; the horsecars were slow and irregular, and stopped short of Manhattan. As the *Record and Guide* observed in 1883, "Proposed parks are well enough in their way, yet . . . rapid transit and more bridges are all important."[42] Without cheap, swift connections to Manhattan, the Bronx would never become the populous, urbanized area of which its boosters dreamed.

Rapid transit to Gotham's core would irrevocably join the western Bronx to Manhattan. There were even suggestions to fill in the Harlem River. Thus bound, the Bronx would share in the city's economic and population growth. Property owners, real estate agents, and aspiring entrepreneurs—Bronx boosters all—proposed, demanded, and invested in elevated lines, streetcars, railroad extensions, and finally subways. In the process, the Bronx gained transportation routes that facilitated commuting to Manhattan but also created and reinforced patterns of dense urban construction.[43]

Acting for the Parks Department with the assistance of J. J. R. Croes, Frederick Law Olmsted designed the first Bronx transit routes in 1877. Olmsted's lines passed through territory "yet wholly unprovided with facilities for access to old New York." His routes foreshadowed future ones, but were not through connections to the city. Olmsted's system bridged the Harlem River at 145th Street, circled all the sections of the Bronx, and returned to Manhattan by its original lateral crossing, avoiding streets and densely settled areas in order to open up more land for housing with the lowest possible fare and the least damage to private property and public thoroughfares. Not being direct extensions of the Manhattan els, the proposed railways did not provide the quickest transport downtown.[44]

In the 1870s, only the elevated steam railroad could handle the long travel distances to uptown and the Bronx as well as the severe congestion of Manhattan streets. By 1880 there were elevated trains reaching up to the Harlem River on Second, Third, and Ninth avenues. As the els traversed the length of Manhattan Island, they stimulated building activity and property values and created whole new residential zones for those who worked downtown. These trains proved that rapid transit, dirty and noisy as it was, promoted the northward expansion of the metropolis and thus enlarged the scope of the old "walking city."[45]

In the late nineteenth century, however, rapid transit was a private affair. The city granted charters for transit companies and franchises for routes on which to operate, providing a fertile field for enterprising land speculators and local boosters. In Manhattan, capitalists fought for control of the transit companies; in the Bronx, local interests fought for control of the transit commissions that granted routes and company charters. The Morris, Mott, and Tiffany families were well represented in the first two transit commissions of 1879 and 1880, which chose routes favorable to their undeveloped land holdings. But the last transit commission of 1881 sided with north Bronx landowners and residents of the most settled parts, both of whom demanded rapid transit along Third Avenue. By 1882, the Bronx had two transit companies on the books, the Suburban Rapid Transit and the New York, Fordham, and Bronx Railway, but no transit facilities in sight.[46]

The first two transit commissions laid out "a comprehensive system" of transit lines loosely based on those Olmsted had devised for the Parks Department. Designed to develop "the less populous parts of the districts," these routes went over private property and connected directly with the els in Manhattan, avoiding Olmsted's circuitous east/west routing (see map 3.2). The last commission, in contrast, claimed its Third Avenue line served "the greatest need of the greatest number" since it passed through the already developed region paralleling the Harlem Railroad. The first group's network—embodied in the Suburban Rapid Transit's east, west, and central branches—would have opened up more of the Bronx, including the higher ground originally set aside for suburban homes. The second group's transit line went directly north through areas better suited for city buildings. Though both sides backed routes that favored their self-interest, they differed over the extent and manner in which the Bronx should be developed. In one form or another, however, all later mass transit proposals incorporated the same general routes of the early transit commissions.[47]

Between 1886 and 1905, the Suburban Rapid Transit's Third Avenue line was the only one to serve the Bronx. The company managed to build the

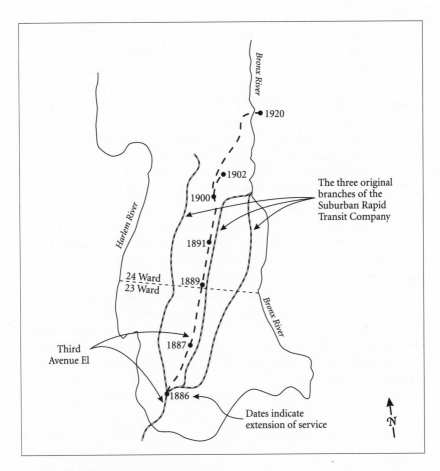

MAP 3.2 Suburban Rapid Transit, 1886–1920

first leg of its original system through the vacant North New York subdivision of Mott Haven before swinging west at 145th Street. From 1887 on, however, the SRT abandoned its original plan and proceeded slowly up the Third Avenue route leased from its former competitor, the New York, Fordham, and Bronx, finally reaching Tremont in 1891.[48]

By then, it was clear that the SRT would not build its other branches. Despite all their efforts, Bronx interests had lost out to Manhattan-based capitalists. At the time of the el's actual construction, in 1885, transportation mogul Jay Gould controlled both the Suburban Rapid Transit and the New York, Fordham, and Bronx Railway. Gould was not interested in extending service to the whole Bronx, only to the Third Avenue corridor, where "an elevated road . . . would be immediately profitable." In 1891, the SRT was directly connected to Gould's Manhattan Railway Company, making the Bronx elevated an extension of a Manhattan transit line.[49]

The Third Avenue El stimulated construction immediately. In 1887, a year after the elevated trains began running in the Bronx, the number of proposed building plans rose dramatically, threefold in the Mott Haven neighborhood alone. Fed by a systemwide five-cent fare in 1894 and direct trains in 1896, building activity continued throughout the 1890s, only lessening momentarily at the onset of the 1893 depression. Construction clustered around the stations but occurred at a greater rate in the undeveloped regions along its track, such as lower Mott Haven and around Claremont Parkway. In these sections, construction of closely built city houses was the rule, with apartments dominating from 1890 on. Along other parts of the transit route, there was a slow insertion of frame and brick structures, with newer brick apartments often replacing older frame housing. The process led to dense concentrations of new settlement accompanied by an intensive infilling of the older localities, giving an urban cast to the Third Avenue corridor of the Bronx years before the subway appeared in 1905.[50]

The next round of improved transportation in the Bronx was the streetcar. The trolley network grew out of the first horsecar "Huckleberry Road" (originally the Harlem River, Morrisania, and Fordham Railway), which in 1892 was electrified and newly incorporated as the Union Railway Company. Owned from its inception by Democratic Party stalwarts, the "Huckleberry" easily obtained permission to cross the Harlem Bridge in 1878, to extend lines away from its original route in the 1880s, and later to incorporate anew with a most favorable charter. Within a year after its reorganization, the streetcar line almost doubled its ridership, from 3.5 million in 1892 to 6.5 million in 1893. In the mid-1890s, the "new and solid tracks" of the trolley spurred some growth in the harder-to-reach, hilly spots along Boston Road, Westchester Avenue, and Southern Boulevard.[51]

The el and the streetcar worked as a unified transit network in the lower Bronx, making the elevated trains accessible to sections farther away from Third Avenue. The Bronx trolleys shuttled commuters to the el stations at 133rd, 138th, 149th, and 161st streets before crossing the Harlem River and connecting with the Manhattan streetcars. By the time the Union Railway had electrified and renovated all its lines, the el had lowered its fare and initiated direct, nonstop service downtown.[52]

This early transit caused dense growth in only a small portion of the Bronx. Unlike the streetcar suburbs of Boston, neither the trolley nor the el extended their lines much beyond settled areas. The el took four years to reach Tremont, at 177th Street, and remained there until 1900 when train service to Fordham was introduced. Streetcars were no better. Once the

"Huckleberry" received its franchises, it delayed putting tracks on radiating avenues until there was a substantial population along the route. When new trolley lines were added in the late 1890s, the long travel distances over single-track right-of-ways kept them from inducing the kinds of building activity that the el had done in the lower Bronx. Hence promoters of areas with fledgling trolley service also wanted the speedier, cheap transportation a subway would provide.[53]

In the late 1890s, however, transit was hard to get. Not until fifteen years after the el's arrival did the subway enter the Bronx, in 1905. During those years, transit companies, the city, the public, and the courts argued over who should own transit, how it should be built and paid for, and where it would go.[54] It was less possible for Bronx interests to create transportation companies or determine routes in such a setting. When, in 1884, the Board of Aldermen regained power to give out surface railway grants, Bronx entrepreneurs bombarded the council with requests for new streetcar franchises. This system ended when the Union Railway gained ascendancy after the mid-1890s.[55] And subways, the agreed-upon mode of construction after 1891, were costly, large-scale undertakings that required huge financial resources.

Unable to create the lines themselves and so profit directly, Bronx boosters worked incessantly to get others to build transit for them. During this struggle, routes were proposed, altered, or scrapped by each new plan or commission. The uncertainty over Bronx routes kept the rapid transit issue before the public, for once an area had been designated for service, no matter how tentatively, it would anticipate and continue demanding that line in the future. Bronx interests thus organized and lobbied constantly, since, as stated in the motto of their Rapid Transit League, "It is only by agitation that Rapid Transit can be secured."[56]

Bronxites wanted transit at all costs. As James Lee Wells declared in 1890, "We want rapid transit beyond the Harlem and I don't care who gives it to us, provided it is the proper kind of rapid transit." Four years later, Wells represented the North Side Board of Trade before the Rapid Transit Commission. "The people in my neighborhood," testified Wells, "prefer an underground or elevated road, but would not object to an open cut if that seemed to the commission the most advisable." By 1901, the ubiquitous Mr. Wells and Bronx Borough President Louis Haffen were "particularly gratified" by the planned subway extension but wondered if it could be built cheaper as an el, thus allowing for another elevated line on Jerome Avenue to provide "all the transit facilities needed by this rapidly growing borough." To Wells and Haffen, the "proper kind of rapid transit" meant anything that moved on wheels.[57]

Behind it all was the hope, and for some the certainty, of enhanced land values. Transit lines transformed suburban acres into urban lots, immediately raising the price of land.[58] A 1907 advertisement for Bronx lots bluntly stated the concern with higher property rates:

Three Secrets of increase in real estate values are:
1st—Rapid Transit
2nd—More Rapid Transit
3rd—Most Rapid Transit

Not surprisingly, there were no misgivings, no qualms, and certainly no questions about how rapid transit would affect the Bronx. While civic reformers decried congestion in the inner city, Bronx real estate circles hoped that congestion would push "the increasing exodus of Manhattan's population" to their borough. "But," argued booster and architect Alfred E. Davis, "we cannot, in reason, expect to attract population hither unless we provide safe, comfortable and rapid means of transit."[59]

And what the Bronx received were els and subways built on viaducts. Once past the Mott Haven and North New York section, the early Bronx subways ran on elevated tracks, in essence, el lines with all the attendant discomforts and inconveniences of dirt and noise. The first el roads spewed cinders and smoke from steam engines. The subway viaducts were cleaner but as noisy as the elevated trains. Both cut off light and made the affected thoroughfares good for only businesses and poorer tenements. While great in the 1880s, the els were undesirable in the 1890s and obsolete by 1905.[60] Yet, because els were cheaper, they were proposed and accepted in 1904 and 1913 by Bronx promoters, residents, and everyone concerned with building them. As the *New York Evening Post* observed in 1905, it did not matter that twenty or thirty years later Bronx "streets in which elevated roads are now proposed will be important business thoroughfares."[61] The need for rapid transit was great, but the ability to provide it when subway costs were so prohibitive was not. Hence, in the Bronx, elevated tracks became unalterable features of the urban landscape.

The subways came to the Bronx after much maneuvering between transit interests and the city (see map 3.3). By 1900, it was decided that the city would own and finance construction of a new transit system, but lease it to a private company for operation. This compromise allowed the city to build two subways in the Bronx in 1905. One was an extension of the Broadway line that passed through upper Manhattan before entering the northwest Bronx at Kingsbridge (the current 1 and 9 trains). The other, the more important of the two, entered the borough at 149th Street and ran

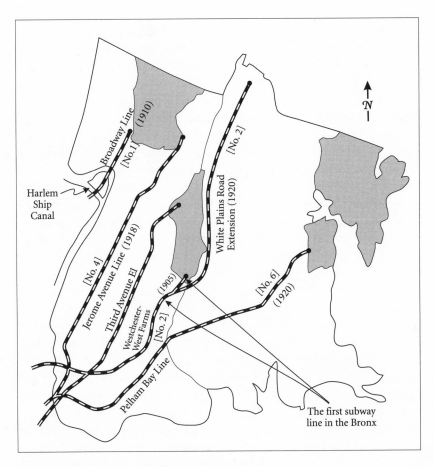

Harlem
Ship
Canal

Broadway Line
[No. 1]
(1910)

[No. 2]

White Plains Road
Extension (1920)

Jerome Avenue Line (1918)
[No. 4]

Third Avenue El
Westchester-
West Farms
(1905)
[No. 2]

[No. 6]
(1920)

Pelham Bay Line

N

The first subway
line in the Bronx

MAP 3.3 Subway Routes in the Bronx, 1905–1920

over Westchester Avenue and Southern Boulevard to West Farms (the current 2 train).[62] The demand for more transit lines was met when a movement to relieve congestion in lower Manhattan resulted in plans for a vast expansion of mass transportation in four of the city's boroughs. The Dual Contracts of 1913 eventually gave the Bronx two new transit routes, the Jerome Avenue and Pelham Bay lines (the current 4 and 6 trains) and extensions of its older ones, the White Plains and Gun Hill roads additions to the Westchester Avenue/Southern Boulevard subway and the Third Avenue El, respectively.[63] By 1930, continued strife between transit companies and the city government led to the construction of the only fully underground subway in the Bronx, the city-owned Independent D line under the Grand Concourse.[64]

Both the el and later subways increased land values and building activity wherever they ran and left dense urban areas in their wake. All the lines plowed through settled districts and vacant blocks, thus causing infilling of previously built sections and creating whole new urban neighborhoods in the undeveloped areas beside their tracks. Since they arrived years apart, after long negotiations between transportation companies and the city, the el and the subway did not distribute growth evenly throughout the borough as envisioned by the early Bronx transit commissioners. Every subsequent introduction of transit stimulated development within an irregular lineal strip, resulting in progressively newer and denser urban neighborhoods. As more subways and trolleys were introduced, these intensely built-up corridors widened, eventually merging with previously developed areas. It was rapid transit, arriving in this staggered nature, that helped make the Bronx urban in its construction and density of population.[65]

El and subway tracks bound the Bronx firmly to New York City. Every rail line ran over transportation arteries that radiated from bridge and tunnel crossings to Manhattan. With none of Olmsted's circular routing that buffered as well as served neighborhoods, these subway routes were designed to funnel commuters downtown; the "view was to link the important parts of Manhattan with the important parts of the Bronx."[66] The borough's irregular topography reinforced this pattern. With the el and subway, it was simply easier to travel downtown, despite improved crosstown trolley service. The linear traffic flow helped re-create a Manhattan-style environment north of the Harlem River that because of its density, housing type, and elevated tracks was conducive to a continued outward movement of people, and thus to settlement by progressively lower income groups. Mass transit had made a difference in the Bronx.

By the turn of the century, the Bronx had many of the urban amenities for which its boosters had long striven, and more on the way. Thus when the borough began getting the population figures its promoters had long wanted, it was fully prepared to handle all who wished to settle there. Transit would bring them, parks would serve them, and all would fit snugly on straightened, paved, and sewered streets.[67]

4 EMERGING NEIGHBORHOODS

During the late nineteenth and early twentieth centuries, the estates and villages of the early Bronx became urban neighborhoods. The basic, underlying factors that had permitted them to develop in the first place—the city's economy, population, and transit systems—were shared by all areas. The timing, pace, and conditions under which they grew differed. But the primary agent for neighborhood creation and growth was "the real estate operator [who] . . . gets hold of tracts of land here and there which he can map and cut up into blocks and building lots and advertise and sell." "He is the man," concluded Elihu Root, "who very largely determines the growth of a city."[1] These real estate operations created the city neighborhood by neighborhood.

MOTT HAVEN

One such neighborhood was Mott Haven, the southernmost area of the Bronx. Cheap rapid transit spurred its development. The Suburban Rapid Transit Company—the later Third Avenue El—reached Mott Haven in 1886 and made the area accessible to Manhattan's swelling population. From then on, Mott Haven had higher land values, much construction of residential and business buildings, a rapid pace of public improvements, and population growth. The combination of private and public endeavors transformed it into an urban neighborhood.[2]

In the immediate postannexation years, the Mott Haven area languished with the rest of the Bronx. With time, however, proximity to Manhattan gave it an edge in the competition for public and private improvements. Its street system was too long established to lend itself to wholesale change. Consequently, the Parks Department left Mott Haven to the same purposes its early developers had—for "commercial and manufacturing" facilities and "for inexpensive residences for the working classes." By the late 1880s, as Parks Commissioner William R. Martin had predicted, Mott Haven was well prepared to receive Manhattan's overflow population and to be "the centre of the greatest suburban activity and growth . . . of this metropolitan city." And by the 1890s, well ahead of other neighborhoods, practically every street in central Mott Haven was paved, sewered, and lit by electricity.[3]

Booster efforts for the Bronx as a whole and the neighborhood in particular worked in Mott Haven's favor.[4] Mott Haven gained a park, new bridges, a railroad depot, and depressed tracks on the Harlem and Port Morris railroads. Carved out of the Wilton tract, St. Mary's Park reduced the acreage available for buildings yet enhanced adjacent property values by creating an area more suited for better residences. The Harlem River span at 138th Street, soon to be under the "constant presence of the trolley cars," was the first of many new crossings that brought Mott Haven closer to Manhattan. The elimination of grade crossings and a modern, "artistic" depot at 138th Street relieved the "depressing" effect of the storage yards along the Mott Haven Canal—one reporter claimed "the whole neighborhood will in a few years assume a different aspect." These measures focused the neighborhood's center more firmly on the Third Avenue corridor, with 138th Street as the main crosstown thoroughfare.[5]

Rapid transit was Mott Haven's greatest advantage. The Third Avenue El entered the neighborhood between Alexander and Willis avenues in May 1886. By passing east of Third Avenue, the elevated trains of the Suburban Road avoided the developed portions of Mott Haven proper, going instead through the "virgin territory" of North New York, where empty lots beckoned to speculators, builders, and home seekers alike. Until the later part of 1887, the el served Mott Haven exclusively. And during that time alone, though private dwellings suffered from the "rumble of trains and sharp-edged cinders from the locomotive," the el "increased the valuation of property along the line of the road from 35 to 50 per cent."[6] Lots east of Willis Avenue in lower North New York that in 1881 sold for less than $2,000 were selling for twice that amount ten years later. Prices continued to increase during the 1890s, raising land values on streets farther away from the el's route.[7] While some of the upsurge in land prices, and later in tax assessments, was caused by the ongoing installation of urban amenities, the sustained rise was fueled primarily by the el—first by the expectations it generated and later by the accessibility it provided.[8]

In anticipation of higher land values, construction activity predated the actual running of the elevated line. Before 1886, builders erected a few scattered rows of brick and brownstone houses on Alexander and Willis avenues. For example, William O'Gorman, a well-known builder in the

Bronx and the first large-scale operator in Mott Haven, built more than a hundred brownstone dwellings in the first half of the 1880s.[9] Housing operations were spurred on by numerous sales of North New York lots and the ready availability of construction loans.[10] So intense was the building activity in some quarters that in 1894 the *New York Evening Post* marveled at how speedily streets were lined with solid structures, prematurely depicting Willis Avenue as "continuously built up on both sides." Construction spread from the vicinity of the el stations (from 134th to 142nd Streets, between Lincoln and Willis avenues) to the entire central core of North New York (132nd to 148th Streets, between Third and St. Ann's avenues), leaving most blocks there completely filled in by 1898 (see map 4.1). As the streets farthest from the el—those south of St. Mary's Park—remained

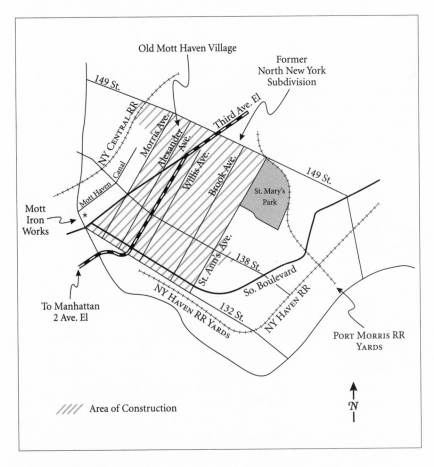

MAP 4.1 Mott Haven, 1898

largely undeveloped and the older, upper portions of Mott Haven village and North New York contained numerous empty lots and frame structures that could easily be removed, Mott Haven approached the new century with enough land to sustain subsequent construction.[11]

Building shifted from the wood frame houses predominant in the 1870s to the brick, multistory, multifamily structures of the post-el years. Between 1880 and 1887, most buildings were one-family, two- to three-story, brick or brownstone row houses. With the onset of el service and the concomitant rise in land values, three- to five-story multifamily buildings began to outnumber single-family dwellings.[12] A single five-cent fare in 1894 reinforced this trend by making the commute to Manhattan affordable for everyone. Though private attached dwellings continued to be erected, by 1897 Mott Haven builders preferred multifamily housing.[13]

The new housing ranged from frame row houses and cold-water flats to modern townhouses and "model" apartments with heating, hot water, and electric lights, many, if along the main arteries, with stores at street level. All the new structures, however, were on narrow lots. One-family dwellings were often fitted snugly into 15-foot-wide spaces, allowing the builder to squeeze five houses into every three standard lots. Flats were more expansive, covering the entire 25-foot width of a lot and extending as far back as circumstances and the law afforded, and sometimes farther. Though far uptown, Mott Haven resembled lower Manhattan in this respect.[14]

Factory construction accompanied residential building. Between 1880 and 1898, seventy factory plans were filed for the Mott Haven area, all but one or two in the vicinity of the Mott Haven Canal, Port Morris, and along Southern Boulevard. Land that, years before, Mott and Morris set aside for business and industry, that Mott Haven realtor George C. Goeller described as "one of the finest and most convenient locations that can be found anywhere," and that the *Record and Guide* considered "especially favorable for manufacturers" became by 1895 "the great manufacturing district, where nearly everything, from a piano to a refrigerating machine, is made."[15]

No definite boundary separated residences from these "important manufacturing plants." Mott Haven's most vocal proponent of industry, the Port Morris Land and Improvement Company, stressed that its lots were suited for business purposes or residences. As new factories came in, builders put up "small single dwellings and a good class of tenements to accommodate the influx of skilled Mechanics," so that, as Port Morris industrialist John De La Vergne put it, "workingmen can live near their place of work."[16] Real estate dealers, builders, and businessmen agreed with Alexander Avenue resident and realtor James Lee Wells, who in 1889 was ecstatic because the Bronx was "becoming more self-sustaining year by year, [with] no less than thirty factories between Harlem Bridge and 138th Street alone." Though complaints of industrial pollution were becoming commonplace, entrepreneurial interests in both Mott Haven and the western Bronx foresaw no danger in juxtaposing better-class flats and houses with cheap tenements and factories. In their minds, Mott Haven as the most downtown area of the Bronx was analogous to lower New York City, not to a suburb for commuters.[17]

New buildings brought new people. Gotham's population growth and Mott Haven's lower rents created a consistent demand for small houses and flats within walking distance of the elevated trains throughout the period. Speaking about the Bronx in 1895, real estate broker J. Clarence Davies explained that families "got more for the same rent" across the Harlem River than south of it.[18] By 1900, with 85 to 90 percent of its new construction in place, Mott Haven had approximately 53,000 inhabitants, a more than sevenfold increase from 1875 levels and an 86 percent increment since 1892 (see table 4.1). As it spread outward from the el stations, this population filled in the older, settled portions and created new communities in the North New York sector. Two subneighborhoods sprang up somewhat independently of the elevated route, a working-class area of frame tenements along the curve of Southern Boulevard and a middle-class townhouse district on Mott and Walton avenues—the former an offshoot of the many new factories, the latter almost isolated from Mott Haven proper, dependent on the New York and Harlem Railroad. The neighborhood's central core now stretched from the Mott Haven Canal to St. Ann's Avenue and contained many of the schools, churches, hospitals, and stores necessary for its larger population. Mott Haven, at the turn of the century, was a full-fledged urban neighborhood.[19]

TABLE 4.1 Population of Mott Haven, 1875–1900

| Year | Population | Percent | |
		Foreign Born	Aliens
1875	7,263		8%
1892	28,460		15%
1900	53,027	30%	

Source: Frank Rice, Secretary of State, New York State, "Exhibits Showing the Enumeration of the State by Counties, Cities, Towns and Election Districts for the Year 1892," in New York State, *Senate Documents, 1892*, no. 60; "Population of the County of New York, Bronx Borough, 1900–1905," in John O'Brien, Secretary of State, New York State, *Manual for the Use of the Legislature of the State of New York, 1906*, 238.

In the beginning, the new residents resembled the earlier inhabitants. In 1892, Mott Havenites were largely of old-stock American, Irish Catholic, and Christian and Jewish German ancestry, with a sprinkling of Eastern European Jews and Italians. Eighty-five percent of these residents were native-born or naturalized American citizens (see table 4.1). The locality's interior had few un-Americanized aliens, but here and there certain streets and houses evinced a definite ethnic or cultural cast that intensified with time.[20] As the 1890s wore on, the Irishness of lower Mott Haven increased—St. Jerome's Catholic Church had become the largest congregation in Mott Haven by 1901—while a growing German presence permeated the entire neighborhood, spawning three new German-speaking churches. In 1897, there were enough Jewish residents in the area to form the Temple Hand-in-Hand, the first synagogue in North New York. And by 1899, Mott Haven's northern boundary teemed with Italians and was, according to the *New York Evening Post*, "in every way worthy of an Italian quarter."[21] The foreign-born segment of the neighborhood doubled to almost one third of the total population by 1900. The varied ancestry of its residents meant Mott Haven had become a zone of emergence for Americanized immigrants and their American-born children and became a haven for new immigrants of similar background as foreign immigration into New York City continued.[22]

Mott Haven, during the 1890s, was a growing and vital neighborhood. Never mind that trains girded the waterfront, or that the Mott Haven Canal was still "a public nuisance, dangerous to life and detrimental to health," about which nearby property owners and residents had been complaining for years.[23] The neighborhood's tree-lined streets offered all the conveniences of the lower city and were the business and commercial center of the Bronx. The proportion of new immigrants may have been rising, but Mott Haven entered the borough years with a high status, embracing well-off townhouse districts where many of its business and political leaders lived as well as much new housing affordable by the "ordinary family." The older, village portions had wooden cottages interspersed with apartment buildings. The thoroughfares near the factories were lined with neat, orderly rows of shining new wood frame or brick houses. Although they were small, cramped, and packed together, they seemed to be on wider streets than lower Manhattan and had no pervasive odor of decay. New, with vacant land, and therefore still "parklike," the neighborhood conveyed a sense of openness, not of hemmed-in tenements. Mott Haven was considered a good place to live, notwithstanding that it had been developed as a mixture of factories and residences, of working and middle classes, with few recreational facilities and a noisy elevated line.[24]

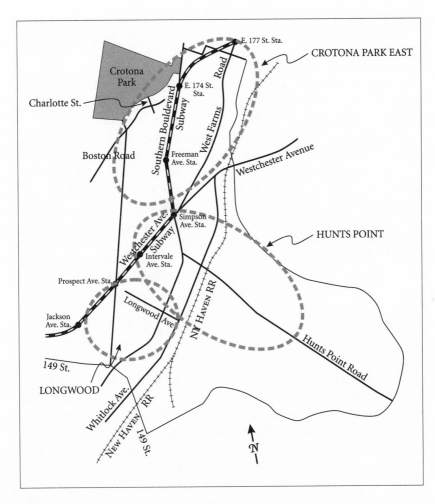

MAP 4.2 Hunts Point–Crotona Park East, 1879–1905

HUNTS POINT–CROTONA PARK EAST

The Hunts Point–Crotona Park East sector developed later than its southwestern neighbor. This area—the old Hunts Point–West Farms tract of township days, the later Southern Boulevard District or East Bronx of the thirties, and the Fort Apache precinct of the sixties—lay east of Prospect Avenue and contained large estates, few houses, and hardly any streets. Though the region's heavily wooded uplands and grassy tidal marshes were slated for transit development from 1880 on, the territory did not receive fast, reliable transportation until the early twentieth century. Only when the subway arrived in 1905 did the Hunts Point–Crotona Park East section become the site of the up-and-coming neighborhoods of the Bronx (see map 4.2).[25]

In the immediate postannexation years, however, the territory seemed ripe for development. It was not far from the city's core, but because it was slightly off the beaten track, its property owners were deeply involved in gaining urban services for the Bronx. The Tiffany, Faile, Hoe, Simpson, Spofford, and Vyse families—all politically active owners of large tracts—were ably represented on the Park Board and the many transit commissions. Petitions for public improvements invariably carried the signatures of Lyman and Henry D. Tiffany, Charles V. Faile, and J. L. Spofford, as representatives of the Fox, Faile, Vyse, Simpson, Hoe, Dickey, Spofford, White, and Rogers estates. These owners were influential enough to get a branch of the el plotted through their land and to keep the street plan of the Fox estate unchanged by either the Department of Parks or the Department of Street Improvements. However, the area's potential could not be realized without actual transit service.[26]

Without transit, Hunts Point's undeveloped acres lay fallow for twenty years. Whenever installation seemed imminent, an estate was carved up and auctioned off with much fanfare (see map 4.3). The Fox estate in 1884, the Longwood Park property of the White and Rogers estates in 1887 and 1888, and the Vyse estate in the 1890s were all put up for sale in anticipation of rapid transit.[27] When those prospects dimmed, the offered parcels wound up as city lots with no access to the city. These lots increased in value only as surrounding valuations rose. The result, therefore, was a slow increase instead of the boom in land values occurring elsewhere in the Bronx. This was true for the whole period even though the trolley stimulated a slow accretion of housing from the late 1890s on. In those years, the Fox and Vyse estates gained scattered rows of small, narrow frame dwellings along Prospect Avenue, while Longwood received a few blocks of semidetached brick townhouses. In both instances, however, the new buildings were too few and too small to alter the area's nonurban status.[28]

The subway changed things somewhat. So long as subdivision inevitably led to cheap suburban lots, there was little incentive to put other estates on the market. But immediately after the Interborough Rapid Transit contract was signed in January 1900, those lowly suburban lots beyond Prospect Avenue became prime urban property. The 86-acre Hoe-Simpson tract, for example, changed hands just before the transit agreement. A scant month later, the property was right on the line of the subway and therefore "nearer the City Hall in point of time and at a five-cent fare, than the corresponding section served by the elevated roads." While estate sales once again "assumed

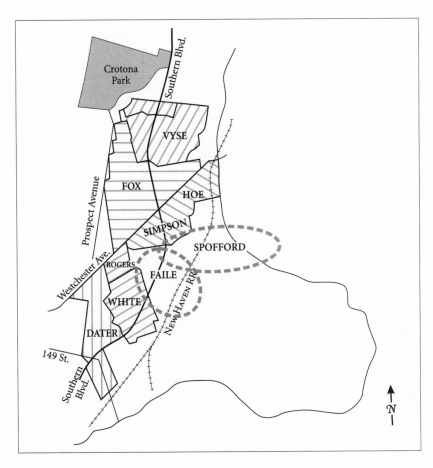

MAP 4.3 Estates in Hunts Point–Crotona Park East, 1879–1905

special importance," the region remained largely undeveloped. Up to 1904, there were houses only on the Fox, Vyse, and Longwood subdivisions. Despite the area's new "metropolitan status," the experience of the previous decades stifled boom conditions until subway construction actually began.[29]

The boom finally arrived in 1904. The subway traversed the district on a route that paralleled the once-planned eastern branch of the el, running high above Westchester Avenue, Southern Boulevard, and Boston Road before reaching West Farms (see map 4.3). As construction of the Interborough Rapid Transit's elevated tracks progressed, a "most feverish activity" set in. Land was sold, resold, and quickly sold again—each time at a profit because of the certainty of rising prices. As early as June 1904—a full year before subway service began—a reporter noted that "nothing is for sale in this neighborhood at prices within reason," and absolutely "nothing can be bought along the line of the [Southern] Boulevard."[30]

Building activity followed. Between 1904 and 1906, applications for building permits skyrocketed, precipitating a wave of construction that continued almost unabated until 1918. Construction began south of Westchester Avenue, around the Prospect Avenue and Simpson Street stations, and spread northward along both sides of the subway trestle. A new crop of entrepreneurs accounted for much of this building, but those who had formerly built in the lower borough were also "going out along the Rapid Transit." In 1910 Bronx booster W. W. Gill exclaimed that "blocks and blocks of handsome flats and residences have sprung up as if by magic." To increase real estate opportunities, Hunts Point property owners paid for an additional subway station at Intervale Avenue. "It's simply marvelous," declared Colonel John D. Jones at the station's 1910 opening ceremony. Jones, a resident of the area, observed that it reminded him of a California prairie town receiving the railroad for the first time. The Hunts Point–Crotona Park East sector had at last come into its own.[31]

Beyond Prospect Avenue, the transit-induced boom cycle resulted in a totally urban environment of buildings, sidewalks, and streets. What was new about the Hunts Point–Crotona Park East region was its building pattern and, of course, the severity of the resulting city landscape. Though private dwellings were built before and after the subway, there was no transition from smaller housing to flats, as had happened elsewhere. From the beginning, the five- to six-story apartment house was the predominant form. Apartment buildings went up on vacant land and among the existing housing of the Fox and Vyse subdivisions, where they often replaced recent frame dwellings. All at once, the area was covered with multifamily buildings, in groups of ten to twenty at a time, on Southern Boulevard; on Charlotte, Freeman, Kelly, and Fox streets; and on Intervale, Hunts Point, and Hoe avenues.[32] In 1913, for example, Harry T. Cook described how "four of the largest operators and home-makers in the Bronx"—the American Real Estate Company, Henry Morgenthau, George F. Johnson, and James F. Meehan—had "swept away" the "neglected estates" of the Hunts Point region, spending over a million dollars "in transforming this territory into city property, [with buildings that could] house more than one hundred thousand persons." By 1920, unbroken walls of brick stretched from the tracks of the New Haven Railroad northward to Crotona Park and from Prospect Avenue almost to the Bronx River.[33]

The Southern Boulevard region was to be "chiefly a tenement-house section." The subway's link to Manhattan, the booming land prices, and the city's burgeoning population predisposed the area to multifamily housing.

But the apartment buildings of Hunts Point–Crotona Park East were bigger and better than ever, because the Tenement House Law of 1901 (also known as the New Law) mandated more fire protection, light, and air, and separate toilet facilities within each family unit. Designed to eliminate dark and unsanitary dumbbell tenements, the new code made it unprofitable to build multifamily dwellings on anything less than a 40 x 100-foot lot. The combination of tenement legislation, high property costs, empty acres, and thousands of eager prospective tenants spurred construction of larger rental structures.[34]

Builders quickly discarded the narrow tenement layout and turned instead to apartments, ranging in width from 40 feet to an entire city block and differing in quality from the unheated cold-water flat to the warm, roomy—often luxurious—elevator building. But whether plain or fancy, big or small, these New Law apartments were densely built. Jammed side by side and relieved only by occasional frame dwellings, churches, schools, and retail outlets (those ubiquitous "taxpayers"), the buildings housed the largest amount of people in the smallest amount of space. When, in 1920, the new Pelham Bay subway made lower Southern Boulevard and Hunts Point more accessible, the center of Hunts Point–Crotona Park East was already one solid mass of urban humanity.[35]

The Hunts Point–Crotona Park East district was primarily a place to live. It was practically uninhabited until the turn of the century, and had only

TABLE 4.2 Population of Hunts Point–Crotona Park East, 1892–1920

Year	Total Population	Percent of	
		Foreign Born	Foreign Ancestry[b]
1892	2,559[a]		
1905	19,527		
1910	56,875	34%	77%
1915	119,691		
1920	153,651	44	91

[a] Figures were computed from election district statistics and adjusted to reflect the boundaries of the Hunts Point–Crotona Park East neighborhood.

[b] Includes foreign born and those of foreign parentage.

Source: New York State, "Exhibits Showing the Enumeration of the State by Counties, Cities, Towns and Election Districts for the Year 1892"; Laidlaw, *Population of New York City, 1890–1930*, 54–56; Laidlaw, *Statistical Sources for Demographic Studies of Greater New York, 1910*; Laidlaw, *Statistical Sources for Demographic Studies of Greater New York, 1920*.

19,000 residents when the subway arrived in 1905. Fifteen years later, by 1920, the streets in and around Southern Boulevard housed more than 153,000 people, with most of this growth occurring between 1905 and 1915 (see table 4.2).[36]

Higher densities followed. In 1915, 14 census tracts had 100 people to the acre, two of which had more than 200 per and one more than 300. By 1920, there were 15 tracts with more than 100 people to the acre, within which six hovered around 200 to 350 persons per. Population was greatest in the section centered around Westchester Avenue and in the region immediately southeast of Crotona Park, namely, in those very spots that were later abandoned and synonymous with urban decay but that in 1920 contained 200 to 300 people per acre, living in blocks of fully tenanted apartment buildings.[37] In a 1909 address on Bronx real estate, James Lee Wells had predicted "that this will soon become one of the most populous sections of The Bronx." But in the same year, the *North Side News* lamented that the "tenement house law is permitting as horrible congestion [in the Bronx] as that which damns Manhattan," and outlined how a Crotona Park East block went from empty lots to solid tenements in about a year. That block—on Charlotte Street—was the very one visited by Presidents Carter and Reagan 70 years later.[38]

In 1905, the area's few residents were largely of German extraction, both Christian and Jewish, with a few Irish and old-stock Protestant Americans thrown in. This early population was a spillover from the trolley neighborhoods of East Morrisania and Woodstock. The subway residents, however, differed markedly. From the beginning, the district was a full-grown immigrant neighborhood—a zone of emergence for those who had lived in lower Manhattan and Harlem that attracted the newly arrived. By 1910, immigrants and their children accounted for over three quarters of the inhabitants, and of these, almost a third were Jews from Russia and Eastern Europe. Ten years later, when the Bronx Board of Trade called for the "'Americanization' of alien residents of the community," the foreign-parentage group had risen to over 90 percent of the total (see table 4.2). Eastern European Jews of foreign birth constituted more than a third of the neighborhood's population all by themselves. Other nationalities added to the international flavor of Hunts Point and Crotona Park East. From 1907 on, small pockets of Italians, Germans, Scandinavians, Irish, and British lived among the larger Jewish population. While predominantly Russian and Eastern European Jewish, the area had some diversity.[39]

It was a "swell" area at first, particularly around Prospect Avenue, the Longwood section, and the Southern Boulevard–Hunts Point Road locality.[40] This is where the first elevator apartment buildings stood, where architect John DeHart and flashy builder James F. Meehan lived, and where the status-conscious Longwood and Pioneer clubs met. The early residents were comfortable in income and middle class in outlook and aspirations. They founded churches and synagogues, demanded schools and public improvements, formed social and religious clubs, and transformed sterile buildings and streets into a vibrant, viable social environment. But as more buildings went up and more immigrants moved in, the neighborhood became a working-class section, still quite good because its housing was new, "with every improvement in a new clean district," but not as upscale as before. For workers who earned a decent wage, the density and growing congestion did not lessen the neighborhood's appeal, for it had residential units to suit every taste and budget, all meeting the minimum standard for good housing. By 1920, Hunts Point–Crotona Park East was a varied, diverse urban community, in which families ranked each other by their street, building, floor, or even by whether they lived at the front or the back. To newcomers from downtown, the old East Bronx was a step up. Those who wanted better still moved on along the subway line that had first brought them there.[41]

MELROSE AND MORRISANIA

Melrose, Morrisania, and the Woodstock–East Morrisania section fared differently from the introduction of transit (see map 4.6). Because of local conditions, these areas grew piecemeal, in ways that left them with more housing and more people, yet less of an urban character than their counterparts, Mott Haven and Hunts Point–Crotona Park East. Despite the el, the trolley, and the subway, the interior streets of Melrose, Morrisania, and Woodstock–East Morrisania had a village air about them. Each wave of transit development filled in the open spaces of these neighborhoods further, yet left them in a seemingly transitional stage in which they were never wholly new or fully of one type or another.[42]

Melrose was the best example of this. It was northwest of Mott Haven, between the New York Central's Harlem line and Third Avenue (see map 4.4). During the late nineteenth century, Melrose benefited from the same public improvements that had helped its southern neighbor, including a spanking new freight yard at its southwest corner.[43] It gained no parks, but from late 1887 on, Melrose had elevated transit along its eastern edge. As it wound its way up Third Avenue, the el reinforced the existing commercial and business character of the thoroughfare and spurred some residential construction in the adjacent streets. Building activity spread slowly west-

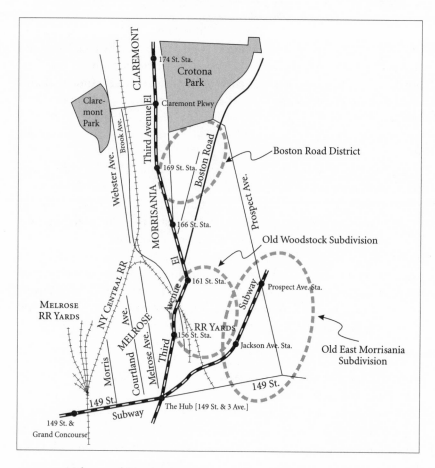

MAP 4.4 Melrose and Morrisania, 1915

ward and petered out in the less desirable blocks near the yards and tracks of the New York Central. Because it had been the most populous community, with many cottages on small parcels, Melrose did not have the empty blocks that Mott Haven and later Hunts Point had. New buildings went up on vacant lots among the older village structures in those areas, but in Melrose, the three- to four-story tenement predominanted. Taller ones were built when the subway became more of a reality, but at the time, the smaller tenements, both brick and frame, were the early neighborhood builders' response to the higher land prices and housing demand brought by the el (see table 4.3). These tenements were profitable and fitted nicely within the close-knit community. But they did not give it an urban look, for there were too many village buildings. Until the subway, Melrose remained a

TABLE 4.3 Population of Melrose, 1892–1920[a]

Year	Total Population	Percent of		
		Alien	Foreign Born	Foreign Ancestry[b]
1892	15,189	29%		
1905	35,553			
1910	47,735		40%	81%
1915	49,787			
1920	50,528		33%	77%

[a] Figures were computed from election district statistics for 1892 and census tracts for all other years. Totals were adjusted to reflect boundaries of Melrose.

[b] Includes foreign born and those of foreign parentage.

Source: New York State, "Exhibits Showing the Enumeration of the State by Counties, Cities, Towns and Election Districts for the Year 1892"; Laidlaw, *Population of New York City, 1890–1930*; Laidlaw, *Statistical Sources for Demographic Studies of Greater New York, 1910*; Laidlaw, *Statistical Sources for Demographic Studies of Greater New York, 1920*.

sort of cul-de-sac, hemmed in by train tracks, with a freight yard instead of a park. Because it was in place when transit arrived, the el intensified what the neighborhood already was.[44]

With the coming of the subway, old Melrose village became "the hub of the entire Bronx." Before it surfaced, the Interborough Rapid Transit crossed under the Third Avenue El at 149th Street and provided a free transfer between the subway and el stations. A few years before, 149th Street had been "little more than a cowpath." By 1911, however, the intersection was "the great business centre of the north borough" and "the most prominent shopping district in the Bronx." Reporters predicted that Melrose "will continue to grow as an important center for retail business, warehouses, factories and railroads" and so "values will increase on a sound and honest basis." The view by then was that "large business buildings" would be in greater demand than residential housing, though New Law apartments had been gradually replacing frame structures since subway service began. Yet the cross streets north and west of the Hub retained that small town look and feel. Melrose Avenue was "very poorly improved," while Courtlandt Avenue, "some years ago the most busy and prosperous little lane on the North Side, ha[d] gone backward instead of forward." Much of the early village remained because the old residents of Melrose were still there. They lived in Melrose partly out of sentiment and partly in the hope of "a greater increment than even the present has brought." Thus as 1920 neared, the neighborhood had an urbanized downtown business zone and a small-townish interior, encircled by railroads and rapid transit. Melrose, for all its uneven growth, was a community whose residents were comfortable with the present and confident of the future.[45]

Morrisania was something else again. Straddling Third Avenue just beyond Mott Haven and Melrose, it contained many distinct communities cut off from one another by topography and the large breweries built into the ridge east of Third Avenue (see map 4.4). As a well-established area with homes, stores, and businesses, Morrisania eventually wound up with a little of everything—tenements, dwellings, and village housing in Morrisania proper, blocks of tenements and apartments in its Claremont section, frame row houses in Woodstock, and brick flats and attached dwellings in East Morrisania.[46]

The el first reached Morrisania in 1887, and by 1891 served its central core with three additional stations along North Third Avenue. There was plenty of space, but a double fare, a change of trains, and topography kept parts of the region inaccessible. However, the neighborhood had been improved with paved streets, sewers, utilities, more schools, and two large parks, Crotona at the northeast corner and Claremont just slightly to its west. Although churches acquired sites to be used "when the neighborhood is well built up," there was little building activity. But there were expectations, for local promoters were dazzled by Mott Haven's ongoing building boom and fully expected it to move north.[47]

In the late 1890s, a boom of sorts began in the Morrisania region, with cheaper and improved transit after 1894. The *Record and Guide* reported that "a heavy immigration of small householders from below the Harlem immediately followed," because the five-cent fare represented "a saving . . . of some $30 a year in house rents."[48] In upper Morrisania, or Claremont as the northernmost section came to be called, the breakup of the Bathgate estate in 1897 was a further stimulus. Just west of Crotona Park on Third Avenue and Claremont Parkway, the former estate was soon covered with Old Law tenements. All of Claremont and lower Morrisania were too, with leftover space among the one-family homes earmarked for tenements and later larger apartment buildings. By 1910, the North Side Board of Trade marveled at how Morrisania was "slowly but surely being improved with modern apartment houses." As 1920 approached, Morrisania had breweries and commercial establishments on Third Avenue, some factories near the railroad tracks, and blocks and blocks of tenements and apartments intermingled with old and new frame buildings.[49]

On the higher ground east of Third Avenue and west of Prospect, the electrified streetcar provided access via Boston Road and Westchester Avenue. This area consisted of East Morrisania, Woodstock, and the former well-to-do, eastern portion of Morrisania village "where lived those whose means permitted them to have large grounds" and the "finest" of residences.[50] Combined with the el's lower fare and faster trains, the trolley induced the building of rows of narrow, one- to three-family frame houses. This type of building provided the amenities of the city in a less crowded setting and, because it fit in with what was already there, nurtured the illusion that the area was still a suburb of sorts.[51]

After 1905, the subway on Westchester Avenue caused a burst of apartment house construction in East Morrisania that spread northward toward Boston Road. Blocks that had required a little more time and money to reach were now suitable for multifamily construction, despite the presence of lower-density housing. The el and the trolley had increased land values enough to make narrow attached dwellings the most fitting and profitable alternative. The el, trolley, and subway combination did the same for New Law apartments. As local promoter W. W. Gill explained in 1910, "Nearly all the buildings in this section are large apartment houses, fitted with all the latest improvements, and well filled with the choicest kinds of tenants." A year later, reporter William R. Brown described how "the palatial homes of the former owners of the land" in the Boston Road section "have likewise been driven out by the development which has taken place." By 1920, the neighborhood was completely filled in. It was solely residential except for commercial strips on Boston Road and Westchester Avenue. But its mix of low- and high-density housing set the area off from the Third Avenue corridor on the one hand and the Southern Boulevard district on the other.[52]

By the time the subway arrived in 1905, Melrose's population had more than doubled, to more than 35,000 inhabitants (see table 4.3). It increased more slowly afterward and hardly at all in the two subsequent census periods. Indeed, population declined in some spots because of public improvements and the growth of the business and commercial center. By 1920, Melrose had more than 50,000 inhabitants, most clustered just beyond the Hub in the central portion of the neighborhood, where density reached higher than 200 people to the acre.[53]

Morrisania also had its greatest rate of population increase prior to 1905, but continued gaining residents during the following fifteen years (see table 4.4). Its population jumped from 16,000 in 1892 to more than 137,000 in 1920, for an overall growth rate of over 700 percent. While Claremont, the Boston Road district, and the old town of Morrisania more than doubled their population between 1905 and 1920s, the old town section grew at a slower pace and became the less densely settled area of the neighborhood.

TABLE 4.4 Population of Morrisania, 1892–1920[a]

Year	Total Population	Percent of		
		Alien	Foreign Born	Foreign Ancestry[b]
1892	16,135	16%		
1905	55,264			
1910	94,723		39%	83%
1915	125,687			
1920	137,789		40	87

[a] Figures were computed from election district statistics for 1892 and census tracts for all other years. Totals were adjusted to reflect boundaries of Morrisania.

[b] Includes foreign born and those of foreign parentage.

Source: New York State, "Exhibits Showing the Enumeration of the State by Counties, Cities, Towns and Election Districts for the Year 1892"; Laidlaw, *Population of New York City, 1890–1930*; Laidlaw, *Statistical Sources for Demographic Studies of Greater New York, 1910*; Laidlaw, *Statistical Sources for Demographic Studies of Greater New York, 1920*.

Claremont had the most people in the smallest area and contained, by 1920, census tracts with more than 200 residents to the acre, including the only one in Morrisania with more than 300 residents per.[54]

Melrose and Morrisania were peopled by immigrants and their children (see tables 4.3 and 4.4). In both 1910 and 1920, over three quarters of their residents were of foreign ancestry and over one third of alien birth. From the late 1890s on, Melrose was populated by Germans and Italians. By 1910, southwestern Melrose was almost totally Italian, while eastern and northern Melrose were almost all German. This remained true in 1920, though Eastern European Jews were living amid the older inhabitants of German descent. Morrisania, on the other hand, was largely German and Eastern European, with almost equal numbers of each in 1910. Christian Germans abounded in the old town of Morrisania and the Boston Road section, while a small group of Irish concentrated in East Morrisania. A few Italians were scattered throughout the entire neighborhood. Eastern European Jews, meanwhile, were in the majority in Claremont, an area that in 1915 was described as "a foreign district . . . with Hebrew characters and strange tongues." By 1920, Jews from Russia and Eastern Europe had increased throughout Morrisania. In contrast, the German and Irish presence lessened as the numbers of their alien born sharply declined. Both decennial censuses reveal small pockets of blacks along the rail yards and tracks that girded Melrose and Morrisania.[55]

Melrose and Morrisania were never described as classy. Claremont was working class from the first—a fact underscored by the pushcart market along Bathgate Avenue. Lower Morrisania had a seedy air about it despite its many new public buildings, such as a county courthouse, an armory, and the much praised lecture and assembly hall, the Bronx Church House. Melrose, for all its business, commercial, and entertainment buildings at the Hub, was not where the elite lived—the immigrant laborers and factory workers, yes; the craftsmen and better-paid brewery hands, perhaps; but certainly not the well-to-do.[56] The Boston Road district, Woodstock, and East Morrisania were a cut above those areas. They had Morris High School, brewer John Eichler's mansion, better-grade apartment buildings, and privately owned row houses. The latter would give more permanency than would later exist in either Melrose or the rest of Morrisania. In the early years, active social and civic clubs imparted a genteel tone to the neighborhood, but here, too, with time there was a slight lowering in class. In spite of these differences, each area had spots with better-quality housing to which residents could aspire, thus enabling them to move up without moving out.[57]

MOTT HAVEN AGAIN

Mott Haven, the earliest neighborhood to develop, continued growing after 1900. Although no longer new, it still contained plenty of vacant land and was easier to reach when the subways arrived in 1905 and later in 1920.[58] Thus new housing occupied practically every nook and cranny, increasing Mott Haven's population from the more than 53,000 it had in 1900 to almost 99,000 twenty years later. During that time, population rose everywhere between Third Avenue and Southern Boulevard, extending the neighborhood's central core eastward through the previously empty blocks near St. Mary's Park. The most densely settled spots, from 1910 on, were near the 149th Street/Third Avenue Hub and along the length of 138th Street, south of which was the only census tract in Mott Haven with more than 300 people to the acre. By then, however, Mott Haven no longer had the newest buildings. Most of its urban housing stock was pre-1901 cold-water flats, with some frame structures east of Third Avenue. As the 1920s neared, there was an increasing disparity between Mott Haven's old and new residential housing.[59]

From 1910 on, the population of Mott Haven was over three-quarters of foreign birth or parentage. The neighborhood still had Irish, Italians, Germans, and Eastern European Jews. Each group predominated in certain areas, though they were found throughout the entire neighborhood. Italians were mostly in the village part of Mott Haven, that is, in the streets east of Third Avenue that blended into Melrose's Italian quarter. The Irish concentrated mainly around Alexander Avenue in the parish of St. Jerome's, with a smaller working-class section near Port Morris. The Germans, both Christian and Jewish, lived in the central portion of Mott Haven, between Willis and St. Ann's avenues, while Jews from Russia and Eastern Europe spread throughout the center of Mott Haven. There were very small pockets of Scandinavians, and even smaller isolated groups of blacks around the rail tracks and yards near Port Morris, the Mott Haven Canal, and the lower parts of Park and Third avenues. All in all, a varied group of inhabitants.[60]

Despite the area's aging housing stock, Mott Havenites had confidence in the future. Business and industry continued to move in. Land prices stayed high and apartments had few vacancies. While business and community organizations worked tirelessly to eliminate pushcarts, garbage dumps, and the run-down zone at the area's southwestern tip, Eugene McGuire, the local Democratic Party boss, bragged in 1907 that "there has never been a dive, gambling house or disreputable resort in the district." Promoters had faith in Mott Haven because of its proximity to Manhattan and the new subway beneath 138th Street. The South Bronx Property Owners Association, for one, had been calling for this subway for years. In 1910, its president, Sigmund Feust, claimed it was needed "first, on account of the density of the population dwelling in the district and, second, on account of the

TABLE 4.5 Population of South Bronx Neighborhoods, 1892–1920[a]

Year	Mott Haven	Melrose	Hunts Point–Crotona Park East	Morrisania
1892	28,460	15,189	2,559	16,135
1900	53,027 [86%]			
1905	65,534 [24%]	35,553 [134%]	19,527 [663%]	55,264 [243%]
1910	89,226 [36%]	47,735 [34%]	56,875 [191%]	94,723 [71%]
1915	90,770 [2%]	49,787 [4%]	119,691 [110%]	125,687 [33%]
1920	98,712 [9%]	50,528 [1%]	153,651 [28%]	137,789 [10%]

[a] With percent of growth from previous population.

Source: New York State, "Exhibits Showing the Enumeration of the State by Counties, Cities, Towns and Election Districts for the Year 1892"; Laidlaw, Population of New York City, 1890–1930.

many factories in existence in this territory." Banking on the coming subway, the North Side Board of Trade built its new headquarters at 138th Street, confident that the vicinity would "be transformed into an attractive centre which will become the pride of the borough." Mott Haven, while not as elite as it once had been, was not yet ready to be abandoned.[61]

By 1920, the neighborhoods of the southern Bronx were fully developed (see table 4.5). Their built environment consisted of residential housing, industrial and commercial structures, schools, churches, a few hospitals, and civic buildings. They had a growing and vital downtown business center, thriving commercial strips, and a few parks, with railroads, freight yards, and el and subway transit all over the place. Their population was diverse, reflecting the heterogeneity of the city at large. Yet in each of the neighborhoods, there were conditions that would worsen as time went by. Mott Haven, Melrose, and Morrisania were saddled with aging and outmoded housing. Claremont and the Hunts Point/Southern Boulevard district were overcrowded. And all had areas that were starting to decline in income and status. Although still newish, these Bronx neighborhoods had begun to change.

BOOSTING A BOROUGH

BOOSTERS

Antebellum President John Tyler once said, "There is nothing like the elbow room of a new country." To Bronx promoters, there was nothing like a new borough. For decades, they promoted their area with a booster spirit reminiscent of early frontier cities, claiming that "geography and topography have predestined the old county towns of Westchester as the business centre of the metropolis of the Western Hemisphere."[1] Boosters expected monetary gain but believed progress and growth would benefit all. Thus they welcomed and encouraged the northward expansion of the city. As long as the city grew, progress would indeed be good for the Bronx.[2]

Bronx residents believed their area was "the logical line of expansion of New York City."[3] Since the trend of the city's growth had always been northward, the boosters applauded whatever promoted that "natural" tendency and opposed anything that aided migration to other parts of the metropolitan area. Over the years, they opposed bridges and transit connecting Manhattan to Brooklyn and Queens and the consolidation of Brooklyn, Queens, and Richmond counties into a Greater New York City.[4] In 1897, that most vocal of Bronx boosters, James Lee Wells, argued against the move because the city "is already confronted by the very serious problem of how to take care of the recently acquired territory to the northward." That territory was the Bronx, an area he and other promoters described as the "natural accretion" of New York.[5]

Consequently, throughout village, ward, and borough years, Bronx interests linked themselves to Manhattan. Their first efforts culminated in the 1874 annexation of Morrisania, West Farms, and Kingsbridge. Afterward, owners of land east of the Bronx River called for annexation of the towns of Westchester and portions of Eastchester and Pelham because, as the *Record and Guide* wrote, "these places [were] practically part of New York City as it is."[6] Their demands resulted in annexation in 1895. The subsequent 1897 Charter of Greater New York created the Borough of the Bronx out of the two former halves of lower Westchester and kept the new borough in the county of New York.[7] Realtor J. Clarence Davies reiterated this long-standing policy of Bronx promoters in a protest against a 1904 proposal for county status. Calling the county movement "a radical departure from that which we have pursued for the last thirty years," Davies explained that "it has been our constant effort to make ourselves a part of the county and city of New York."[8]

Proud of being North Siders and later Bronxites, its leaders sought local autonomy whenever city policies hampered the borough's growth. They gained authority over street improvements in 1890, lost it when the borough was created in 1897, and pressured continuously until the borough regained control of local improvements. The 1901 charter revision gave the borough presidents powers like those originally held by that former Bronx official, the Commissioner of Street Improvements of the Twenty-third and Twenty-fourth Wards.[9] Local control intensified local pride and became a prime ingredient in the effort to create the county of the Bronx, which originated when residents of the new borough objected to being lumped into Manhattan assembly districts. The movement revived in 1902 when the newly formed Bronx Bar Association took up the cause as a way to eliminate traveling downtown for all legal and real estate proceedings. Despite their concerted actions, county status was not achieved until 1914 because of political infighting.[10]

Landowners, businessmen, realtors, architects, builders, local politicians, and the just plain civic minded worked alone and in concert to enhance the condition, prospects, and image of the Bronx. Over the years, Mott, McGraw, Cauldwell, and Morris gave way to the likes of James Lee Wells, J. Clarence Davies, Louis Haffen, Alfred E. Davis, and Henry Morgenthau, as they worked to gain public improvements, urban services, transit connections, and political representation. They lobbied successively at the federal, state, and city levels for all manner of improvements and amenities. Therefore, they were a potent force in the growth of the borough, in large part responsible for its densely built urban environment.[11] In 1904, the North Side Board of Trade claimed that the "remarkable advance in prices of real estate, the many sales and large number of new buildings projected in the Bronx, resulting from Rapid Transit and other improvements, are largely due to the efforts of this Board in furthering such improvements."[12]

Booster organizations were everywhere. The first, the North Side Association, was formed in 1874. Twenty years later, in 1894, local taxpayers' and property owners' associations formed a loose coalition called the Taxpayers' Alliance that continued informally until well into the twentieth century.[13] The North Side Board of Trade, a longer-lasting businessmen's group, began in 1894 and quickly became "one of the most influential bodies in the upper section of Greater New York." The first president, John C. De La Vergne, explained that "the scope of our task should be to make the North Side the most important and attractive part of the City of New York." Years later, another president, Alfred E. Davis, advised the members to "strive to make this the healthiest, the most prosperous, the most beautiful, the grandest of all the boroughs." The organization became the Bronx Board of Trade in 1914 when some members split off over the issue of whether to remain at its 138th Street headquarters or move to the new retail and business "Hub" at 149th Street and Third Avenue. The splinter group existed separately as the Bronx Chamber of Commerce until the organizations reunited in the 1960s under that name.[14]

Property owners found auctions an effective way of selling both their land and the borough. As more and cheaper transit reached the Bronx, estates went on the auction block in anticipation of future growth. Advertisements, brochures, and broadsides stressed the profits to be made in the resale of lots. An 1869 auction broadside claimed that "these lots will triple in value." Similarly, a brochure for a 1910 auction of Hunts Point property told the public to "Look at the prices lots brought at [their 1908] auction sale . . . [and] ask any real estate expert what they are worth today." Since "History repeats itself," "Now is the Time to Buy and Make a Big Profit."[15]

Local politicians also boosted their area with published reports and public ceremonies. The borough presidents were particularly adept at this: witness Louis F. Haffen's Annual Reports, published speeches, and lengthy tract on the achievements of the Bronx during his tenure. Subsequent borough presidents were just as unflagging in their promotional efforts. Borough President Cyrus C. Miller was often in the press with his plans for an industrial zone along the southern rim of the Bronx, a project that allowed him to herald the suitability of the borough for industrial pursuits. Similarly, from the 1930s on, Borough President James J. Lyons turned every public event and ceremony into a media photo session.[16]

As Manhattan grew from a million residents in 1875 to almost two million in 1900, Bronx interests waged propaganda campaigns to attract population. Both the North Side Board of Trade and the Taxpayers' Alliance published newspaper supplements boosting the borough. The former was exceptionally active. Its yearbooks and annual reports were public relations tracts. The board also organized opening day ceremonies for new civic improvements and public works and placed feature articles about the borough in the newspapers. The more people came to the Bronx, the more opportunities there would be to provide services—in housing, retailing, education, entertainment, and health care.[17]

Bronx promoters welcomed the larger population brought by improved transit. Though the number of residents had risen twelvefold between 1875 and 1910, local boosters felt the borough could hold many more. In 1897, as the population fast approached the 200,000 mark, realtor James Lee Wells claimed, "The territory can easily accommodate a population ten or even fifteen times as great." Borough President Haffen went one better in 1909 when he declared that "The goal at which we are all aiming is A Million Population before the next State census in 1915." Yet at the time, the Bronx had almost 431,000 people and enough congestion to warrant its very own exhibit by the Committee on Congestion of Population and a public hearing of the Mayor's Commission on Congestion a year later. Nevertheless, local leaders endorsed the North Side Board of Trade's annual assertions that "A large mass of people are waiting to come to the Bronx and every opportunity should be offered to encourage this much desired end."[18]

Manhattan's population followed transit into the Bronx. By 1905, over half of the borough's population lived in the census tracts through which the Third Avenue El ran. During the following ten years, the first subway spurred an almost trebling of the population in the census tracts along the 149th Street–Westchester Avenue–Southern Boulevard route (part of the current 2 train route). Another round of subway construction between 1915 and 1930 brought population increases of 200 to 600 percent along the viaduct routes of the Broadway, Jerome Avenue, White Plains Road, and Pelham Bay lines (the current 1, 4, 2, and 6 trains) and made the Bronx between 1910 and 1920 "The Fastest Growing Borough of the City of New York." By 1920 the borough had 700,000 people, enough to make it the ninth largest city in the United States if it had been a separate municipality. Ten years later, it contained almost 1.3 million residents and would have ranked as the fifth largest city in the nation. The borough continued gaining population in the following decade when an additional subway—the D train beneath the Grand Concourse—increased the number of inhabitants along its length by 30 percent despite the economic depression and the earlier stimulus of the nearby Jerome Avenue subway tracks.[19]

APARTMENTS

To boost the Bronx, promoters had to boost apartments. Despite calls for manufacturing and industrial pursuits, the borough's function was to provide "dwellings for its citizens who labor outside of the borough."[20] And though there were large numbers of one- and two-family dwellings in the outlying sections of the Bronx, apartment buildings housed the most people and received the most publicity. Newspaper articles increasingly spotlighted the amenities of the newest apartment buildings, first those in the Hunts Point–Longwood section and later those in Tremont, Fordham, and the Grand Concourse. From the turn of the century on, Bronx apartments were prominently displayed in the *Real Estate Record and Builders' Guide* and the *Architects and Builders' Magazine*.[21] The city's newspapers, meanwhile, ran front-page articles on the evils of tenements, while featuring glowing accounts of Bronx apartments in the real estate pages in the rear. After 1920, more and more of these positive articles headlined the separate Sunday real estate sections. As the years went on, the barrage of propaganda imparted to Bronx apartments, and by extension the borough in general, an aura of modernity and better living.[22]

It was not always so. In 1900, Manhattan builder Peter Herter explained that "flats, apartments, everything of that kind . . . from the humblest to the grandest, are, legally speaking, tenement houses." And tenements, while necessary, were not socially acceptable. Apartments were generally tenanted by the upper and middle classes and rented for over $20 a month. Tenements, on the other hand, were the homes of working-class folk or the less well-off and cost anywhere from $20 on down.[23] In either case, people often lived in a multifamily setting out of necessity, not choice, for the ideal residence remained the one-family suburban home or the two- to three-story row house.[24] In 1901 the *Record and Guide* wondered if the Bronx "will be very largely encased with the kind of two-story and basement residences which are so numerous in Brooklyn" or "will the flat system prevail." Nevertheless, concluded the paper, if builders could make flats popular north of the Harlem, "it would be a good thing for property in the Bronx."[25]

The question of Bronx apartments had to do with New York City's housing needs. As Gotham's economy grew, the central business district expanded, land prices increased, and residential housing and population moved outward. The resulting scarcity of housing seriously affected low-income city dwellers, who crowded into the lower wards. Speculators subdivided former private homes or erected buildings specifically designed to house many families under one roof. From the 1830s on, "multifamily arrangements were often connected to deprivation." Those who could afford better were not that much better off, for "a place in the respectable middling class was signified by a single family house." But high land prices kept the narrow, attached city house or the small cottage way uptown or in the suburbs, beyond the means of most New Yorkers. The solution was a middle-class version of the tenement, that is, the French flat or apartment house.[26]

Multifamily housing was profitable. The landowner hiked his price if the lots were suitable for flats or tenements, the builder sold his buildings based on the expected rent rolls, and the landlord had a ready market for his apartments because of congestion downtown. Squeezing the most rent from the least space, tenements yielded from 10 to 25 percent annually on the initial capital investment. They remained profitable throughout the nineteenth century despite progressively restrictive building codes and legislation geared to improve the worst tenement conditions. In 1900, a builder could easily earn a 10 percent profit simply "by exercising good judgement, carefully studying the section in which he is going to build, and putting up a building that meets the requirements of the particular tenants he is catering to."[27] Countless articles appeared in real estate journals explaining how to make a tenement or flat pay. Architects revealed how to design a building, irrespective of lot size, that conformed to the Tenement House Laws. Thus architects, builders, and real estate interests "sold" the flat to New Yorkers and Bronxites alike.[28]

To make apartments more acceptable to middle-class families, architects and builders redesigned the French flat to meet middle-class sensibilities. Because "the apartment is the substitute for the house," wrote noted architect Ernest Flagg, "it should therefore be planned to supply as far as possible what the house gives."[29] Every new design feature and technological advance was thus incorporated, by grouping living quarters away from sleeping areas, planning public halls and lobbies to minimize social contact with strangers, and installing elevators, telephones, steam heat, electric lights, kitchen ranges, and private bathrooms. The apartment, by the early twentieth century, epitomized all that was modern and desirable in living quarters, its only drawback being that it was not a house.[30]

At the other end of the scale, restrictive legislation and building codes gradually upgraded the housing standards of tenements. The tenement became an apartment in its own right after the 1901 Tenement House Law. New minimum standards of light, air, and indoor plumbing forced builders to construct bigger tenements with rental rates that compensated for the greater investment the new buildings required. In the Bronx, such apartments were found in Hunts Point and the Boston Road district by 1910, and in select streets and avenues throughout the borough by the mid-1920s. Less-fancy apartments continued to be built, though in decreasing numbers, but the standards they now had to meet kept conditions and rents a cut above the Old-Law tenements.[31]

Whether Old-Law (pre-1901) or New-Law (post-1901), Bronx housing was plentiful, and of relatively high quality. The borough had city and suburban-type dwellings for one to three families in brick, stone, or frame, none of which were for the lowest income group. Its flats ranged from the cheapest to the best, but were usually newer, cleaner, and lower in rent than those downtown. After the coming of new tenement laws in 1901 and the subway in 1904, the Bronx continued to supply both housing and transit in a different manner. In 1904, it was widely believed that the "subway's patronage will come from the working class." As the *Record and Guide* saw it, "Bronx Borough is an especially interesting part of the city this year, now that the gates are about to be thrown open that will let in the multitude pressing up from the south." Yet, in large part, Bronx builders were aiming for a higher-income clientele. Their "new-law flats," never less than 37½ feet wide, had "improvements which have not generally been put into flats," with rents from $38 to $45 a month.[32] These apartments attracted an upwardly mobile, status-conscious group—whether blue collar, professional, or entrepreneurial, from the Lower East Side, Harlem, or Mott Haven—who were quick to move to better dwellings as soon as they were able. Those who earned less moved into new low-rent flats for about $16 a month or into the former apartments of those who had left for better quarters. By the 1920s, new construction in the Bronx was geared to the middle class. Lower-income groups had to find housing units vacated by those who had moved up in status.[33]

Better living quarters, therefore, filtered down to the lower-income tenant in a trickle-down process that matched up new vacancies with the different social classes of the city. Every dwelling unit, residential building, and even every neighborhood fit into "a fixed hierarchical order . . . in terms of their desirability, with all units eventually taking their place at the bottom of the pecking order." As long as there were newly vacated apartments, due to either new construction or population decline, undesirable units dropped out of the market. The low end of the housing scale, therefore, tended to improve. In this way, everyone would have better quarters—as long as the supply exceeded the demand. This analysis assumes that new housing would be of higher quality and that it would be built on the periphery, as was usually the case, thereby assuring that the vacated apartments would be in the central core's oldest housing, which in the Bronx meant in Mott Haven, Melrose, Hunts Point, and Morrisania. This filtering process provided low-income housing, but it could also, with time, lower the class and tone of the building, the neighborhood, and eventually the entire Bronx.[34]

From the 1920s on, government policies encouraged the building of apartments for the middle class. Prior to World War I, New York City's increasing population and improved transit service were all that Bronx builders needed. During the war years, construction slumped as labor and building materials were diverted to the war effort. This virtual halt in building caused severe housing shortages, rent gouging, and tenant evictions. In response to tenant complaints, the state legislature provided tax exemptions for residential construction during the 1920s. To qualify for these tax exemptions, landlords agreed to limit their dividends or profits by charging slightly lower rents.[35]

In the Bronx, this legislation caused a burst of apartment-house building. By 1924, construction of apartment buildings was "Breaking All Records" and creating new neighborhoods along University, Morris, Bainbridge, and Sedgwick avenues, on Pelham and Mosholu parkways, and on the Grand Concourse, none of which was in the older South Bronx. After 1926, these laws also promoted the building of limited dividend and cooperative apartment complexes in the far reaches of the borough. These projects led to other co-op housing ventures, which, during the Depression of the 1930s, often relied on federal New Deal financing. By 1940, Amalgamated Housing, Thomas Gardens, the Shalom Aleichem Houses, the Workers Cooperative Colony (or Coops for short), Academy Housing, Hillside Homes, and Parkchester had added thousands of middle-income units to the supply of Bronx apartments.[36] The lower-income tenant in the Bronx still had to rely on whatever units were left.[37]

Each boom made the earlier housing obsolete, the older neighborhoods less desirable, and their streets shabbier by comparison. The process was ongoing and inevitable given that in the nineteenth and early twentieth centuries, businessmen were unfettered, progress was considered good, and any construction was deemed an "improvement." To hold their own amid such conditions, people had to be constantly on the move. Since housing was a reflection of social status and standard of living and since "different neighborhoods and dwelling types were occupied by different classes," status-conscious New Yorkers and Bronxites moved from neighborhood to neighborhood or from apartment to apartment.[38] In 1921, social worker Helen Kempton observed that "as they become more prosperous [borough residents] move over to the better sections of the Bronx and finally to Riverdale . . . and on out into the country."[39] Thus the aspiring middle-class family aimed for the Bronx only until something better came along.

As long as new apartments were being built and new neighborhoods were beginning to grow, the Bronx was all right. The borough's reputation had been built upon the waves of apartment-house construction that had accompanied each new transit route. Decade after decade, something was always being built, torn down, or installed—buildings, public works, sports arenas, or utilities and streets that were repeatedly dug up for water, gas, electricity, and sewers. Seemingly forever under construction, the Bronx projected an image of newness and modernity.[40] In 1931, in the throes of the Depression, the Bronx Board of Trade wrote glowingly about the "building operations" of the previous thirty years, which had left housing "of comparatively modern construction." By 1939, after years of economic decline, the Board of Trade was citing "The Amazing Growth Achieved By The Bronx During The 45 Years in Which The Board had been serving The Borough."[41] If the Bronx was unfinished, still being built, there was nothing to worry about. In time, all would be well. Such a view allowed many to gloss over imperfections as temporary and not the true Bronx at all.

DENSITY

What *was* true about the Bronx was its shifting population. In aggregate numbers the borough continued to grow, but not all over or all the time. In the 1920s, population declined along the Third Avenue corridor, particularly in the oldest portions of Mott Haven, Melrose, and Morrisania, as residents moved into the newer neighborhoods. For instance, 70 percent of the tenants in the new Amalgamated Houses were from the Bronx. This population loss was checked during the 1930s by severe economic hard times, but areas outside of the Mott Haven–Melrose–Morrisania–Hunts Point core continued gaining residents.[42] Whether fed by the lower Bronx or the Lower East Side, the outer ring of the borough was growing, while its southern tip was not. This was as it should be. The southernmost Bronx was supposed to have been the downtown center, the central business district that was to have superseded lower Manhattan as the locus of the metropolitan area. The Bronx was simply following the pattern of urban growth and neighborhood change that was so familiar to boosters and real estate interests. If that meant population loss at its lowest end, so be it; there was still plenty of vacant land in the east and north of the borough.[43]

The city's growth had transformed the suburban villages of the 1850s into the urban neighborhoods of the late nineteenth and early twentieth centuries. In this process, estate auctions shifted from the core to the old Hunts Point–East Bronx area and thenceforth to the west, north, and east of the borough and were fed and intensified by the timing and direction of the transit lines that entered the Bronx.[44] Real estate business cycles, which had had so much to do with urbanization in the first place, had been either mild or short-lived, enough so that the main participants fully expected a renewed burst of building activity after each downturn. According to Alfred

E. Davis, population came to the Bronx because "living conditions make it attractive." Thus up to the 1930s and even beyond, confidence in the borough was never shaken.[45]

The notion of the suburb also worked in the borough's favor. Despite an early grid layout, the Bronx had been touted as the city's suburb from the 1850s, with "villa-sites" hawked by Mott, Morris, and sundry others. Years later, Olmsted's street layouts had been based on that very same premise, reinforced by the acquisition of an extensive park and parkway system during the 1880s. When the Third Avenue El began rumbling overhead, real estate dealers predicted that streets close to the el would soon be "dotted quite numerously with . . . desirable little cottages." Instead those cottages were often attached frame row houses—more citylike than suburban—which would soon be either replaced by or sandwiched between rows of apartments.[46]

The image of parklike surroundings held despite the repeated waves of apartment building. In her 1915 study of Morrisania's Claremont section, Ada H. Muller explained that some of the reasons residents moved to the Bronx were "the comparative freedom from congestion, the better air, [and] the greater quiet and openness of surroundings." Yet according to Stephen Jenkins, in 1913, Wendover Avenue, the soon to be Claremont Parkway in the very heart of Claremont, "had more adults and children— children especially—to the square inch than in almost any other place in the city." That vacant lot or two that had not yet been developed or those vast tracts that went up for sale as each new transit line gave access belied the increasing density and urban character of the settled area of the borough and harbored the illusion that it still was "a pretty, healthful, rural retreat."[47]

To be sure, cottages continued to be built along the railroads up to the early twentieth century and even more after the el and subway made the Bronx more accessible.[48] Between 1902 and 1937, the number of small dwellings, ranging from single-family bungalows to one- to three-family row houses. surpassed multifamily buildings in all but six years. Small homes were feasible wherever land prices were low enough to allow low-density construction and still provide a return on investment. This usually meant they were built some distance from the el or subway but on or near surface transit, allowing just enough accessibility to sell the houses but not enough to preclude building them in the first place. This remained the case even after the automobile began influencing the design and location of small homes during the 1920s. From then on, the "Own-your-own-home" campaign of the United States Department of Labor and the tax-exemption laws that spurred much apartment-house construction prompted the building of many "Small Home Centers" in the eastern Bronx, where, according to developer Joseph P. Day, "any good American citizen will be glad to live with his family." The eastern Bronx received more dwellings in the 1930s, when FHA mortgages caused a "revival of building in the small home field." The Bronx seemed, indeed, a "Borough of Homes."[49]

But by and large, apartments lined the subway routes, filled in open spaces, and elbowed out low-density housing, even in outlying sections far from transit, where huge apartment complexes grew amid open fields.[50] Despite the many smaller homes, the Bronx had fewer owner-occupied units in 1940 than in any other borough except Manhattan. And it was also the outer borough with the most apartment buildings housing twenty or more families, again second only to Manhattan. In 1938, "cliff dweller blocks of multi-family buildings comprise[d] . . . nearly 70 percent" of the total in the Bronx. Similarly, a 1944 study found that "three quarters of the dwelling units in [the] Bronx are in the larger apartments (10 families or over) whereas only a quarter of Brooklyn's families live in larger apartment buildings." Manhattanization existed beyond the normal imperatives of urban growth. In a borough where development occurred piecemeal, boosters foresaw the least accessible areas as sites of future development. The expectations generated were enough to enhance land values long before actual conditions would have. When coupled with the press of population in the city's tenement districts, multifamily structures made demographic and economic sense.[51]

They also made for a denser environment. Boroughwide figures are misleading about what was happening within the Bronx. Between 1900 and 1940, the population west of the Bronx River never dropped below 77 percent of the borough total, and at times reached as high as 89 to 91 percent (see table 1.1). This population, moreover, was concentrated in the central core served by mass transit, underscoring that much of the Bronx continued to be developed for the el and subway masses long after the automobile began influencing residential growth patterns in the metropolitan area.[52]

Ironically, measures instituted to reduced congestion had had the opposite effect. Thus, while the 1901 Tenement Law led to bigger apartment buildings, the use, height, and area restrictions of the 1916 Zoning Law still allowed for a future city population of 55 to 77 million, depending on whose estimates one used, and did nothing to curtail apartment-house construction.[53] Similarly, up to the 1930s, the Bronx had more land devoted to parks than the other boroughs. Yet the edges of that land were "where housing was built to the highest densities," with "great urban walls facing equally impressive parks." As a result, portions of the Bronx had solid blocks of apartment buildings that housed thousands of families but provided little or no off-street public spaces or parking sites.[54]

The construction of apartment complexes in the far reaches of the borough reflected boosters' and builders' continuing assumption that the Bronx would receive more of Manhattan's population—whence their reliance on cheap rapid transit. As realtor J. Clarence Davies expressed it in 1908, "The reason Bronx values are high today and will be higher in the near future is that many sectors are densely populated, and the density is growing." But in boosting their area to hold the masses, promoters lost sight of the future adaptability of the housing, the neighborhoods, and the borough itself, for the better-quality apartments of the Bronx existed within structural and neighborhood densities that were usually reserved for downtown and could not be sustained—or welcomed, for that matter—as tenants continually sought better living quarters and higher economic status.[55]

Density, in and of itself, was not necessarily bad. Crowding within the home, for example, occurred in a small, private familial environment that could shield a person from external conditions. Neighborhood crowding, on the other hand, took place in a public setting and often added to the cohesiveness of immigrant communities. Though crowded neighborhoods usually have "more congestion, competition, and environmental degradation," they also provide more services, activities, and opportunities for their residents. Within the Bronx, residents created social areas often composed of a street, a "social block," or even one apartment house, within which they socialized with kin, friends, and compatriots, right in the midst of other socializing groups. Crowding, therefore, does not automatically lead to anomie, social conflict, or mental stress, as urban sociologist Louis Wirth had argued. City living does affect people, but they in turn "cope, manipulate and change environments," adapting to crowding and minimizing its stress. In truth, "critical masses" allow for development of social groupings, networks, or subcultures, and in the end result in "greater, not lesser social organization."[56]

Density alone was not to blame for the residential mobility that characterized the Bronx. As Mark Baldassare believes, "social position and economic status are more significant determinants of well-being than household or neighborhood crowding."[57] And the Bronx, by accident and by design, had become one of the places to which one moved in order to improve living standards. Hence its apartments had to meet the "housing aspirations" of residents at every stage. Living in the new was fine, but the not so new was another matter: satisfaction with a neighborhood or apartment building depended upon the ethnic and class composition of its inhabitants and their particular ethos or lifestyle. As that changed over time, so too did the residents' perceptions of the livability of their neighborhoods.[58]

Density, however, was crucial to future viability. Along with age and condition, crowding affected how an area fared in the latter stages of neighborhood evolution—whether it went into stagnation, decay, and abandonment or renewal, rehabilitation, and gentrification.[59] That the lower Bronx was eminently suited to house progressively lower-income tenants was known and accepted, but it meant that much of the borough would become poorer with normal growth patterns. The issue was whether the apartment-house neighborhoods of the Bronx could satisfy the "housing aspirations" of later decades, and if not, whether these neighborhoods were adaptable to meet higher living standards.[60]

Everyone noted how crowded parts of the Bronx were. But it was no more so than the Lower East Side, Hell's Kitchen, East Harlem, or other tenement districts in Manhattan. Long-time residents of the Bronx just moved away from the increasing congestion and went into newer areas. Their part of the Bronx, therefore, was always open and pristine. Both new and current residents were comfortable with the Bronx. Each had improved their situation, albeit just a little. And each was in an area that had the necessary urban amenities and services that made for more convenient living, away from Manhattan yet still in the city.[61]

The Bronx instilled a sense of improvement and pride in both its residents and its boosters. To long-time resident and educator Dr. James F. Condon, it was "the most beautiful borough in the world." To Borough President James J. Lyons, it was "the most beautiful and healthiest borough."[62] Such sentiments were echoed through the years as Bronx promoters stressed that it was "moral" and "prosperous," and had parks, universities, homes, and apartments as well as room in which to build and invest. No one admitted there were slums. In 1910, Henry Morgenthau, one of the Bronx's largest investors, believed "that section to be a desirable home-centre for the over-flow of New York's population." And a "home-centre" it was, for in each area residents created neighborhoods where they were comfortable until their circumstances changed. Bit by bit, the Bronx's image became multifaceted, different things to many.[63] The substance it conveyed was that, despite the multifamily housing, the constant and pervasive residential mobility, the aging housing of some spots, and the urban density, the borough was a good place in which to live.[64]

The Bronx became a collection of neighborhoods that differed in age, construction, ethnicity, and affordability. Each new transit route created new residential areas and filled in the older ones further. These neighborhoods reflected the city's heterogeneity. Some people followed the transit lines northward; others followed family and friends into the existing ethnic communities. And still others were steered into whole new areas by contractors who built housing specifically for their compatriots and, in the process, created ethnic communities, which in turn attracted their fellows. A Bronx that in the 1880s had been mostly old-stock American with a large German community and a few Irish was by 1930 almost half Jewish, with sizable contingents of Irish, Germans, and Italians. By 1940, a million and a half Bronxites were joined irrevocably to Manhattan by bridges, railroads, pipelines, and transit.[65]

URBAN NEIGHBORHOODS

During the twenties and thirties, the Bronx evolved into a collection of urban neighborhoods. By 1920, Mott Haven, Melrose, Morrisania, and Hunts Point–Crotona Park East had become the urban neighborhoods of the future South Bronx. Between 1920 and 1940, moreover, a host of newly built city neighborhoods increased the urbanized area of the borough. Mott Haven and Melrose were by this time often called the Lower or South Bronx, while Morrisania and Hunts Point–Crotona Park East were lumped together as the "East Bronx." Apart from nomenclature, the most salient feature of these South Bronx neighborhoods was that they were no longer the same. They had evolved from suburban villages to established city communities and would continue changing in the decades to come.

The Bronx itself was in flux. In these decades, its population increased almost everywhere (see table 1.1).[1] Moreover, from the 1920s on, and along with more people, houses, and even more transit, the borough gained institutions, businesses, and public works that enhanced its economy and reputation. In 1923 alone, it gained a lavish hotel and major-league baseball club and stadium. By the late twenties, it was known far and wide as the home of the New York Yankees, the Bronx Zoo, and New York and Fordham universities. By the thirties, it was still known for the Yankees (by then nicknamed the Bronx Bombers), but also for the Lindbergh kidnapping case, and to a lesser extent, for Edward J. Flynn, the Bronx Democratic Party boss who was a close friend and ally of President Franklin D. Roosevelt. Flynn's control of a solid Democratic vote made the Bronx an essential campaign stop for all manner of aspiring politicians. Adding to its new nationwide fame was the humor of *The Goldbergs*. Set in a mythical Bronx apartment in a typical Bronx neighborhood, the weekly NBC radio show kept the name of the Bronx on the air for two decades.[2]

The major change in the Bronx of the twenties and thirties was the rise of new neighborhoods (see map 6.1) due to the opening of new transit lines

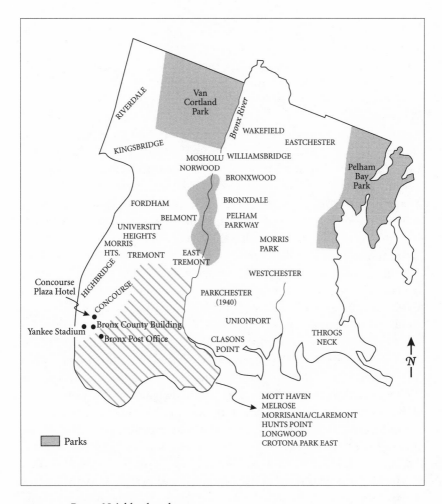

MAP 6.1 Bronx Neighborhoods, 1940

and to state efforts to spur residential construction. Whole new apartment communities arose to the west, north, and east of the older settled area, peopling the streets near Jerome and Westchester avenues, White Plains Road and Broadway, and the Grand Concourse. The once fashionable spots in Mott Haven and Hunts Point began to be surpassed by the Concourse, Highbridge, Morris and University Heights, Kingsbridge, Fordham, Norwood, and Bronxdale–Bronxwood stretches, all of which had better, more up-to-date housing.[3] These neighborhoods reflected the city's heterogeneity, with some contractors building housing specifically for their compatriots. In the 1880s, the Bronx had been mostly old-stock American with a large German community and a few Irish; by 1930, it was 46 percent Jewish, with sizable contingents of Irish, Germans, and Italians. By 1940, with almost 1.4 million residents, the borough was over 38 percent Jewish, still with Irish, German, and Italian neighborhoods.[4]

As the new development bypassed the borough's former political and geographic centers, the Third Avenue corridor lost many municipal and county offices. By 1934, when the Bronx County Building opened, up the hill from Yankee Stadium and across from the Concourse Plaza Hotel, the lower Concourse became where most of the political, civic, business, and sporting events of the Bronx took place. With this at its southern end, quality apartments along its entire length, and a rising upscale shopping center at its northern tip, the Grand Concourse became the urban Bronx's highest status area. By 1940, the shift from the southern Bronx to the newer "West Bronx" was complete.[5]

Bronx Democratic Party head Edward J. Flynn brought many federally sponsored projects to the borough during the 1930s Depression.[6] Except for Crotona Pool, the Triborough Bridge, and a scattering of local playgrounds, these improvements were outside of the South Bronx. The central post office, the Bronx County Building, the county jail, Hunter College (the current Lehman College campus), Orchard Beach, the Bronx Terminal Market, the Hutchinson River and Henry Hudson parkways, the Whitestone Bridge, and even a new subway heightened the growing disparity between the older and newer areas of the Bronx.[7]

Some public works enhanced the industrial tone of certain spots or relegated them to undesirable uses, as happened with the Terminal Market, the Bronx County Jail, and the approaches to the Triborough Bridge. Meanwhile, the parkways and bridges allowed travelers to bypass the Bronx completely as they drove to Westchester County or Connecticut. Orchard Beach, Crotona Pool, and the numerous local playgrounds, moreover, were recreational facilities that had to be shared with the general public. These improvements addressed the needs of crowded Bronx communities, but they also accentuated the working-class character of many of its residential areas and were potential trouble spots if the race and ethnicity of that public changed. The improvements of the twenties and thirties plus the added population and new transit that accompanied them would promote and later accelerate change within the borough.[8]

While the rest of the borough was growing, the South Bronx was not. Mott Haven, Melrose, and Morrisania steadily lost population (see table 6.1). Only the Hunts Point–Crotona Park East district had more people in 1940 than it had had in 1920, making up for the losses of the other neighborhoods. The new subway (the current 6 train) running underneath Mott

TABLE 6.1 Population of South Bronx Neighborhoods, 1920–1940

Neighborhoods	1920	1930	1940
Mott Haven	98,712	93,635	91,208
Melrose	53,188[a]	42,858	43,212
Morrisania	135,830[a]	125,675	125,727
Hunts Point–			
Crotona Park East	153,651	196,638	192,144
South Bronx	441,381	458,806	452,291

[a]This differs from the 1920 population of Melrose and Morrisania shown in chapter 4. For comparison with earlier decades, the 1920 totals shown in chapter four were computed from 1905–1910 census tracts rather than the 1920–1940 census tracts used in the current chapter and were adjusted to reflect actual neighborhood boundaries.

Source: Laidlaw, *Population of New York City, 1890–1930*, 55–56, 103–8; Bureau of the Census, *Census Tract Data on Population and Housing, New York City: 1940*, 6–14.

Haven gave the streets south of St. Mary's Park new housing and residents at the expense of those nearer Third Avenue. That subway also spurred population gains in the Longwood section of Hunts Point, and the older subway line did the same for the most northerly blocks of Crotona Park East. These new areas drained people from the oldest spots in Mott Haven, Melrose, and Morrisania–Claremont, particularly along the Third Avenue corridor. In Morrisania–Claremont and around Prospect Avenue the steady loss was only reversed on the blocks where black residents increased. The pattern was familiar: Bronxites were leaving the older built areas of the southern Bronx by moving farther out along the subway tracks.[9]

There was also much transiency because the South Bronx was an area of young tenants. By 1940, over 92 percent of the area's dwelling units were rental apartments, while over 70 percent of the population in each neighborhood was under 44 years old.[10] More important, perhaps, was the presence of rooming houses, particularly in Mott Haven where some of the original townhouses had been converted into single-room rentals—all the more underscoring the changing nature of the southern Bronx. It was easier to pick up and move when one was young and did not own the property.[11]

Mott Haven, Melrose, Morrisania, and Hunts Point–Crotona Park East were neighborhoods of European immigrants and their children (see table 6.2). Collectively, they had a greater proportion of foreign-born residents between 1910 and 1940 than the borough as a whole; individually, they were never less than one third alien born and often much more. Even more telling, the foreign ancestry group, consisting of immigrants and their

TABLE 6.2 Percentage of Foreign Born in the South Bronx, the Bronx, and New York City, 1910–1940

	1910	1920	1930	1940
South Bronx Neighborhoods:				
Mott Haven	34%	35%	39%	33%
Melrose	40	33	35	32
Morrisania	39	44	43	33
Hunts Point– Crotona Park East	34	44	48	41
South Bronx	38	41	44	36
The Bronx	35	36	38	33
New York City	40	35	33	28

Source: Laidlaw, *Statistical Sources for Demographic Studies of Greater New York, 1910*; Laidlaw, *Statistical Sources for Demographic Studies of Greater New York City, 1920*; Laidlaw, *Population of New York City*, 34, 51, 102–5, 179; Bureau of the Census, *Census Tract Data on Population and Housing, New York City: 1940*, 15–23; Rosenwaike, *Population History of New York City*, 141, 194.

American-born children, was 80 percent or more of the population of the entire South Bronx and of its individual neighborhoods between 1910 and 1930, and there is evidence that it may have been so in the next decade as well. The proportion of residents of foreign ancestry remained high despite decennial variations and despite the federal government's cutoff of immigration with the 1921 and 1924 quota laws. These predominantly immigrant communities were a factor in the continued migration of new residents to the borough. The foreign born and their offspring displaced by early slum clearance or public works in downtown Manhattan found affordable, fully established, ethnically compatible communities in the southern Bronx. The neighborhoods were there, in place, with all the necessary infrastructure and institutions, and ready-made compatriot neighbors.[12]

These neighbors, as before, were Russian and Eastern European Jews, Christian and Jewish Germans, Irish Catholics, Italians, and a bit of everything else. Jews from Russia and Eastern Europe were by far the most numerous. During the 1930s, historian Beth Wenger found that "the East Bronx housed almost half of the Jewish population of the Bronx." Yet not every neighborhood was Jewish. South-central Mott Haven was mostly Irish, lower Melrose was almost completely Italian, and upper Melrose and lower Morrisania still had Germans. Within this hodgepodge of peoples were small, scattered groups of English, Scots, Scandinavians, Greeks, French, African Americans, and, by 1940, the Spanish speaking. Between 1920 and 1940, a walk through the streets of the South Bronx revealed a host of racial and ethnic immigrant communities consisting of a building, a block, or an even larger area.[13]

By 1940, there were fewer Russian and Eastern European Jews in the South Bronx. As measured by foreign-born heads of families, Jewish residents were not only declining within each neighborhood but also shifting from place to place, moving along the subway tracks into the upper reaches of Crotona Park East and beyond to Tremont, west to the Concourse corridor, and with the new subway (the 6 train) across the Bronx River. Germans, English, Scots, and Scandinavians—those from England and Northern Europe who had been few to begin with—also lessened throughout the South Bronx. The void was filled by the Italians and the Irish. Though their numbers never rivaled those of their Russian and Eastern European counterparts, there were more Irish and Italians in 1940 than in 1920. By that time, both groups had spread to practically all portions of the South Bronx.[14]

Into this mélange of peoples came blacks and Puerto Ricans. There were only 4,100 blacks in the Bronx in 1910, when they represented less than one percent of the borough's population and only 2 percent of the city's total of African Americans (see table 6.3). Their numbers increased to almost 13,000 in 1930 and 23,500 ten years later, comprising less than 2 percent of Bronx residents in 1940. In the South Bronx, the totals started with 2,700

TABLE 6.3 Population of Blacks in the South Bronx, the Bronx, and New York City, 1910–1940

	1910	1920	1930	1940
Mott Haven	989	550	1,546	1,269
Melrose	1,134	639	511	576
Morrisania	546	959	3,413	6,666
Hunts Point– Crotona Park East	108	613	2,776	8,397
The South Bronx	2,777	2,761	8,246	16,908
The Bronx	4,117	4,803	12,930	23,529
New York City	91,709	152,467	327,706	458,444

Source: Rosenwaike, *Population History of New York City*, 133; Laidlaw, *Statistical Sources for Demographic Studies of Greater New York, 1910*, vol. 1; Laidlaw, *Statistical Sources for Demographic Studies of Greater New York, 1920*, 139–86; Bureau of the Census, *Census Tract Data on Population and Housing, New York City, 1940*, 6–14.

TABLE 6.4 Population of Puerto Rican Born in New York City, 1910–1940

Year	New York City	Bronx	Manhattan	Brooklyn
1910	554			
1920	7,364			
1930	44,908	1,273	34,715	7,985
1935	49,500			
1940	61,463			

Source: C. Wright Mills, Clarence Senior, and Rose Kohn Goldsen, *The Puerto Rican Journey: New York's Newest Migrants* (1950; reprint, New York: Harper & Brothers, 1961), 187; Lawrence Chenault, *The Puerto Rican Migrant in New York City* (1938; reprint, New York: Columbia University Press, 1970), 58, 63; Rosenwaike, *Population History of New York City*, 139.

blacks in 1910, mostly in Mott Haven and Melrose; rose to more than 8,000 in 1930, chiefly in Morrisania and Hunts Point–Crotona Park East; and doubled to almost 17,000 by 1940, still mainly in Morrisania and Hunts Point–Crotona Park East.[15]

The number of Puerto Ricans is harder to pinpoint. Beginning with 554 in 1910, the Puerto Rican–born population of the city grew to more than 7,000 in 1920, jumped to almost 45,000 in 1930, and passed 61,000 ten years later (see table 6.4). Although Puerto Ricans were American citizens from 1917 on, their number was probably much higher than these totals. In 1926, for example, contemporary sources estimated there were 100,000 to 200,000 Puerto Ricans in New York City.[16] The majority of these were in Manhattan, but in 1930, the Health Department found almost 1,300 Puerto Rican–born residents in the Bronx, while a 1939 study observed that "in the northern part of Health Area 41 [which was just south of Westchester and Prospect avenues], there has recently been an influx of Puerto Rican families." A look at census tracts that tally foreign-born, white heads of families from Spain, Latin America, and the Caribbean also indicates where the Spanish-speaking were in 1940, in three main spots in the South Bronx—central Mott Haven, along the first subway in Hunts Point–Crotona Park East, and Claremont—in sum, in those same census tracts where a Welfare Council study estimated there were almost 72,000 Puerto Ricans in 1948.[17]

In 1940, the small black population of the Bronx was more segregated than ever. To begin with, almost three quarters were in the South Bronx. As their numbers increased after 1920, blacks regrouped. In Morrisania's Claremont district, for example, every census tract gained small numbers of blacks between 1920 and 1930. But in the subsequent decade, only two did so while all the others lost. By 1940, 86 percent of Claremont's African American residents were between East 169th Street and Claremont Parkway near the Park Avenue railroad tracks. Surrounding streets, meanwhile, had hardly any blacks. Elsewhere, most African American residents were at the juncture of Morrisania and Hunts Point–Crotona Park East. In 1940, more than 10,000 black Americans lived in the blocks that straddled Prospect Avenue—quite a change from the 2,000 that had been there in 1930 or the 300 or so of the previous decade. Away from Prospect, however-er, blacks were fewer and fewer.[18]

In all cases, blacks lived in the poorest housing. A 1927 survey found that one of the worst tenements in Mott Haven, a three-story frame structure with no heat, hot water, or toilet facilities, was full of African Americans.[19] Similarly, by 1940, blacks were also living around Prospect Avenue in the older frame houses of the former Fox estate. This area was the only exception to a settlement pattern that relegated blacks to the factory and warehouse sections near the riverfronts and the tracks and train yards on Park, Third, and Brook avenues. But it was not anomalous in terms of its housing stock, for every census tract with blacks had a solid core of not-so-new, second-rate housing. The Hispanic population occupied more substantial structures—the New-Law apartments that flanked the subway trestle along Westchester Avenue and Southern Boulevard, those around Claremont Parkway, and the ones near Brook Avenue and 138th Street. Blacks and Puerto Ricans often occupied the same areas but not the same streets or houses.[20]

From the 1920s on, the South Bronx was "fast becoming a slum."[21] In 1934, over half of its structures had been built before the 1901 Tenement House Law. Indeed, the neighborhoods, both individually and collectively, scored worse than the borough in every category that measured the quality of the city's housing. A 1939 study concluded that the area's housing did "not have the minimum standards for decent, safe and sanitary housing which are at present a legal requirement."[22] However, when compared to areas of Manhattan and Brooklyn, the housing stock of the Bronx's oldest neighborhoods was not so bad. For this reason, no part of the Bronx was designated for slum clearance in the 1930s by the Slum Clearance Committee, a group of housing reformers. Even as late as 1942, one study concluded that the "reconstruction problem, so vitally important in Manhattan, is negligible in the Bronx."[23]

The neighborhoods were also poorer because better-off residents moved away. In the 1920s, new transit lines made it easy to reach new areas. The Irish of Mott Haven aspired to Fordham and Kingsbridge; the Italians of Melrose to Williamsbridge or Morris Park; the Germans of Melrose and

Morrisania to Unionport, Eastchester, Wakefield, or even Mount Vernon on the other side of the city line; and the Jews of Claremont and Hunts Point–Crotona Park East (the old "East Bronx") to University Heights, Tremont, the Grand Concourse, or Pelham Parkway. It was a sure sign of status to leave the old neighborhood. By the end of the decade, the South Bronx was a working- and lower middle-class immigrant district with pockets of middle-class housing in Hunts Point, Alexander Avenue, and the Boston Road district, and south of St. Mary's Park. By then, the Bronx's southernmost area had become the counterpart of Manhattan's Lower East Side—still a step up from the downtown slums, but no longer able to satisfy the housing aspirations of many residents.[24]

The area was also poorer because of the Depression. The economic collapse lasted throughout the decade and affected the entire city. In 1940, 18 percent of the city's total labor force—more than 635,000 people—was still unemployed.[25] The average annual expenditure of a Bronx family decreased from $3,259 to $2,624 during the decade. As late as 1940, on the eve of World War II, 18 percent of the borough's labor force was out of work (the same unemployment rate as the whole city). It was no accident that in 1934, Bronx Borough President James J. Lyons proposed a bill requiring that city employees be city residents.[26]

The neighborhoods of the South Bronx were the least well off. In 1930, the Association for Improving the Condition of the Poor noted that "a very large proportion" of its clients lived within a three-quarter-mile radius of 149th Street and Third Avenue.[27] Four years later, in 1934, Rabbi Herman Saville of the nearby Sinai Congregation reported that many of his flock were "coping with disheartening economic conditions."[28] By 1939, the lower Bronx had 66 percent of the relief cases in the borough, and in 1940, with the exception of the Hunts Point peninsula, it had the smallest average annual expenditure in the entire borough. The Hunts Point–Crotona Park East section was slightly better off, but some blocks around Prospect and Westchester avenues—those where blacks and Puerto Ricans were—had incomes and rents comparable to those in Gotham's poorest neighborhoods.[29]

But even the cheapest rents were hard to pay. In the early 1930s, Bronx tenants organized and forcibly resisted evictions by using rent strikes, picket lines, and violent confrontations with city marshals and the police, in essence pitting Jewish tenants against Jewish landlords. These tenant protests began far from the South Bronx, in the Workers Cooperative Colony known as the "Coops" on Allerton Avenue in Bronx Park East and the Sholem Aleichem Apartments south of Van Cortlandt Park—both inhabited by Jews steeped in socialist ideals and labor activism. By late 1932, rent strikes had spread to the poorer and heavily Jewish Morrisania and

Crotona Park East, particularly in and around Charlotte Street, as well as to Harlem, the Lower East Side, and Brooklyn. In one Crotona Park East incident on Franklin Avenue, the police "were overrun, kicked, clawed and scratched [as] for more than an hour, the battle raged." The eviction crisis eased during 1933 when some Bronx landlords compromised with their tenants and Mayor John O'Brien provided rent checks from New Deal emergency relief funds. Tenant activism led to the City-Wide Tenants League, a group formed to assist working-class tenants with their housing complaints. In late 1936, City-Wide helped 600 Irish, Italian, and Jewish families in lower Mott Haven who were ordered to leave their homes two weeks befor Christmas. The families lived in tenements condemned for the Bronx approaches to the Triborough Bridge, which was being built by Robert Moses. City-Wide organized demonstrations, press coverage, and delegations to public officials and obtained tenants a stay of demolition and emergency expenses for moving and for food, clothing, and medical care. A 1939 study of the lower Bronx revealed that these families moved into similar tenements on adjoining blocks.[30]

Assessments of the borough often overlooked the increasing poverty of the lowermost neighborhoods. In 1942, Fred Allen's real estate survey concluded that the "outstanding characteristic of the county is the fact that the great majority of the people" were of "moderate means." Basing his premise on 1933 statistics, the author asserted that there was "less [economic] diversification in the status of the population in the Bronx than there [was] in the other 4 boroughs."[31] Such findings, however, were based on boroughwide percentile groups, which were quite broad and accommodated wide variations in monthly rent and annual spending.[32] Residents of the South Bronx knew full well they were in the borough's poorest spots.

There were still factories in the area. According to Allen's survey, the borough lost manufacturing jobs during the thirties "more rapidly" than Manhattan, Brooklyn, or Queens. By the early forties, Allen concluded that "the part played by the Bronx in City-wide industry is very small, considering how much territory is taken up by scattered plants of all types." What remained—milk plants, laundries, retail outlets, and the Con Ed power plant—was largely in Mott Haven, Morrisania, and Hunts Point. Prohibition had eliminated the breweries of Morrisania and Melrose, and only two reopened after the 1933 repeal. Mott Haven, by 1939, was still a piano center of sorts, but the number of factories had declined as the economy, changing tastes, and new modes of entertainment affected piano sales. In their place, however, came "a large number of smaller plants, or 'sweat shops' . . . along the older and more blighted parts of Third Avenue." World War II revived manufacturing in the borough for a few years, but

after the war, Bronx industry continued to decline. The lower Bronx's industrial rim and spine, which at one time had represented growth and
prosperity, was by the forties contributing to an increasingly seedier look
and feel.[33]

Because of the Depression, fewer South Bronx residents were able to realize their housing aspirations. Having little choice, Jews, Italians, Irish,
Germans, blacks, and Hispanics lived more or less side by side in many
spots. Those who could afford to leave did so, and those who could not
separated themselves physically and psychologically as much as possible
from the other groups—hence the growing segregation of blacks despite
their small numbers and the continued existence of disparate ethnic social
networks within the same general area. Hence also the sporadic ethnic conflict that occurred during the 1930s and early 1940s.[34]

In the 1930s, the severe economic difficulties that beset all ethnic and
racial groups exacerbated Old World rivalries, while job competition and
political displacement at times led to violent confrontations in the city's
streets. Specifically, ethnic tensions intensified because Jews and Italians
wanted more political power, Germans feared another outbreak of anti-
German hysteria as had occurred during World War I, the Irish resented
the growing Jewish threat to their control of New York City politics, and
Jews contended with growing anti-Semitism from Nazi-sponsored groups
and Christian extremists. Most of the time and especially within the more
homogeneous neighborhoods, such conflict took place in the normal city-
wide political arena. In the lower Bronx of the late thirties and early forties,
however, local conditions resulted in "an intense, prolonged, and violent
conflict" between the Irish and the Jews.[35]

The social geography of the southernmost Bronx was a prime factor in
intergroup problems. The Depression hit unskilled laborers the hardest.
The least affected were members of the civil service and the professions,
which by the late twenties had been increasingly filled by Jews. The Irish,
Italians, and Germans of the South Bronx, in contrast, were mostly in the
less-skilled positions and also in the lowest rent blocks of the area. Most
Italian and German Americans rejected blatant anti-Semitic appeals because they were linked to fascism. The Irish, however, knew they had lost
ground to the Jews in civil service jobs, political patronage, the mayoralty,
and the Democratic Party leadership. Politically and economically frus-
trated, they could easily believe that Jews "seemed to be taking everything
away from them."[36]

These interethnic politics, plus the severe economic crunch and the resulting lack of mobility, created a fertile climate for ethnic hostility. Violent
conflict usually erupted wherever mixed groups of disparate classes rubbed

elbows. In the lower Bronx, there were many spots in Mott Haven and east Melrose where varied groups, the Irish and Jews in particular, lived close together and where the former were constantly confronted with the seemingly better housing and slightly better-off economic position of the latter. And it was in those same places where gangs of Irish youths roamed the streets during the late 1930s and early 1940s, vandalizing Jewish businesses and physically attacking Jewish-looking people.[37]

In a way, the Irish-Jewish conflict was a portent of things to come. The Depression had reversed the upward mobility of many families. For the Irish, the seemingly higher economic position of nearby Jews was a constant reminder that they had not achieved better and that the area was no longer their old neighborhood. The easy solution to the conflict was for one group or the other to leave the locale, as would happen decades later. But at the time, neither could do so. They had to live together whatever the consequences and thus had to be concerned about their neighborhoods, regardless of their long-term aspirations. Local leaders tried to lessen the conflict because they knew the social fabric would be torn apart if the violence increased or lasted too long. Stressing cooperation and good neighbor policies, politicians, clergymen, and leading citizens organized tolerance committees, held demonstrations, joined interfaith movements, and spoke out against Nazism and anti-Semitism. Despite these efforts, Irish-Jewish hostilities did not end until the mid-1940s, when the economy improved and Nazi atrocities in Europe were made known.[38]

During the war years, however, there was an increase in juvenile delinquency. The violence between Irish and Jewish teens began to include Italian, black, and Puerto Rican youths. As early as 1944, there were "more than 500 conflict gangs of boys in New York City."[39] A year later, the 41st Police Precinct counted at least 23 teen gangs in its Hunts Point–Crotona Park East district, many of which were black and Puerto Rican. By 1946, South Bronx residents were complaining to the city authorities about "racial gang-warfare among the children," resulting in fights, shootings, and an occasional killing. In response, social welfare agencies called for more police presence, recreation centers, vocational training, interracial councils, and neighborhood meetings. This youth violence and gang warfare would increase during the fifties and eventually feed into the drug-related street crime of the sixties. But in the forties, it was another incentive to move away from the borough's southern neighborhoods.[40]

Despite the conflict, residents considered the South Bronx their home. Mott Haven, Melrose, Morrisania, and Hunts Point–Crotona Park East were the places from which they left to go to work, school, or church and back again. They enjoyed the amenities the Bronx had to offer and shopped at the Hub; played ball at Crotona and St. Mary's parks; relaxed at the botanical gardens, Yankee Stadium, Starlight Amusement Park, and the zoo; swam at the newly opened Crotona Pool and Orchard Beach; and, in short, made themselves at home. But the neighborhoods had changed. Each one contained significant pockets of poorer residents. The ethnic makeup of their populations had begun to shift, enclaves of different races and groups of people had begun to emerge, and the housing had begun to decline. Moreover, the ongoing relocation of South Bronx residents at all class levels revealed a transiency and a concern with status that boded ill for the future viability of the neighborhoods. Residents were proud of their borough and immediate neighborhood and of every new improvement that came to the Bronx during the twenties and thirties. But they would be quick to improve themselves even more by moving out whenever their circumstances permitted.[41]

By the early 1940s, Mott Haven, Melrose, Morrisania, and Hunts Point–Crotona Park East were deteriorating. The elevated tracks of both the el and the subway had by 1940 lowered the tone and the land values of the thoroughfares above which they ran and were the means by which residents moved away.[42] Depression-era public works worsened matters. In Mott Haven, for instance, the building of the Triborough Bridge and the elevated highway approaches removed substandard housing but increased traffic congestion and left darkened streets in their wake, making both the industrial zone and adjacent housing dirtier than before. Built for mass transit, the area lacked parking, which would be inconvenient in later years. But these neighborhoods had not been built to last. They had been built because it was lucrative for the landowner, the speculator, the builder, and eventually the landlord, and only coincidentally supplied the housing needs of an increasing population. The speculator or builder followed the dictates of the market economy and thought nothing of the consequences of the physical environment they were creating.[43]

Clearly the neighborhoods had stopped growing. It was more than population losses or lower ticket sales at the el and subway stations: there were only three new structures. The massive Bronx Central Post Office was built in 1936 at the extreme western edge of 149th Street and was thus closer to the Grand Concourse than to Third Avenue. The second, the Mott Haven Health Center, was also built in 1936 at East 140th Street and underscored the low-income character of the lower Bronx. The third, the Bronx Grit Chamber, was built in 1937 near the Mott Haven waterfront. The Grit Chamber removed larger solids from sewage and was the "first major project to help reduce pollution in the city's waterways" and the first of many unwanted facilities that the South Bronx would receive.[44] Real estate and business interests had for years viewed lower Mott Haven and the Hub as a business center that would stimulate the profitable conversion or rebuilding of old tenement areas for industrial, business, or commercial use. When that did not occur, the South Bronx was left with an aging housing stock for progressively poorer groups of people. With no new construction in sight, it was only a matter of time before Mott Haven, Melrose, Morrisania, and Hunts Point–Crotona Park East entered the last stage of the neighborhood change process—that of obsolescence or renewal.[45]

Well aware of the dire possibilities, the business and financial communities hoped the public sector would reconstruct "certain old areas." In 1939, the Bronx Board of Trade urged that the blighted spots in the Bronx be replaced by subsidized, low-rent public housing. Three of the four sites proposed were in the South Bronx: between the factory district and 138th Street in Mott Haven; from 165th Street to Tremont Avenue in Morrisania and Claremont; and nearby the Longwood Avenue, Kelly, and Fox streets juncture in Hunts Point.[46] In a few decades, all three of these locations would be poor, drug-infested, and crime-ridden—the last spot smack in the middle of the police precinct that became known as Fort Apache. At the time, however, public housing seemed a viable alternative to the lack of private construction and the failure of the market economy in the lowermost Bronx.[47]

In the late 1920s, the South Bronx Tenants' Association had looked to public housing to fill the need for affordable residential units in the South Bronx. They had seen that even then, new construction in the borough did not satisfy the demand for low-rent housing.[48] That was only being done by the filtering process, as the least desirable units in soon-to-be or already blighted areas, generally in Mott Haven, Melrose, Morrisania, and Hunts Point–Crotona Park East, were vacated as families could afford better. The filtering process allocated housing for the poor. Neighborhood deterioration or blight, on the other hand, determined where that housing would be. Since it provided low-rent housing and the poor had to live somewhere, some blight was "necessary to cope with poverty."[49] And since the poor were already in Mott Haven, Melrose, Morrisania, and Hunts Point–Crotona Park East, it was better if they were in new public housing projects— or so thought the Bronx Board of Trade. But once private enterprise no longer controlled the built environment, it would be harder to achieve changes in land use in the South Bronx. Public housing projects would solidify the low-income character of the area for decades to come.[50]

But in the early 1940s, the neighborhoods remained viable because people still chose to live there. The South Bronx was habitable, but no longer the place to be if standards of living increased. All the signs of imminent obsolescence were there—an aging housing stock, a shifting ethnic and racial mix, an outward movement of population, a weakening economy, and the continuance of an urban environment and infrastructure that from the 1940s on was not considered the ideal. The Board of Trade and all residents were aware that Mott Haven, Melrose, Morrisania, and Hunts Point–Crotona Park East were the oldest, poorest, and least desirable neighborhoods in the borough. The poor had to live somewhere, and that had become the South Bronx.

7 THE SOUTH BRONX

By the 1940s, the South Bronx no longer met middle-class expectations. It was too old, too crowded, and too inconvenient, and for the most part did not offer the option of individual home ownership. More than ever, families had to leave the neighborhood and often the entire borough to improve their standard of living. Although this outward flow of population had been going on for years, sharp demographic changes and pro-suburban government policies further motivated residents to leave and provided them with the means to do so.[1] Meanwhile, the continuance of wartime rent controls lessened the attraction of apartment house ownership. Declining real estate investment, a growing incidence of crime, and an aging housing stock spread the "South Bronx" name beyond its original neighborhoods of Mott Haven, Melrose, Morrisania–Claremont, and Hunts Point–Crotona Park East to everything south of Fordham Road, from Highbridge and the lower Concourse to Tremont, University Heights, and lower Fordham. By the late seventies, this newly defined South Bronx had become the "most extensively abandoned piece of urban geography in the United States."[2]

THE POSTWAR YEARS

After World War II, the most important change in the Bronx was the coming of thousands of Southern blacks and Spanish-speaking Puerto Ricans. Early slum clearance in black and Spanish Harlem reduced the housing available to African Americans and Puerto Ricans just when they began arriving in greater numbers. In the segregated city of the forties, they had nowhere to go but along the subway and the el into the low-rent part of the Bronx, which already had small pockets of blacks and Hispanics and had the least desirable housing.[3] By 1950, there were almost 160,000 African Americans and Puerto Ricans in the borough, 91 percent of them in the

TABLE 7.1 Population of Blacks, Puerto Ricans, and Hispanics in the Bronx, 1950–1980

Year	Total Bronx	Blacks, Puerto Ricans, and Hispanics	
		Bronx[a]	South Bronx[b]
1950	1,451,277	159,676 [11.1%]	145,549 [91.1%]
1960	1,424,815	350,781 [24.6%]	266,988 [76.1%]
1970	1,471,701	674,453 [45.8%]	
1980	1,168,972	745,099 [63.7%]	

[a] Includes number and percentage of blacks and Puerto Rican birth and parentage in the Bronx in 1950, 1960, and 1970, and number and percentage of blacks and those of Hispanic origin in 1980.

[b] Includes number and percentage of blacks and Puerto Rican birth and parentage in th the neighborhoods of Mott Haven, Melrose, Morrisania, Claremont, and Hunts Point–Crotona Park East. Statistics were computed from census tract data.

Source: Rosenwaike, Population of New York City, 133, 139; Welfare and Health Council of New York City, Population of Puerto Rican Birth or Parentage, New York City: 1950; Bureau of the Census, U.S. Census of Population and Housing: 1960, New York City; New York City Department of City Planning, 1980 and 1990 Census Bureau Data, reprinted in New York Times, 22 March 1991.

South Bronx, concentrated around Prospect and Westchester avenues where their compatriots had settled years earlier. Later arrivals joined them as migration from the rural South and Puerto Rico continued. By 1960, the number of blacks and Puerto Ricans in the Bronx had increased to more than 350,000, with almost 267,000 of these—over three quarters—in the South Bronx. As new groups poured in, white ethnics moved out. Twenty years later, by 1980, the borough was almost two-thirds black and Hispanic: 745,000 within a total borough population of over 1.1 million (see tables 1.1 and 7.1). Population change was not new to the Bronx, but the race and rapidity of the turnover was.[4]

African Americans and Puerto Ricans predominated in different parts of the South Bronx. Between 1950 and 1960, blacks filled in central Morrisania, from Webster to Prospect avenues and from 163rd Street to just beyond Crotona Park South, an area that would remain predominantly black for the rest of the century. Puerto Ricans, by contrast, fanned out from 138th Street, Southern Boulevard, Westchester Avenue, and Claremont Parkway, following the subway and elevated train routes into central Mott Haven, lower Morrisania, Claremont, and Hunts Point–Crotona Park East. The rest of the borough was still overwhelmingly white in 1960, still mostly of Jewish, Italian, Irish, and German ancestry.[5]

The postwar suburban housing boom added another incentive for whites to leave the city. As Federal Housing Authority (FHA) and Veterans' Administration programs helped lower mortgage payments for new houses, returning veterans found the ideal of a one-family detached home easier to achieve. Tens of thousands of young families soon moved to Westchester and Nassau counties in New York and to Bergen and Essex counties in New Jersey. The apartments they vacated in the Bronx were quickly filled by black and Spanish-speaking immigrants.[6]

Unfortunately, there was no upgrading of the aging housing of the South Bronx. The FHA and private lending institutions had redlined the area in the 1930s—literally showing the neighborhood in red on area maps—because its ethnic and racial mix was considered too risky for mortgage loans. So much of the Bronx was simply excluded from federal largesse in the postwar years. Although some state loans and city tax incentives were available to rehabilitate apartment buildings, South Bronx landlords typically saw no advantage in improving their structures in low-income, rent-controlled neighborhoods. Instituted by the federal government during the war, rent control was kept by the state and city because of the housing crunch.[7] Some property owners began to look toward federal public housing and urban renewal programs, which would buy their aging buildings, as ways to salvage their investments. Meanwhile, as housing expert Charles Abrams observed at the time, other landlords rented to blacks and Puerto Ricans, often "charging all the traffic [would] bear" and making "high returns because repairs [were] never made."[8]

Public housing was part of the problem. Begun during the Depression, it was necessary because the private sector would not build for the low- to lower middle-income market. By late 1950, New York City Construction Coordinator Robert Moses had already completed 20 housing projects and had at least 15 more under way. Much of this public housing replaced slums with superblocks of multistory "towers in the park," the construction of which tore down neighborhoods before they could be built anew. Demolition for the early housing projects, particularly those in black and Spanish Harlem, displaced many Manhattan tenement dwellers into the Bronx. When public housing came to the South Bronx a few years later, many were pushed out again.[9]

Public housing was accepted at first. Clasons Point Gardens, for example, was built just before the war in an undeveloped part of the Bronx. A "garden apartment"–style complex, it fit in with the few single-family homes nearby. During the 1950s, nine of the sixteen public housing projects completed in the borough went up in less-populated areas in the eastern Bronx (see map 7.1). The first five, completed between 1950 and 1952, encountered little resistance because four were medium-rent apartment houses and the one lower-rent project was in an unsettled area. The last

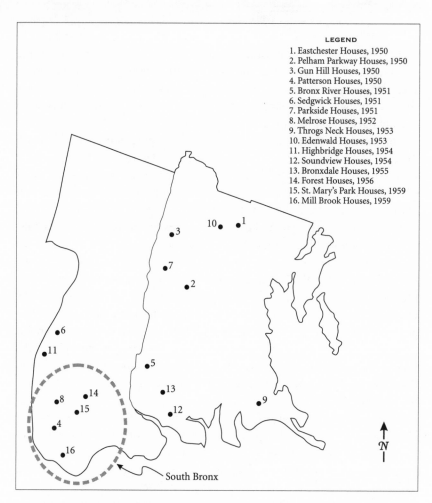

1. Eastchester Houses, 1950
2. Pelham Parkway Houses, 1950
3. Gun Hill Houses, 1950
4. Patterson Houses, 1950
5. Bronx River Houses, 1951
6. Sedgwick Houses, 1951
7. Parkside Houses, 1951
8. Melrose Houses, 1952
9. Throgs Neck Houses, 1953
10. Edenwald Houses, 1953
11. Highbridge Houses, 1954
12. Soundview Houses, 1954
13. Bronxdale Houses, 1955
14. Forest Houses, 1956
15. St. Mary's Park Houses, 1959
16. Mill Brook Houses, 1959

South Bronx

N

MAP 7.1 Public Housing in the Bronx, 1950–1959

four, however, were huge low-rent projects that began introducing blacks and Puerto Ricans into predominately white areas. By 1955, protesting residents of the eastern Bronx succeeded in changing the proposed Castle Hill Houses from low to medium rent. Four of the five projects built in the South Bronx, meanwhile, had lower rentals from the first, which meant they too would house poorer blacks and the Spanish speaking.[10]

Urban renewal also affected the Bronx at this time. In the first decades of the twentieth century, private investors had done most of the subdividing, building, and leasing of apartments. But by the forties, the difficulty of accumulating large tracts, plus the better housing standards mandated by City Hall, made building unprofitable in most of New York City. Housing was a business. In order to make money, builders had to peg rents at a certain level. Essentially, private enterprise could not clear slums, build affordable housing, or renew aging infrastructure in the city or the borough. Accordingly, Washington changed the ground rules with the Housing Acts of 1949 and 1954. From then on, the federal government assumed most of the costs of urban land so that business and institutional sponsors could buy that land below cost and profitably rebuild slum areas and renew the city.[11]

Clearing the slums meant clearing the residents as well. In 1956, Urban League president Sophia Y. Jacobs complained to Robert Moses that urban renewal was displacing thousands of "minority families . . . [who] had to resort to doubling up with relatives and friends, thereby intensifying overcrowding in already deteriorating and segregated neighborhoods." Moses assured her public housing was the answer, but it was difficult to get financing for the projects in "the bad slum areas," despite FHA guarantees. Reporting on the relocation problem a few years later, mayoral advisor J. Anthony Panuch conceded urban renewal had "unhoused thousands" who would "swell the overcrowding of the most dilapidated portion of the City's housing inventory." To handle displaced tenants, future Bronx projects would have to hold more.[12]

Race was critical. In 1940, African Americans and Puerto Ricans together accounted for less than 7 percent of the city's 7.4 million people (see table 7.2). A decade later, that proportion had doubled to 13 percent, with

TABLE 7.2 Population of Blacks and Puerto Ricans in New York City, 1940–1960[a]

Year	New York City	Blacks and Puerto Ricans	Total Blacks and Puerto Ricans
1940	7,454,995	458,444 blacks 61,463 PRs	519,907 [6.9%]
1950	7,891,957	747,608 blacks 246,306 PRs	993,914 [12.5%]
1960	7,781,984	1,087,931 blacks 612,574 PRs	1,700,505 [21.8%]

[a] Statistics for 1940 enumerate Puerto Rican born living in New York City. Statistics for 1950 and 1960 reflect Puerto Rican birth and parentage in New York City.

Source: Mills, Senior, and Goldsen, *The Puerto Rican Journey*, 187; Rosenwaike, *Population History of New York City*, 139, 141.

blacks having less than 748,000 and Puerto Ricans less than 247,000. By 1960, there were a million blacks and more than 600,000 Puerto Ricans, together constituting 22 percent of the residents of New York City.[13] Up through the 1950s, however, the city worried more about Puerto Ricans than blacks.[14] Many New Yorkers believed Puerto Ricans disproportionately settled there, swelled the welfare rolls, and were a drain on the city. This concern was felt in South Bronx neighborhoods. "You can live with Negroes," a Bronx housewife remarked. "The Puerto Ricans are the trouble." While both groups "smashed the mold of residential segregation," it was white Puerto Ricans who paved the way for their darker-skinned brethren and African Americans. The growing influx of black Americans went almost unnoticed by comparison.[15]

At first both groups lived in crowded slums that in many cases had early been designated for slum clearance and housing projects. As vast tracts of Manhattan were cleared during the forties and fifties, slum conditions often moved elsewhere. By 1954, Reverend Ernest Davies claimed the black and Hispanic Claremont section of the South Bronx was "one of the most highly deprived socio-economic areas in the Bronx," filled with unhealthy, overcrowded one-room flats. Unsurprisingly, many white New Yorkers blamed blacks and Puerto Ricans for these worsening conditions.[16]

In the postwar years, white ethnic New Yorkers were concerned with sharing in the American Dream, not with sharing their jobs and housing with darker or non-English speaking groups. The first Puerto Rican and black families in the South Bronx encountered little resistance. But from 1950 on, new migrants began moving into established neighborhoods that were not their own at a time when the city and later the nation would attempt to bring about some form of racial integration and equal housing. As early as 1948, the old East Bronx, according to Samuel Lubell, was "a living experiment in race relations."[17] "We can live together," claimed Borough President James Lyons in 1955, but many in the South Bronx disagreed. "We may have to live together," answered one longtime resident, but "most of us don't like it." Already fearful of being trapped in the slums, many Bronx families resented the imposition of different and often poorer peoples within their midst.[18]

There were attempts to promote tolerance and eliminate racial barriers. During the forties and fifties, community and police groups, city agencies, human rights activists, and faith-based organizations sponsored neighborhood activities and school programs to improve race relations.[19] In the mid-fifties, for example, the Forest Neighborhood Committee interviewed public housing applicants to achieve an interracial mix of tenants for the new, low-income Forest Houses in the South Bronx, and by 1956 claimed that this was the city's first successfully desegregated public housing project. Elsewhere in the Bronx, interracial councils and civil rights groups tried to end discrimination in the all-white, middle-class Parkchester apartment complex and supported the construction of the low-rent Castle Hill project, portraying its opponents as "bigots."[20] The most visible effort was the Mayor's Committee on Unity. Formed in 1944, it was the forerunner of the Committee on Puerto Ricans and its successor, the Commission on Inter-Group Relations, which later became the Commission on Human Rights.[21]

City housing incentives led directly to the passage of fair housing laws. In 1943, a new limited-profit law allowed the Metropolitan Life Insurance Company to build Stuyvesant Town. This development replaced 18 square blocks of East Side tenements with housing for 24,000 white middle-income families, because as Frederick Ecker, chairman of Metropolitan Life, quipped, "Negroes and whites don't mix." In the Bronx, Metropolitan Life's earlier foray into housing had also built the Parkchester complex. But in the midst of a war against Nazi racism, Ecker's comments prompted the City Council to prohibit tax concessions for segregated housing. After the war, the open housing movement was fed by the growing civil rights struggle, the Cold War's spotlight on Jim Crow practices, and the need to house the UN delegates from Third World countries. From 1944 on, the city and the state began enacting progressively more stringent fair housing laws. By 1958, the city had a comprehensive antidiscrimination law on the books with the Commission on Inter-Group Relations as the enforcement vehicle.[22]

Racial change and the housing problem worked against the interracial ideal. For a short time, the South Bronx teemed with different races and ethnicities. After a 1952 fire, a black family stayed with Jewish neighbors until its apartment was repaired. Similarly, as Secretary of State Colin Powell remembered, growing up on Kelly Street in the forties and fifties, there were no minorities or majorities. "Everybody was either a Jew, an Italian, a Pole, a Greek, a Puerto Rican, or as we said in those days, a Negro." But by 1955, even he noticed the old neighborhood was "deteriorating." The heterogeneity of the population vanished as the South Bronx became poorer, blacker, and more Hispanic. Most borough residents and New Yorkers did not understand why the slums spread and housing was still the city's "No. 1 problem." They only saw their neighborhoods changing and dreamed of a private home in the suburbs.[23]

The city fathers feared the exodus of whites. Public housing and urban redevelopment had originally been promoted to keep the middle class from leaving. Indeed, by the late 1950s, income limits for public housing were raised to keep lower middle-class families from being evicted as their incomes rose. In 1955, the Mitchell-Lama law, providing low-cost mortgages and tax incentives to build middle-income housing, was enacted to keep "the heart of the productive working force" in Gotham. Ira Robbins of the New York City Housing Authority claimed Mitchell-Lama was necessary because families earning less than $10,000 could not afford apartments in the city. From 1955 on, therefore, the state subsidized housing for families who were middle class in outlook and aspiration but not quite middle class in income, many of whom felt threatened by racial change and spreading slums. By 1961, 6 of 17 Mitchell-Lama cooperatives completed or under construction were in the Bronx.[24]

Mitchell-Lama housing was a disaster for the borough. Its co-ops siphoned off white families from housing that was still sound, leaving vacancies to be filled by poorer blacks and Puerto Ricans, themselves often displaced or moving away from the worsening slums, and thus spread the blight and the segregation farther. The best example of this was Co-op City, Gotham's biggest housing complex, built during the late 1960s on the northern border of the Bronx. Its 15,500 apartments in 35 buildings allowed fearful white Jewish residents to abandon Grand Concourse neighborhoods almost overnight. Thirty years later, former Bronx resident Harriet Bailer asserted that Co-op City "helped undermine the rich and integral fabric of Bronx neighborhoods" and wondered how the Bronx would have fared had it not been built.[25]

The Cross-Bronx Expressway was also disastrous. The idea for the road emerged even before the Bronx–Whitestone Bridge opened in 1939 because the new span made a direct link to New Jersey possible via the George Washington Bridge. Approved in 1944, the expressway was built in the late 1950s as part of the interstate highway system. Early Bronx parkways enhanced the value of vacant land while later highways followed rail lines or the industrial waterfront. The Cross-Bronx Expressway, in contrast, sliced through "a dozen solid, settled, densely populated neighborhoods" in the borough's western portion, destroying blocks of apartment buildings at a time when every apartment was needed. These neighborhoods were not slums. The expressway swept away housing that was newer and better than that in the South Bronx neighborhoods of Mott Haven, Melrose, Morrisania–Claremont, and Hunts Point–Crotona Park East. Despite protests from residents of the East Tremont neighborhood, over which part of the road ran, by 1955 all the occupants were evicted, and housing adjoining the vacated buildings was less desirable. The expressway was the equivalent of public housing's "towers in the park"; neighborhoods were demolished so travelers could bypass the Bronx completely.[26]

Although increasingly black and Puerto Rican during the 1950s, the South Bronx contained viable communities for many families, whose children in later years would have fond memories of growing up in the Bronx. A former Charlotte Street resident, Renee Sartoris, explained that "There was something special about the Bronx in those days, a feeling. You knew everybody, the butcher, the baker, the candlestick maker, and they knew you."[27] While city officials considered the area a slum, there were no rubble-filled lots or abandoned buildings in Mott Haven, Melrose, Morrisania–Claremont, or Hunts Point–Crotona Park East. New migrants to the city or residents displaced by Manhattan's slum clearance filtered into the housing left by those who moved to better quarters or away from the newcomers. The first Puerto Rican residents of the South Bronx were part of this early outmigration, particularly if they spoke English and were whiter than their incoming poorer brethren. Hispanic bodegas replaced Jewish delicatessens and Spanish films took over the local movie houses, but rent control and scarce housing kept many from leaving. Pockets of earlier Bronxites remained—Jews around the synagogue on Intervale Avenue in Hunts Point–Crotona Park East, Italians near the Church of Our Lady of Pity in southern Melrose, and some Irish nearby St. Jerome's on Mott Haven's Alexander Avenue. Residents still cheered at Yankee Stadium, shopped at the 149th Street–Third Avenue "Hub," and rode the elevated and subway to work, but only for as long as they had to.[28]

DEVASTATED NEIGHBORHOODS

The Bronx had developed along with the city. From the forties on, however, civic and business interests rebuilt Manhattan and downtown Brooklyn, replacing tenements with highways, newer housing, and cultural institutions to keep the white middle class in the city. Every attempt to do so disrupted the city as a whole and the Bronx in particular. Highways, public housing, and urban renewal displaced residents and jobs and spread the slums, while Mitchell-Lama enclaves segregated the white middle class from the disadvantaged. The effect was devastating for the Bronx.[29]

In the 1950s, though, no one envisioned what these citywide policies would do. The borough's population was still growing, its neighborhoods were still densely settled, and its image was one of tightly knit ethnic communities, as portrayed by the 1957 motion picture, *Marty*. A mini–building boom allowed the upwardly mobile to move into high-rises in Riverdale and private homes in the far Bronx, freeing apartments in the better neighborhoods for other aspiring families. Despite its deteriorating southern tip,

the borough had apartment buildings that seemed sound and still had political clout. In 1960, presidential aspirant John F. Kennedy sought support
from Bronx Congressman and Democratic Party boss Charles A. Buckley.
Yet the same conditions that had predisposed South Bronx neighborhoods
to decline existed in the rest of the borough: tightly packed apartment
houses that could not compete with a suburban home, a continued outward movement of residents in search of better living space, a tight housing market that would propel many to the suburbs, and a population of
renters that could move away easily. The spread of different and poorer
groups from the borough's southern neighborhoods exacerbated these
conditions and changed the Bronx.[30]

African Americans and Puerto Ricans were largely unskilled and arrived just when the city's economy began losing the very jobs these new
migrants would need. Between 1947 and 1976, the city lost 500,000 factory jobs as big and small industries left the city. Civil service employment
was often closed to the newcomers as well, even more so after a 1960 law
permitted city workers to live in the suburbs. The other ethnic groups
monopolized jobs in the uniformed services, the schools, and city agencies, while education and language requirements kept many blacks and
Hispanics from other entry-level civil service jobs. Earlier immigrants had
found work building the city's infrastructure. Now, however, any upgrading would be done by heavy machinery rather than strong backs.
New York City had been the "Golden Door" for earlier immigrant
groups, but the means for climbing out of poverty diminished as more
and more African Americans and Puerto Ricans came north. What would
remain was welfare and, from 1964 on, the little that trickled down from
the federal government's "Great Society" programs.[31]

A black and Hispanic South Bronx was doomed to be poor. A 1967 Fordham University study found that the Bronx had become poorer because its
businesses and middle-class families were moving to the suburbs, while "in
their place [had] come thousands of Negro and Puerto Rican families . . .
[who] live in abject poverty with little hope for the future." Noting the
"sluggish performance" of the Bronx economy, the study called for more
help for the borough's businesses and more education and job training to
provide the skills needed by Bronx employers.[32] Despite the 1967 opening
of the huge Hunts Point Terminal Produce Market, the borough continued
losing jobs. Between 1970 and 1977, 300 companies employing 10,000 workers went out of business or moved out of the Bronx. The old industrial waterfront and Third Avenue spine was no more. Bronx businesses had only
employed a small portion of the borough's labor force, but they had helped
sustain nearby streets with part-time and after-school work for many. Such

jobs might have helped residents of the predominantly black housing projects that straddled Third Avenue once the elevated line was removed in 1973. A year later, *New York Affairs* was predicting the Bronx would be "Host to the City's Poor" by the year 2000.[33]

Racial change and deepening poverty went hand in hand, as more welfare recipients wound up in the borough. By 1960, roughly a quarter of the families in the South Bronx were receiving welfare. As a result, the South Bronx was one of the first areas proposed for antipoverty funding in 1964 and the Model Cities program in 1966. Poverty in the 1960s was tied to race, a changing economy, urban decline, and a suburban exodus that accelerated as more blacks and Hispanics came in and as the turmoil resulting from the civil rights struggle and the activism of the sixties engulfed the city. By 1970, a group of clergymen, teachers, and politicians from the Hunts Point neighborhood wanted the South Bronx declared "a disaster area."[34] The mayor's office estimated that in the district south of Fordham Road "one of every three residents was on welfare . . . as much as 25–30 percent of the eligible work force is unemployed" in 1976. Eight years later, by 1984, 55 percent of the families in that same area were below poverty level and 39 percent were receiving welfare.[35]

Poverty also coincided with crime and social disorder. In the 1950s, juvenile delinquency and street gangs continued to increase in the city's poorest neighborhoods. Community services were expanded to check the growing disorder, but these outreach programs could not remove the worsening poverty and segregation of minority communities. There gangs flourished because minority youths felt they needed to defend their turf, their manhood, and their race. Hence in the Bronx, juvenile delinquency rates were greatest in the South Bronx areas where black Americans and Puerto Ricans lived. By the mid-fifties, Secretary of State Powell remembered, his Hunts Point neighborhood had gone "from gang fights to gang wars . . . from marijuana to heroin." By 1955, gang warfare and teen violence had resulted in the fatal mugging of an elderly Bronx resident and several killings of gang members and innocent youths. This violent behavior reflected the fraying social fabric of the black and Hispanic communities of the city and the South Bronx and also prefigured a more violent epidemic of gangs, drugs, and street crime.[36]

By all accounts and along with the rest of the nation, New York City was engulfed by a massive wave of crime and public disorder during the sixties and seventies.[37] Murders, muggings, rapes, break-ins, and car thefts began occurring throughout the city rather than only in the poorest neighborhoods. An outbreak of drug addiction among ghetto youth during the 1960s caused much of the crime. But whatever the reason, demands for greater police protection became commonplace and "law and order" became the catchphrase of politicians, the media, and the average person on the street. "Law and order" was also a code name for race, for the great majority of perpetrators seemed to be minority youths.[38] A 1969 profile of robberies in the Highbridge section of the Bronx found that "more than four-fifths of the robbers . . . were Negroes or Puerto Ricans."[39]

Crime was everywhere, but there seemed to be more of it in the Bronx. Reported assaults in the borough increased from 998 in 1960 to 4,256 in 1969, while burglaries rose from 1,765 to 29,276. Most of this was in the South Bronx. The 41st Police Precinct in Hunts Point–Crotona Park East— a.k.a. "Fort Apache"—led the city in murders and crime from the early sixties on. Fireman Dennis Smith claimed that "there [were] more homicides per square mile in this precinct than anywhere in the United States."[40] By 1967, violent crime was spreading out from the original South Bronx, reaching Highbridge, the lower Concourse, Fordham, Kingsbridge, and Bronx Park. In March of that year, Bronx Councilman Bertram Gelfand claimed the crime spree had created an "atmosphere of terror" in the borough. Weeks later, Deputy Police Commissioner Jacques Nevard admitted that an "improved, more accurate reporting of crime . . . found that the Bronx had the highest increase of any borough in total crime, in felony complaints, and more specifically, in robberies."[41] Conditions were so bad in 1969 that a group of black and Puerto Rican housewives marched to the Morrisania police precinct and demanded gun permits to protect themselves from drug addicts.[42]

Crime worsened when a new wave of youth gangs appeared in the South Bronx during the 1970s. With names such as the Savage Skulls, Cypress Bachelors, Black Spades, Spanish Mafia, and the Reapers, these new groups attacked drug addicts and pushers and asserted they were merely cleaning up the neighborhoods. One leader claimed they were only "a group of guys working together to help out people."[43] Often with ex-inmates and Vietnam vets as members, these gangs terrorized residents, ripped off local shopkeepers, fought with rival gangs, vandalized buildings, and at times hired themselves out to local drug dealers, thugs, or even landlords. Gang membership provided self-esteem and a sense of belonging for Puerto Rican and black youths, most poorly educated, unemployable, and estranged from their families, because as Victor Marrero said in 1973, "The whole atmosphere [of the South Bronx] is geared to crushing a person's spirit, and most people don't have the kind of strength to resist." These gangs were striking evidence that much of the South Bronx was unstable, unsafe, and undesirable.[44]

The city itself was disorderly during the sixties and seventies. Race riots erupted sporadically from 1964 on, as blacks and Puerto Ricans angrily demanded jobs, welfare, housing, and equal rights. Bronx welfare recipients participated in the citywide welfare rights campaign that began in 1966. "We found that welfare people were entitled to more than just the monthly check," explained Bronx organizer Carmen Arroya, so "we prepared forms for every itemized thing . . . and we all got money." By 1968, Bronx welfare mothers were occupying local welfare centers in Melrose, Tremont, and Kingsbridge. City expenditures rose along with the welfare rolls and stirred resentment among white ethnic groups.[45]

In this setting, every issue became a racial confrontation. Teachers clashed with minority groups over local control of schools; policemen resisted a civilian complaint review board; white middle-class communities fought against busing and low-rent public housing; white extremists firebombed homes of blacks who moved into white areas; and minority students closed down the City University system. In Mott Haven, the Young Lords, an organization of Puerto Rican youths, seized the aging Lincoln Hospital and demanded better health care and a new building. Labor conflicts between the city and its employees contributed to the turmoil, as sanitation and transit workers dumped garbage in the streets and shut down the subway. And behind it all were rising inflation and energy prices, and a growing fiscal crisis for the city that necessitated cutting city services. With crime and poverty up and available affordable housing still down, Gotham was a mess.[46]

Amid the crime and social disorder of the 1960s, the South Bronx fell apart. Neighborhoods that had been home to successive waves of immigrants and their children suddenly became unlivable. Hunts Point residents were "literally living in a state of siege," reported *The New York Times* in 1969. Because of crime, people feared for their personal safety, local businesses could not function, and apartment buildings lost tenants. Because of the crime and poverty already there, city services for the poor and the deviant were put in the South Bronx, while fire, police, and sanitation services were cut back, worsening the situation further. People moved to the South Bronx out of necessity, not choice, often installed there by the welfare authorities. All who could move away did so. Those who couldn't often vented their rage on the police, the firemen, the buildings, and the neighborhood. Thus shops closed, landlords abandoned buildings, the population declined, and the neighborhoods of the South Bronx collapsed.[47] Devastation spread to other parts of the borough; as this occurred, seminarian and community activist Paul Brant observed that "welfare people were moving west" (see table 7.3).[48]

TABLE 7.3 Population of South Bronx Neighborhoods, 1950–1980[a]

Neighborhood	1950	1960	1970	1980
Mott Haven	86,718	88,688	80,032	49,146 [-39%]
Melrose	38,114	36,662	34,927	17,840 [-49%]
Morrisania	124,927	106,618	105,773	49,324 [-53%]
Hunts Point–				
Crotona Park East	187,164	173,963	165,329	51,060 [-69%]
South Bronx	436,923	405,931	386,061	167,370 [-57%]

[a] These totals are based on census tracts which incorporated South Bronx neighborhood boundaries used in previous chapters.

Source: Bureau of the Census, *U.S. Census of Population: 1950, New York City*; Bureau of the Census, *U.S. Census of Population and Housing: 1960, New York City*; Bureau of the Census, *1970 Census of Population and Housing, New York, N.Y.*; and Bureau of the Census, *1980 Census of Population and Housing, New York, N.Y.* (Washington, DC, 1983).

Disorder, crime, and poverty came to a head during the July 1977 power blackout. The entire city was subjected to "a night of terror" of widespread looting and arson. But up in the Bronx, District Attorney Mario Merola found there was "almost a state of anarchy." Looters ransacked commercial strips from 138th Street to Fordham Road, even stealing fifty new cars from a Jerome Avenue showroom. Policemen were bombarded with bricks and bottles, a rebellion at the Bronx House of Detention was put down, and one cop was shot. The next day, at Bronx central booking, the line of arrestees stretched into the street. The looting destroyed small businesses throughout the South Bronx, leaving residents without food stores, pharmacies, or small retail shops—all the services needed close to home.[49] Thirteen years later, in 1990, the twenty-block-long retail center on East Tremont Avenue still had not recovered from the blackout's damage.[50]

The social collapse of the South Bronx occurred before its physical destruction. Poverty and old buildings do not inevitably lead to crime, abandonment, and arson, for there had always been slums in the city. As long as the South Bronx contained viable neighborhoods for the poor, of whatever race or ethnicity, its dilapidated housing was in demand. By the mid-sixties, moreover, much of the oldest housing stock had been replaced by low-rent housing projects. The entire upper Morrisania–Claremont area was a solid mass of "towers in the park," while western Melrose, central and lower Mott Haven, lower Morrisania, and the streets near the Westchester Avenue subway trestle contained wide stretches of spanking new public housing (see map 7.2).[51]

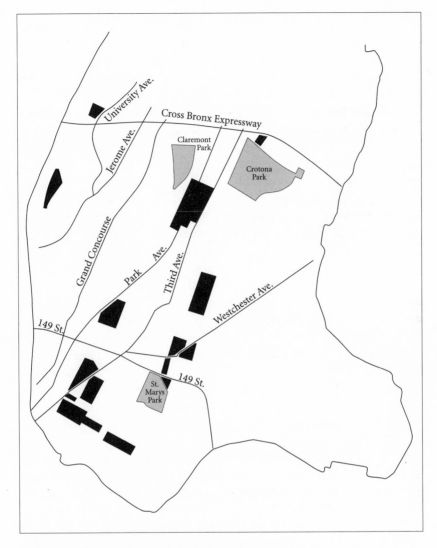

MAP 7.2 Public Housing in the South Bronx, 1969

These projects housed only the poor and no longer screened out unruly or "problem" families. In 1955, the mostly black and Hispanic tenants of the Forest Houses were petitioning for greater police protection even before all the buildings were occupied. The new residents needed to make friends and become neighbors, but the form and design of public housing worked against it. There were too many invisible public spaces where antisocial behavior could take place. Thus it was difficult to monitor young-sters and next to impossible to keep out unwanted strangers. And since everyone was new to the area, who knew who belonged or not? By the six-ties, the only distinction between the projects and the surrounding blocks was the newness of the buildings.[52]

The South Bronx, by then, had become a churning mass of population. An elevated expressway and eleven public housing projects were under con-struction during the first half of the 1960s. People were constantly moving in and out as block after block was demolished, cleared, and rebuilt. In some instances blocks were razed in anticipation of housing that was never built. Afraid their buildings would be next, residents in the adjoining blocks left as well, while landlords skimped on repairs even more.[53] The family, ethnic, and community ties that had earlier sustained the low-income ethnic and racial neighborhoods of the South Bronx could not flourish in such an en-vironment. This excessive transiency prevented the continuation of local networks or the formation of new ones and, as the Women's City Club ob-served, "even denied [residents] the comfort of neighbors." Without the so-cial constraints and community sanctions engendered by such networks, delinquency, alcoholism, drug abuse, and violent behavior increased. Once stability and safety were gone, the neighborhoods of Mott Haven, Melrose, Morrisania–Claremont, and Hunts Point–Crotona Park East disappeared and the blighted area of the South Bronx grew.[54]

Without neighborhoods, the older housing stock of the South Bronx disappeared. From the mid-1960s on, landlords and tenants abandoned, vandalized, and burned apartment buildings that a few years before had been filled to the brim. In the words of Nathan Glazer, "One saw an on-slaught on physical structures that has no parallel in the history of civilized urban life."[55] There was building abandonment in other boroughs, but there was proportionately more in the Bronx because it had more apart-ments, more crime, and a more rapid rate of ethnic and racial change. Be-tween 1970 and 1981, the Bronx lost more than 108,000 dwelling units or one fifth of its housing stock, amounting to one third of the estimated 321,000 dwelling units abandoned in the entire city.[56] As the 41st Police Precinct went from being "Fort Apache" to being "The Little House on the Prairie," surrounded by abandoned, burned-out, and demolished build-ings, abandonment spread to the west and north of the original South Bronx. The destruction of the city's housing stock tapered off during the mid-1980s, but by then, much of the oldest multifamily built environment of the South Bronx had been devastated.[57]

It was not a total blight. The public housing projects remained, and so did blocks of row houses in Mott Haven, Longwood, and around Clay Avenue. The Italian neighborhood of Belmont, flanked by Fordham University, the Bronx Zoo, and Third Avenue, also continued untouched, but its southern neighbors in West Farms and Tremont succumbed. Streets west of Third Avenue in lower Fordham also fared badly. The apartment buildings on the Grand Concourse were too good to abandon; they simply went from mostly white Jewish to mostly African American. The streets radiating away from the Concourse, however, were narrow, treeless, and so closely packed with large apartment buildings that there was extensive abandonment and arson, particularly in the blocks that flanked the elevated tracks of the Jerome Avenue Subway (the present number 4 train) north of Yankee Stadium.[58]

The time between de facto and de jure abandonment obscured the process. The lag between when the landlord stopped paying taxes, providing services, and collecting rents and when the city acquired, demolished, and finally wiped the structure from its books often varied from years to overnight. At each stage of the process, landlords, tenants, and squatters could and often did burn their buildings. The city, moreover, was incapable of stopping the process. The Women's City Club concluded that everything the city did—from fining landlords for building violations to taking a building for nonpayment of taxes—was mere record keeping. Peter Marcuse found the city's own inability "to police its own housing stock . . . create[d] the opportunity to milk a building" and often led to abandonment.[59] Other city policies encouraged arson. In 1969, the city installed a less reliable fire alarm system and shut down firehouses where they were most needed. The delayed fire response time meant that fires increased, so in the words of Deborah and Roderick Wallace, "what could burn did burn." The New York Urban Coalition ultimately concluded the problem was a loss of hope. "The owner loses hope in the building, the banks in the neighborhood, and the tenants in the landlord . . . [thus] the building has no future."[60]

Building abandonment resulted from an interaction between the housing market and the socioeconomic condition of the building, the block, and the locality. It usually occurred in unstable areas where younger, poorer black and Hispanic tenants were replacing older, more affluent white ethnic ones. This was exactly the case in the impoverished, crime-ridden urban environment of the South Bronx. Previously, Bronx apartment buildings had provided homes for families and profits for landlords. But now, despite the continuing citywide housing shortage, Bronx landlords were saddled with apartment buildings no one wanted. The problem was not rent control, but finding any tenant at all. The classic filtering model dictated that as people moved to better housing the least desirable units would disappear from the housing stock. This model did not explain what unwanted buildings would do to a neighborhood or to the tenants who remained. Former resident Clara Rodriguez remembered the "psychic despair" of the time. "One day there was a supermarket to shop at, the next day it [was] closed. Last week, you had friends or relatives up the street, today they too [were] leaving."[61]

One option owners and residents had was to profit from the destruction. Why take care of an older apartment building that seemed to be in the path of public housing or urban devastation? Some landlords used their derelict buildings as tax shelters or transferred their properties back and forth to increase valuation for sale to the city or to acquire second mortgage loans. Others cut down on maintenance, deferred paying taxes, rented to undesirable tenants or "problem families," aggressively collected whatever rents they could get, and "ran for the hills." If cities were places where economic transactions took place, then Bronx neighborhoods were sites for quick profits as well. "South Bronx landlords [were] like California prospectors a hundred years ago," explained Edward Martin of the Bronx Office of Rent Control. "They rushed in, took out the gold, and left a ghost town."[62]

Some, however, went a step further and burned the structures. When low-premium fire insurance became available in the 1970s, many investors bought Bronx apartment buildings with the express intent of burning them, while an "untold number of Bronx property owners bought policies that made their buildings worth more dead than alive."[63] Similarly, some tenants increased their welfare allotments by not paying the rent, others torched their apartments to get first crack at vacancies in public housing; and all the while gangs and addicts stripped vacant, occupied, and rehabilitated buildings alike for the fixtures and scrap metal. These practices accelerated the decay of individual buildings, the housing stock, and the neigborhood, but they also revealed, as the Right Rev. Paul Moore observed, that both owners and residents had "redlined the South Bronx as an area not worth saving."[64]

The collapse of the South Bronx propelled its residents into Jewish, Irish, and Italian neighborhoods already fearful of integration, crime, and neighborhood decline. It did not matter that blacks and Puerto Ricans were themselves fleeing from crime and devastation. As more minorities came in, white ethnic residents moved away. Every mugging, whether rumored or true, became an added incentive to leave. *The New York Times* ran feature articles on the "Once-Grand Concourse" and the "Grand Concourse . . . Undergoing Ethnic Changes," and thus reinforced the fear that the blight would spread. This fear became "a self-fulfilling prophecy" when the mostly Jewish Grand Concourse residents signed up en masse for Co-op City apartments in the mid-1960s.[65]

In 1971, the owner of a building near the New York University campus revealed that race mattered. "Look, let's face it . . . white middle class people just don't want to live in that kind of an area. Look, I certainly don't mind integration, but let's not kid ourselves." Three years later, New York University itself abandoned its Bronx campus. So, landlords rented to welfare families, cut back on service, and continued the South Bronx syndrome beyond the old neighborhood. By 1975, a banker claimed, "You can write off the entire area south of the Cross-Bronx Expressway." By 1978, the South Bronx deterioration reached up to Fordham Road and seemed as if it would continue to the city line.[66]

And this happened in spite of well-meaning policies to arrest poverty and blight. The welfare rights movement of the 1960s achieved benefits for the needy but also introduced families to generations of dependency, depleted city and state coffers, fueled middle-class resentment of welfare recipients and the welfare system, and allowed the blight to continue. Similarly, the city's attempt to harness Bronx gangs to stem neighborhood deterioration collapsed amid charges of fraud and corruption, while the Neighborhood Preservation Program in the West Bronx Concourse area provided information on rehabilitating buildings but did little to stop abandonment. The Municipal Loan Program, likewise, gave landlords another way of bailing out of the South Bronx.[67]

Federal programs had similar results. Antipoverty job training helped residents move away. Model Cities legislation eventually built more subsidized housing and thus further entrenched the poor in the South Bronx. Both of these measures were sporadic, unfocused, limited in scope, and riddled with rancorous infighting, as city agencies, the mayor's office, and the different racial and ethnic groups fought over what should be done and who should control the funding. Conflicts between blacks and Puerto Ricans and between different factions within each group weakened the programs, wasted time and money, allowed the unscrupulous to pocket funds, and in one instance resulted in the death of a Puerto Rican activist. Fraud and abuse by speculators and real estate interests also characterized federal programs for low-income housing rehabilitation during the early 1970s.[68]

Fighting over federal programs continued during the late 1970s after President Jimmy Carter's 1977 surprise visit to Charlotte Street in Crotona Park East resulted in a plan for improving the South Bronx. This time, the other boroughs demanded that the largesse be spent on them because, as Queens Borough President Donald R. Manes said, the South Bronx had already "gone down the drain." The newly elected mayor, Ed Koch, and his appointed head of the South Bronx plan, Herman Badillo, quickly were at odds over how much of the South Bronx should be helped and how it should be done. The South Bronx, meanwhile, continued to decay.[69]

Everyone knew what was happening. From the late sixties on, community activists repeatedly called attention to the borough's plight, often inducing visiting dignitaries, local officials, and candidates to tour the South Bronx. One of the area's most vocal advocates was Father Louis Gigante of St. Athanasius Church in Hunts Point. Father Gigante scolded the City Council, conducted council members around the borough, and eventually served as a City Council member during the 1970s. In 1974, another local activist, Genevieve Brooks, invited then Congressman Herman Badillo and other bigwigs to show them how the Bronx was burning. As she escorted the group, Mrs. Brooks was stunned by their indifference. "Everyone thought that because this was a predominantly minority area it was just junkies and welfare folks. No one in authority was trying to combat arson." Some local officials even denied it was happening. "Fires? What fires?" asked Bronx District Attorney Mario Merola when confronted by a group of Catholic priests. Others, from borough presidents to community leaders and elected representatives, thought nothing could be done and thus did nothing. Accordingly, the South Bronx burned and the devastation spread.[70]

Clearly, no one represented the South Bronx. As a political entity, it had been gerrymandered out of existence and parceled out to adjacent districts.[71] As the city's fiscal crisis worsened in the mid-1970s, officials decided what services to provide knowing that the South Bronx did not matter, eliminating police officers, firehouses, and transit lines alike. One official even proposed shutting down city services until the next round of investment and growth, while another suggested bulldozing the whole area for industrial use.[72] Congressman Badillo denounced this as a "callous disregard of human lives," but Father Luce of St. Ann's Episcopal Church in Mott Haven realized "the policy of shrinkage is the whole motif of the South Bronx."[73]

The borough presidents themselves were totally ineffective in halting the decline. As a Puerto Rican, Borough President Herman Badillo was uniquely placed to aid the South Bronx. Yet Badillo did not seek help from banking and real estate circles because he felt they considered him "the enemy" and thus part of the problem. Instead, he sought another post. After one term as borough president, he was elected to represent one of the newly carved-out congressional districts, where he tried to bring federal programs to the South Bronx and ran repeatedly for mayor. The subsequent borough president, Robert Abrams, fretted more about the Bronx's image than about the actual decay. Abrams ignored the South Bronx, emphasized the good areas of the borough, and eventually became State Attorney General.[74] The next borough president, Stanley Simon, used his office to feather his nest and wound up having to resign. It was politics as usual while the South Bronx collapsed; after all, it was just "junkies and welfare folks."[75]

It was also business as usual, which meant no investment in areas or endeavors that would not yield a commensurate profit. In the urban context this meant some neighborhoods would decay unless something or someone intervened to check the process. But not everyone could invest in the optimum areas, so they profited from existing conditions. In the South Bronx these were a decaying urban infrastructure that was not in demand except by a poor, marginalized minority population. Thus landlords collected rents without paying for services or property taxes, burned buildings for the insurance, and reneged on rehabilitation loans; politicians used political office to secure lucrative contracts and higher posts and ran antipoverty agencies and clinics for personal gain; and residents and gangs looted stores during a blackout or sold drugs on the street.[76]

After the sixties, that former symbol of Bronx greatness, the Concourse Plaza Hotel, went from hosting the Yankees and visiting dignitaries to housing drug addicts and welfare families. The whole nation saw the Bronx burning during TV coverage of the 1977 World Series at Yankee Stadium. As the cameras panned the surrounding streets, Howard Cosell's play-by-play was laced with comments about the fiery Bronx sky. Presidential visits deepened its notoriety. President Jimmy Carter saw Charlotte Street in 1977 and pledged federal aid to rebuild its vacant blocks. Presidential candidate Ronald Reagan stood on still-empty Charlotte Street in 1980 and blamed federal policies for its decline. A year later, the motion picture, *Fort Apache, The Bronx*, forever entrenched its disrepute. "We know of the Bronx from the movies—the police movies," admitted French architect François Bregnac when he visited in 1990. Tourists and movie crews came to gape at and film the ruins, the rubble, and the graffiti, while English tabloids dubbed a drug-torn neighborhood in Manchester, England, "the Bronx."[77] The negative image was so total that when David Rockefeller proposed building affordable housing in the South Bronx, he was greeted with incredulity: "You want to build *where*? You want to build *what*?"[78]

8 THE ROAD BACK

Just when it seemed that the South Bronx would overrun the entire borough, community groups began working to stem the devastation. A coalition of residents, neighborhood organizations, and clergymen came together in response to the increasing severity of conditions. Suddenly realizing what was going on, the newly politicized residents began to say, "Wait a minute, wait a minute, I live here." Up through the sixties and seventies, most just moved away as the area deteriorated, but the continuing decay and the high cost of housing in the rest of the city made that more difficult. "There is no place left to move to," recalled Margaret Terry, a South Bronx resident, "so we have to do it ourselves and make this place work." As Charles Orlebeke has written, borough residents "permanently changed the chemistry of urban politics" by creating grassroots community networks and coalitions and innovative strategies that revitalized Bronx neighborhoods.[1]

They didn't do it alone. As abandonment spread, city officials and downtown interests began to fear for the entire city. They were motivated to find new ways to deal with decay in a time of declining federal support. Abandonment itself, meanwhile, created the conditions that allowed for the turnaround. The abundance of city-owned vacant land and abandoned buildings, along with a multitude of public and private initiatives that had been devised, enacted, or ineffective during the height of the destruction, now made it possible to rebuild whole areas. In addition, a spurt of new black and Spanish-speaking immigrants revived the housing market in the areas where similar groups lived, in this case, the South Bronx. Thus, from the mid-1980s on, public-private housing partnerships, City Hall, the Bronx Borough President, and community groups joined together to improve conditions and build affordable housing. As the neighborhoods stabilized, city initiatives that had failed before because of the extent of the devastation began to work. These efforts rebuilt the South Bronx and saved the borough.[2]

The first priority was to hold devastation at bay and "preserve the North-west Bronx [as] . . . a decent place to live and raise a family." With this in mind, the Northwest Bronx Community and Clergy Coalition (NWBC-CC) began in 1974 as a group of tenant and block associations and sixteen Catholic parishes north of the Cross-Bronx Expressway. "Our problem here is survival," one priest remarked. "If those neighborhoods go up, our parishes go." The group's "spark plug" was Bronx grandmother Anne Devenney. Saying, "Don't move, improve," Devenney energized tenants, parishioners, and community workers to overcome the apathy of the city bureaucracy and the real estate and financial establishment. The NBCCC picketed the offices and homes of city officials, bank directors, and insurance executives, often forcing them to comply with housing codes, fair lending laws, and "good repair" clauses. As they worked, members learned how to use every new law and initiative to ward off and turn back urban blight.[3]

Black landlords also had "a financial stake in the continued existence of the South Bronx." The Reverend George Hoke had owned his Kelly Street apartment building since 1945, while Frank and Nancy Potts bought their four Kelly Street buildings on a shoestring at tax-delinquent sales during the worst of the devastation. Black owners protected their property by keeping their apartments fully rented. Reverend Hoke had a full house of long-time tenants, but the Pottses had to rent to welfare families who "don't give a hoot and holler about anything," as Nancy Potts scornfully observed. "They're the people that's ruining everything." Her husband disagreed, claiming "they are trying to run all the blacks out" so the big developers could come in. Frank Potts believed that if he could hang on, the neighborhood would be rebuilt with "a better class of tenants." Black landlords stood guard over their Kelly Street buildings during the 1977 blackout. The Pottses' son, Leon, became a founding member of the Banana Kelly Community Improvement Association, one of the first groups to begin rebuilding in the South Bronx.[4]

Although much had been leveled, here and there South Bronx residents organized to protect and rehabilitate their buildings and build new housing. Some groups did it on their own, fixing abandoned structures and leveraging this "sweat equity" into further funding. The first to do so was the People's Development Corporation (PDC), formed in 1974 by Ramon Rueda. The PDC took over a vacant city-owned apartment house in the Morrisania section of the South Bronx, secured rehab loans, and restored it completely with oak floors and solar panels. On hand when President

Carter visited Charlotte Street in 1977, Rueda became an instant celebrity. His organization, meanwhile, had shifted its focus from fixing one building to creating "a village of ten thousand people . . . for maybe forty blocks."[5] It was too much too soon—projects failed, monies disappeared, and their buildings were repossessed. By 1982, the PDC was struggling to exist with a reorganized board of directors. The People's Development Corporation, which for a time was a symbol of the resurgence of the South Bronx, became in a few years just another symbol of its decay.[6]

Another sweat-equity group, the Banana Kelly Community Improvement Association, began at the height of the PDC's success. Also adopting the "Don't move, improve" slogan, Banana Kelly organized in 1977 to prevent the demolition of three Kelly Street buildings. "We were looking to block deterioration of our neighborhood," said member Mildred Velez, "transforming them from houses where they had to live to homes where they want to live." Led by Harry De Rienzo and Leon Potts, the association learned from the PDC's mistakes and by 1981 had transformed the three gutted buildings into twenty-one new co-op apartment units. Banana Kelly went on to manage rehabilitated city-owned buildings from the mid-eighties to the present.[7]

Some community initiatives relied on local and federal policies. The Southeast Bronx Community Organization (SEBCO) began in 1968 as part of the South Bronx Model Cities effort. Led by Hunts Point activist Father Louis Gigante, SEBCO began years before the NWBCCC, the PDC, and Banana Kelly, but still "lost the battle of the 1960's and early 1970's."[8] The group was unable to do much until it "engaged in the American way of doing things," explained Father Gigante. After 1975, SEBCO was "allowed to sell tax shelters" to finance rehabilitation for low-rent housing and to share in the Section 8 federal program for low-income rent subsidies. SEBCO opened its first building in September 1976 and by the mid-1980s had 2,100 new and rehabbed units in Hunts Point; it was well on the way to the 3,500 apartments it would manage in 2001.[9]

The Mid-Bronx Desperados (the later MBD Community Housing Corporation) took its cue from SEBCO. Father William Smith and Genevieve S. Brooks created the MBD in 1974 to rebuild the Charlotte Street area of Crotona Park East. However, the extreme devastation, the city's fiscal crunch, and its own inexperience kept the MBD from building housing until the early 1980s, when it too could sell tax shelters and get Section 8 rent subsidies. Improving the South Bronx took more than money. "This only works," explained Brooks, "because I interview each and every family who moves in." By 1983, the corporation was helping tenants buy and restore the last apartment house left on the Charlotte Street block and screening prospective buyers of the suburban houses that would fill the rest of that area. By 2001, the MBD was managing 38 buildings with 1,170 units throughout the South Bronx.[10]

The Longwood Community Association used historic district designation to preserve their neighborhood. The late nineteenth-century brownstones on Dawson, Beck, and Kelly streets had always been a cut above their surroundings and had had a sprinkling of black middle-class homeowners since the 1940s. Thirty years later, with 90 percent of the homes still owner-occupied and most owners elderly on fixed incomes, the area was totally black and Hispanic and threatened by the adjoining blight. Inspired by the success of nearby Banana Kelly, long-time black homeowners Thomas Bess and Marilyn Smith organized the Longwood Community Association and applied for historic status. The area became the Longwood Historic District in 1980 and expanded with the Longwood Historic District Extension in 1983. The designation allowed them to get government funds for exterior improvements and to rescue the derelict city-owned brownstones within their neighborhood. These homes were needed, Tom Bess believed, "to attract young, stable moderate-to-middle income families" to Longwood. Landmarking began in the Bronx right after the 1965 landmarks law, with the Alexander Avenue area of Mott Haven the first historic district in 1969, but after the Longwood designation, civic and community groups sought landmark status to counter the Bronx's pervasive negative image and instill pride in their borough.[11]

These fledgling efforts to restore the South Bronx emerged from the grassroots activism of the 1960s. The War on Poverty dispensed funds for social services, economic development, educational programs, and job training through a network of locally organized community action agencies. Those involved gained valuable administrative and leadership skills, like Evelina Lopez Antonetty, who founded United Bronx Parents in 1965, and Ramon Velez, who began the Hunts Point Multi-Service Center in 1967 and later transformed it into his personal antipoverty empire. As the devastation continued, Genevieve Brooks noted that "We needed everything, especially decent housing." Thus, community action groups reemerged as nonprofit community development corporations (CDCs), primarily working for new and rehabilitated housing. Although they began during the nadir of the South Bronx, the Northwest Bronx Community and Clergy Coalition, the PDC, Banana Kelly, the Longwood Community Association, SEBCO, and the Mid-Bronx Desperados were in the vanguard of the borough's resurgence.[12]

These community groups fitted well with local initiatives and decentralization of city services. In 1973, the nonprofit Urban Homesteading Assistance Board (UHAB) began training sweat-equity groups like the PDC and Banana Kelly in seeking grants and managing buildings; it has continued to do so under city contract until the present. Similarly, in 1975, New York State began funding the operating costs of all local housing CDCs through its Neighborhood Preservation Companies Program. This policy was later reinforced by the federal 1988 McKinney Homeless Amendments and the 1990 Home Program.[13] The community focus was also seen in the local school districts and community planning boards that emerged during the 1960s and 1970s. Both defused conflict by creating forums for community concerns. Community planning boards evolved into the community district boards that became part of the city's land use decision-making process in 1977. Meanwhile, however, the South Bronx school districts have featured prominently in corruption scandals and in Jonathan Kozol's exposés of underfunded and poorly performing schools.[14]

Housing policy changes affected rebuilding efforts. Indeed, from the 1960s on, a new array of federal rent supplements, mortgage guarantees, interest subsidies, and tax shelters had made it profitable for private developers to build low-rent housing, even as urban renewal and public housing construction continued. In the Bronx, these led to a peak of 11,923 housing units completed in 1972. The many programs, combined with antipoverty and Model Cities funding and municipal loans, allowed for mismanagement and rip-offs at all levels and resulted in a host of scandals during the early 1970s. The upshot was a presidential freeze on all housing funds in 1973 and housing acts in 1974 and 1977 that emphasized community development and neighborhood preservation, but provided less federal spending to achieve it. The new laws replaced urban renewal and Model Cities with community block grants, transformed rent supplements into Section 8 rent subsidies, reduced the low-interest mortgage programs, provided some grants for larger economic redevelopment schemes in distressed cities after 1977, and, most important, required private funds to make up for federal cuts.[15] Although the federal urban programs were gone, Father Gigante continued planning for when "Federal money again becomes available." The mayor's office also believed that "nothing short of a major, federally-directed and coordinated urban strategy [could] . . . restore areas like the South Bronx."[16]

Other initiatives ultimately benefited Bronx CDCs. Nationally organized community interests persuaded Congress to pass the Home Mortgage Disclosure Act of 1975 (HMDA) and the Community Reinvestment Act of 1977 (CRA). HMDA directed banks to reveal their mortgage lending practices and the CRA required them to make loans in their neighborhoods. From the late 1970s to the present, the Northwest Bronx Community and Clergy

Coalition used these laws to pressure Bronx banks for loans.[17] Similarly, nonprofit intermediaries provided money and expertise to local groups. These intermediaries arose because of the increasing complexity of the housing and community block grants programs and the need to match public funds with private money. The first national one, the Local Initiatives Support Corporation (LISC), began in 1979 with help from the Ford Foundation. LISC first tested its strategy in the South Bronx and by 1982 had financed sixteen organizations, including Banana Kelly and the Longwood Community Association, "to deliver in their own neighborhoods." LISC's Anita Miller believed that in time these "micro efforts . . . [would] have a macro impact." Two others began in that same year—the Enterprise Foundation helped CDCs in the city and nationwide, and the New York City Housing Partnership worked locally. From the eighties on, these intermediaries fostered the "public-private partnerships" that community interests would use to restore their areas.[18]

President Carter's visit to Charlotte Street eventually led to a major improvement in the South Bronx. What remained of the grandiose plans that had ensued in the wake of that visit was Edward J. Logue's South Bronx Development Organization (SBDO). Logue relied on free abandoned, city-owned land to bring jobs and housing to the borough. He created Bathgate Industrial Park as an eight-block area of industrial sites on Third Avenue, but his most important project was Charlotte Gardens, a group of 89 suburban-style ranch houses built on the desolate blocks where Carter and Reagan had stood. Low-cost federal and state mortgage subsidies reduced the average price to $52,000 and prescreening of prospective buyers by Genevieve Brooks ensured the venture's success. The first ranch homes of Charlotte Gardens opened in 1983, complete with white picket fences, and quickly became the focal point of the borough's resurgence, proving, as Logue believed, that "home ownership is key to a neighborhood's survival." In 1997, President Bill Clinton visited Charlotte Gardens and found tree-lined suburban streets and homes that were worth almost $200,000, quite a change from what President Carter had seen 20 years earlier.[19]

These improvements were still few and far between in the mid-1980s. Abandoned buildings were everywhere, but money to fix them or build new was not, for President Ronald Reagan had drastically curtailed federal housing funds and the Section 8 rent subsidy program. Although Congress tried to lessen the impact with Low Income Housing Tax Credits (LIHTC) in 1986, the steep cuts represented a $16 billion loss to the city between 1981 and 1987. Instead of housing money, the city received grants for vinyl window decals to cover the gaping holes in buildings facing the Cross-Bronx

Expressway. "This is a terrible thing," said Robert Jacobson, director of the Bronx office of the City Planning Commission. "Decals aren't going to solve people's problems . . . [or] give them jobs." While the city had rebounded from its fiscal crisis and abandonment had tapered off, drug addiction had continued, the housing shortage had worsened, and a new problem of homelessness had arisen.[20] In the midst of it all, a citywide scandal revealed the illegal schemes of Bronx politicians, from party leaders to borough presidents and congressmen. Now more than ever, civic and community interests had to find alternative means to renew the South Bronx.[21]

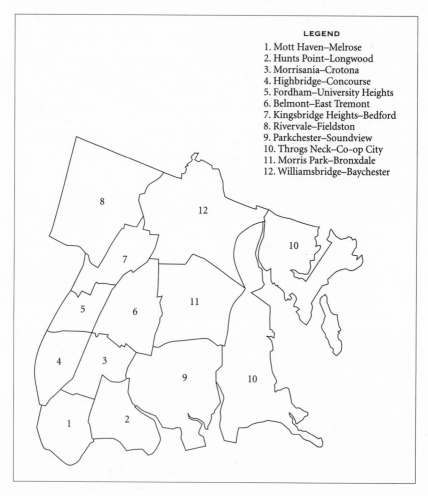

LEGEND

1. Mott Haven–Melrose
2. Hunts Point–Longwood
3. Morrisania–Crotona
4. Highbridge–Concourse
5. Fordham–University Heights
6. Belmont–East Tremont
7. Kingsbridge Heights–Bedford
8. Rivervale–Fieldston
9. Parkchester–Soundview
10. Throgs Neck–Co-op City
11. Morris Park–Bronxdale
12. Williamsbridge–Baychester

MAP 8.1 Bronx Community Districts, 2000

TABLE 8.1 Population of South Bronx Community Districts, 1970–2000[a]

CD	1970	1980	1990[b]	2000
1	138,600	78,441 [-43.4%]	77,214 [-1.6%]	82,159 [+6.4%]
2	93,900	34,397 [-63.4%]	39,443 [+14.7%]	46,824 [+18.7%]
3	150,600	53,638 [-64.4%]	57,162 [+6.6%]	68,574 [+20.0%]
4	144,200	114,309 [-20.7%]	119,962 [+4.9%]	139,563 [+16.3%]
5	123,000	107,997 [-12.2%]	118,435 [+9.7%]	128,313 [+8.3%]
6	114,100	65,014 [-43.0%]	68,061 [+4.7%]	75,688 [+11.2%]

[a] Includes percentage change from previous decade.

[b] The 2000 Census has different 1990 population figures for Community Districts 3 and 4 than those published in Department of City Planning, *Community District Needs, The Bronx, Fiscal Year 2000*.

Source: Department of City Planning, *Community District Needs, The Bronx, Fiscal Year 2000* (City of New York, 2000); New York City Department of City Planning, *2000 Census Community Districts*, Table PL P–103, "New York City Community Districts, 1990 and 2000," http://www.nyc.gov/html/dcp/html/popstart.html.

REBUILDING THE BOROUGH

And renew it they did, for by the late 1980s the borough once again had the ingredients necessary to rebuild its southern neighborhoods—land, people, and political support. The large inventory of empty blocks and abandoned vacant buildings provided "the raw clay" for new construction and rehabilitation. Meanwhile, a new wave of immigration into New York City increased the demand for affordable housing. Five of the six community districts in the expanded South Bronx grew in population between 1980 and 1990 (see table 8.1 and map 8.1). The Hunts Point–Longwood section, Community District 2, had "the largest margin of growth of any community in the Bronx," increasing 14.7 percent after losing over 63 percent or almost 60,000 residents in the previous decade. Similarly, the Morrisania–Crotona Park East area, Community District 3, increased its population by 6.6 percent after declining almost 65 percent or 97,000 residents during the previous decade. The combination of concerned long-time residents and new Spanish-speaking and black migrants brought back property values and a stronger mortgage and housing market. Finally, the Bronx had a supportive political climate again. It had a growing crop of experienced community organizations eager to take advantage of the improved mortgage market, new borough politicians untainted by scandal, and city and state leaders willing to work with civic interests and local entities to improve conditions.[22]

The critical year was 1987 and the catalyst was Mayor Ed Koch's $5.1 billion capital housing program. In April 1986, Mayor Koch announced the city would rehabilitate its entire stock of city-owned buildings, both abandoned and occupied, and build new housing on its vacant city-owned land. Funded largely from city capital monies with some help from New York State, this plan would produce and preserve more than 250,000 units of affordable housing for low- to moderate-income people and the homeless throughout the city. Government help was needed because private developers only built for the affluent. Since "Federal support of housing is now just a memory," Koch said, "we have been forced to find ways to offset those losses." To accomplish this, he proposed a multifaceted approach that combined old and new mechanisms to deal with differing locales and housing conditions but relied for its implementation on private and nonprofit developers, local and national intermediaries, the new Bronx Borough President, Fernando Ferrer, and those ubiquitous community groups. By early 1989, the plan had produced 15,600 apartments in the South Bronx, nearly 80 percent of the 19,800 vacant units the borough had had when the program began in 1986. "We're moving like gangbusters," crowed Housing and Preservation Commissioner Abraham Biderman. "After two decades of decline in the Bronx, we're seeing rebirth of entire neighborhoods."[23]

This rebirth occurred because by the 1980s all the players had finally learned how to deal with abandonment. For example, a West Tremont group based in St. Edmund's Episcopal Church went through "a difficult, frustrating process" to renovate four vacant buildings for low-income housing. Their first efforts failed because of Reagan cuts and the corruption scandals that engulfed Borough Hall and City Hall alike. Beginning anew in 1986 with help from the Northwest Bronx Community and Clergy Coalition and LISC, they organized a community development corporation (the Mount Hope Housing Company), obtained financing from Low Income Housing Tax Credits and the Community Preservation Corporation (a consortium of city banks), and opened 110 apartments to low-income tenants in 1989. In the process, the Mount Hope Housing Company went from seeking federal handouts to strengthening itself and finding alternative means to achieve its goals.[24]

The New York City Housing Partnership (NYCHP) went through a similar process. Concerned about the worsening blight, David Rockefeller created the NYCHP to build affordable housing in the city's devastated areas. As the partnership developed from 1982 on, recalled its president Kathy Wylde, "home ownership turned out to be the *best* way to do what David Rockefeller wanted to do." That way was worked out over a five-year period, during which the NYCHP learned how to acquire city property; obtain financing from public and private coffers; select community sponsors and developers; build a few projects of owner-occupied homes, two of them in the Bronx; and lower the purchase price with subsidies, grants, and rebates. By 1987, after many delays, the housing partnership had regularized its relations with city agencies, institutionalized its New Homes Program, and increased its pace of production. By the early 1990s, NYCHP homes were being built throughout the city and were completely filling in the empty acres of Crotona Park East and Hunts Point.[25]

The city, too, had learned from past mistakes. It used tried-and-true private and nonprofit developers, intermediaries, and community groups to produce, own, and manage the housing built under the mayor's program. Two of the nonprofits in the Bronx—Phipps Houses and the Settlement Housing Fund—had long track records in the city and the borough and by the nineties were producing apartments in Highbridge, Morris Heights, East Tremont, and West Farms.[26] The intermediaries, LISC and Enterprise, were also part of the housing program. The city provided the vacant building and a direct loan. LISC and Enterprise then augmented the city money by selling Low Income Housing Tax Credits to private corporations, and selected and trained a CDC to manage and eventually own the renovated structure. These intermediaries became so adept at converting tax credits into financing that they created a new nonprofit, the New York Equity Fund, to do just that. By 2000, community groups that wanted to renovate or build could only convert their tax credits through the equity fund because "never has one of its projects failed."[27]

The city's housing program contained a home ownership component as well. Years earlier, Father Gigante realized that "we have to bring an economic class in that can sustain the neighborhood," otherwise "what would happen is the same thing that happened in the 1960s." Also believing that owner occupancy was the "cornerstone" of rebuilding neighborhoods, Mayor Koch utilized the New York City Housing Partnership to construct affordable homes to give moderate-income residents "a chance of owning a piece of the Big Apple" and hence a stake in their neighborhoods. In the 14 years from 1987 to 2000, the housing partnership produced 5,300 dwelling units in the Bronx, mostly in two- and three-family attached townhouses, with an assortment of co-ops and condominiums. The NYCHP worked with community groups and contractors to market the homes and guide the applicants through the mortgage process. In 1990, a $50,000 subsidy lowered the price so a family earning between $32,000 and $53,000 could buy a two-family attached home in West Farms. Ten years later, the subsidy had risen to $97,000 and the family income to between $43,000 and $70,000 for a similar home in Hunts Point. Along with new apartments and the rehabilitated city-owned housing stock, these owner-occupied homes completely transformed the South Bronx.[28]

South Bronx Churches (SBC) claimed it could build owner-occupied row houses more cheaply. Organized in 1985 by Reverend John Heinemeier of St. John's Lutheran in Morrisania, SBC was a group of 40 assorted congregations ,many of which were African American, that wanted I. D. Robbins to build hundreds of his Nehemiah Homes in the South Bronx. Robbins, a long-time builder and housing advocate, had successfully produced low-cost, one-family homes in Heinemeier's former Brooklyn parish by using church funds and high-volume, mass-production techniques on city-owned land. In 1989, South Bronx Churches decided to build on Site 404, a vacant three-block Melrose parcel already slated for housing partnership condominiums. Since that site was part of the higher-density Melrose Commons Project, the city offered SBC several alternative plots. Charging that the city's housing plan was "a give-away program to developers," the church group insisted on the larger, ready-to-build Site 404 because "we are building community . . . not just building housing," thus creating a new environment for lower-income city employees rather than for the higher-income families who were the housing partnership's customers.[29]

The conflict continued until Mayor David Dinkins negotiated a settlement in 1991. But it revealed how things had changed. Community groups were now highly professional and worked within the system. Nehemiah Homes were cheaper, but the confrontational tactics used by South Bronx Churches put off many—Mayor Koch, his housing team, and the housing partnership—and set back its housing goals for years. In the end, South Bronx Churches built on the land first offered to them north of St. Mary's Park and compromised on its Nehemiah Plan to include higher-density three-family condominiums. South Bronx Churches finally completed the last of its 512 homes in 1996. By then the original price of $50,000 had risen to $73,000, but it was still affordable for owner Felix Santiago, a $20,000-a-year custodian. "I don't have to live on Park Avenue to see the Empire State Building," Santiago said, "I can see it from my house." In 1997, SBC broke ground for a new Nehemiah Project south of St. Mary's Park. With prices for one- and two-family homes at $75,000 and $130,000 and qualifying minimum incomes at $21,000 and $26,000, many at the groundbreaking took applications to buy the houses.[30]

As the city asserted that Site 404 was central to Melrose Commons, Melrose residents began questioning the plan itself. The Melrose project was part of an even larger Bronx Center Plan to revive the area from Yankee Stadium to Third Avenue with a new police academy, a courthouse and detention center, and the 2,600 housing units of Melrose Commons. Although much of Melrose was vacant, including Site 404, the plan would still destroy hundreds of homes and businesses. When it was presented in

1992, Melrose residents objected and organized themselves into a community group called Nos Quedamos, Spanish for "we stay." They were helped by Borough President Ferrer, who had finally realized that planning must come from a "community-based process." By 1994, after hundreds of community meetings, the new plan set guidelines for density, building heights, and income levels, and placed new construction among the existing buildings. This allowed 90 percent of the residents to stay in their homes because, as Nos Quedamos director Yolanda Garcia declared, "you can't throw people away." The first phase, a group of 35 three-family housing partnership homes priced for families earning from $32,000 to $71,000 and called Plaza de los Angeles, was sold out a year before its completion in late 2000.[31]

The dispute over Site 404 had many levels. To South Bronx Churches, it was about housing for those who had "jobs that will never pay that much money." To Nos Quedamos, it was about Melrose residents staying in their neighborhood. To the city, it was about population density or, as city housing official Sam Kramer explained in 1990, "a political problem," because "we have churches that need a congregation . . . [and] politicians . . . who need jobs."[32] But to Billy Procida, the contractor who built the condos on Site 404 and the Plaza de los Angeles for Melrose Commons, "It's not about saving the world. . . . It was about the city making money, the banks making money, and the developers, the retailers, and the minority contractors making money." Of course there was a commitment to house the poor, the homeless, and the elderly, especially by Mayor Koch, Mayor Dinkins, and all the nonprofit community groups. But "this is not just another free lunch," declared Borough President Ferrer. "We're convincing people that there's a market here, a work force here, and that they can make money."[33]

Bit by bit, the South Bronx was rebuilt with a mix of housing types, densities, and people. The West Farms neighborhood south of Bronx Park was a case in point. The area deteriorated steadily during the seventies and eighties, almost overwhelming Lambert Houses, the 1970s housing development built by Phipps Houses. Lambert "residents were less educated, less stable, and less able to fend for themselves in society," recalled Lynda Simmons, then head of Phipps Houses. By the mid-eighties, one third of West Farms was city-owned and vacant and "outdoor public life was virtually destroyed." The turnaround began in the late 1980s, when Phipps Houses built apartments for lower-income families and homeless mothers with children under the city's housing program and also developed 33 two-family homes for moderate-income families with the housing partnership. Other developers soon joined Phipps and the NYCHP in rebuilding. By the time the faith-based Aquinas Housing Corporation built an art deco–style building for the elderly in 1999, there were only a few undeveloped parcels left, and area developers openly joked about the "Manhattanization" of West Farms.[34]

And so it went throughout the borough. The city program, Nehemiah Homes, the housing partnership, all the church and community nonprofits, and even private developers had built over the rubble and fixed the derelict structures from Highbridge to Hunts Point and across the Bronx River. Construction was everywhere. It completely remade Crotona Park East into a neighborhood of small homeowners, and inserted new and rehabbed apartments and owner-occupied homes wherever there was space and community support. There were even new owner-occupied homes in Belmont, the Italian area that had remained stable because its merchants and residents had not left.[35] As the areas stabilized, the city's ongoing tenant ownership efforts had a greater chance of success, making it easier for Bronx tenants to restore, manage, and own their troubled buildings, and hence contributed even more to residential stability. These were not the new neighborhoods of the past. But "compared to what it was in the 1970's and 1980's," said Teresa Melendez in her new Hunts Point apartment, "it's come a long way."[36]

Revitalizing the Bronx also meant alleviating the social ills that had contributed to the devastation in the first place. South Bronx Churches wanted to do this by sweeping away the old and building anew—something akin to the urban renewal model of the past. The housing partnership would do this by filling in the vacant spots with an aspiring class of homeowners. Other groups had always gone beyond mere housing. Phipps Houses was "extremely careful" about who it accepted as tenants or owners, but it also provided a wide range of social services, what Ronay Menschel of Phipps called "our human-services strategy." Noting that "it takes more than bricks and mortar," a 1997 assessment concluded that Phipps Houses worked "to foster a sense of community and family well-being" to help their housing developments survive. In a similar vein, groups like Banana Kelly, MBD Housing, Bronx ACORN (Association of Community Organizations for Reform Now), Highbridge Community Life Center, Mount Hope Housing, the Mid-Bronx Senior Citizens Council, Promesa Inc. (a social service provider spun off from Banana Kelly), and SOBRO (South Bronx Overall Economic Development Corporation)—to name a few—provided job training, drug rehab, day-care centers, health clinics, and classes in English, life skills, citizenship, and whatever else was needed. Along with the new housing, these efforts helped stabilize the borough's neighborhoods.[37]

Because of such activities, the Bronx won the All-America City Award in 1997. Each year the National Civic League recognized 10 cities for grass-roots innovations in solving urban problems. Prepared by the borough president's office, the winning Bronx entry described the borough's over-all improvement as "a journey from a community of hopelessness to a community of possibilities being built on a base of local citizen action."[38] The entry used three grassroots initiatives as examples: the Undercliff–Sedgwick Neighborhood Safety Service Council, which cleaned up litter, graffiti, and vandalism in the Morris Heights–West Bronx area; the Wo-men's Housing and Economic Development Corporation (WEDCO), which renovated the run-down and vacant Morrisania Hospital into a low-income housing and social service facility called Urban Horizons; and the Mid-Bronx Senior Citizens Council, which restored the Andrew Freedman Home, a once-grand mansion for "persons of quality" who had lost their fortunes, into a multiservice Grand Concourse residence for the elderly poor. "We've worked long and hard to bring the Bronx back," said a proud Borough President Ferrer, "and this recognition demonstrates that our hard work is paying off."[39]

Private foundations also recognized the borough's grassroots endeavors and local participation. Throughout the 1990s, Bronx community groups received grants and program assistance from a bewildering array of foun-dations and community-building ventures that sought "to strengthen all sectors of neighborhood well-being." In 1992, for example, the Surdna Foundation's seven-year "Comprehensive Community Revitalization Pro-gram" awarded grants to six well-known Bronx CDCs—Banana Kelly, MBD Housing, the Mid-Bronx Senior Citizens Council, Mount Hope Housing, Phipps CDC, and Promesa. Likewise, in 1996, the Edna Mc-Connell Clark Foundation's "Neighborhood Partners Initiative" support-ed the Mid-Bronx Senior Citizens Council, Bronx ACORN, and the High-bridge Community Life Center. Another six-year community-building effort, the Neighborhood Strategies Project of the New York Community Trust, sponsored the Mott Haven Collaborative, which coordinated and helped sixty community entities to create jobs, improve businesses, and strengthen citizen involvement. The Bronx was indeed unique. "The peo-ple really care . . . about the children and the community," said Eddie Calderon-Melendez, Phipps education coordinator. "The volunteerism and the energy of the people here is incredible."[40]

It was not all sweetness and light. Crime dropped throughout the 1990s, but there were bouts of criminal behavior, police shootings, and black-white youth conflict.[41] In 1990, a patron set fire to the Happy Land Social Club in West Farms, killing 87 people. Nine years later, four plainclothes

TABLE 8.2 Population by Race and Hispanic Origin in the Bronx, 1990–2000[a]

	1990	2000
Bronx	1,203,789 [100%]	1,332,650 [100%]
White Nonhispanic	272,503 [22.6%]	193,651 [14.5%]
Black/African American		
Nonhispanic	369,113 [30.7%]	416,338 [31.2%]
Hispanic Origin	523,111 [43.5%]	644,705 [48.4%]

[a] Includes percent of total Bronx population.

Source: New York City Department of City Planning, *Citywide and Borough Population, 1990 & 2000*, 1–2, http://www.nyc.gov/html/dcp/html/popstart.html.

police officers mistakenly killed a West African immigrant, Amadou Diallo, in the doorway of his home in the Soundview neighborhood.[42] In both instances, community interests and local governments stepped in to help the victims and improve relations between residents and the police. In the 1990s, black, Puerto Rican, and Albanian youths clashed over turf in their Pelham Parkway neighborhood.[43] Scandals over fraudulent mortgage loans and management of subsidized housing also surfaced regularly. An especially vexing problem was the Jose de Diego Beekman Houses, one of the earliest private housing developments to receive tax shelters and rent subsidies from the federal Department of Housing and Urban Development (HUD). Beekman's tenants fought for decades to get repairs and eliminate drug gangs, and in the late 1990s tried to wrest ownership of the repossessed buildings away from HUD. Similarly, in March 2001, after many tenant complaints, Father Gigante's SEBCO took over management of Banana Kelly's stock of rehabilitated housing, saying, "I'm not going to see this neighborhood fail." Reporter Amy Waldman noted that this ended "Banana Kelly's role as a developer and manager of housing, and closes a chapter in the South Bronx's history."[44]

Who were the people of the South Bronx? It had become the borough with the most residents of Hispanic origin (644,705 or 48.4 percent), the least residents of white European ancestry (193,651 or 14.5 percent), and the third most residents of African descent (416,338 or 31.2 percent), going from over 90 percent white in 1950 to almost 80 percent black and Hispanic in 2000 (see tables 8.2 and 8.3). After the devastation of the sixties and seventies, however, the population of the borough began to rise again (see tables 1.1 and 8.1). Whites continued to leave, but from 1980 on new groups of blacks and Hispanics moved in. African Americans were joined by blacks from the Caribbean and Africa, called "Los Africanos" by their

Lady Washington Volunteer Fire Co., Morrisania, 1868.

Row houses, East 138th Street, Mott Haven, William O'Gorman, 1881.

East 167th Street, looking west across Park Avenue, Morrisania, 1882.

Collection of The New-York Historical Society.

East 167th Street, looking west across Park Avenue, Morrisania, 1936.

Collection of The New-York Historical Society.

NOTE: These are before and after shots of the same location.

The "North Side" apartment house, Third and Lincoln aves. and 136th St., Mott Haven, Alfred E. Davis, Architect. *Real Estate Record and Builders' Guide*, December 10, 1892.

The Haffen family and workers in front of the Haffen Brewery, 152nd St. and Melrose Ave., Melrose, late 1890s.

Old Law tenements, East 138th Street, Mott Haven, Harry T. Howell, 1898.

Collection of The New-York Historical Society.

Louis F. Haffen, Bronx Borough
President, circa 1899.

Courtesy of The Bronx County Historical Society.
The Bronx, New York.

"The Great North Side: Its Past and Future," title page of *North Side News*, May 18, 1901, supplement "North Side Board of Trade" edition.

St. Regis apartment house, southwest corner Prospect Ave. and 163rd St., Hunts Point–
Crotona Park East, J. F. Meehan, Architect. *Real Estate Record and Builders' Guide*,
April 4, 1908. *Avery Architectural and Fine Arts Library, Columbia University.*

Advertisement for "The Hunts Point"
apartment house, in Taxpayers' Alliance,
The New North End: Bronx Borough,
New York, 1910.

Milstein Division of United States History,
Local History & Genealogy, New York Public Library,
Astor, Lenox, and Tilden Foundation.

South side East 138th Street, Mott Haven, showing Third Avenue El entrance, 1913.

Collection of The New-York Historical Society.

St. Jerome's Church,
East 138th St. and Alexander
Ave., Mott Haven, 1913.

*Collection of The New-York
Historical Society.*

Breaking ground for a Bronx subway station, May 27, 1916. Bronx Borough President
Douglas Mathewson is at right front center. *Collection of The New-York Historical Society.*

The Bronx County Building, 161st St. and the Grand Concourse, May 14, 1940.

Fiorello H. LaGuardia Photographs, NYC Municipal Archives.

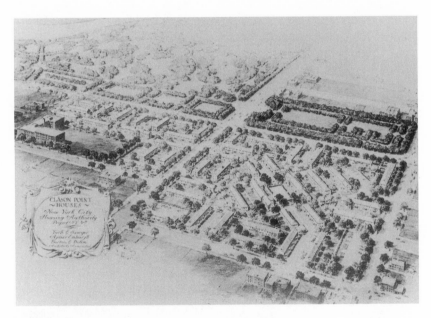

Artist's rendering of Clason Point Houses, a public housing project, Story, Metcalf, and Lafayette aves., Clason Point, Bronx, circa 1940.

Municipal Archives Collection, NYC Municipal Archives.

Metropolitan Oval, Parkchester apartments, Bronx, October 30, 1941.

Courtesy of The Bronx County Historical Society. The Bronx, New York.

President Franklin Delano Roosevelt Bronx campaign headquarters, 188th St. and the Grand Concourse, 1944.   *Fiorello H. LaGuardia Photographs, NYC Municipal Archives.*

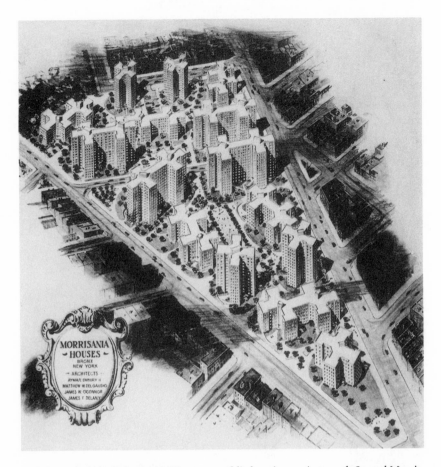

Artist's rendering of Morrisania Houses, a public housing project, 145th St. and Morris and Third aves., Mott Haven, circa 1946 (renamed the Lester W. Patterson Houses when completed).

Concourse Plaza Hotel, 161st St. and the Grand Concourse, Bronx, circa late 1940s.

Courtesy of The Bronx County Historical Society. The Bronx, New York.

El Teatro Puerto Rico, 138th St. and Brown Place, the South Bronx, 1955.

The Justo A. Martí Photographic Collection, Centro de Estudios Puertorriqueños, Hunter College, CUNY.

Charlotte Street seen from Boston Road, March 1981.

Photograph by Camilo José Vergara. Fernando Ferrer Collection.
Courtesy of The Bronx County Historical Society. The Bronx, New York.

View west along Charlotte Street from Southern Boulevard and Jennings Street,
October 1995.

Photograph by Camilo José Vergara. Fernando Ferrer Collection.
Courtesy of The Bronx County Historical Society. The Bronx, New York

NOTE: These are before and after shots of the same location.

139th St. and Brook Ave., northwest corner, June 1980.

139th St. and Brook Ave., northwest corner, October 1995.

NOTE: These are before and after shots of the same location.

Corner of Fulton Ave. and Crotona Park North, showing window decals facing the
Cross-Bronx Expressway, April 1986.   *Photograph by Camilo José Vergara. Fernando Ferrer Collection.*
Courtesy of The Bronx County Historical Society. The Bronx, New York.

Corner of Fulton Ave. and Crotona Park North, facing the Cross-Bronx Expressway,
October 1995.   *Photograph by Camilo José Vergara. Fernando Ferrer Collection.*
Courtesy of The Bronx County Historical Society. The Bronx, New York.

NOTE: These are before and after shots of the same location.

Sale brochure, Nelson Gardens townhouses, 2000, New York City Housing Partnership's New Homes Program. *Nelson Avenue Development LLC. and New York City Housing Partnership.*

TABLE 8.3 Population of Hispanics in the Bronx, 2000

Mexicans	34,377
Puerto Ricans	319,240
Cubans	8,233
Dominicans	133,087
Central Americans	21,408
South Americans	20,782
Other Hispanics	107,578
Total Hispanics	644,705

Source: *New York City Latino Population: Census 2000,*
http://www.lehman.cuny.edu/depts/latinampuertorican/latinoweb/Census2000/NYC/main.htm.

Spanish-speaking neighbors, while Puerto Ricans were augmented by other Hispanics: Dominicans, Cubans, Colombians, and the latest newcomers, Mexicans. By 2000, this new Hispanic community extended beyond the South Bronx to Fordham, Kingsbridge, and Norwood and across the Bronx River to Clasons Point, Soundview, and Castle Hill. The black population, meanwhile, spread across the South Bronx from Sedgwick Avenue to Crotona Park and across the Bronx River into Williamsbridge, Wakefield, and Eastchester. Each of these groups predominated in certain spots, but both lived alongside each other throughout the borough. Whites lived in Riverdale and in the farthest parts of the eastern Bronx.[45]

Within this populace, as Kathy Wylde explained, there was "an emerging African American and Puerto Rican middle class." The Bronx was still the poorest borough, but welfare dependency declined throughout the 1990s as the economy of the city and the nation improved. There were more opportunities in community development groups, in retail establishments catering to new immigrants, and in low- and mid-level civil service positions whites had left. In the Bronx, many low-income jobs and low- and mid-level civil service positions were concentrated in health care and hospital staffing—the biggest employment sector in the borough.[46] This new class was still inchoate, often at the low end of the middle-class scale, but it was not on welfare and many were buying houses in the South Bronx. "People really want to live where they are," explained Billy Procida. Those who bought his Melrose Court Homes at Site 404 were cleaning women, bus drivers, secretaries, and maintenance men who home buyer Sara Morales described as working people with a "vested interest in the community." They distanced themselves from the negative connotations and images of the South Bronx. As a recent buyer of a Charlotte Street house acknowledged, "They're not going to be South Bronx kids—they're going to be Charlotte Gardens kids."[47]

New and old residents had made a home in the Bronx. "This is a dream," asserted hotel worker David Garcia after buying a house in the South Bronx. "Wouldn't you want to own your own home rather than live in the projects with 10,000 other people?" Even the troubled Beekman buildings had sheltered extended families for decades. "I love my community," exclaimed long-time tenant Delfina Cruz in 1997. "It was always a Beekman." To these residents, the borough was home. It was a place to live and to do business, not a place to escape from or move to on the way to somewhere else. There was life in the Bronx once again.[48]

SUMMARY

The Bronx epitomizes American urban history. It began in the 1840s when early rail lines allowed Manhattan residents to build homes and businesses in lower Westchester County. These budding suburbs opened up investment possibilities in subdivision and community building. To ensure continued growth, local interests worked for public improvements and annexation to New York City. Once the Bronx was part of Gotham, els and subways converted vacant land into city property and provided access to it, again stimulating transactions of property, buildings, and businesses. Bronx promoters enhanced these opportunities by boosting the borough, its neighborhoods, and its housing, and linked real estate development with the public good. Booster F. Austin admitted landlords built apartments for profit, but that they "should find profit in the business of improving the standard of existence and appealing to the pride of the folk was to [him] a wondrous sign of the essential vigor of American civilization."[49] With cheap transit, accessible jobs, and a good press, the borough grew from a few thousand in 1850 to more than 1.3 million inhabitants by 2000, and changed from old-stock Protestant American to German and Irish, then to Italian and Jewish, and later to African American and Hispanic. In the process the Bronx passed through stages of urban and neighborhood growth.

The communities that evolved were densely populated and closely built. Every transit line created whole new neighborhoods and filled in the older ones further. Each new route spurred construction of different city housing: the early row houses of Mott Haven, the narrow tenements of Morrisania–Claremont, the wider New Law apartment buildings of Hunts Point–Crotona Park East, and the better apartments of the Grand Concourse, University and Kingsbridge Heights, Norwood, Pelham Parkway, and Parkchester. Such structures filled entire streets with unbroken building lines and prompted architectural critic Montgomery Schuyler to disparage the Bronx in 1917 as "simply an extension of the tenement house district of Manhattan." Although smaller family homes predominated in the eastern portion of the borough, by the 1930s the Bronx conveyed an urban image of brick and concrete.[50]

The people, meanwhile, made the area their own. The early villages soon gained an indigenous work force to serve the commuting segment of the populace, and together both groups became a nucleus for a community. The later Bronx neighborhoods also developed a network of hospitals, schools, clubs, stores, churches, and synagogues that provided local jobs and the comforts of home. Every major transit station or streetcar transfer point became a business and entertainment center. And every locality had social ties based on family, ethnicity, or business. In essence, the neighborhoods were self-contained. While many residents worked downtown, their lives were centered in the borough. "Your neighborhood," recalled former borough president Robert Abrams, "was your universe."[51]

The Bronx, however, was "a social and economic ladder." From its beginnings, it was "a story of shifting people" who moved in to better their lot and left as soon as they improved. Writing about the "Bronxward trek" in 1948, Samuel Lubell noted that without "rooted shelter belts of homeowners, there was little to check the uptown surge which pushed the Bronx's development steadily northward." Lubell likened the borough to "a rags-to-riches escalator" that went from its southern slums to the swank homes of Riverdale at its northwestern tip. "There was no standing still," he observed, "a family either climbed or was engulfed by the pursuing slum."[52]

Yet it was said that the borough had no slums. Each wave of construction in the Bronx had included the latest amenities of the time. Bronx families upgraded their housing by simply moving to newer buildings. At first, the new were built near the old. But with time, the most modern apartments were found only in the borough's newest neighborhoods and at rentals that excluded many. By the early 1940s, the streets and tenements of lower Bronx neighborhoods paled when compared to the model apartment complexes of the north, Amalgamated Houses (1927), Hillside Homes (1935), and the grandest of all, Parkchester (1940), and even to the borough's first public housing project, Clason's Point Gardens (1941). With favorable press coverage, the borough's image remained strong—except for the southern Bronx. It had been the least desirable part of the borough since the thirties. In the decades that followed, many residents remained because of the Depression, World War II, and a severe postwar housing shortage. The South Bronx held its own during those years only because its main characteristics did not change too much or too soon.

From 1950 on, however, the city took advantage of new urban policies and attitudes toward housing to rebuild its aging downtown and clear its slums. This occurred just at the onset of a massive exodus of white urban dwellers into the suburbs and an equally massive migration of different racial and cultural groups into the city. As Southern blacks and Puerto Ricans poured into existing African American and Hispanic ghettos, countless blocks were being razed and rebuilt with high-rise, low-income public housing projects. The newcomers thus spilled over into adjacent low-rent neighborhoods in Manhattan, the Bronx, and Brooklyn only to be displaced again by highway construction, urban renewal, and another round of public housing construction. In the Bronx those areas were in the southern part of the borough, in Mott Haven, Melrose, Morrisania–Claremont, and Hunts Point–Crotona Park East. At first, blacks and Puerto Ricans occupied apartments vacated by families who were leaving for the northern Bronx or the suburbs. But as more came, more and more white Bronx residents moved away from the newcomers.

The urban environment of the South Bronx did not meet the postwar expectations of white, upwardly mobile Bronx residents. Its housing, though structurally sound, lacked modern amenities, and its image was of an old, poor area of cheap rents. The only thing that kept the South Bronx marketable in the 1940s and 1950s was a housing shortage and the influx of new racial and non-English speaking groups who had to settle wherever they could. Rent control was not an issue.[53] Landlords could not have rented South Bronx apartments for more. Elimination of rent control might have helped the more upscale Concourse, Tremont, and Fordham, but not Mott Haven, Melrose, Morrisania–Claremont, or Hunts Point–Crotona Park East. Those neighborhoods had already been set aside for the poor, who from the 1950s on would be nonwhite and Spanish-speaking. To continue to earn from their South Bronx properties, landlords cut down on maintenance, rented to welfare and problem families, induced tenant turnover, failed to pay taxes, and then either walked away or sold the building to the city for another round of slum clearance—again causing continuous, massive residential displacement and devastation.

Government policies and economic restructuring often worsened matters. Urban renewal and the shift away from manufacturing eliminated the very jobs and opportunities for which the newest migrants had come to the city. Public housing projects caused displacement of tenants; destroyed stable neighborhoods, both white and minority; installed a large stock of low-income apartments; and, along with social welfare initiatives, seemed to foster a cycle of poverty. At the same time, Mitchell-Lama Co-ops drew white Bronx residents into subsidized apartment enclaves that were either in the far reaches of the borough, as was Co-op City, or walled off from the surrounding area, as was Concourse Village. When Co-op City fully opened up for occupancy in 1971, seminarian Paul Brant remarked that "it just siphoned people out of there like a vacuum cleaner." Similarly, federal programs to eliminate poverty, rebuild decaying areas, and encourage low-income home ownership resulted in numerous scandals and waste, and discredited the use of public sector policies to improve the inner city.[54]

Crime was another problem. Black and Hispanic areas had high rates of juvenile delinquency in the 1950s and street crime from the 1960s on. That the majority of those arrested may have been African American and Puerto Rican youths did not mean that most blacks and Hispanics were criminals, but this was the perception held by most white New Yorkers and Bronxites as well. The racial stereotyping lent itself to blaming the victims—it was "they" who ruined the housing, the neighborhoods, and by extension the city—and thus led to even more white flight. To the larger metropolis, the South Bronx did not matter. So why extend services to areas where residents stoned the police, firemen, and street cleaners? Unloved by its residents, its landlords, and City Hall, the South Bronx became older, poorer, crime-ridden, drug-infested, and finally vacant in spots.

In the postwar years, the lower Bronx could have been renewed or could have continued to deteriorate. It did both. It was renewed in a way that reinforced the most negative aspects and results of the neighborhood change process. Removal of the el left the Third Avenue corridor without cheap transit to downtown jobs. New highways and public housing projects displaced tenants who might not all have left with low-income black and Spanish-speaking tenants who could not afford to leave. Older apartment buildings continued deteriorating and remained profitable only by means that spread the blight farther. Drugs and crime sealed the South Bronx's fate.

The area, however, had been written off even before blacks and Hispanics moved in. After 1940, local banks and federal lending institutions only financed new construction in the suburbs or the borough's outer reaches. The South Bronx was dismissed by its residents because they aspired to better housing and perceived the borough as a way station, and also because of the race of the new incoming groups. The people had made the area their own, but only for a short time. Industry too followed the citywide trend and left Mott Haven's industrial zone. Thus, there was little demand for land and housing except by the latest round of incoming migrants to New York City—African Americans and Hispanics. Any demand for older, low-rent areas was more easily satisfied in more convenient

Manhattan or in the closer parts of Brooklyn or Queens. This demand eventually led to much gentrification in downtown neighborhoods, but not way uptown in a borough known for crime, poverty, and decay, and as nonwhite. Once European immigration ended, the South Bronx was seen as a site for poorer and poorer groups of nonwhite and non-European peoples. For all practical purposes, it had become a continuation of Harlem.

In the end, the South Bronx lost out because deterioration is "an essential part of urban development" and the neighborhood change process.[55] The lower Bronx had been declining steadily since the 1920s, but this was not inevitable. The decline could have been arrested at any stage by the conscious decisions of residents, business interests, and the city at large. But all followed the dictates of the market economy, the business cycle, and the prevailing sociocultural mores and aspirations. Thus in the Bronx, every policy and decision ensured that the cycle would continue to its most negative result and in the end guaranteed deterioration. As long as the borough was on the growing periphery of the city and receiving the upwardly mobile, it was all right. Once the demand for its land came only from the poorest, no one would invest there and the Bronx would suffer. Neighborhoods are not inanimate; the devastation that occurred in the South Bronx destroyed people and homes as well as property and businesses. It did, however, set the scene for renewal in the future.

This renewal started when local forces joined in a common effort to save the borough. As 1980 approached and the South Bronx reached up to Fordham Road, a host of community groups and nonprofit organizations sprang up in response to the ongoing decay. Noting, as Borough President Ferrer did in 1990, that "the absence of resources doesn't excuse inaction," city and Bronx groups creatively used an array of housing and social initiatives that had been put in place over the years by federal and local governments but that had not worked well before. Helped by a resurgence in housing demand caused by new immigration to the city, their work brought new housing, new businesses, and eventually even more residents. To change the "dumped-on look" of the Bronx, much of this new housing was lower-scaled and owner-occupied; some, like Charlotte Gardens, was even suburban. This emphasis was deliberate, for it was believed that the preponderance of rentals in the borough had fostered the neighborhood decay and building abandonment that had destroyed the South Bronx and almost the entire borough as well.[56]

The Bronx still has a dense population, 1.3 million in 2000, and despite the co-ops and owner-occupied homes, a high rate of tenantry. Eighty percent of the borough is black and Hispanic, but the whites that are left live in Riverdale, Throgs Neck, Morris Park, the Country Club district, and Co-op City, though the latter now has a strong black and Spanish-speaking presence. There are pockets of Italians, Albanians, Irish, and Asians. Many Jews remain in Riverdale and the Amalgamated Houses near Van Cortlandt Park, and scattered throughout. Working- and middle class blacks and Hispanics from America, the Caribbean, and Africa live in the northern Bronx, the Grand Concourse area, and the rest of the borough, while upwardly mobile blacks and Hispanics are in Co-op City, rehabbed Grand Concourse buildings, and the now co-op and newly renovated Parkchester Apartments.[57]

Today, the Bronx has neighborhoods again. In 2000, the 16th Congressional District, which contains the South Bronx, Fordham, and Kingsbridge, was the poorest congressional district in the city.[58] There were still rubble-filled lots a few streets away from where President Clinton praised Charlotte Gardens as a model for the nation. But now crime is down and South Bronx land is in demand. "There is literally no place where people can move," said organizer Lee Stuart of South Bronx Churches in 1998. "It's just tight, tight, tight." Local housing advocates continue to build affordable rows of owner-occupied attached homes wherever they find space and funding, even fighting for control of community gardens. A budding new crop of entrepreneurs, meanwhile, snaps up whatever structures the city auctions off. Blacks and Hispanics are investing in the South Bronx neighborhoods from which whites divested themselves decades ago.[59] Thus, as Emanuel Tobier has recently written, "There is no great prosperity, but the borough is on the mend." A new Bronx is rising from the ashes of the old.[60]

NOTES

1. THE BRONX AND ITS NEIGHBORHOODS

1. Robert Jensen, ed., *Devastation/Resurrection: The South Bronx* (New York: Bronx Museum of the Arts, 1979), 13; Jill Jonnes, *South Bronx Rising: The Rise, Fall, and Resurrection of an American City* (New York: Fordham University Press, 2002), 311–23, 333–36; Bureau of the Census, *U.S. Census of Population: 1950, New York, New York* (Washington, DC, 1952); Welfare and Health Council of New York City, *Population of Puerto Rican Birth or Parentage, New York City: 1950* (New York, 1952); Bureau of the Census, *U.S. Census of Population and Housing: 1960* (Washington, DC, 1962); New York City Department of City Planning, *Citywide and Borough Population, 1990 & 2000*, New York City government Web site, www.nyc.gov/html/dcp.

2. Quotes are from Craig Horowitz, "A South Bronx Renaissance," *New York*, 21 November 1994, 54; Borough President of the Bronx, *The 2000 State of the Borough Report* (New York, 2000), 1. Fernando Ferrer quoted in Barbara Stewart, "The Bronx: An All-America City, Thonx," *New York Times*, 19 November 1997.

3. For examples of these interpretations see Jonnes, *South Bronx Rising*; Thomas J. Sugrue, *The Origins of the Urban Crisis: Race and Inequality in Postwar Detroit* (Princeton: Princeton University Press, 1996); Herbert Meyer, "How Government Helped Ruin the South Bronx," *Fortune*, Nov. 1975, 140–54. The widespread black/white conflict that Sugrue described in Detroit did not occur in the Bronx.

4. Roy Lubove, "The Urbanization Process: An Approach to Historical Research," *Journal of the American Institute of Planners* 33 (Jan. 1967): 34.

5. The Bronx received its name from the Bronx River, which had earlier been named for the first European settler in lower Westchester, the Swedish-born Jonas Bronk. Stephen Jenkins, *The Story of The Bronx: From the Purchase Made by the Dutch From the Indians in 1639 to the Present Day* (New York: G. P. Putnam's Sons, 1912), 7–10, 26, 366 (hereafter cited as Jenkins, *The Bronx*); Lloyd Ultan, "1776–1940, The Story of The South Bronx," in Jensen, *Devastation/Resurrection*, 14–36.

6. "Memorial by Lewis Morris, of Morrisania, To his Excellency the President and the Honorable the Members of the Congress of the United States of America, 1790," in John Thomas Scharf, *History of Westchester County, New York: including Morrisania, Kingsbridge, and West Farms which Have Been Annexed to New York City*, 2 vols. (Philadelphia: L. E. Preston & Co., 1886), 1:823.

7. Jenkins, *The Bronx*, 2–4; Louis F. Haffen, *Address by Louis F. Haffen, President Borough of the Bronx, Delivered at Complimentary Dinner at the Longwood Club, October 2, 1905* (Bronx, NY, 1905), 14–15.

8. Between 1890 and 1910, the Bronx's population increased at greater decennial rates than those of any U.S. city of comparable or larger population. In the next decade, only Detroit had a greater proportional gain. See Walter Laidlaw, *Population of the City of New York, 1890–1930* (New York: Cities Census Committee, 1932), 12–14; Louis F. Haffen, *Borough of The Bronx: A Record of Unparalleled Progress and Development* (New York, 1909), 3–7, 23–27; President of the Borough of the Bronx, *Annual Report for the Year 1912* (New York: M. B. Brown Printing & Binding Co., 1913), 151, 171; The Bronx Board of Trade, *"The Nation's Ninth City," The Bronx: New York's Fastest Growing Borough* (New York: Bronx Board of Trade, 1922), 3.

9. North Side Board of Trade, *The Great North Side or Borough of The Bronx* (New York: Knickerbocker Press, 1897), 113; Haffen, *Address to the Longwood Club, 1905*, 10–11; Haffen, *Borough of The Bronx, 1909*, 45; Taxpayers's Alliance, *The New North End: Bronx Borough* (New York: Diagram Publishing Company, 1910), 33; Martha Golden, "The Grand Concourse: Tides of Change" (New York: New York City Landmarks Preservation Commission, 1976), 48; Katherine Jeannette Meyer, "A Study of Tenant Associations in New York City, with Particular Reference to The Bronx, 1920–1927," (M.A. thesis, Columbia University, 1928), 29.

10. Lloyd Ultan, *The Beautiful Bronx (1920–1950)* (New Rochelle, NY: Arlington House, 1979); Clara Rodriguez, "Growing Up in the Forties and Fifties," in *Devastation/Resurrection*, ed. Jensen, 45–50; Brian J. Danforth and Victor B. Caliandro, *Perception of Housing and Community: Bronx Architecture in the 1920s* (Bronx, NY: West Bronx Restoration Committee, Graduate Program in Urban Planning, Hunter College, CUNY, 1977).

11. Thomas Glynn, "The South Bronx," *Neighborhood*, August 1982, 3–25; Donald G. Sullivan, "1940–1965, Population Mobility in the South Bronx," in *Devastation/Resurrection*, ed. Jensen, 37–44; Donald G. Sullivan, "The Process of Abandonment," in *Devastation/Resurrection*, ed. Jensen, 69–71; Nathan Glazer, "The South Bronx Story: An Extreme Case of Neighborhood Decline," *Policy Studies Journal* 16 (winter 1987); Jim Rooney, *Organizing the South Bronx* (Albany: State University of New York, 1995), 45–61.

12. See for example, Jon Bradshaw, "Savage Skulls," *Esquire*, June 1977; Meyer, "How Government Helped Ruin the South Bronx"; Ira Rosen, "The Glory That Was Charlotte Street," *New York Times Magazine*, 1 October 1979;

Robert A. Caro, *The Power Broker: Robert Moses and the Fall of New York* (New York: Knopf, 1974), 839–43.

13. By 1915, the Bronx had 53 census tracts with residential densities of over 100 people to the acre; 17 of these had more than 200 per acre, and one lucky Hunts Point tract had 300 plus. In 1992 the Bronx had 28,443.2 people per square mile, the third highest density in the nation. Densities were compiled from census tract areas and population statistics in Laidlaw, *Population of New York City, 1890–1930*, 55–56, 210. For later statistics see Joseph R. Passonneau and Richard Saul Wurman, *Urban Atlas: 20 American Cities* (Cambridge: MIT Press, 1966), unpaged; and Bureau of the Census, *County and City Data Book, 1994*, 12th ed. (Washington, DC, Aug. 1994), xii.

14. Laidlaw, *Population of New York City, 1890–1930*, 34, 82; Fred H. Allen, ed., *New York City, Westchester, and Nassau Counties in Relation to Real Estate Investments, 1942* (New York: Sponsored by The Bank for Savings, Bowery Savings Bank, Group Five Mortgage Information Bureau, 1942), 104.

15. See for example, Fred Ferretti, "After 70 Years, South Bronx Street Is at a Dead End," *New York Times*, 21 October 1977; Rosen, "The Glory That Was Charlotte Street"; Suzanne Daley, "Lost Neighborhood Found in Memory," *New York Times*, 25 April 1983; Michael Dorman, *The Making of a Slum* (New York: Delacorte, 1972). For semifictional accounts of this nostalgia, see the three memoirs by Jerome Charyn, *Bronx Boy* (New York: St. Martin's Press, 2002); *The Black Swan* (New York: St. Martin's Press, 2000); and *The Dark Lady of Belorusse* (New York: St. Martin's Press, 1997).

16. The conceptual literature on neighborhood encompasses many fields. See Suzanne Keller, *The Urban Neighborhood: A Sociological Perspective* (New York: Random House, 1968); Terrence Lee, "Urban Neighborhoods as a Social-Spatial Schema," in *Environmental Psychology: Man and His Physical Setting*, eds. Harold M. Proshansky, William H. Ittleson, and Leanne G. Rivlin (New York: Holt, Rinehart and Winston, 1970), 349–70; Randolph T. Hestor, *Neighborhood Space* (Stroudsburg, PA: Dowden, Hutchinson & Ross, 1975), 7–13; Barry Wellman and Barry Leighton, "Networks, Neighborhoods, and Communities: Approaches to the Study of the Community Question," in *Internal Structure of the City: Readings on Urban Form, Growth, and Policy*, ed. Larry S. Bourne, 2nd ed. (New York: Oxford University Press, 1982), 245–59; Howard W. Hallman, *Neighborhoods: Their Place in Urban Life* (Beverly Hills, CA: Sage, 1984).

17. Walter Firey, "Sentiment and Symbolism as Ecological Variables," *American Sociological Review* 10 (April 1945): 140–48; Walter Firey, *Land Use in Central Boston* (Cambridge: Harvard University Press, 1947); Rolf Goetze, *Understanding Neighborhood Change: The Role of Expectations in Urban Revitalization* (Cambridge, MA: Ballinger, 1979).

18. Kenneth T. Jackson, *Crabgrass Frontier: The Suburbanization of the United States* (New York: Oxford University Press, 1985); John R. Logan and Harvey

L. Molotch, *Urban Fortunes: The Political Economy of Place* (Berkeley: University of California Press, 1987). The quote is from Robert A. Beauregard, *Voices of Decline: The Postwar Fate of U.S. Cities* (Cambridge, MA: Blackwell, 1993), 20.

19. William G. Flanagan, *Contemporary Urban Sociology* (New York: Cambridge University Press, 1993); Homer Hoyt, *The Structure and Growth of Residential Neighborhoods in American Cities* (Washington, D.C.: Federal Housing Administration, 1939); David Ward, *Cities and Immigrants: A Geography of Change in Nineteenth-Century America* (New York: Oxford University Press, 1971); David Ward, *Poverty, Ethnicity, and the American City, 1840–1925: Changing Conceptions of the Slum and the Ghetto* (New York: Cambridge University Press, 1989); Kristy Maher McNamara and Robert P. McNamara, eds., *The Urban Landscape: Selected Readings* (New York: University Press of America, 1995).

20. Edgar M. Hoover and Raymond Vernon, *Anatomy of a Metropolis: The Changing Distribution of People and Jobs Within the New York Metropolitan Region* (Cambridge: Harvard University Press, 1959), 183–98; *The Dynamics of Neighborhood Change*, by James Mitchell (United States Department of Housing and Urban Development, Office of Policy Development and Research, San Francisco, May 1975); Leo Grebler, *Housing Market Behavior in a Declining Area* (New York: Columbia University Press, 1952), 14; Jackson, *Crabgrass Frontier*, 286–87.

21. Lubove, "The Urbanization Process," 33–39; Charles L. Leven, James T. Little, Hugh O. Nourse, and R. B. Read, *Neighborhood Change: Lessons in the Dynamics of Urban Decay* (New York: Praeger, 1976), xii–xvi, 3–50; Hoover and Vernon, *Anatomy of a Metropolis*, 198–229; Ira S. Lowry, "Filtering and Housing Standards: A Conceptual Analysis," *Land Economics* 36 (Nov. 1960): 362–70; Wallace F. Smith, *Filtering and Neighborhood Change*, Research Report No. 24 (Berkeley: Institute for Urban and Regional Development, University of California, 1964); Paul F. Cressey, "Population Succession in Chicago, 1898–1930," *American Journal of Sociology* 44 (July 1938): 56–59. On population invasion and residential mobility in New York see Ronald H. Bayor, "The Neighborhood Invasion Pattern," in *Neighborhoods in Urban America*, ed. Ronald H. Bayor (Port Washington, NY: Kennikat Press, 1982), 86–102; Peter H. Rossi, *Why Families Move* (Glencoe, IL: Free Press, 1955); William Michaelson, *Environmental Choice, Human Behavior, and Residential Satisfaction* (New York: Oxford University Press, 1977). For recent treatments of racial neighborhood change, see Gerald Gamm, *Urban Exodus: Why the Jews Left Boston and the Catholics Stayed* (Cambridge: Harvard University Press, 1999); Louis Rosen, *The South Side: The Racial Transformation of an American Neighborhood* (Chicago: Ivan R. Dee, 1998).

22. See "Needs of South Bronx," in Haffen, *Borough of The Bronx, 1909*, 59–60; Bronx Council of Social Agencies, *A Study of The Lower Bronx* (New York: Bronx Council of Social Agencies, 1939), 2.

23. Since the borough's east/west axis was Jerome Avenue, neighborhoods on or near it—as long as they were on or near the Grand Concourse ridge—were in the "West Bronx." See Golden, "The Grand Concourse," 48–51; Deborah Dash Moore, *At Home in America: Second-Generation New York Jews* (New York: Columbia University Press, 1981), 41–57, 73–74; Glynn, "The South Bronx." By the 1930s, the distinctness had class connotations, as the oldest housing of the borough was in the "East Bronx." The inherent class tensions among various parts of The Bronx in the 1950s are revealed in Eliot Wagner, *Grand Concourse: A Novel* (New York: Bobbs-Merrill, 1954); see also Julius Jacobs, *Bronx Cheer: A Memoir* (Monroe, NY: Library Research Associates, 1976).

24. See descriptions of residential sections in *Real Estate Record and Builders' Guide*, 30 March 1907 (hereafter cited as *Record and Guide*); Taxpayers' Alliance, *The New North End*; *North Side News*, Bronx County Progress Section, 17 May 1914.

25. See discussion in Seth Kugel, "Is Melrose a Melrose By Any Other Name?", *New York Times*, 23 June 2002; and an earlier effort to clarify area names by The Bronx County Historical Society in *New York Times*, 9 September 1964.

26. New York State, *Census for 1865* (Albany, NY, 1867), xl–xli. Laidlaw, *Population of New York City, 1890–1930*, 51, estimated the population of the Bronx for 1840 as 5,346. Most of this population was east of the Bronx River. Frederick Shonnard and W. W. Spooner, *History of Westchester County, New York, From Its Earliest Settlement to the Year 1900* (New York: New York History Company, 1900), 562; *Westchester Herald*, 10 Sept. 1839. Jenkins erroneously puts the installation of the Mott works in 1828; the correct date was 1841. See Jordan L. Mott to Committee on Roads and Bridges, April 1866, Mott Papers, Columbia University Library, New York.

27. All three roads and their connecting spur, the Spuyten Duyvil and Port Morris Railroad built in 1867, became part of Cornelius Vanderbilt's New York Central Railroad system. The New York and New Haven Railroad entered lower Westchester in 1848 on the tracks of the Harlem line, and thus had little influence on the area's growth. In early 1872 the New Haven gained direct rail access up to the Harlem River via the eastern half of the future Bronx area. Jenkins, *The Bronx*, 229–37; Shonnard and Spooner, *History of Westchester County*, 591; Joseph Warren Green Jr., "New York's First Railroad, The New York and Harlem, 1832 to 1867," *New York Historical Society Quarterly Bulletin* 9 (January 1926): 107–23.

28. Shonnard and Spooner, *History of Westchester County*, 576–77, 584–85, 591; New York State, *Census for 1865*, xl–xli, xlix–lvi. In 1870, the most populous areas in West Farms were the villages of Fordham and Tremont, both on the route of the New York and Harlem Railroad.

29. Edward K. Spann, *The New Metropolis: New York City, 1840–1857* (New York: Columbia University Press, 1981), 176–204, 308–11, 394–95. On the commuter villages see John Homer French, *Gazetteer of the State of New York*, Empire

State Historical Publications Series No. 72 (1860; reprint, Port Washington, NY: Ira J. Friedman, 1969), 696–707.

30. See *Sunday Mercury*, 19 July 1863, 4 Nov. 1866, 20 Jan. 1867, 3 May, 6 Dec. 1868; and *New York Times*, 1 March 1869.

31. *New York Herald*, 15 March 1851; Joel Schwartz, "Community Building on the Bronx Frontier: Morrisania, 1848–1875" (Ph.D. diss., University of Chicago, 1972), 39–46 (hereafter cited as Schwartz, "Morrisania"); and "Copy of Memo on file in Town Clerk's Office [West Farms, Westchester County]," 3 July 1855, Mott Papers, CU. See ads in *New York Tribune*, 3 July 1850, 6 Sept. 1853; also the Mott Papers, CU; and the Chauncey Smith Papers, New-York Historical Society.

32. Quoted in John A. Henry, ed., *Henry's Directory of Morrisania and Vicinity for 1853–4* (Morrisania, NY: Spratley's Westchester Gazette Print, 1853), 6. See also Schwartz, "Morrisania," 63–67; D. B. Frisbee and William T. Coles, eds., *Morrisania and Tremont Directory, 1871–2* (Morrisania, NY: Times Print, 1871), xv; Scharf, *History of Westchester County*, 2:624–26. The phrase "corner lots" was used in a discussion of springtime in Morrisania in the *Sunday Mercury*, a paper owned and edited by Morrisania resident and town supervisor William Cauldwell. See *Sunday Mercury*, 8 March 1859.

33. Jackson, *Crabgrass Frontier*, 63–72; Neil Harris, *The Artist in American Society: The Formative Years, 1790–1860* (New York: George Braziller, 1966), 208–16. For an in-depth account of Andrew Jackson Downing, see David Schuyler, *Andrew Jackson Downing, 1815–1852* (Baltimore: Johns Hopkins University Press, 1996).

34. Henry, *Henry's Directory*, 5.

35. "Report of the Special Legislative Committee on Building Associations in the City of New-York," 29 Jan. 1856, New York State, *Assembly Documents, 1856*, vol. 3, no. 46, pp. 1–10; Schwartz, "Morrisania," 46–48. Building associations were part of the various land reform schemes aired during the 1840s and 1850s. On these see Norman Ware, *The Industrial Worker, 1840–1860: The Reaction of American Industrial Society to the Advance of the Industrial Revolution* (1924; new ed., Chicago: Quadrangle, 1964), 180–84; Helene Sara Zahler, *Eastern Workingmen and National Land Policy, 1829–1862* (New York: Columbia University Press, 1941).

36. Schwartz, "Morrisania," 1–114, 154–60; *New York Times*, 4 Dec., 30 Dec. 1870; *Sunday Mercury*, 9 Sept. 1866, 22 Nov. 1868. The effort to make the Harlem River "navigable to ocean going vessels" surfaced periodically from the 1850s on. The plan was first sponsored as a private endeavor and later as a state and federal project. See Louis G. Morris, *Harlem River; Its Use Previous to and Since The Revolutionary War and Suggestions Relative to Present Contemplated Improvement* (New York: J. D. Torrey, 1857); "An Act to Incorporate the Hudson and Harlem River Canal Company," New York State, *Laws of 1863*, chap. 365; *Sunday Mercury*, 6 Dec. 1868; 10 Jan., 11 April, 26 June, 18 Dec. 1870; *New York Times*, 20 July 1869, 12 Dec., 23 Dec. 1873, 17 March 1874.

37. *Sunday Mercury*, 29 April, 13 May, 1 July 1866.
38. Laidlaw, *Population of New York City, 1890–1930*, 51; "Second Annual Report of the Metropolitan Board of Health of the State of New York, 1867," New York State, *Assembly Documents, 1868*, vol. 9, no. 122, pp. 146–47, 213; Robert Greenhalgh Albion, *The Rise of New York Port, 1815–1860* (New York: Charles Scribner's Sons, 1939); Spann, *The New Metropolis*.
39. "Report of the Select Committee appointed to examine into the condition of Tenement Houses in New-York and Brooklyn, 9 March 1857," New York State, *Assembly Documents, 1857*, vol. 3, no. 205; "Report . . . [on] the public health of the counties of New York, Kings and Richmond, and the waters thereof, 7 February 1861," New York State, *Assembly Documents, 1861*, vol. 2, no. 59; Edward Ewing Pratt, *Industrial Causes of Congestion of Population in New York City* (New York: Columbia University, Longmans, Green & Co., 1911), 9–44; Spann, *The New Metropolis*, 117–38; Richard B. Calhoun, "New York City Fire Department Reorganization, 1865–1870: A Civil War Legacy," *New York Historical Society Quarterly* 40 (Jan./April 1976): 7–34; James F. Richardson, *The New York Police: Colonial Times to 1901* (New York: Oxford University Press, 1971); Harry James Carman, *The Street Surface Railway Franchises of New York City* (New York: Columbia University Press, 1919); James Blaine Walker, *Fifty Years of Rapid Transit, 1864 to 1917* (New York: Law Printing Company, 1918); "New York City's Future," clipping, ca. 1851, Mott Papers, CU.
40. "Report . . . [on] the public health of the counties of New York, Kings and Richmond, 7 February 1861," 10; Roy Lubove, *The Progressives and the Slums: Tenement House Reform in New York City, 1890–1917* (Pittsburgh: University of Pittsburgh Press, 1962), 1–28; Laidlaw, *Population of New York City, 1890–1930*, 51; New York State, *Census for 1875* (Albany, NY, 1877), 258.
41. See comments to that effect by Dr. Stephen Smith, *New York Times*, 7 Jan. 1874; *Sunday Mercury*, 12 March 1865. Quotes are from the *New York Times*, 2 Aug. 1869; *Record and Guide*, 2 Nov. 1872.
42. *New York Times*, 11 Dec., 13 Dece. 1870, 4 Jan. 1871; Schwartz, "Morrisania," 277, 285–86; Andrew H. Green, "Communication of the Comptroller of the Park Relative to Westchester County, Harlem River, and Spuyten Duyvil Creek, December 30, 1868," in *Twelfth Annual Report of the Board of Commissioners of the Central Park for the Year Ending December 31, 1868* (New York: Evening Post Steam Presses, 1869).
43. "New York City's Future," clipping, ca. 1851, Mott Papers, CU; *New York Times*, 15 Feb. 1869, 27 Dec. 1870; *Sunday Mercury*, 3 Feb. 1861; Daniel Curry, *New York: A Historical Sketch of the Rise and Progress of the Metropolitan City of America, by a New Yorker* (New York: Carlton & Phillips, 1853), 337. On the eve of annexation, Westchesterites estimated that 40,000 inhabitants left New York City annually because they could not find "suitable homes in this island." See *Record and Guide*, 1 Nov. 1873.
44. New York State, *Laws of 1869*, chap. 826, passed 11 May 1869; *New York Times*, 20 July 1869.

45. *New York Times*, 29 Dec. 1870, 14 Jan. 1871, 6 Jan. 1873; William Cauldwell, "Annexation," in North Side Board of Trade, *The Great North Side*, 19–24. The Democratic leaders of Morrisania and West Farms feared they would lose their power under Tweed's plan. See Schwartz, "Morrisania," 283–89.

46. Thomas H. Edsall, *History of the Town of Kingsbridge: Now part of the 24th Ward, New York City* (New York: the author, 1887), 43–44; French, *Gazetteer of the State of New York*, 708; Schwartz, "Morrisania," 328; Frisbee and Coles, *Morrisania and Tremont Directory*; William A. Tieck, *Riverdale, Kingsbridge, Spuyten Duyvil: A Historical Epitome of the Northwest Bronx* (Old Tappan, NJ: Fleming H. Revell, 1968), 115–17.

47. New York State, *Census of 1875*, 245. Of the 5,451 dwellings within the three former towns, 55 percent were valued between $1,000 and $5,000 and 38 percent were valued at $5,000 and over. In 1857, a suburban or rural cottage cost from $1,500 to $4,200. Edgar W. Martin, *The Standard of Living in 1860* (Chicago: University of Chicago Press, 1942), 42–43. As 1875 was also a depression year, and since in 1868 Morrisania Town homes and lots were still being advertised as advantageous to "persons of moderate means" (*Sunday Mercury*, 6 Dec. 1868), it is reasonable to assume that most of the dwellings were comfortable, if not middle class, by the standards of the day.

48. Schwartz, "Morrisania," 268–73; Matthew P. Breen, *Thirty Years of New York Politics* (New York: the author, 1899), 722–24; *New York Times*, 25 Dec. 1870, 3 May, 14 May 1873; and quoted in *Record and Guide*, 1 Nov. 1873, 31 May 1873.

49. New York State, *Laws of 1873*, chap. 613, passed 23 May 1873.

50. *New York Times*, 6 Nov. 1873; Breen, *Thirty Years of New York Politics*, 724–27; Cauldwell, "Annexation," 24–27.

51. *Record and Guide*, 1 Nov. 1873. On the aversion to being called the "Annexed District" see *Morrisania Gazette*, 30 Oct. 1874; *New York Times*, 28 July 1891.

52. *Peremptory Sale at Auction: Estate of Lewis G. Morris, Monday, March 15, 1869*, Auction Pamphlet, New York Public Library.

53. Land prices rose considerably during the community-building period. Morrisania village land sold for $173 an acre in 1848, while comparable property went for $3,000 per in 1867. *Sunday Mercury*, 20 Jan. 1867. The cultural tradition of the city as the sphere of profit making, i.e., "privatism," is ably described in Sam Bass Warner, *The Private City: Philadelphia in Three Periods of Its Growth* (Philadelphia: University of Pennsylvania Press, 1968), 3–21. For the theoretical underpinnings of this, see Logan and Molotch, *Urban Fortunes*; Neil Smith, *Uneven Development: Nature, Capital, and the Production of Space* (Cambridge, MA: Blackwell, 1991); David Harvey, *The Urbanization of Capital* (Baltimore: Johns Hopkins University Press, 1985).

2. EARLY BEGINNINGS

1. *Sunday Mercury*, 12 March 1865; Jordan L. Mott quoted in "Report of Committee Relative to the Reformed Dutch Church Edifice Erecting at Mott

Haven," 2, Chauncey Smith Papers, NYHS; New York City Planning Commission, *Plan for New York*, vol. 2, *The Bronx* (New York: New York City Planning Commission, 1969), 36.

2. Stephen Jenkins, *The Story of The Bronx: From the Purchase Made by the Dutch From the Indians in 1639 to the Present Day* (New York: G. P. Putnam's Sons, 1912), 360–64 (hereafter cited as Jenkins, *The Bronx*); Dumas Malone, ed., *Dictionary of American Biography*, 23 vols. (New York: Charles Scribner's Sons, 1934), 13:209–12; John W. Reps, *The Making of Urban America: A History of City Planning in the United States* (Princeton: Princeton University Press, 1965), 297; Paul Sann, *Kill the Dutchman! The Story of Dutch Schultz* (New Rochelle, NY: Arlington House, 1971).

3. Jenkins, *The Bronx*, 2, 229; John Thomas Scharf, *History of Westchester County, New York: including Morrisania, Kingsbridge, and West Farms which Have Been Annexed to New York City*, 2 vols. (Philadelphia: L. E. Preston & Co., 1886), 1:823; F. W. Beers, *Atlas of New York and Vicinity, 1868* (New York: F. W. Beers, A.D. Ellis, & G. G. Soule, 1868); Jared Sparks, *The Life of Gouverneur Morris with Selections From his Correspondence and Miscellaneous Papers*, 3 vols. (Boston: Gray & Bowen, 1832), 1:495, 505; Joel Schwartz, "Community Building on the Bronx Frontier: Morrisania, 1848–1875" (Ph.D. diss., University of Chicago, 1972), 39–46 (hereafter cited as Schwartz, "Morrisania"), 37–46.

4. "Testimony of Jordan L. Mott," in Westchester County Board of Supervisors, *Reports of the Special Committee on the New Harlem Bridge* (New York: Press of Wynkoop, Hallenbeck & Thomas, 1864), 110; J. Leander Bishop, *A History of American Manufactures, From 1608 to 1860*, 3 vols. (1868; reprint, New York: Johnson Reprint Corporation, 1967), 2:443, 498, 576–78; Second American Building Association to Jordan L. Mott, 4 October 1852, Mott Papers, CU; D. B. Frisbee and William T. Coles, eds., *Morrisania and Tremont Directory, 1871–2* (Morrisania, NY: Times Print, 1871), vi–ix; Schwartz, "Morrisania," 5–25.

5. Jordan L. Mott to Committee on Roads and Bridges, April 1866, Mott Papers, Columbia University Library, New York; "Jordan L. Mott to John York and John Deen, Deed, Lot 144," 11 Nov. 1853; "Jordan L. Mott to N.Y. and Harlem Railroad, Deed," 22 Sept. 1852; J. W. Adams to J. L. Mott, "Estimate for the Building of the Mott Haven Canal," 29 May 1852; Andrew Findlay, Surveyor, "Map of the Village of Mott Haven in the Manor of Morrisania, Town of West Farms," Westchester County, New York: 1 Jan. 1850, Mott Papers, CU; *New York Tribune*, 3 July 1850; *Westchester Gazette*, 13 Sept. 1850. An overall assessment is in Schwartz, "Morrisania," 14, 42–53.

6. Schwartz, "Morrisania," 27.

7. Mott Papers, CU; Westchester County Board of Supervisors, *Reports of the Special Committee on the New Harlem Bridge*, 12–14.

8. *New York Tribune*, 6 Sept. 1853; Schwartz, "Morrisania," 38, 54–55, 325; Jenkins, *The Bronx*, 21; John McNamara, *History in Asphalt: The Origin of Bronx*

Street and Place Names, Borough of The Bronx, New York City (Harrison, NY: Harbor Hill Books in collaboration with The Bronx County Historical Society, 1878), 243, 479–80.

9. Schwartz, "Morrisania," 76, 325. By 1860, Wilton had become the home of "fourteen or fifteen members of the theatrical profession." See *Sunday Mercury*, 15 January 1860.

10. Schwartz, "Morrisania," 78–81.

11. F. W. Beers, *Map of 23rd Ward, New York City, 1876* (New York: J. B. Beers & Co., 1876); William Cauldwell, "Annexation," in North Side Board of Trade, *The Great North Side: Its Past and Future, Its Advantages as a Commercial and Manufacturing Centre, North Side News*, Supplement, 18 May 1901, 20.

12. "J. L. Mott to N.Y. & Harlem Railroad, Deed," 22 Sept. 1852; American Danamora Iron Company to J. L. Mott, ca. 1864; L. S. Mott to S. S. Marshall, 11 Oct. 1864, Mott Papers, CU; Schwartz, "Morrisania," 52–54, 242.

13. Schwartz, "Morrisania," 55–56, 77.

14. Ibid., 78–81, 253; Jenkins, *The Bronx*, 239. Ad was in the *Sunday Mercury*, 19 July 1863. For the Harlem Bridge, Morrisania, and Fordham Railroad Company and the Southern Boulevard, see New York State, *Laws of 1863*, chap. 361; *Laws of 1867*, chap. 290; and *Laws of 1869*, chap. 804; *New York Times*, 4 Dec. 1870.

15. "Annual Report of the Railroad Commission for the Fiscal Year Ending September 30, 1856," in New York State Engineer and Surveyor, *Accompanying Documents* (Albany, NY: C. Van Benthuysen, 1857), 487; Schwartz, "Morrisania," 116–18, 183, 280; Jenkins, *The Bronx*, 232. On the 1870s see *New York Times*, 14 Aug. 1871; Frisbee and Coles, *Morrisania and Tremont Directory*, vi–vii.

16. "Communication from the Secretary of State Showing the Population in Each Election District of the City of New York," in New York State, *Assembly Documents, 1876*, vol. 6, no. 55, p. 14; Works Projects Administration, *Historical Records Survey, Guide to Vital Statistics in the City of New York, Borough of The Bronx, Churches* (New York: Works Projects Administration, 1942), 1–10.

17. St. Augustine's Roman Catholic Church in Morrisania village served the Irish laborers in the Mott Haven area up to the mid-1860s. A few years after its founding, St. Jerome's started a parochial school. For the subsequent identification of St. Jerome's with the Irish see New York City Landmarks Preservation Commission, "Mott Haven Historic District–Borough of The Bronx," Number 1, July 29, 1969, LP–0451 (New York: NYC Landmarks Preservation Commission, 1969), 2; Brian J. Danforth, *Mott Haven: Nineteenth-Century Landmark District in The South Bronx* (New York: West Bronx Restoration Committee, Hunter College, 1976), 7, 17.

18. Joel Schwartz, "Morrisania's Volunteer Firemen, 1848–1874: The Limits of Local Institutions in a Metropolitan Age," *New York History* 55 (1974): 159–78; Schwartz, "Morrisania," 166–75, 181–98. The fire crews were middle class in character at first, for few laborers could afford the membership fees and

monthly dues. As late as 1866, only two members of Jackson Engine No. 4 were laborers. From 1870 on, however, more fire volunteers were coming from lower social and economic strata.

19. Mott Haven's Buena Vista team was organized in the 1850s. Schwartz, "Morrisania," 21, 88–100, 162–65, 191.

20. Since other villages in the town experienced a slight lowering of ethnic barriers by 1870, with a few intermarriages between Irish and German Catholics, it is likely this could have been true for Mott Haven. See Schwartz, "Morrisania," 115–25.

21. Jenkins, *The Bronx*, 368; Schwartz, "Morrisania," 133, 211, 302–4; L. S. Mott to S. S. Marshall, 11 Oct. 1864, Mott Papers, CU. Louis B. Brown dealt in Manhattan West Side property. *Record and Guide*, 25 Dec. 1875. J. L. Mott Jr. was a road commissioner for the township from 1859 on. In 1869 he served without pay as a "Special Police Constable." By 1870, Mott Jr. was dispensing local patronage for the Democratic Party. *Sunday Mercury*, 24 April, 8 May, 24 July 1859.

22. Mott joined with the Morris and Bathgate families and Robert H. Elton in laying out streets throughout Morrisania Township. "Copy of Memo on File in Town Clerk's Office," 3 July 1855, Mott Papers, CU. Gouverneur Morris was on the commission to build Southern Boulevard in 1867 and was a partner in the Spuyten Duyvil and Port Morris Railroad. New York State, *Laws of 1867*, chap. 290; *Laws of 1868*, chap. 194; "Report of The Board of Commissioners of the Department of Public Parks of the City of New York, March 15, 1871," New York State, *Assembly Documents, 1871*, doc. 88; "Annual Report of the State Engineer & Surveyor of the State of New York," New York State, *Assembly Documents, 1870*, doc. 154.

23. Andrew Findlay, surveyor, "Map of the Village of Mott Haven in the Manor of Morrisania, Town of West Farms," Westchester County, New York, 1 Jan. 1850, Mott Papers, CU; Beers, *Atlas of New York and Vicinity, 1868*; Beers, *Map of 23rd Ward, 1876*; Reps, *The Making of Urban America*, 296–99. Gouverneur Morris's father was one of the commissioners who drew up the 1811 grid plan of New York City.

24. New York State, *Laws of 1868*, chap. 841; "Memorandum by General George S. Greene, Engineer, relating to plans for streets and avenues in the Twenty-fourth Ward, between the Hudson River and the Croton Aqueduct, September 1875," in New York City, Department of Parks, *Documents*, no. 74, 28 Feb. 1877, 20; *Record and Guide*, 23 Nov. 1872. The earliest row houses were built in 1863, at 276–94 Alexander Avenue between 139th and 140th streets; #280 belonged to developer Edward Willis. New York City Landmarks Preservation Commission, "Mott Haven Historic District," 3. Among the commissioners were Jordan L. Mott, Gouverneur Morris, and William Cauldwell. See Westchester County, New York, *Map of the Town of Morrisania, made in pursuance of "An Act for the laying out, Opening and closing of Streets, Roads and Avenues, in the Town of Morrisania, in the County of Westchester, Passed May*

19, 1868," 6 Jan. 1871, Map Room, NYPL; Frisbee and Coles, *Morrisania and Tremont Directory.*

25. Beers, *Map of 23rd Ward, 1876*; Jenkins, *The Bronx*, 235, 268–69; *New York Times*, 20 July 1874.

26. *New York Times*, 17 March 1874. A letter to the *Times* in support of annexation claimed Port Morris had "ample" warehouse space and freight service to benefit New York City. *New York Times*, 17 May 1873.

27. Beers, *Atlas of New York, 1868.*

28. Schwartz, "Morrisania," 46, 69–73.

29. *Westchester Gazette*, 3 Oct. 1851; Schwartz, "Morrisania," 69–73, Elton quote is on 72.

30. Schwartz, "Morrisania," 46–48, 58–61; Robert Ernst, *Immigrant Life in New York City, 1825–1863* (New York: King's Crown Press, Columbia University, 1949), 132.

31. Schwartz, "Morrisania," 71–76. After 1853, the state legislature supervised the sale of Melrose lots when a defect was found in the will that had given William H. Morris title. See New York State, *Laws of 1853*, chap. 14.

32. This last premise is based on the location of two black churches within Melrose—St. Paul's African Methodist Church and the Second Congregational Church. The former began in Melrose in 1868 but by the turn of the century was at a Morrisania address. The latter's parishioners were originally in the First Congregational Church of Morrisania. Both were listed in directories and area newspapers during the 1870s. Frisbee and Coles, *Morrisania and Tremont Directory*, xxvi, 134; Special Term of the County Court of Westchester County, 27 June 1873, "In the Matter of the application of the religious Society known as 'St. Paul's African Methodist Episcopal Church' of Morrisania for leave to sell certain Real Estate and also to Mortgage certain other real estate," Chauncey Smith Papers, NYHS; *Westchester Clarion*, 28 Feb. 1873; *Westchester Times*, 20 Nov. 1874; *Morrisania Gazette*, 18 Sept. 1874; "List of Churches," *Federation* 2 (Dec. 1902): 60.

33. Immaculate Conception Church, *Diamond Jubilee Souvenir, 1853–May 1928* (Bronx, NY: Immaculate Conception Church, 1928), 15; Ultan, "1776–1940: The Story of the South Bronx," 31; WPA, Historical Records Survey, *Bronx Churches*, 3–11; "Bronx Borough Churches," in North Side Board of Trade, *The Great North Side*, 33–35; Colman J. Barry, *The Catholic Church and German Americans* (Milwaukee: The Bruce Publishing Company, 1953), 36–37; Schwartz, "Morrisania," 104–10, 181–83, 220–21, 333–35; Westchester County Bible Society, *Annual Report, 1864* (White Plains, NY: Westchester County Bible Society, 1864), 19.

34. Barry, *The Catholic Church and German Americans*, 4; Charles Dawson Shanley, "Germany in New York," *Atlantic Monthly* 19 (1867): 555–64; Jay P. Dolan, *The Immigrant Church: New York's Irish and German Catholics, 1815–1865* (Baltimore: Johns Hopkins University Press, 1975), 6–26; Ernst, *Immigrant Life in New York*, 41–42.

35. Schwartz, "Morrisania," 60–75; Frisbee and Coles, *Morrisania and Tremont Directory*.

36. Except for Dunham's piano factory and a few beer gardens, holdings larger than two or three lots were few in Melrose. Enterprises and institutions needing larger sites had to acquire lots bit by bit or look elsewhere. See Immaculate Conception Church, *Diamond Jubilee Souvenir*, 15.

37. The *Vereine* movement also extended to reform efforts, credit unions, and benevolent endeavors. See Ernst, *Immigrant Life in New York City*, 130–31; Barry, *The Catholic Church and German Americans*, 27; Carl Wittke, *We Who Built America: The Saga of the Immigrant* (New York: Prentice Hall, 1939), 219–28, 240; Augustus J. Prahl, "The Turner," in A. E. Zucker, ed., *The Forty-Eighters: Political Refugees of the German Revolution of 1848* (New York: Columbia University Press, 1950), 79–110.

38. *Sunday Mercury*, 14 Aug. 1859; Schwartz, "Morrisania," 107–14, 216–18; Dolan, *The Immigrant Church*, 31–32.

39. Frisbee and Coles, *Morrisania and Tremont Directory*; "Annual Report of the Railroad Commission for 1856," 487.

40. Of the 1,562 who listed occupations in Melrose, a full 33 percent (536) were in the building trades, with 301 laborers making up almost two thirds of that amount. The next largest occupational groups were tailors with 112, shoemakers 41, cigar makers 37, and piano makers with 34. Frisbee and Coles, *Morrisania and Tremont Directory*.

41. The original developer, Rober H. Elton, moved on to other village schemes in Eltona, Bensonia, and Wilton, and died at his Eltona home in 1863. Those from Melrose who would be influential in later years—as the Haffen and Bruckner families—were not yet at the forefront of community affairs. None of the commissioners for Morrisania's street plan came from Melrose. *Sunday Mercury*, 28 June 1863; Westchester County, *Map of the Town of Morrisania*, 1871.

42. M. Dripps, *Map of the Southern Part of Westchester County, 1853* (New York: M. Dripps, 1853).

43. New York City Planning Commission, *Plan for New York*, vol. 2, *The Bronx*, 36–42; South Bronx Development Organization, *South Bronx Industrial Fair* (New York: City of New York, State of New York, Port Authority of New York and New Jersey, no date).

44. Frisbee and Coles, *Morrisania and Tremont Directory*, v–vii; Schwartz, "Morrisania," 1–20, 23–28; "List of Original Lot Owners of Morrisania," MS, NYHS.

45. Schwartz, "Morrisania," 6–13, 20; Frisbee and Coles, *Morrisania and Tremont Directory*, v–vii.

46. "Gouverneur Morris to the several owners of Lots in village of Morrisania, Deed of Release," 25 July 1849; "Gouverneur Morris to Caroline E. Bovay, Benjamin J. Timms and others, Release in the Condition in the Deeds," 25 July 1849, Chauncey Smith Papers, NYHS.

47. Schwartz, "Morrisania," 20–27; *List of Original Lot Owners of Morrisania*; Frisbee and Coles, *Morrisania and Tremont Directory*, vi–vii, xi–xiii; "Gouverneur Morris to the several owners of Lots in village of Morrisania, Deed of Release," 25 July 1849, Chauncey Smith Papers, NYHS.

48. Dripps, *Map of the Southern Part of Westchester County, 1853*; John A. Henry, ed., *Henry's Directory of Morrisania and Vicinity for 1853–4* (Morrisania, NY: Spratley's Westchester Gazette Print, 1853), 5; H. R. Serrell, surveyor, "Map of the Village of Eltona," 6 June 1851, revised 14 Feb. 1852, Westchester County Maps Folder, NYHS; Schwartz, "Morrisania," 325.

49. Surveyed and laid out in early 1851, Central Morrisania was often overlooked by contemporary mapmakers because it was sandwiched between the more populated areas of Morrisania and Tremont. See reference to "Map of Central Morrisania," surveyed by A. Findley, 1 Feb. 1851, in J. H. Weyer to Chauncey Smith, 13 March 1868, Chauncey Smith Papers, NYHS; *Assessment Roll of the Town of West Farms for the Year 1857*, MSS, NYHS; description of the locality in John Homer French, *Gazetteer of the State of New York*, Empire State Historical Publications Series No. 72 (1860; reprint, Port Washington, NY: Ira J. Friedman, 1969), 707.

50. "Copy of Memo on File in Town Clerk's Office," 3 July 1855, Mott Papers, CU; Town of West Farms to Chauncey Smith, "Bill for laying out Highways in West Farms on the Bathgate Farm," Nov. 1863, Chauncey Smith Papers, NYHS. The premise that the Bathgates were haphazard real estate promoters is based on an overall reading of the sources, none of which deals specifically with the Bathgate family.

51. See Jordan L. Mott's comments in *Report of Committee Relative to the Reformed Dutch Church Edifice Erecting at Mott Haven*, 2, Chauncey Smith Papers, NYHS; Dripps, *Map of the Southern Part of Westchester County, 1853*; Henry, *Henry's Directory*, 5.

52. *New York Evening Post*, 26 Sept. 1849; Henry, *Henry's Directory*, 5; *Sunday Mercury*, 28 June 1863; Bert Sack, "Bensonia Cemetery," 1967, in Bert Sack, "Miscellaneous Historical Material," in Vertical File, NYPL; R. Henwood, surveyor, "Map of the Village of Grove Hill in the Town of West Farms, County of Westchester and State of New York," 1853, Westchester County Maps Folder, NYHS; Dripps, *Map of the Southern Part of Westchester County, 1853*; Schwartz, "Morrisania," 54; *New York Tribune*, 6 Sept. 1853; Beers, *Map of Town of Morrisania, ca. 1864*; Beers, *Atlas of New York and Vicinity, 1868*.

53. Dripps, *Map of the Southern Part of Westchester County, 1853*; N. Parker Willis, *Hurry-Graphs or, Sketches of Scenery, Celebrities and Society, Taken From Life*, 2nd ed. (New York: Charles Scribner, 1851), 130–31; New York City Planning Commission, *Plan for New York*, 1964, vol. 2, *The Bronx*, 26.

54. Henry, *Henry's Directory*.

55. New York State, *Census for 1865*, xliv–lvi, 15–16.

56. "Communication from the Secretary of State Showing the Population in Each Election District of the City of New York," 1876; Beers, *Map of the Town of*

Morrisania, ca. 1864; Bromley, *Atlas of the Entire City of New York, 1879* (New York: Geo. W. Bromley & E. Robinson); *Sunday Mercury*, 20 Nov., 29 Nov. 1859; 6 Sept. 1868; Henry B. Dawson, "Rambles in Westchester County, New York, A Fragment," in Henry B. Dawson, ed., *The Gazette Series* 5 (Yonkers, NY, 1866): 2.

57. Frisbee and Coles, *Morrisania and Tremont Directory.*

58. Mott bought and sold lots all over lower Westchester County. Elton dealt in Melrose and Wilton properties; McGraw speculated in West Morrisania, South Fordham, Westchester, Upper Morrisania, Adamsville, Fairmount, Brooklyn, and the Bathgate farm; while East Morrisania investor D. Winton also sold Harlem lots. See Mott Papers, CU; Chauncey Smith Papers, NYHS; *New York Tribune*, 1 March 1851; *Sunday Mercury*, 18 Sept. 1859; 28 June 1863; Frisbee and Coles, *Morrisania and Tremont Directory*, xi.

59. The Morrisania area bridged the gap between the mostly old-stock American population of Mott Haven and the predominantly German composition of Melrose.

60. WPA, Historical Records Survey, *Bronx Churches*, 1–10; "Bronx Borough Churches," 31–37; St. Augustine's Church, *Golden Jubilee, 1849–1899* (New York, 8 Oct. 1899). Most Catholic Germans in the vicinity attended St. Augustine's until the creation of the German Catholic church in Melrose in 1853.

61. Giordano, "A History of the Morrisania Section of the Bronx in Three Periods: 1875, 1925, 1975" (M.A. thesis, Columbia University, 1981), 37–44; Schwartz, "Morrisania," 117–18.

62. Occupational and thus class patterns by village or section can be discerned in the listings of the *Morrisania and Tremont Directory*. See also Schwartz, "Morrisania," 83–127; Giordano, "A History of the Morrisania Section of the Bronx," 44–50.

63. Schwartz, "Morrisania," 83–127.

64. An example of this character type was attorney Chauncey Smith. An early resident of Morrisania and a small-time speculator in lower Westchester property, Smith was a founder of the Centenary Methodist Church of Morrisania and a member of the school board who also belonged to many reform associations and Morrisania's baseball club. See Chauncey Smith Papers, NYHS; Schwartz, "Morrisania," 87–100; Morrisania Bible Society, *Constitution and By-Laws* (Morrisania, NY: Morrisania Bible Society, 1860); *Morrisania Gazette*, 18 Sept. 1874.

65. The German community of Morrisania village and its environs was intimately connected to that of Melrose. Morrisania village Germans had a *Turnverein* that drew recruits from the entire town but also had local singing and shooting societies, the Morrisania Mannechor and the Schutzen Gilde. *Sunday Mercury*, 10 July 1859, 3 June 1860, 30 June 1866; Schwartz, "Morrisania," 139.

66. East Morrisania's Monitor Engine Co. No. 2 attracted local Irish and German residents. (That three of its members were laborers in 1866 underscores the slightly more working-class aspect of East Morrisania vis-à-vis Eltona and the

elevated portions of Morrisania village.) Morrisania village's three fire crews were more diverse; only one—in the more compact "downtown" area—was over two-thirds German. Fire Department of the Town of Morrisania, *Annual Report of the Chief Engineer* (Morrisania, NY, 1866); Schwartz, "Morrisania," 170–72, 181–89, 332, 336–37.

67. The Irish were consistently third in number throughout the preannexation years. While far from the Catholic churches of the area, East Morrisania and Woodstock did have significant pockets of Irish-surnamed residents. Schwartz, "Morrisania," 83–127, and passim. The columns of the short-lived *Morrisania Gazette*, August to December 1874, published by Henry B. Dawson, dealt exclusively with the doings of the native-born, Protestant American community. The Germans had their own newspaper, the *Deutsches Volksblatt*. There is one, unfortunately mutilated, copy in the New-York Historical Society.

68. Schwartz, "Morrisania," 128–65; Stephen Wray, "Westchester's Only Draft Riot," MS, NYHS; New York State, *Laws of 1864*, chap. 277.

69. Frisbee and Coles, *Morrisania and Tremont Directory*, xviii, xxii; *Sunday Mercury*, 30 Oct., 13 Nov. 1859. The premise that most township residents, regardless of class, ethnicity, or section, had a unanimity of thinking on certain subjects is based on an overall reading of the primary sources. Incorporation papers, New York State laws, and the company listings of the *Morrisania and Tremont Directory* are only a few of the documents that reveal the varied and shifting coalitions that backed rail lines, horesecars, river improvements, road building, street pavings, and annexation to New York City.

70. It could not have been otherwise when improvements from rapid transit to paving were judged on the number of people they would attract to the area. See Henry B. Dawson's lament in *The Plain Dealer*, Jan. 1869. On real estate expectations throughout the newly annexed region, see the newspaper articles reprinted in Potter Brothers, Brokers for the Sale of Real Estate in the new wards, *Map of the Northern Portion of the City of New York, Comprising the 12th Ward, and the new 23rd and 24th Wards* (New York, 1873), Map Room, NYPL.

71. Frisbee and Coles, *Morrisania and Tremont Directory*, xviii–xxi; Jenkins, *The Bronx*, 368–69; J. L. Mott to Morrisania Township Board, 25 March 1865; *New York Times*, 25 Feb., 29 March 1873; 26 March, 29 Sept. 1874; *Morrisania Gazette*, 14 Aug. 1874; J. L. Mott to Morrisania Township Board, 25 March 1865; J. L. Mott to the Committee on Roads & Bridges, April 1866, Mott Papers, CU. See also Schwartz, "Morrisania," 15, 164–270. The quote by Dr. Harris is on 249–50.

72. The presence of two black churches indicated some African Americans lived in the Melrose vicinity.

3. THE CHANGING LANDSCAPE

1. Matthew P. Breen, *Thirty Years of New York Politics* (New York: the author, 1899), 726–29; *New York Evening Post*, 27 March 1897.

2. John Foord, *The Life and Public Services of Andrew Haswell Green* (Garden City, NY: Doubleday, Page & Company, 1913), 71–75; George Alexander Mazaraki, "The Public Career of Andrew Haswell Green" (Ph.D. diss., New York University, 1966), 94–100, 104. Quotes from Green; "Communication . . . Relative to Westchester County, Harlem River, and Spuyten Duyvil Creek, 30 December 1868," 148; New York State, *Laws of 1869*, chap. 826, 11 May 1869.

3. *New York Times*, 6 Nov. 1873; New York State, *Laws of 1874*, chaps. 329 and 604.

4. "Report of the Commissioners of the Central Park in Compliance with the Provisions of 'An Act for the Improvement of Certain Parts of Westchester County, Harlem River and Spuyten Duyvil Creek, passed 11 May 1869,' 24 March 1870," in New York State, *Senate Documents, 1870*, vol. 3, no. 76; "Report of the Commissioners of Department of Public Parks, 15 March 1871"; Henry G. Stebbins quoted in "Appendix A, 31 December 1872," New York City, Department of Public Parks, *Documents*, no. 54, p. 10 (hereafter cited as *Parks Documents*); *Third General Report of the Board of Commissioners of the Department of Public Parks, From May 1st, 1872, to December 31st, 1873* (New York: William C. Bryant & Co., 1875), quote on 23.

5. William H. Grant, Civil and Topographical Engineer, quoted in "Appendix E," in *Third General Report of the Board of Commissioners of the Department of Public Parks, May 1st, 1872, to December 31st, 1873*, quote on 233.

6. "Report of Hon. Wm. R. Martin, President, upon the subject of laying-out the Twenty-third and Twenty-fourth Wards, 20 December 1876," *Parks Documents*, no. 73, pp. 2–3. The progress of the plans during the 1870s can be followed in the reports, memoranda, and communications of the Department of Parks in *The City Record*. On Olmsted, see Laura Wood Roper, *FLO: A Biography of Frederick Law Olmsted* (Baltimore: Johns Hopkins University Press, 1973), 360; Frederick Law Olmsted Jr. and Theodora Kimbal, eds., *Forty Years of Landscape Architecture*, 2 vols. (New York: G. P. Putnam's Sons, 1928), 2:104–55.

7. Department of Public Parks, "Abstract of the Proceedings of the Board of Commissioners, January 5, 1878" (hereafter cited as "DPP Proceedings") in *The City Record*, 16 Jan. 1878; Department of Public Parks, "Reports for the Quarters June 30, 1877, June 30, September 30, 1878, March 31, 1879" (hereafter cited as "DPP Quarterly Report") in *The City Record*, 20 Aug. 1877, 30 July, 9 Dec. 1878, 10 April 1879; Breen, *Thirty Years of New York Politics*, 728–29; *Record and Guide*, 23 Oct. 1886, 10 Dec. 1887, 18 Feb., 1 Dec. 1888. Mayor Grant quoted in *Record and Guide*, 9 March 1889.

8. "Communication from Commissioner Martin relative to public improvements, 5 March 1875," *Parks Documents*, no. 64; "A communication from Commissioner William R. Martin relative to the plans and improvement of the Fort Washington district, and the 23rd and 24th Wards, 30 March 1875," *Parks Documents*, no. 65, especially quotes on 24–26; "Report of Wm. R. Martin upon the Twenty-third and Twenty-fourth Wards, 20 December 1876"; *New York Times*, 21 March 1874; *Record and Guide*, 31 Jan. 1880. Martin urged that all streets in a district be opened at once, thus saving time and

expense. This was eventually done late in the 1890s. See *Record and Guide*, 20 Feb. 1897.

9. See Olmsted and Croes's reports for 1876, 1877, and 1887, in *Parks Documents*, nos. 72, 75, and 76. Documents 72 and 75 and the map that accompanies the latter are conveniently reprinted in Albert Fein, ed., *Landscape Into Cityscape: Frederick Law Olmsted's Plans for a Greater New York City* (Ithaca, NY: Cornell University Press, 1968). For Olmsted's urban planning concepts see Fein, ed., *Landscape Into Cityscape*; Albert Fein, "Frederick Law Olmsted: His Development as a Theorist and Designer of the American City" (Ph.D. diss., Columbia University, 1969). For the zoning aspect of Olmsted's work see Irving David Fisher, "Frederick Law Olmsted and the Philosophic Background to the City Planning Movement in the United States," 2 vols. (Ph.D. diss., Columbia University, 1976), 2:358–60; Olmsted Jr. and Kimbal, *Forty Years of Landscape Architecture*, 2:191–92; David Schuyler, *The New Urban Landscape: The Redefinition of City Form in Nineteenth-Century America* (Baltimore: Johns Hopkins University Press, 1988), chapter 8.

10. John W. Reps, *The Making of Urban America: A History of City Planning in the United States* (Princeton: Princeton University Preas, 1965), 296–99; Gunther Barth, *City People: The Rise of Modern City Culture in Nineteenth-Century America* (New York: Oxford University Press, 1980), 30–31.

11. "Report of Commissioner Stebbins upon the plans for laying out that part of the Twenty-fourth Ward lying west of Riverdale Road, 28 February 1877," in *Parks Documents*, no. 74, especially 6–12, quotes from 7, 9–11; "Memorandum by George S. Greene for streets between the Hudson River and the Croton Aqueduct, September 1875," in previous report cited, 16; Olmsted and Croes, "II. Report Accompanying a Plan . . . for west of the Riverdale Road, 1876,"in *Parks Documents*, no. 72, p. 14.

12. *Proceedings of the North Side Association of the 23rd and 24th Wards of the City of New York for the Year 1874* (New York: Torrey Brothers, 1875), quote from 2; *Minutes of the Board of Estimate and Apportionment of the City and County of New York, 1880*, quote from "October 1880, Petition of Property Owners," 598–602. The Parks Department proceedings in the *City Record* and the minutes of the Board of Estimate and Apportionment are littered with calls for street openings and improvements between 1874 and the early 1880s.

13. Seymour J. Mandelbaum, *Boss Tweed's New York* (New York: Wiley, 1965), 89–130; Mazaraki, "Public Career of A. H. Green," 213–88. The depression's effect on real estate lasted six years. *Record and Guide*, 24 May 1879. Street openings were restricted to thoroughfares that were already in use and shorter than a mile. According to a 1874 law, the city would pay half the cost of opening streets longer than a mile in the new wards. Enacted as a concession to Bronxites, this law proved a further impediment to public improvements until it was repealed in the 1890s. *Record and Guide*, 18 Oct. 1890, 14 Jan. 1893.

14. See Department of Parks Quarterly Reports and Proceedings in *The City*

Record and *Minutes of the Board of Estimate and Apportionment* from 1874 to 1890; *Record and Guide*, 18 Dec. 1880.

15. "Report of the Special Committee of the Senate in Relation to the Public Affairs of the Twenty-third and Twenty-fourth Wards of the City of New York, 26 February 1890," in New York State, *Senate Documents*, 1890, vol. 4, no. 36, p. 6.

16. Quoted in *Record and Guide*, 9 June 1888; "Report of the Special Committee, 26 February 1890," 5.

17. The commissioner was elected for a six-year term. Though he was not responsible to the mayor, his proposals had to be approved by the Board of Street Openings and Improvement, to which both he and the mayor belonged. New York State, *Laws of 1890*, chap. 545; *Record and Guide*, 19, 26 April, 2 Aug. 1890; Breen, *Thirty Years of New York Politics*, 738–42.

18. *New York Evening Post*, 5, 6 Dec. 1889; 7 Oct. 1890; Breen, *Thirty Years of New York Politics*, 730–45. The only two who opposed "the remedy proposed by the taxpayers' association" at the Senate committee hearings were William Caudwell, long associated with back-room Democratic politics, and Louis L. Delafield, a wealthy, influential Riverdale property owner. See "Report of the Special Committee, 26 February 1890," 7.

19. The Citizens' Party was guided by knowledgeable politicians—assemblyman and later magistrate Matthew P. Breen was counsel, Republican John H. Knoeppel led the party, and former Tammany district leader John H. J. Ronner headed the finance committee. The party continued running candidates in 1891. James Lee Wells, a real estate broker and auctioneer and once rumored as candidate for Commissioner of Street Improvements, became the new assemblyman for the Twenty-fourth District. Heintz was nephew and partner of John Eichler, another committee member and a leading brewer in the northern wards. Breen, *Thirty Years of New York Politics*, 744–50; *New York Evening Post*, 25 Oct. 1890; *Proceedings of the Board of Estimate and Apportionment*, 1890, 270–71; *Record and Guide*, 24 Oct. 1891.

20. *New York Times*, 24 Jan. 1891. The layout was finished in 1895. *Record and Guide*, 27 May, 1 April 1893; Department of Street Improvements, Twenty-third and Twenty-fourth Wards, *Report for the Three Months ending December 31, 1895, and Summary for the Year* (New York: Martin B. Brown, 1896) (hereafter cited as "DSI Quarterly Report").

21. *New York Times*, 11 Oct. 1891; *Record and Guide*, 3 July, 17 Oct. 1891; "DSI Quarterly Report, 31 December 1891," in *The City Record*, 26 March 1892, 1046. See also map of Hunts Point in *Record and Guide*, 16 April 1892.

22. *Record and Guide*, 16 June 1888, 3 July 1891 (Risse was the Chief Engineer of the Department of Street Improvements).

23. *New York Times*, 4 Jan., 11 Oct. 1891; *Record and Guide*, 10, 17 Oct. 1891.

24. The extent of the Department of Street Improvements' operations is revealed in the quarterly reports from 1891 to 1897, published separately; in *The City Record*; and in the columns of the *Record and Guide*. See especially "DSI

Quarterly Report, 31 December 1891," in *The City Record*, 26 March 1892, 1047; *Record and Guide*, 9 April 1892, 18 March 1893; *New York Evening Post*, 8 June 1895, quotes from 8 July 1893.

25. "DSI Quarterly Reports, 31 December 1893, 31 December 1895," in *The City Record*, 24 May 1894, 5 June 1896; *New York Evening Post*, 27 March 1897. The Grand Concourse was originally conceived by Louis A. Risse, laid out by Heintz, and eventually begun by Haffen. Landowners along its route unanimously approved the project. *New York Evening Post*, 16 March 1895.

26. "DSI Quarterly Report, 31 December 1893"; North Side Board of Trade, *Address of John C. De La Vergne, President of the North Side Board of Trade, delivered at its first meeting held at the Melrose Lyceum, March 6th, 1894*. The more suburban portion of the Bronx that was annexed in 1895 would also get an urban street pattern. Its original street plan, designed by Louis A. Risse and approved in 1898, was replaced in 1903 by a loose grid of streets between the old meandering thoroughfares that still existed. See *Report of the President of the Borough of The Bronx, December 31, 1903* (New York: Martin B. Brown, 1904), 84–85; *Report of the President of the Borough of The Bronx, December 31, 1902* (New York: Mail and Express Company, 1903), 24; Albert E. Davis, *The Borough Beautiful: A Bronx Opportunity being a paper read before the New York City Improvement Commission, July 27, 1904* (New York, 1904).

27. John Mullaly, *The New Parks Beyond the Harlem* (New York: Real Estate Record and Builders Guide, 1887), 42–43, 112, quotes on 16, 43; *Record and Guide*, 20 May 1882; *New York Herald*, 17 May 1882.

28. Mazaraki, "Public Career of A. H. Green," 101–5; *Third General Report of the Department of Public Parks, May 1, 1872 to December 31, 1873*, 235–37. Quoted in Letter to the editor, signed AN OLD NEW-YORKER, *New York Times*, 6 Sept. 1869.

29. *New York Times*, 6 Feb. 1874; "DPP Proceedings, 26 January 1874," in *The City Record*, 6 Feb. 1874; Frederick Law Olmsted and J. J. R. Croes, "Communication from the Landscape Architect and the Civil and Topographical Engineer, in relation to the proposed plan for laying out the Central District of the Twenty-fourth Ward, lying east of Jerome Avenue and west of Third Avenue and the Harlem Railroad, 7 November 1877;" *Parks Documents*, no. 76; "Communication from Commissioner William R. Martin relative to the plans and improvement of the Fort Washington district, and the 23rd and 24th Wards, 30 March 1875"; "Report of Wm. R. Martin upon the Twenty-third and Twenty-fourth Wards, 20 Dec. 1876."

30. Luther R. Marsh, *New Parks: Luther R. Marsh's Reply to the Memorial of Mayor Grace Against the New Parks Act* (New York: C. G. Burgoyne, 1885), 14–15.

31. *New York Herald*, 18 Sept., 9, 23 Oct., 12 Nov. 1881.

32. *New York Herald*, 18 Sept., 23 Oct. 1881.

33. The New York Park Association was formed two months after Mullaly's first article on November 26. *New York Herald*, 27 Nov. 1881. A list of officers and

executive committee members are in Mullaly, *The New Parks Beyond the Harlem*, 111. Nine of the twenty-nine members were prominent Bronxites. Many supporters were members of the North Side Association. *New York Herald*, 2, 12, 19 March 1882.

34. The meetings were extensively reported in the *New York Herald*, 5, 12, 17, 19 March 1882, quote is from 23 Oct. 1881; *Record and Guide*, 8 April, 20, 27 May, 3 June 1882. See also the pamphlets published by the New York Park Association, all probably written by Mullaly, including the ones attributed to Park Association president Luther R. Marsh. *More Public Parks: How New York Compares with other Cities, Lungs for the Metropolis, The Financial and Sanitary Aspects of the Question* (New York, 1882); *The Demand of the People for More Public Parks* (New York, 1884); *The Park Question* (New York, ca. 1884); *New Parks: Luther R. Marsh's Reply to Mayor Grace*; and "[Unsigned petition to the Mayor, William R. Grace,] upon the subject of the advisibility of a public park for said district," William R. Grace, Mayors' Papers, no date, Box 111, New York City Municipal Archives.

35. New York Park Association, *More Public Parks*, 14; *New York Herald*, 23 Oct. 1881.

36. New York State, *Laws of 1884*, chap. 522. Governor Grover Cleveland signed the act on June 14, 1884. *Record and Guide*, 21 June 1884; *Report to the New York Legislature of the Commission to Select and Locate Lands for Public Parks in the Twenty-third and Twenty-fourth Wards of the City of New York, and in the Vicinity Thereof* (New York: Martin B. Brown, 1884), 32–33, quote on 33; *Sunday Mercury*, 23 Sept. 1883; *New York Herald*, 23 Oct. 1881.

37. Fordham Morris's comments are quoted in the *New York Herald*, 17 May 1882. The argument, however, was propounded in all the articles and pamphlets of Mullaly and the New York Park Association. The reference to children rather than sheep alluded to the Sheep Meadow in Central Park. See also *Record and Guide*, 20 May 1882; *New York Herald*, 2 March 1882.

38. This opposition is described in Mullaly, *New Parks Beyond the Harlem*, 117–61. The park bill was eventually upheld by the courts on April 20, 1886. See also the letters, petitions, and testimony in Mayor Grace Papers, Box 111, NYC Municipal Archives; Simon Sterne, *The Park Act of 1884: Its Dangers and Consequences, An Open Letter to the Citizens of New York* (New York: Committee of Twenty-five Taxpayers Appointed at the Mass Meeting at Chickering Hall, [1885]). Supporters fought back with their own propaganda. See *New Parks: Luther R. Marsh's Reply to the Memorial of Mayor Grace Against the New Parks Act*; Luther R. Marsh, *The Sinking Fund and the New Parks* (New York, 1885?); *The Future of New York: Remarks by Luther R. Marsh at the First Panel Sheriff's Dinner, 14 January 1885* (New York: Dempsey & Carroll Print, 1885); and E. B. Hinsdale, *The New Parks: Opinion of E. B. Hinsdale On the Question Raised as to the Power of the City of New York to Issue Bonds for Public Improvement by Reason of the Constitutional Amendment* (New York: C. G. Burgoyne, 1884).

39. *New York Evening Post*, 31 March 1900, 12 June 1901; Chas. H. Ludewig, *A Quiet Holiday in the Bronx* (New York: the author, 1899), unpaged, pamphlet at NYPL.

40. Mullaly, *New Parks Beyond the Harlem*, 38–47; *New York Herald*, 23 Oct. 1881.

41. *Report to the New York Legislature of the Commission to Select and Locate Lands for Public Parks in the Twenty-third and Twenty-fourth Wards.* This last premise is based on an overall assessment of all the sources.

42. *Proceedings of the North Side Association, 1874,* 10–16; *New York Times*, 10 Jan., 16 March 1879; *Record and Guide*, 3 Feb. 1883.

43. Bronx interests were investing in transit proposals years before annexation. James Blaine Walker, *Fifty Years of Rapid Transit: 1854 to 1917* (1918; reprint, New York: Arno Press and *New York Times*, 1970), 69, 94–96, 101–5. On filling in the Harlem River, see *Record and Guide*, 16 June 1883; *New York Times*, 4 Jan. 1891.

44. Olmsted and Croes, "Report for local steam transit routes," *Parks Documents*, no. 75, quotes on 4, 8.

45. *The Minutes of Proceedings of the Board of Commissioners of Rapid Transit, in the City of New York, From July to December, 1875* (New York: Martin B. Brown, 1877); *New York Tribune*, 28 Dec. 1879; William Fullerton Reeves, *The First Elevated Railroads in Manhattan and the Bronx of the City of New York: The Story of Their Development and Progress* (New York: The New-York Historical Society, 1936), 24–32. The Third Avenue line reached 129th Street in December 1879, the Second Avenue one, a year and a half later in August 1880. The Ninth Avenue El arrived at the Harlem River at 155th Street and Eighth Avenue on November 7, 1879. If continued across, this line would have entered the 23rd Ward in a less populous area, at the spot where Yankee Stadium would later stand.

46. "Resolutions passed by the Commissioners of Rapid Transit, in session June 10, 1879," in New York City, *Proceedings of the Board of Aldermen, 1879* (New York: Martin B. Brown, 1879), vol. 154, p. 814; "Report of the New Rapid Transit Commissioners, 8 December 1879," reprinted in *New York Times*, 11 Dec. 1879; "Report of the Rapid Transit Commissioners, of 16 June 1881," New York City, *Proceedings of the Board of Aldermen, 1881–1882*, vol. 164, p. 453; *New York Tribune*, 28 Dec. 1879; *Record and Guide*, 10 April 1880, 27 Aug. 1881, 18 March 1882.

47. Quotes in *New York Tribune*, 28 Dec. 1879. See also "Report of the Rapid Transit Commissioners, of 16 June 1881."

48. Reeves, *The First Elevated Railroads in Manhattan and the Bronx*, 34–38.

49. *Commercial and Financial Chronicle*, 5 Dec. 1885; *Record and Guide*, 3 Feb. 1883, 12 Dec. 1885, quote from 12 Jan. 1884; Julius Grodinsky, *Jay Gould: His Business Career, 1867–1892* (Philadelphia: University of Pennsylvania Press, 1957), 288–316, 572. In 1891, the Suburban Rapid Transit became part of the Manhattan Railway Company, the owner of the Manhattan els. See Reeves, *The First Elevated Railroads in Manhattan and the Bronx*, 38.

50. E. Robinson and R. H. Pidgeon, *Robinson's Atlas of the City of New York, 1885* (New York: E. Robinson, 1885); George W. Bromley and Walter S. Bromley, *Atlas of The City of New York, 23rd & 24th Wards, 1897* (Philadelphia: G. W. Bromley and Co., 1897); the Buildings Projected listings in the *Record and Guide*, 1879 to 1898; Reeves, *The First Elevated Railroads in Manhattan and the Bronx*, 36–41.

51. *New York Evening Post*, 23 Aug. 1892, 24 March 1894, 20 Jan. 1896, 9 Jan. 1900; *Record and Guide*, 7 March 1891, quote in 25 Aug. 1894; Bromley, *Atlas of The City of New York*, 1897; Buildings Projected listings in *Record and Guide*, 1879 to 1898. For more on the Union Railway, see Gustavus Myers, *The History of Public Franchises in New York City (Boroughs of Manhattan and the Bronx)* (New York: Reform Club Committee on City Affairs, 1900), 136–37, 150–51; Robert Clarkson Brooks, "History of the Street and Rapid Transit Railways of New York City" (Ph.D. diss., Cornell University, 1903), 283–88.

52. Bronx surface lines crossed the Harlem River at the Third Avenue Bridge and thus reached the el trains before meeting the Manhattan trolleys. In 1898, the Third Avenue Railroad Company took over the former Huckleberry line. Reeves, *The First Elevated Railroads in Manhattan and the Bronx*, 36–41; *New York Evening Post*, 14 Jan. 1898.

53. Reeves, *The First Elevated Railroads in Manhattan and the Bronx*, 35–38; *Record and Guide*, 15 Aug. 1899, 7 April 1900; *New York Evening Post*, 30 Oct. 1901. On Boston transit, see Sam Bass Warner Jr., *Streetcar Suburbs: The Process of Growth in Boston, 1870–1900* (Cambridge: Harvard University Press and MIT Press, 1962).

54. Walker, *Fifty Years of Rapid Transit*; Chamber of Commerce of the State of New York, *Rapid Transit in New York City and in Other Great Cities* (New York: Chamber of Commerce of the State of New York, 1906).

55. Brooks, "History of the Street and Rapid Transit Railways of New York City," 252; petitions in New York City, *Proceedings of the Board of Aldermen, 1885 to 1887*, vols. 179, 181, 183, 184.

56. *Report of the Board of Rapid Transit Railroad Commissioners in and for the City of New York to the Common Council of the City of New York: In pursuance of the provisions of section 5 of Chapter 4 of the Laws of 1891, October 20, 1891* (New York, 1891); *Record and Guide*, 17 Nov. 1894, 7 April 1900; *Third Annual Report of the Secretary of the North Side Board of Trade of the City of New York* (New York, March 6, 1897), 8; *Address of Albert E. Davis, president of the North Side Board of Trade, delivered at its Meeting Held at 520 Willis Avenue, January 27, 1903* (New York: North Side News Book and Job Print, 1903). See petitions by the Taxpayers' Association of Morrisania and Chester, the Jerome Avenue Property Owners' Association, the North Side Board of Trade, the Association of Bronx Real Estate Brokers, the Bronx Board of Brokers, the Bronx Committee of One Hundred, and the Taxpayers' Alliance, *Record and Guide*, 11 Feb. 1905, 12 Oct., 28 Dec. 1907, 15 Feb. 1908. In 1891, the Rapid Transit League's president was long-time booster and property owner Jordan L.

Mott, son of the original developer of Mott Haven. *Record and Guide*, 7 March 1891.

57. Quotes from *Record and Guide*, 24 May 1890, 17 Nov. 1894, 6 April 1901.

58. For the link between land values and rapid transit see Edwin Harold Spengler, *Land Values in New York in Relation to Transit Facilities* (1930; reprint, New York: AMS Press, 1968); James Leslie Davis, *The Elevated System and the Growth of Northern Chicago* (Evanston, IL: Department of Geography, Northwestern University, 1965). Specific examples of the Bronx are found in *Record and Guide*, 11 June 1894, 3 March 1900.

59. Rapid transit quote in *New York Times*, 14 April 1907. North Side Board of Trade, *Address of Albert E. Davis*, 27 Jan. 1903.

60. *New York Evening Post*, 10 Jan., 11 Feb. 1905; City Plan Committee, Municipal Art Society of New York, *A Discussion of the Rapid Transit Problem in and About New York City* (New York: Municipal Art Society of New York, 1905), Bulletins No. 14 and 20.

61. *New York Evening Post*, 20 Feb. 1905.

62. The compromise was a direct outcome of the Rapid Transit Act of 1894, which gave the transit commmmissioners the right to build and operate rapid transit routes for and on account of the city. Walker, *Fifty Years of Rapid Transit*; Chamber of Commerce of the State of New York, *Rapid Transit in New York City and in Other Great Cities*. In 1907, the Broadway subway stopped just north of the Harlem Ship Canal at 225th Street; it inched across Spuyten Duyvil Creek into Kingsbridge in 1908. Bion J. Arnold, *Reports Upon Interborough Subway* (New York: Martin B. Brown Press, 1908), Report no. 6, pp. 10–11; William A. Tieck, *Riverdale, Kingsbridge, Spuyten Duyvil: A Historical Epitome of the Northwest Bronx* (Old Tappen, NJ: Fleming H. Revell Co., 1968), 41–46, 136–40.

63. This premise is in Peter Derrick, *Tunneling to the Future: The Story of the Great Subway Expansion That Saved New York* (New York: New York University Press, 2001), 90–185; but see also City Plan Committee, Municipal Art Society of New York, *A Discussion of the Rapid Transit Problem in and About New York City*, Bulletin No. 14; John Martin, *Rapid Transit: Its Effect on Rents and Living Conditions and How to Get It* (New York: The Committee on Congestion of Population, March 1909); Pratt, *Industrial Causes of Congestion of Population in New York City*, 192–96; State of New York, *Dual System of Rapid Transit for New York City* (New York: Public Service Commission for First District, September 1912).

64. Peter E. Derrick, "The New York City Transit Crisis of 1918–1925" (M.A. thesis, Columbia University, 1967).

65. These observations are based on an analysis of insurance maps, projected building plans, Department of Buildings reports, and accounts in the contemporary press.

66. Quoted in James L. Wells, Louis F. Haffen, and Josiah A. Briggs, eds., *The Bronx and Its People: A History, 1609–1927*, 3 vols. (New York: The Louis Historical Publishing Co., 1927), 2:807.

67. The city built water mains, 20 schools, and 8 bridges between 1879 and 1908. The Third Avenue, McCombs Dam, and Broadway bridges replaced older crossings; the Willis Avenue, Madison Avenue, 149th Street, Washington, and University Heights bridges created new links to Manhattan. The Harlem Ship Canal was completed in 1895. *Record and Guide*, 12 Feb. 1887; *New York Evening Post*, 24 March 1894; *New York Times*, 24 March 1895; New York City Department of Bridges, *Report of the Commissioner of Bridges, December 31, 1898* (New York: The Martin B. Brown Company, 1899); Jenkins, *The Bronx*, 188–208; James L. Wells, *The Completion of the Harlem Ship Canal: Statement Submitted to the Committee on Rivers and Harbors, House of Representatives* (New York: The North Side Board of Trade, January 1907).

4. EMERGING NEIGHBORHOODS

1. Plan of New York and Its Environs, *Plan of New York and Its Environs: The Meeting of May 10, 1922* (New York: Russell Sage Foundation, 1922), n.p.
2. William Fullerton Reeves, *The First Elevated Railroads in Manhattan and the Bronx of the City of New York: The Story of Their Development and Progress* (New York: The New-York Historical Society, 1936), 35.
3. William H. Grant to Henry G. Stebbins, "Appendix A, 31 December 1872," *Parks Documents*, no. 54, pp. 18–19; "Communication from Commissioner Martin relative to the Fort Washington district and the 23d and 24th Wards, 30 March 1875"; "Report of Wm. R. Martin upon the Twenty-third and Twenty-fourth Wards, 20 December 1876," quotes on 19; *Record and Guide*, 24 Oct. 1891, 16 April 1892; Department of Street Improvements, Twenty-third and Twenty-fourth Wards, *Report for the Three Months ending December 31, 1896, and Summary for the Year* (New York: Martin B. Brown, 1897). The main improvement in Mott Haven was diverting the "stagnating" Mill Brook into a covered drain. See E. B. Van Winkle, "A Report from the Topographical Engineer on the drainage of the Twenty-third and Twenty-fourth Wards, 2 March 1881," *Parks Documents*, no. 88, p. 48.
4. Mott Haven interests continued supporting policies that would enhance their holdings. In the 1880s and 1890s, such old standbys as Jordan L. Mott Jr., Lewis B. Brown, and Gouverneur Morris were joined by William Reynolds Brown, William O'Gorman, and John K. Knoeppel. See *Minutes of the Board of Estimate and Apportionment, 1880*, 600–601; *Proceedings of the Board of Estimate and Apportionment, 1890*, 260. John J. Crane, owner of property south of St. Mary's Park, was on the Board of Directors of the Suburban Rapid Transit Company. *Record and Guide*, 13 Oct. 1883.
5. *Minutes of the Board of Estimate and Apportionment, 1884* (New York: Evening Post Job Printing Office, 1885), 116–17; Department of Bridges, *Report of the Commissioner of Bridges, 1898*, 43–48; Marsh, *The Sinking Fund and the New Parks*, 36, 42–43; *Record and Guide*, 31 Oct. 1885, 9 April, 13 Aug., 24 Sept., 29 Oct. 1887, 14 June 1890, 31 Oct. 1896. Mott Haven boosters

had pressed for the 138th Street bridge right after annexation. *New York Times*, 29 Sept. 1874.

6. The Mott Haven el stations were at 133rd Street (opened on May 17, 1886), 138th Street (opened on January 1, 1887), and 143rd Street (opened on May 23, 1886). The 149th Street Station was not opened until late summer 1887. Reeves, *The First Elevated Railroads in Manhattan and The Bronx*, 35–36; E. Robinson and R. H. Pidgeon, *Robinson's Atlas of the City of New York, 1885* (New York: E. Robinson, 1885); *Record and Guide*, 17, 31 Oct. 1885, 11 June 1887.

7. Beyond proximity to el stations and the el line, land values depended upon whether the lot had full urban services and whether it was on an avenue or cross street, on a corner or within the block. The real estate columns of the *Record and Guide*, 1880 to 1898, reveal the amount and extent of rising land prices in Mott Haven. See also *New York Times*, 31 March 1895.

8. Streetcar lines did not materially affect the neighborhood's growth in this period, because they were slow and unreliable before their electrification in 1894 and had higher fares than the el trains. New trolley routes that might have had some input were not completed until later in the 1890s. *Record and Guide*, 7 March 1891, 16 July 1892; *New York Times*, 24 March 1895.

9. O'Gorman and sometime partner Herman Stursberg continued planning more rows of houses in the neighborhood after 1887, eventually building as many as 300 houses from 138th to 142nd streets. *Record and Guide*, 23 Oct. 1880, 9 April 1881, 11 April 1885, 19 March 1887, 24 April 1897.

10. Sales of land belonging to early Bronx investors continued throughout the 1880s and 1890s. In 1889, the Brown Estate, consisting of 124 separate lots on Southern Boulevard, Alexander, and Brook avenues, sold for a total of $3,056 per lot. Edward Hirsch specialized in buying and reselling lots with loans to builders. *Record and Guide*, 23 March, 13 April 1889, 2 May 1991, 27 Aug. 1892.

11. Construction peaked dramatically in 1887, continued high until the sharp economic downturn of 1893, and increased steadily after the mid-1890s. In the late 1890s, builders from distant Brooklyn and New Jersey joined the host of Bronx builders operating in Mott Haven. This and following descriptions of building activity are based on the Buildings Projected listings in the *Record and Guide*, 1879 to 1898; Robinson and Pidgeon, *Robinson's Atlas of New York, 1885*; George W. and Walter S. Bromley, *Atlas of the City of New York, 23rd & 24th Wards, 1893* (Philadelphia: G. W. Bromley and Co., 1893); Bromley, *Atlas of The City of New York, 23rd & 24th Wards, 1897*. Quote in *New York Evening Post*, 24 March 1894.

12. Nicholas and John Cotter, the largest builders of apartment houses in this period, built groups of flats throughout North New York. After concentrating on private dwellings, William O'Gorman and Edward D. Bertine began erecting flats in the beginning of the 1890s. Buildings Projected, 23rd and 24th Wards, in *Record and Guide*, 1880 to 1898; Robinson and Pidgeon, *Robinson's Atlas of New York, 1885*; Bromley, *Atlas of the City of New York, 1893 and 1897*.

13. Reeves, *The First Elevated Railroads in Manhattan and The Bronx*, 39; *New York Times*, 24 March 1895.

14. Buildings Projected, *Record and Guide*, 1880 to 1898; Bromley, *Atlas of the City of New York, 1893 and 1897*; *Record and Guide*, 13 Aug. 1892.

15. Buildings Projected, *Record and Guide*, 1880 to 1898; *Record and Guide*, 1 Jan. 1887; *New York Times*, 31 March 1895. Goeller quoted in *Record and Guide*, 26 June 1880. During the 1890s, Mott Haven became "a small center of piano manufacturers," with 8 piano factories by 1897. See *Record and Guide*, 14 Nov. 1891; Bromley, *Atlas of the City of New York, 1897*. With more than 1,000 workers, the Mott Iron Works remained a major employer in Mott Haven until 1904. Jordan L. Mott died in 1915, but his Iron Works was already operating in Trenton, New Jersey. See *Record and Guide*, 20 April 1889; *Harlem Local Reporter and Bronx Chronicle*, 17 Sept. 1904; *Bronx Home News*, 29 July 1915; John T. Cumbler, *A Social History of Economic Decline: Business, Politics, and Work in Trenton* (New Brunswick, NJ: Rutgers University Press, 1989), 90.

16. *Record and Guide*, 1 Jan. 1887, 4 Feb. 1888, 18 Jan. 1890, 21 Dec. 1895; John C. De La Vergne, "A Manufacturing Centre," in North Side Board of Trade, *The Great North Side*, 98.

17. *Record and Guide*, 20 April 1889, 3 Aug. 1895. Believing that manufacturing enterprises would be "a very decided advantage to any community," Albert E. Davis, architect and soon-to-be president of the North Side Board of Trade, stressed that Mott Haven "will become the theatre of a fair share of the business development which is steadily pushing and crowding the residence section from the main portion of Manhattan Island." "Mott Haven Advantages," in North Side Board of Trade, *The Great North Side, North Side News, Supplement*, 18 May 1901, 23.

18. A flat with five rooms and bath rented for $10 to $18 a month in Mott Haven, a small two- or three-story house with basement was $20 to $60 a month. In Manhattan a comparable house was $75 a month. But Bronx rents were never as low as many would have wished. From 1881 on, Manhattan families besieged Mott Haven realtors for small houses with rents far below the prevailing rates. *Record and Guide*, 16 April 1881, 24 April 1897; *New York Times*, 24 March 1895, 31 March 1895; *New York Evening Post*, 16 March 1895.

19. Population statistics are from New York State, "Exhibits showing the Enumeration of the State by Counties, Cities, Towns and Election Districts for the Year 1892," in New York State, *Senate Documents, 1892* (Albany: James B. Lyon, 1892), no. 60 (hereafter cited as "Enumeration of the State"); "Population of the County of New York, Bronx Borough, 1900–1905," in New York State, *Manual for the Use of the Legislature of the State of New York, 1906* (Albany: Brandow Printing Company, State Department Printers, 1906), 238; the 1893 and 1897 editions of Bromley, *Atlas of the City of New York*. Election district boundaries are in the *City Record*, 24 Oct. 1891.

20. Ethnicity was ascertained by contemporary references and analysis of names from 1874 and 1891 voter registration lists. Davenport, *Registry of Voters in the*

City of New York, 1874; List of Registered Voters for the Year 1891 in the City Record, Supplement, 28 Oct. 1891; American Council of Learned Societies, Report of Committee on Linguistics and National Stocks in the Population of the United States, in American Historical Association, Annual Report 4 (1931); Edward MacLysaght, A Guide to Irish Surnames (Baltimore: Genealogical Book Company, 1964); Benzion C. Kaganoff, A Dictionary of Jewish Names and Their History (New York: Schocken, 1977).

21. There were two other Catholic churches in Mott Haven by 1901, but St. Jerome's, with more than 9,000 members, was the largest. The four German churches were in the central portion of Mott Haven. WPA Historical Records Survey, Bronx Churches, 7, 11–12; "List of Churches," in Federation 2 (Dec. 1902), 59; North Side Board of Trade, The Great North Side, North Side News, Supplement, 18 May 1901, 31–33; New York Evening Post, 18 July 1899; Record and Guide, 5 May 1900, 8 May 1897.

22. Statistics on the number of foreigners in Mott Haven are from "The Federal Census of New York," Federation 2 (April–June 1902), 18, 22.

23. The Board of Health had long urged the city to fill in the canal. Record and Guide, 19 July 1890, 12 May 1894, 21 Nov. 1896.

24. Record and Guide, 9 April 1881; New York Times, 24 March 1895. In the 1890s, voter registration lists in the City Record reveal that architects, builders, realtors, and politicians lived around the Mott Avenue area or around the Alexander and Willis avenues/138th Street locus.

25. Bronx Home News, 8 July 1909; Taxpayers' Alliance, The New North End, n.p. In 1919 the area was already being described as the "East Bronx." See Absolute Auction Sale, To Close Estate of George F. Johnson, . . . Building Lots and Plots on Southern Boulevard, Longwood and Westchester Avenues, Bronx Boro, Monday, November 3, 1919, Bronx Auction Pamphlet, Map Room, NYPL. This is part of an extensive collections of maps and brochures of Bronx land auctions. On the Fort Apache label, see Jill Jonnes, South Bronx Rising: The Rise, Fall, and Resurrection of an American City (New York: Fordham University Press, 2002), 226–27.

26. New York Tribune, 28 Dece. 1879; Minutes of the Board of Estimate and Apportionment, 1880, 598–602; Record and Guide, 22 Oct. 1887, 21 July 1888, 22 Feb. 1890. On the subdivision of the Fox estate and the street plan see Minutes of Proceedings of the Board of Commissioners of the Department of Public Parks for the Year Ending April 30th, 1879 (New York: Evening Post Steam Presses, 1879), 59, 71, 475; Minutes and Documents of the Board of Commissioners of the Department of Public Parks for the Year Ending April 30, 1883 (New York: Martin B. Brown, 1883), 181; Robinson and Pidgeon, Robinson's Atlas of the City of New York, 1885; Bromley, Atlas of the City of New York, 1897.

27. Record and Guide, 21, 28 June, 5 July, 27 Sept. 1884, 9 April 1887, 28 April 1888, 25 July 1891, 27 May 1893; Bromley, Atlas of The City of New York, 1897; George W. and Walter Bromley, Atlas of the City of New York, 1905 (Philadelphia: G. W. Bromley and Co., 1905).

28. This assessment is based on a perusal of the Bromley maps of 1897 and 1905 and the Buildings Projected columns in the *Record and Guide*. New housing on the Fox and Vyse estates often sat on unopened, unsewered streets. The Intervale Avenue trunk sewer was not completed until 1897. See reports of the Department of Street Improvements, 1894 through 1897.

29. *Record and Guide*, 3 March 1900; Bromley, *Atlas of the City of New York, 1905*. The Hoe–Simpson tract was bought by the American Real Estate Company—A-Re-Co for short—which became a major developer in the vicinity of Southern Boulevard and Hunts Point. See *Record and Guide, A History of Real Estate, Building and Architecture in New York City During the Last Quarter Century* (New York: Arno Press, 1967), 168–69; F. Austin, "Real Estate Development of Bronx County," *North Side News*, Bronx County Progress Section, 17 May 1914.

30. Quotes from *Record and Guide*, 11 June 1904. See also *Record and Guide*, 22 Oct., 12 Nov. 1904, 27 May 1905. In 1900, the 1,000 lots of the Hoe–Simpson tract sold for slightly more than $1,000,000. Five years later, the 300 lots of the Bathgate–Beck estate went for the same figure, some of the plots selling for as much as $44,000. Similarly, 12 lots on the corner of Longwood and Westchester avenues were bought for $39,000 before the 1905 boom and were sold, in 1908, for about $145,000, netting the seller a neat 73 percent price increase. The rise in land prices continued despite a momentary lull during the banking crisis of 1907. See *Record and Guide*, 3 March 1900, 27 May 1905; James Lee Wells, *Bronx Real Estate, An Address to the North Side Board of Trade* (New York: North Side Board of Trade, 1909), 3–4.

31. Wells, *Bronx Real Estate*; *Record and Guide*, 16 July, 22 Oct. 1904, 14 Jan. 1905, 30 March, 16 Nov. 1907, 16 May 1908. Quotes from *Record and Guide*, 11 June 1904; W. W. Gill, "Residential Sections," in Taxpayers' Alliance, *The New North End: Bronx Borough* (New York: Diagram Publishing Co., 1910); *Bronx Home News*, 5 May 1910.

32. Compare Bromley, *Atlas of the City of New York, 1905*, with G. W. Bromley & Co., *Atlas of the Borough of The Bronx, 1912* (New York: G. W. Bromley & Co., 1912). See also Wells, *Bronx Real Estate*; Louis F. Haffen, *Borough of the Bronx: A Record of Unparalleled Progress and Development* (New York, 1909); Taxpayers' Alliance, *The New North End*; Bronx Borough President, *Annual Report, 1912*; and the real estate columns of the *Record and Guide*.

33. Harry T. Cook, *The Borough of The Bronx, 1639–1913: Its Marvelous Development and the Historical Surroundings* (New York: the author, 1913), 38–39; George W. & Walter Bromley, *Atlas of the City of New York: Borough of the Bronx, 1923* (Philadelphia: G. W. Bromley and Co., 1923).

34. *Record and Guide*, 14 Jan., 27 May 1905; Roy Lubove, *The Progressives and the Slums: Tenement House Reform in New York City, 1890–1917* (Pittsburgh: University of Pittsburgh Press, 1962), 134–36; Anthony Jackson, *A Place Called Home: A History of Low-Cost Housing in Manhattan* (Cambridge: MIT Press, 1976), 122–38; North Side Board of Trade, *Inaugural Address of the President*

for the Year 1911 and Annual Reports of the Standing Committees and of the Secretary for the Year 1910 to the North Side Board of Trade in the City of New York (New York: North Side Board of Trade, 1911), 49–50 (hereafter cited as North Side Board of Trade, *Annual Report, 1910*).

35. North Side Board of Trade, *Inaugural Address of the President for the Year 1910, Address of the Retiring President and Annual Reports of the Standing Committees and of the Secretary for the Year 1909 to the North Side Board of Trade in the City of New York* (New York: North Side Board of Trade, 1910), 52 (hereafter cited as North Side Board of Trade, *Annual Report, 1909*); *New York Times*, 30 March 1924; Bromley, *Atlas of the City of New York, 1923*. Rents varied from $18 to $100 a month, with most falling within the $25 to $35 range. The better-quality elevator apartments rented for $35 to $100 a month. This compared favorably with similar housing in Manhattan, where monthly rents ranged from $50 to $150. See *Record and Guide*, 13 Sept. 1907, 8 July 1909.

36. Laidlaw, *Population of New York City, 1890–1930*, 54–56.

37. Ibid.

38. Wells, *Bronx Real Estate*, 4; *Record and Guide*, 16 Nov. 1907; *North Side News*, 28 June 1909, the latter article in Community Service Society Records, Box 176, Clipping File, CU.

39. Bert Sack, "I Grew Up With The Bronx," *The Bronx County Historical Society Journal* 1 (Jan. 1964): 35; Walter Laidlaw, ed., *Statistical Sources for Demographic Studies of Greater New York, 1910*, 2 vols. (New York: The New York Federation of Churches, 1910), vol. 1; Walter Laidlaw, ed., *Statistical Sources for Demographic Studies of Greater New York, 1920* (New York: Cities Census Committee, 1922); The Bronx Board of Trade, *Yearbook, 1920* (New York: The Bronx Board of Trade, 1920), 45; WPA Historical Records Survey, *Bronx Churches*. The *Bronx Home News* regularly mentioned the ethnic makeup of the neighborhood's churches and social clubs during 1908 and 1909.

40. *Bronx Home News*, 7 July 1910.

41. This assessment is based on a thorough reading of the *Bronx Home News*, and the publications of the North Side Board of Trade, the Bronx Board of Trade, and the *North Side News*. The quote is by J. Clarence Davies, *Bronx Home News*, 6 Jan. 1910. See also Louis F. Haffen, *Address by Louis F. Haffen, President Borough of the Bronx Delivered at Complimentary Dinner at the Longwood Club, October 2, 1905* (Bronx, NY, 1905); and the description of the working-class neighborhood around Vyse Avenue in 1917, Leon Trotsky, *My Life* (New York: Grosset & Dunlap, 1930), 271.

42. *Record and Guide*, 4 November, 18 Nov. 1911.

43. Its street plan was adopted without any changes, many streets were paved and sewered, Melrose Avenue was cut through, and the encircling railroad tracks were depressed. See the reports of the Department of Street Improvements and *Record and Guide*, 1887 to 1893.

44. The development of Melrose can be ascertained in the Buildings Projected columns of the *Record and Guide* and in Robinson and Pidgeon, *Robinson's*

Atlas of the City of New York, 1885; Bromley, *Atlas of the City of New York, 1893, 1897, and 1905.* The railroad tracks that encircled Melrose were, in the late nineteenth century, no longer such a vital link. Only 48 commuters paid $35 a year for the 6-mile trip to downtown Manhattan. Instead, the lines made the adjacent streets unsuitable for better-grade housing. See *Record and Guide,* 19 July 1890.

45. Quotes are from feature articles in *Bronx Home News,* 3 April 1908, 7 Dec. 1913; and in *Record and Guide,* 4 Nov. 1911. Lots in the Hub had sold for slightly more than $4,000 in 1901. Ten years later, by 1911, these lots were selling for $30,000 each.

46. Bromley, *Atlas of the City of New York,* for the years 1893, 1897, 1905.

47. Reeves, *The First Elevated Railroads in Manhattan and the Bronx,* 38–39; *Record and Guide,* 26 May, 8 Sept. 1888, 20 April, 15 June 1889, quoted from 21 July 1888; *New York Times,* 24, 31 March 1895.

48. *Record and Guide,* 3 Sept. 1898.

49. Bromley, *Atlas of the City of New York, 1897; Record and Guide,* 12 Feb. 1887, 27 Nov. 1897; North Side Board of Trade, *Annual Report, 1910,* quote on 46; Bromley, *Atlas of the City of New York, 1923;* Ada H. Muller, "A Study of a Bronx Community" (M.A. thesis, Columbia University, 1915). The latter describes the neighborhood around Claremont Parkway.

50. William R. Brown, "Reminiscences of the Central Bronx," in *Record and Guide,* 18 Nov. 1911.

51. Bromley, *Atlas of the City of New York,* for the years 1893, 1897, and 1905; *Record and Guide,* 18 March 1899.

52. Gill, "Residential Sections," in Taxpayers' Alliance, *The New North End,* 38; Brown, "Reminiscences of the Central Bronx," in *Record and Guide,* 18 Nov. 1911; Bromley, *Atlas of the City of New York,* for the years 1912 and 1923.

53. Laidlaw, *Population of New York City, 1890–1930,* 54–56.

54. Ibid.

55. Laidlaw, *Statistical Sources for Demographic Studies of Greater New York, 1910;* Laidlaw, *Statistical Sources for Demographic Studies of Greater New York, 1920;* Muller, "A Study of a Bronx Community," quote on 10. See also reports of social and church activities in the *Bronx Home News* and the list of churches in WPA Historical Records Survey, *Bronx Churches.*

56. Muller, "A Study of a Bronx Community"; *Record and Guide,* 4 Nov., 18 Nov. 1911, 2 Jan. 1915; "The Bronx Church House," *Architectural Record* 22 (Dec. 1907): 509–10; Montgomery Schuyler, "An Oasis in The Bronx," *Architectural Record* 41 (Feb. 1917): 177–82. In 1920, the Bronx Church House was sold to the Young Men's Hebrew Association. *New York Times,* 9 Aug. 1920.

57. Built at a cost of $70,000 in 1887, the Eichler Mansion stood on the brewery grounds at the corner of 169th Street and Fulton Avenue, on the high ridge that set off the Boston Road District from the old town section of Morrisania. *Record and Guide,* 3 Dec. 1887. For Morris High school see *Record and Guide,* 26 Jan. 1901; *The Morris Annual,* 1905, Morris High School, Bronx, New York,

booklet at Bronx County Historical Society; Mark Price, *A History of the Bronx Public Schools (From Consolidation to the Present) 1898–1944* (New York: Board of Education, 1945), 13–14; Lloyd Ultan and Gary Hermlyn, *The Bronx in the Innocent Years, 1890–1925* (New York: Harper & Row, 1985), 108. For activities of civic and social clubs in the Boston Road area see Women's Municipal League, *Bulletin,* for the years 1902 through 1910; *Bronx Home News,* 1910 to 1914.

58. Blocks south of St. Mary's Park were "entirely unimproved" prior to the auction sale of the Crane Estate in 1905. See *Bronx Home News,* 6 April 1911; *Public Auction Sale of 150 Valuable New York City Lots known as the Crane Estate . . . Tuesday, November 14, 1905,* Bronx Auction Pamphlet, Map Room, NYPL.

59. *Record and Guide,* 30 March 1907; *Bronx Home News,* 8 July 1909; Laidlaw, *Population of New York City,* 54–56; Bromley, *Atlas of the City of New York,* for the years 1897, 1905, 1912, and 1923.

60. Laidlaw, *Statistical Sources for Demographic Studies of Greater New York, 1910;* Laidlaw, *Statistical Sources for Demographic Studies of Greater New York, 1920.*

61. This assessment is based on a thorough reading of the *Bronx Home News,* the *Record and Guide,* the publications of the North Side Board of Trade, and the *Annual Reports* of the Bronx Borough President. Quotes from *Bronx Home News,* 20 Sept. 1907, 4 Aug. 1910, and 4 May 1911.

5. BOOSTING A BOROUGH

1. For boosterism in general, see Daniel J. Boorstin, *The Americans: The National Experience* (New York: Random House, 1965) 113–23, President Tyler quote is on the title page; Daniel J. Boorstin, *The Americans: The Democratic Experience* (New York: Random House, 1973), 268. For a specific example of Bronx boosterism, see Harry T. Cook, *The Borough of The Bronx, 1639–1913: Its Marvelous Development and Historical Surroundings* (New York: the author, 1913), 24–27. Quote is from North Side Board of Trade, *The Great North Side: Its Past and Future, Its Advantages as a Commercial and Manufacturing Centre, North Side News. Supplement,* 18 May 1907.

2. Reformers believed this unbridled entrepreneurship contributed to the increased congestion and chaotic nature of the city. See Edward Ewing Pratt, *Industrial Causes of Congestion of Population in New York City* (New York: Columbia University, Longmans, Green & Co., 1911), 18–19.

3. Quoted in *Public Auction Sale, Prevost Estate, . . . Oct. 26, 1912,* Bronx Auction Pamphlet, Map Room, NYPL.

4. North Side Board of Trade, *Where New York's Future Lies* (New York: Press of The North Side News, 1903); North Side Board of Trade, *Address of Albert E. Davis, president of the North Side Board of Trade, delivered at its Meeting held at 520 Willis Avenue, 27 January 1903* (New York: North Side News Book and Job Print, 1903); *Address of Olin J. Stephens, president of the North Side Board of Trade of the City of New York, Delivered at its meeting held at Me-*

tropolis Theatre Building, 3rd & 142th Street, January 24, 1906; Record and Guide, 25 Jan. 1896, 12 Oct. 1907.

5. Wells quoted in *Record and Guide,* 20 March 1897; *First Real Estate Auction Sale AT NIGHT . . . October 11th, 1910, 297 Bronx Lots, by Order of Hunts Point Estates,* Bronx Auction Pamphlet, Map Room, NYPL.

6. Stephen Jenkins, *The Story of The Bronx: From the Purchase Made by the Dutch from the Indians in 1639 to the Present Day* (New York: G. P. Putnam's Sons, 1912), 6–7; William Cauldwell, "Annexation," in North Side Board of Trade, *The Great North Side,* 19–27. The annexation of the area east of the Bronx River was almost achieved in the 1870s and was portended anew by the city's acquisition of Pelham Bay Park and Pelham Parkway in the 1880s. See *Report to . . . Select and Locate Lands for Public Parks,* 113–21. Bills for annexation were introduced regularly in the state legislature. Large landowners in lower Westchester—the Messrs. Huntington, Lorillard, Havermeyer, and Waterbury among them—were the prime movers behind all attempts for acquiring the territory for New York City. *Record and Guide,* 24 Dec. 1887.

7. *Record and Guide,* 4 April 1885, 24 July 1886, 21 May 1887, 13 Jan. 1894; Jenkins, *The Bronx,* 7–8; Barry Jerome Kaplan, "A Study in the Politics of Metropolitanization: The Greater New York City Charter of 1897" (Ph.D. diss., State University of New York, Buffalo, 1975), 141–42, 153, 186, 202.

8. *Record and Guide,* 30 Jan. 1904.

9. See chapter 3 for the 1890 struggle. Despite the protests of Bronx promoters, the 1897 Charter replaced the Bronx's Department of Street Improvements with a centralized Board of Public Improvements. Each borough was given a number of local improvement boards (much like the community boards of today) and a largely ceremonial borough president's office, both of which were ineffective. For the 1897 Greater New York Charter and its 1902 Revision see Wells, et al., *The Bronx and Its People,* 23–24, 384, 689; North Side Board of Trade, *Third Annual Report of the Secretary of the North Side Board of Trade of the City of New York. March 6th, 1897* (New York: North Side Board of Trade, 1897), 10; *Record and Guide,* 24 Nov., 8 Dec. 1900; P. Tecumseh Sherman, *Inside the Machine—Two Years in the Board of Aldermen, 1898–1899: A Study of the Legislative Features of the City Government of New York City Under the Greater New York Charter* (New York: Cooke & Fry, 1901), 13–16, 63–84.

10. The county bill was passed because upstate Republicans wished to loosen Tammany's grip on the Bronx. Jenkins, *The Bronx,* 10; Herman Gerald Chapin, *Bronx Borough a Separate County: Address delivered before the North Side Board of Trade, November 25, 1903* (New York: North Side Board of Trade, 1903); Henry K. Davis, "History of Bronx County," in *North Side News,* Bronx County Progress Section, 17 May 1914; George M. Zoebelein, "The Bronx: A Struggle for County Government," *Bronx County Historical Journal* 1 (Jan. 1964): 3–24.

11. See publications of the North Side Association and the North Side Board of Trade, especially *Proceedings of the North Side Association of the 23rd and 24th*

Wards of the City of New York for The Year 1874 (New York: Torrey Brothers, 1875); North Side Board of Trade, *Third Annual Report . . . March 6th, 1897*; Mc-Dougall Hawkes, *The Improvement of the Bronx Waterfront* (New York: North Side Board of Trade, November 23, 1903); Fordham Morris, *Address of . . . the Opening of the Harlem Ship Canal, June 17, 1895* (New York: North Side Board of Trade, 1895).

12. *Annual Report of the Secretary of the North Side Board of Trade for the Year 1904, Charles E. Reid, Secretary* (New York: North Side Board of Trade, 1904), 9.

13. *Proceedings of the North Side Association of the 23rd & 24th Wards of the City of New York, for the Year 1875* (New York: Press of Bedell & Bro., 1876); *Proceedings of the North Side Association . . . for the Year 1874.* Taxpayers' Alliance, *The New North End: Bronx Borough* (New York: Diagram Publishing Co., 1910), 10, 19–28; *Record and Guide*, 19 Jan. 1889. The North Side Association fell into disuse a few years after 1885. See reference to its president, Samuel Filley, who was also the head of the Third Avenue El's founding company, the Suburban Rapid Transit, in *Record and Guide*, 10 Oct. 1885.

14. Cook, *The Borough of The Bronx*, 24–27, quote on 24; *Address of John C. De La Vergne, President of the North Side Board of Trade, delivered at its first meeting held at the Melrose Lyceum, March 6th, 1844* (New York: North Side Board of Trade, 1894); *Address of Albert E. Davis, president of the North Side Board of Trade, delivered at its Meeting held at 520 Willis Avenue, January 28, 1902* (New York: North Side Board of Trade, 1902), 4; *Bronx Home News*, 4 April 1915; *Bronx and Business Directory of the Bronx Chamber of Commerce, 1929* (New York: The Bronx Chamber of Commerce, 1929), 384.

15. Quotes from *Peremptory Sale at Auction: Estate of Lewis G. Morris, March 15, 1869*; and *First Real Estate Auction Sale AT NIGHT . . . October 11th 1910, 297 Bronx Lots, by Order of Hunts Point Estates*, Bronx Auction Pamphlet, Map Room, NYPL.

16. Louis F. Haffen, *Borough of The Bronx: A Record of Unparalleled Progress and Development* (New York, 1909); Haffen, *Address by Louis F. Haffen, President Borough of the Bronx Delivered at Complimentary Dinner at the Longwood Club, October 2, 1905* (Bronx, NY, 1905); the annual and quarterly reports of the president of the borough of the Bronx, from 1902 until the 1940s; *New York Times*, 5 Oct. 1913; *Record and Guide*, 19 June 1915; *Bronx Home News*, 20 June 1915; Lloyd Ultan, *The Beautiful Bronx (1920–1950)* (New Rochelle, NY: Arlington House, 1979), 44–45; Jill Jonnes, *South Bronx Rising: The Rise, Fall, and Resurrection of an American City* (New York: Fordham University Press, 2002), 79–81. Haffen's 1909 discourse on the merits of the Bronx was, in reality, a defense of his administration after he had been removed from office because of maladministration. *New York Times*, 30 Aug. 1909; *Bronx Home News*, 2 Sept. 1909.

17. Walter Laidlaw, ed., *Population of the City of New York, 1890–1930* (New York: Cities Census Committee, 1932), 51; Morris, *Address of . . . the Opening of the Harlem Ship Canal*; North Side Board of Trade, *The Great North Side or Bor-*

ough of The Bronx (New York: North Side Board of Trade, 1897); North Side Board of Trade, *The Great North Side, North Side News Supplement*, 18 May 1901; North Side Board of Trade, *Where New York's Future Lies*; James Lee Wells, *The Growth of The Bronx, New York City, Since Consolidation, January 1, 1898 to January 1, 1906* (New York: The Bronx League, 10 January 1906); Bronx Board of Trade, *"The Nation's Ninth City": The Bronx, New York's Fastest Growing Borough* (New York: Bronx Board of Trade, 1922); Taxpayers' Alliance, *The New North End*; *North Side News*, Bronx County Progress Section, 17 May 1914. The actions of the North Side Board of Trade's Literature and Publicity Committe are revealed in the annual reports for the years 1906 until 1914. In 1915, the Board of Trade's Publicity Bureau placed 813 articles in the city's newspapers. Bronx Board of Trade, *Yearbook, 1916* (New York: Bronx Board of Trade, 1916), 25.

18. Laidlaw, *Population of The City of New York, 1890–1930*, 51; Wells quoted in "Addenda: The Growth of the North Side," v, at rear of North Side Board of Trade, *The Great North Side*; Haffen, *Borough of The Bronx, 1909*, 63; "To Avoid City Congestion," *North Side News*, 28 June 1909; "Congestion Commission's First Hearing," *Municipal Facts*, 10 June 1910; the latter two articles are in clipping file on Congestion of Population, Community Service Society Records, Box 176, CU; North Side Board of Trade, *Address of Olin J. Stephens, president, delivered on February 2, 1905*, 7.

19. Laidlaw, *Population of New York City, 1890–1930*, 51, 54–56. Bronx Board of Trade, *"The Nation's Ninth City,"* 3; T. J. Mack, "The Bronx Grows, 1894–1939," *Bronxboro*, Feb.–March 1939, 8; U.S. Bureau of the Census, *Census Tract Data on Population and Housing, New York City: 1940* (New York: Welfare Council Committee on 1940 Census Tract Tabulation for New York City, September 1942), 5, 50–51.

20. *Record and Guide*, 19 June 1915. Realtors and builders were also held in high esteem. See their biographies in Randall Comfort, *History of Bronx Borough: City of New York* (New York: North Side News Press, 1906), 213–71.

21. *Record and Guide*, 10 Dec. 1892, 18 May 1901, 8 Feb. 1902, 5 Nov. 1904; *Architect and Builders' Magazine*, Old Series, 40 (Feb. 1908): 241.

22. *New York Times*, 30 March, 22 June 1924, 26 April, 1 Nov. 1925, 7 March 1926, 6 March 1927, 4 March 1928, 3 March 1929.

23. Herter claimed that all buildings with apartments renting for $20 or less were tenements. See "How to Invest in Tenement Property: Where to Build and What to Build," *Record and Guide*, 5 May 1900. On the distinction among flats, apartment houses, and tenements see Gwendolyn Wright, *Building the Dream: A Social History of Housing in America* (New York: Pantheon, 1981), 94, 145; Elizabeth Collins Cromley, *Alone Together: A History of New York's Early Apartments* (Ithaca, NY: Cornell University Press, 1990), 5–6.

24. In 1903, architect Ernest Flagg observed that "the apartment house is the result of high priced land." He acknowledged that "humanity prefers separate houses. It is only when they become too costly that the expedient of placing

several families under the same roof is resorted to." Ernest Flagg, "The Planning of Apartment Houses and Tenements," *Architectural Review* 10 (1893): 85–90. For the ideal housing being the single-family home, see Wright, *Building the Dream*, 93–113, 134–51.

25. *Record and Guide*, 18 May 1901.

26. "Report of the Select Committee . . . of Tenant Houses in New York and Brooklyn, 9 March 1857," 1–62; Anthony Jackson, *A Place Called Home: A History of Low-Cost Housing in Manhattan* (Cambridge: MIT Press, 1976), 78; "The Evolution of the Tenement House," in *Record and Guide*, 28 Sept. 1889. Quoted in Cromley, *Alone Together*, 13.

27. Reginald Pelham Bolton, *Building for Profit: Principles Governing the Economic Improvement of Real Estate* (New York: De Vinne Press, 1911; 3rd ed. 1922), 41; Roy Lubove, *The Progressives and the Slums: Tenement House Reform in New York City, 1890–1917* (Pittsburgh: University of Pittsburgh Press, 1962), 112–13; Jackson, *A Place Called Home*, 82–83; *Record and Guide*, 5 May 1900, quote on 765.

28. *Record and Guide*, 28 Sept. 1889, 7 Jan. 1899, 5 May 1900, 21 April 1901, 5 Nov. 1904.

29. Flagg, "The Planning of Apartment Houses and Tenements," quote on 89–90.

30. Bromley, *Alone Together*, 128–211; Wright, *Building the Dream*, 135–51.

31. Jackson, *A Place Called Home*, 138–41; Lawrence Veiller, "Two New-Law Flats," *Record and Guide*, 8 Feb. 1902; *New York Times*, 26 April 1925.

32. *New York Evening Post*, 9 April, 12 Nov. 1904; *Record and Guide*, 11 June 1904; North Side Board of Trade, *Tree Planting and Housing Accommodations, Being a Report of the Committee on Literature and Publication to the North Side Board of Trade of the City of New York, 27 September 1905* (New York: Kieling Bros., 1905). Quotes from *New York Evening Post*, 12 Nov. 1904 and *Record and Guide*, 11 June 1904.

33. Deborah Dash Moore, *At Home in America: Second-Generation New York Jews* (New York: Columbia University Press, 1981), 25, 48–58, 73–78; Homer Hoyt, *The Structure and Growth of Residential Neighborhoods in American Cities* (Washington, DC: Federal Housing Administration, 1939), 121–22.

34. Peter D. Salins, *The Ecology of Housing Destruction: Economic Effects of Public Intervention in the Housing Market* (New York: New York University Press, 1980), 25–33, quote on 27. See also Anthony Downs, *Neighborhoods and Urban Development* (Washington, D.C.: The Brookings Institution, 1981), 1–3, 8, 37–48; Ira S. Lowry, "Filtering and Housing Standards: A Conceptual Analysis," *Land Economics* 36 (Nov. 1960): 362–70; Wallace F. Smith, *Filtering and Neighborhood Change* (Research Report No. 24. Berkeley: Center for Real Estate and Urban Economics: Institute of Urban and Regional Development. University of California, 1964).

35. Bolton, *Building for Profit*, 1–3; Katherine Jeannette Meyer, "A Study of Tenant Associations in New York City with particular Reference to The Bronx, 1920–1927" (M.A. thesis, Columbia University, 1928); *New York Times*, 2 Oct.

1921. Building statistics are in the annual reports of the Bronx borough president for 1902 to 1937.

36. *New York Times*, 30 March 1924, 19 Feb. 1927, 11 March 1928, 30 Nov. 1930; *Record and Guide*, 4 March, 1 April 1939; Victor H. Lawn, "House for the Goose, House for the Gander," *Survey* 57 (15 De. 1926): 371–73; Asher Achinstein, State of New York, *Report of the State Board of Housing on The Standard of Living of 400 Families in a Model Housing Project: The Amalgamated Housing Corporation* (New York: Burland Printing Co., 20 July 1931); "Hillside Homes," *American Architect* 148 (Feb. 1936): 17–33; Calvin Trillin, "U.S. Journal: The Bronx, The Coops," *The New Yorker*, 1 August 1977, 49–54. See also Richard Plunz, "Reading Bronx Housing, 1890–1940" in *Building A Borough: Architecture and Planning in The Bronx, 1890–1940*, ed. Timothy Rub (New York: Bronx Museum of the Arts, 1986), 49–55, 67–76.

37. According to Roy Lubove, the tax exemption law "failed to limit profits or rentals. [Instead] it proved to be a speculative bonanza which increased the housing supply in New York City but did not benefit low-income groups." The Limited-Dividend Housing Act of 1926, which was prompted by the continued shortage of low-cost housing, did "encourage good site-planning of multifamily dwellings." See Roy Lubove, *The Urban Community: Housing and Planning in the Progressive Era* (Englewood Cliffs, NJ: Prentice-Hall, 1967), 17.

38. Hoyt, *The Structure and Growth of Residential Neighborhoods in American Cities*, 95; Bolton, *Building for Profit*, 5–9, 36–44; Cromley, *Alone Together*, quote on 13.

39. Helen P. Kempton, "A Study of The Bronx," March 1921, 15, Community Service Society Papers, Box 21, File 37–13, Columbia University Library; Milton Kaplan, "Private Enterprise in The Bronx: Rags to Riches on Washington Avenue," *Commentary* 10 (Aug. 1950): 162–66. See also Philip Cowen, *Memories of An American Jew* (New York: The International Press, 1932), 104–6, 297.

40. Virtually every issue of the *Bronx Home News* and the *Record and Guide* had some items on the "titanic progress" of the Bronx. See for example, *Bronx Home News*, 4 Oct. 1907, 3 Dec. 1908, 8 April 1909; Cook, *The Borough of The Bronx*, 38–39; and the annual reports of the North Side Board of Trade, the Bronx Board of Trade, and the Bronx borough president.

41. Bronx Board of Trade, *The Bronx in the City of New York: A Comprehensive General and Industrial Survey* (Bronx, NY: Bronx Board of Trade, 1931), 4; T. J. Mack, "The Bronx Grows, 1894–1939," *Bronxboro*, Feb.–March 1939, 8. *Bronxboro* was published by the Bronx Board of Trade.

42. Census tract statistics are from Laidlaw, *Population of New York City, 1890–1930*, 54–56; and Achinstein, *Report of the State Board of Housing on the Standard of Living of 400 Families in a Model Housing Project: The Amalgamated Housing Corporation*, 19.

43. North Side Board of Trade, *The Great North Side, North Side News, Supplement*, 18 May 1901, 7; F. Austin, "Real Estate Development of Bronx County," *North Side News*, Bronx County Progress Section, 17 May 1914, 85.

44. Bronx Auction Pamphlets, Map Room, NYPL.

45. E. B. Boynton, "Confidence in Bronx Real Estate Unshaken," *North Side News*, Bronx County Progess Section, 17 May 1914, 86–87; *New York Times*, 7 March 1926.

46. *Record and Guide*, 5 May 1886. See also the various editions of the Bromley land use maps between 1893 and 1923.

47. Ada H. Muller, "A Study of a Bronx Community" (M.A. thesis, Columbia University, 1915), 6, 21; Jenkins, *The Bronx*, 371.

48. The first suburban-style dwellings after the 1874 annexation continued to follow the railroads: Tremont, Fordham, Bedford Park, Williamsbridge, and Woodlawn Heights along the New York Central's Harlem line; Park Versailles, Van Nest, and Westchester along the New Haven Railroad; Highbridge and Morris and Fordham Heights along the New York Central's Putnam line; and in the early twentieth century, Morris Park and Eastchester along the New York and Boston Railroad.

49. See building statistics in the annual reports of the Bronx borough president, 1902 to 1937; Plunz, "Reading Bronx Housing," 38–41, 56–59; Wright, *Building the Dream*, 196; *New York Times*, 30 July 1922, 3 Feb., 6 April 1924, 13 Aug. 1939.

50. Plunz, "Reading Bronx Housing," 40–56.

51. Theodore T. McCrosky, *Residential Area Analysis* (New York: Works Progress Administration, August 1938), 13–14; Bureau of the Census, *Census Tract Data on Population and Housing, New York City: 1940*, 5; William H. Ludlow, *Population Densities for New York City: A Technical Study of Urban Population Densities in Relation to City Planning* (New York: Citizens' Housing Council, May 1944), 31.

52. Bureau of the Census, *Census Tract Data on Population and Housing, New York City: 1940*, 5–14; Consolidated Edison, *Population Growth of New York City by Districts, 1910–1948* (New York: Consolidated Edison, December 1948), Table 2; Ludlow, *Population Densities for New York City*, 29–30; Laidlaw, *Population of New York City*, 54–56.

53. The densely packed nature of New-Law tenements in the Bronx was noted in "To Avoid City Congestion," *North Side News*, 28 June 1909, clipping in scrapbook on Congestion of Population, Box 176, Community Service Society Records, CU. The article spoke of an exhibit on Bronx congestion presented by the Committee on Congestion of Population in New York. On zoning see Lubove, *The Progressives and the Slums*, 237–45; T. T. McCrosky, *Zoning for the City of New York* (New York: Works Progress Administration, August 1938). Estimates on the maximum population allowed by the 1916 Zoning Law are in Lubove, 244, and McCrosky, 6.

54. Bronx Board of Trade, *The Bronx . . . A Comprehensive General and Industrial Survey*, 4; 1912 and 1923 editions of the Bromley land use maps. Plunz, "Reading Bronx Housing," quote on 35.

55. J. C. Davies quoted in *Bronx Home News*, 10 April 1908.

56. Quotes from Mark Baldassare, *Residential Crowding in Urban America* (Berkeley: University of California Press, 1979), 32; Mark Baldassare, "Introduction: Urban Change and Continuity," in *Cities and Urban Living*, ed. Mark Baldassare (New York: Columbia University Press, 1983), 8, 18. See also Louis Wirth, "Urbanism as a Way of Life" *American Journal of Sociology* 44 (1938): 1–24; Pratt, *Industrial Causes of Congestion of Population in New York City*, 23; D. Stokols, "A Social Psychological Model of Human Crowding," *Journal of the American Institute of Planners* 38 (1972): 72–84.

57. Baldassare, *Residential Crowding in Urban America*, 35.

58. Sam Bass Warner Jr., *Streetcar Suburbs: The Process of Growth in Boston, 1870–1900* (Cambridge: Harvard University Press and MIT Press, 1962), 105–6; Moore, *At Home in America*, 24–58; Baldassare, *Residential Crowding in Urban America*, 11–14, 29–35.

59. Edgar M. Hoover and Raymond Vernon, *Anatomy of a Metropolis:The Changing Distribution of People and Jobs Within the New York Metropolitan Region* (Cambridge: Harvard University Press, 1959), 183–203.

60. Baldassare, *Residential Crowding in Urban America*, 15–35; Warner, *Streetcar Suburbs*, 105–6.

61. Ultan, *The Beautiful Bronx*; Neil Edward Hart, "The Sidewalks Were Red" (1972), postscript, Grand Concourse Vertical File, No. 2, Bronx County Historical Society Library; Rocky D'Erasmo, *Fordham was a Town: A Nostalgic Look into Fordham's Little Italy during the Twenties and Thirties* (Bronx, NY: the author, 1978).

62. Dr. Condon was testifying at the trial of Bruno Hauptmann for the kidnap and murder of the Charles Lindbergh baby. A few months later, the Bronx Board of Trade elected Dr. Condon an honorary life member for praising the borough. See *New York Times*, 10 Jan., 27 March 1935. Borough President Lyons quoted in *New York Times*, 7 Feb. 1935.

63. Haffen, *Borough of The Bronx*, 1909, 45; Dollar Savings Bank, *Golden Anniversary Commemorating Fifty Years of Progress in the Bronx, 1890–1940*; Bronx Board of Trade, *The Bronx . . . A Comprehensive General and Industrial Survey*; Meyer, "A Study of Tenant Associations," 29; "Few Bronx Slums Merit Clearance," *New York Times*, 23 March 1934; Henry Morgenthau, *All in a Lifetime*, in collaboration with French Strother (New York: Doubleday, Page & Company, 1922), 117.

64. In later years, Bronx interests were just as aware of the importance of a positive image. For example, protesting a 1966 *New York Times* article on the beginning of deterioration on the Grand Concourse, J. Clarence Davies told the *Times* editor, "Your paper will be responsible for the ruination of this neighborhood with that story." Twelve years later, Borough President Robert Abrams objected to the telecasting of a burning Bronx building nearby Yankee Stadium during network coverage of the World Series. "That picture," Abrams recalled in 1978, "reinforced the image people have of the Bronx." By

the late 1980s, Fordham University found it had to project a more positive image of the Bronx in order to compete successfully for new students. See Jonnes, *South Bronx Rising*, 272–73; *New York Times*, 6 July 1978, 10 June 1986.

65. C. Morris Horowitz and Lawrence J. Kaplan, *The Estimated Jewish Population of the New York Area, 1900–1975* (New York: The Demographic Study Committee of the Federation of Jewish Philanthropies of New York, 1915), 22, 29–31, 43–44, 96; The News, The New York Times, Daily Mirror, and Journal American, *New York City Market Analysis* (New York: News Syndicate Co. Inc., The New York Times Co., Daily Mirror Inc., Hearst Consolidated Publications Inc., 1943); Bureau of the Census, *Census Tract Data on Population and Housing, New York City: 1940*, 5, 15–24. The neighborhood descriptions and statistics in the New York City Market Analysis reveal the various subareas within the neighborhoods of the Bronx.

6. URBAN NEIGHBORHOODS

1. The exception was the population decreases in parts of Third Avenue. Walter Laidlaw, ed., *Population of the City of New York, 1890–1930* (New York: Cities Census Committee, 1932), 54–56, 96–108; U.S. Department of Commerce, Bureau of the Census, *Census Tract Data on Population and Housing, New York City: 1940* (New York: Welfare Council Committee on 1940 Census Tract Tabulation for New York City, September 1942), 6–14.

2. Presidents Franklin Delano Roosevelt, Harry S. Truman, and John F. Kennedy came to the Bronx to win votes. *The Goldbergs* followed a working-class immigrant family as it gradually moved up the socioeconomic ladder. Lloyd Ultan, *The Beautiful Bronx (1920–1950)* (New Rochelle, NY: Arlington House, 1979), 27–30, 34, 44–47; Jill Jonnes, *South Bronx Rising: The Rise, Fall, and Resurrection of an American City* (New York: Fordham University Press, 2002), 41–92, 128–31.

3. The construction of new neighborhoods can best be seen in census tract population statistics and land use maps. See also the neighborhood descriptions and statistics in The News, New York Times, Daily Mirror and Journal-American, *New York City Market Analysis* (New York: News Syndicate Co., New York Times Co., Daily Mirror, and Hearst Consolidated Publications, 1943).

4. From 1930 to 1950, the estimated Jewish population of the Bronx never dropped below 500,000. C. Morris Horowitz and Lawrence J. Kaplan, *The Estimated Jewish Population of the New York Area, 1900–1975* (New York: Demographic Study Committee of the Federation of Jewish Philanthropies of New York, 1959), 22, 29–31, 43–44, 96; Bureau of the Census, *Census Tract Data on Population and Housing, New York City: 1940*, 5, 15–24.

5. Timothy Rub, "The Institutional Presence in The Bronx," in Timothy Rub, ed., *Building A Borough: Architecture and Planning in The Bronx, 1890–1940* (New York: Bronx Museum of the Arts, 1986), 83–84; Ultan, *The Beautiful Bronx.*

6. President Franklin D. Roosevelt appointed Flynn regional administrator of public works for New York, New Jersey, and Pennsylvania with control of $3.3 billion earmarked by Congress. From 1935 to 1937, almost $58 million was spent for dozens of projects in the Bronx. See Jonnes, *South Bronx Rising*, 65–84.

7. Photographs of these improvements are in Ultan, *The Beautiful Bronx*. The Independent D subway was planned and funded before the Depression and began running beneath the Grand Concourse in 1933. The Bronx Terminal Market was constructed in the 1920s and renovated in 1935 during Mayor Fiorello LaGuardia's first term. See John F. Hylan, *Seven Years of Progress: Important Public Improvements and Achievements by the Municipal Borough Governments of the City of New York, 1918–1925, Report Submitted to the Board of Aldermen, March 1925* (New York: Office of the Mayor, 1925), 17–19, 53–54; Peter E. Derrick, "The New York City Transit Crisis of 1918–1925" (M.A. thesis, Columbia University, 1967), 60–63.

8. Photographs and maps of highways and the Triborough Bridge approaches are in James J. Lyons, *Traffic in The Bronx: Studies and Recommendations for Preventing Congestion—Factors, Objections, Conclusions* (New York: Office of the President of The Borough of The Bronx, September 1947), 4–7.

9. Laidlaw, *Population of New York City, 1890–1930*, 55–56, 103–8; Bureau of the Census, *Census Tract Data on Population and Housing, New York City: 1940*, 6–14, 24–33. There were lower ticket sales on the Third Avenue El and the lower route of the old subway. In contrast, the new subway line's 143rd Street Station gained more riders. See Fred H. Allen, *New York City, Westchester and Nassau Counties in Relation to Real Estate Investment, 1942* (New York: Sponsored by The Bank for Savings, Bowery Savings Bank, and Group Five Mortgage Information Bureau, 1942), 112.

10. Walter Laidlaw, ed., *Statistical Sources for Demographic Studies of Greater New York, 1920* (New York: Cities Census Committee, 1922), 139–86; Bureau of the Census, *Census Tract Data on Population and Housing, New York City: 1940*, 4, 6–14, 25–49. In 1922, the Bronx had the next lowest percentage of owned homes among all the boroughs—8.2 percent as opposed to Staten Island's 42.7 percent, Queens's 36.7 percent, and Brooklyn's 19.3 percent. Manhattan, of course, had the lowest: only 2.1 percent of its homes were privately owned in 1922. See New York Herald, *The New York Market* (New York: New York Herald, 1922), 40. The percentage of owned homes in the Bronx had increased to 10.5 percent by 1930, but it was still behind the other boroughs. Manhattan continued last in this category. See Welfare Council of New York City, Research Bureau, *Study of Neighborhood Statistics: Homes by Tenure and Value or Monthly Rental, by Health Areas, New York City, 1930* (New York: Welfare Council of New York City, 1933), unpaged.

11. New York City Housing Authority, *Real Property Inventory: City of New York, Bronx* (New York: The New York City Housing Authority, 1934), xv, 1A–8A. The inventory's census tract statistics on duration of occupancy reveal that

many of the residents were at their present addresses less than two years. See the discussion on population mobility due to age and tenancy in Anthony Downs, *Neighborhoods and Urban Development* (Washington, DC: The Brookings Institution, 1981), 27–33.

12. Walter Laidlaw, ed., *Statistical Sources for Demographic Studies of Greater New York, 1910* (New York: New York Federation of Churches, 1910); Laidlaw, *Statistical Sources for Demographic Studies of Greater New York, 1920*, 139–36; Laidlaw, *Population of New York City*, 34, 102–5, 179; Bureau of the Census, *Census Tract Data on Population and Housing, New York City: 1940*, 15–23; *The New York Market: 1922*. See Allen, *New York City, Westchester, and Nassau Counties*, 105, for the decade of the thirties.

13. Laidlaw, *Statistical Sources for Demographic Studies of Greater New York, 1920*, 139–86; Bureau of the Census, *Census Tract Data on Population and Housing, New York City: 1940*, 15–23; Welfare Council of New York City, *Population in Health Areas, New York City, 1930* (New York: Welfare Council of New York City, 1931), 11–16; Welfare Council of New York, *Heads of Families by Color and Nativity and Country of Birth of Foreign Born Head, by Health Areas, New York City, 1930* (New York: Welfare Council of New York City, 1934), 15–21; Laidlaw, *Population of New York City, 1890–1930*, 102–5; Horowitz and Kaplan, *The Estimated Jewish Population of the New York Area, 1900–1975*; Beth S. Wenger, *New York Jews and the Great Depression: Uncertain Promise* (Syracuse, NY: Syracuse University Press, 1999), 92. The area had many nationality groups, among them a small Greek community around Forest Avenue in Morrisania. Department of Parks and Recreation Records, box 102386, NYC Municipal Archives.

14. Laidlaw, *Statistical Sources for Demographic Studies of Greater New York, 1920*, 139–86; Laidlaw, *Population of New York City*, 51, 54–56; Welfare Council of New York, *Heads of Families by Color and Nativity and Country of Birth of Foreign Born Head, By Health Areas, New York City, 1930*, unpaged; Bureau of the Census, *Census Tract Data on Population and Housing, New York City: 1940*, 15–23.

15. Laidlaw, *Statistical Sources for Demographic Studies of Greater New York, 1920*, 139–86; Laidlaw, *Population of New York City, 1890–1930*, 102–5; Bureau of the Census, *Census Tract Data on Population and Housing, New York City: 1940*, 6–14; Bronx Council of Social Agencies, *A Study of the Lower Bronx* (New York: Bronx Council of Social Agencies, 1939), 5–6, 52.

16. There was no separate classification of Puerto Ricans in the U.S. Census until 1950. Earlier statistics were gleaned from the number of people born in Puerto Rico and living in the continental United States. See C. Wright Mills, Clarence Senior, and Rose Kohn Goldsen, *The Puerto Rican Journey: New York's Newest Migrants* (1950; reprint, New York: Russell & Russell, a Division of Atheneum House, Inc., 1967), 187; Lawrence R. Chenault, *The Puerto Rican Migrant in New York City* (1938; reprint, New York: Russell & Russell, 1970), 53–63. For the 1926 estimates see Virginia E. Sanchez Korrol, *From Colonia to*

Community: The History of Puerto Ricans in New York City, 1917–1948 (Westport, CN: Greenwood Press, 1983), 59–62.

17. Ira Rosenwaike, *Population History of New York City* (Syracuse, NY: Syracuse University Press, 1972), 139; Bronx Council of Social Agencies, *A Study of the Lower Bronx*, 6; Bureau of the Census, *Census Tract Data on Population and Housing, New York City: 1940*, 29–49. A 1948 Welfare Council study estimated that between 71,00 and 72,000 Puerto Ricans lived in the Bronx, mostly in Mott Haven, Melrose, and Morrisania. Welfare Council of New York City, *Report of the Committee on Puerto Ricans in New York City* (1948; reprint, New York: Arno Press, 1975), 25.

18. Laidlaw, *Statistical Sources for Demographic Studies of Greater New York, 1920*, 139–86; Laidlaw, *Population of New York City*, 102–5; Bureau of the Census, *Census Tract Data on Population and Housing, New York City: 1940*, 6–14; Richard William Giordano, "A History of the Morrisania Section of the Bronx in Three Periods: 1875, 1925, 1975" (M.A. thesis, Columbia University, 1981), 105–7.

19. Katherine Jeannette Meyer, "A Study of Tenant Associations in New York City with Particular Reference to The Bronx, 1920–1927" (M.A. thesis, Columbia University, 1928), 205–6.

20. New York City Housing Authority, *Real Property Inventory: Bronx, 1934*; 1A–8B; Bureau of the Census, *Census Tract Data on Population and Housing, New York City: 1940*, 24–39.

21. Milton Kaplan, "Private Enterprise in The Bronx: Rags to Riches on Washington Avenue," *Commentary* (Aug. 1950): 162.

22. See the classification of residential structures by condition in New York City Housing Authority, *Real Property Inventory: Bronx, 1934*, xv, 1A–8B; Bronx Council of Social Agencies, *A Study of the Lower Bronx*, 87–94, quote is on 3.

23. Allen, *New York City, Westchester, and Nassau Counties*, 116; Bronx Council of Social Agencies, *A Study of the Lower Bronx*, 87–94. See also "Few Bronx Slums Merit Clearance," *New York Times*, 23 March 1934.

24. Ultan, *The Beautiful Bronx*, 13–15; Deborah Dash Moore, *At Home in America: Second-Generation New York Jews* (New York: Columbia University Press, 1981), 19–58, 73–84; *New York City Market Analysis, 1943*; Bronx Board of Trade, *The Bronx in the City of New York: A Comprehensive General and Industrial Survey* (Bronx, NY: Bronx Board of Trade, 1931), 23.

25. Regional Plan Association, *The Economic Status of the New York Metropolitan Region in 1944* (New York: The Regional Plan Association, Inc., 1944), 9, 69.

26. Community Service Society Records, box 38, files 222, 222–2, 222–5, CU. Family expenditures for 1930 and 1940 are in Bronx Board of Trade, *The Bronx . . . A Comprehensive General and Industrial Survey*, 6, 23; *New York City Market Analysis, 1943*. Unemployment figures are from Regional Plan Association, *The Economic Status of the New York Metropolitan Region in 1944*, 69. The proposed bill and correspondence about it are in Board of Aldermen, Bernard S. Deutsch, Correspondence, 1934–1935, box 1739, NYC Municipal Archives.

27. Bronx Board of Trade, *The Bronx . . . A Comprehensive General and Industrial Survey*, 23; S. Max Nelson, "The A.I.C.P. in the Bronx: Establishing a Bronx Office," 2 Sept, 1930; Bronx Division AICP, Case Load Map, 15 Feb, 1931, both items in Community Service Society Papers, box 38, file 222–2, CU. The entire box is replete with references to poverty in the South East Bronx during the 1930s.

28. *Sinai Echo*, [newsletter of the Sinai Congregation of the Bronx], 1 April 1934, Department of Parks and Recreation Collection, box 102385, folder: Permits—Bronx, NYC Municipal Archives.

29. Allen, *New York City, Westchester, and Nassau Counties*, 107; *New York City Market Analysis, 1943*; Community Service Society Papers, box 38, file 222–5, CU; Bureau of the Census, *Census Tract Data on Population and Housing, New York City: 1940*, 23–49.

30. Mark Naison, "From Eviction Resistance to Rent Control: Tenant Activism in the Great Depression," in *The Tenant Movement in New York City, 1904–1984*, ed. Ronald Lawson and Mark Naison (New Brunswick: Rutgers University Press, 1986), 94–133, Wenger, *New York Jews and the Great Depression*, 107–23; Bronx Council of Social Agencies, *A Study of the Lower Bronx*, 4. Quote is from the *Bronx Home News*, 7 Dec. 1932, quoted in Naison, "From Eviction Resistance to Rent Control," 108.

31. Allen, *New York City, Westchester, and Nassau Counties*, 104, 106.

32. For example, noting that 61 percent of Bronx families in 1943 had an annual expenditure of $1,800 to $2,999 glosses over the gap between the lowest and highest figures and obscures the many standard-of-living levels contained within that category. See *New York Market Analysis, 1943*.

33. Allen, *New York City, Westchester and Nassau Counties*, 108–9; Bronx Council of Social Agencies, *A Study of the Lower Bronx*, 85–86; *New York Times*, 1 Nov. 1942, 31 Jan. 1943.

34. Jonnes, *South Bronx Rising*, 66, 75; Ronald H. Bayor, *Neighbors in Conflict: The Irish, Germans, Jews, and Italians of New York City, 1929–1941* (Baltimore: Johns Hopkins University Press, 1978), 151–62. See figures for duration of occupancy in New York Housing Authority, *Real Property Inventory: Bronx, 1934*, 1A–8B.

35. On the stages of neighborhood change see Ronald H. Bayor, "The Neighborhood Invasion Pattern," in Bayor, ed., *Neighborhoods in Urban America* (Port Washington, NY: Kennikat Press, 1982), 86–102. On ethnic tensions see Bayor, *Neighbors in Conflict*, quote is on 160.

36. The analysis is from Bayor, *Neighbors in Conflict*, quote on 160.

37. Ibid., 157–62.

38. Because of its multiethnic constituency, the Democratic Party needed to resolve the conflict between Jews and the Irish. Ibid., 161–62.

39. Eleanor Lake, "Trouble on the Street Corner," *Common Sense* 12 (May 1943): 147–49; Bradford Chambers, "Boy Gangs of New York: 500 Fighting Units," *New York Times Magazine*, 10 Dec. 1944, quote is on 16.

40. New York City Youth Board folders in the papers of New York City Mayors Fiorello LaGuardia, William O'Dwyer, Vincent R. Impelliterri, and Robert F. Wagner, NYC Municipal Archives; three *New York Times* articles: "12 Accused of Rape in a Bronx Theatre," 1 April 1943, "2 Youths Convicted of 'Mugging' Attack," 2 April 1943, "Six Youths Convicted of Rape," 22 May 1943; and box 1615, Mayor's Committee on Unity Papers, NYC Municipal Archives, which has newspaper articles, community studies, press releases, police reports, and accounts of interracial neighborhood meetings about teen gangs in the South Bronx during 1945–1946. The quotation is from a July 1946 press release on conditions in the Prospect Avenue area of the South Bronx.

41. Ultan, *The Beautiful Bronx*; Jonnes, *South Bronx Rising*, 51–84.

42. After initially increasing land values, elevated transit lines exerted a depressing effect upon properties along which they were built. By 1929, lower Third Avenue looked like portions of Third and Sixth avenues in Manhattan "where it seems that el structures keep land values down." Values in the more northerly reaches of the elevated line were still rising, however. See Edwin Harold Spengler, *Land Values in New York in Relation to Transit Facilities* (1930; reprint, New York: AMS Press, 1968), 83–84, 92.

43. On the streets near the Triborough Bridge see Jonnes, *South Bronx Rising*, 80–84. For the lack of future adaptability because of the automobile, see Edgar M. Hoover and Raymond Vernon, *Anatomy of a Metropolis:The Changing Distribution of People and Jobs Within the New York Metropolitan Region* (Cambridge: Harvard University Press, 1959), 203.

44. Allen, *New York City, Westchester and Nassau Counties*, 112; Ultan, *The Beautiful Bronx*, 58; Jonnes, *South Bronx Rising*, 80–81. For the need for a public health center in the lower Bronx, see Community Service Society Records, box 39, file 227, CU. Designed by McKim, Mead, and White, the Bronx Grit Chamber was designated a New York City Landmark for its distinctive architecture in 1982. See Leslie Bennetts, "Panel Declares Treatment Plant City Landmark," *New York Times*, 9 June 1982.

45. Kenneth T. Jackson, *Crabgrass Frontier: The Suburbanization of the United States* (New York: Oxford University Press, 1985), 286; Hoover and Vernon, *Anatomy of a Metropolis*, 183–200.

46. "Bronx Board Plans Six Year Program," *New York Times*, 22 Jan. 1939; Allen, *New York, Westchester, and Nassau Counties*, 120.

47. See map of public housing in New York City, Office of the Mayor, *Summary, The South Bronx: A Plan for Revitalization* (New York: New York City, Office of the Mayor), 49.

48. Meyer, "A Study of Tenant Associations in New York City with Particular Reference to the Bronx, 1920–1927," 33–34.

49. For filtering in New York City see Anthony Jackson, *A Place Called Home: A History of Low-Cost Housing in Manhattan* (Cambridge: MIT Press, 1976), 285–91. On filtering and the need for some deterioration see Downs, *Neighborhoods and Urban Development*, 5–6, quote is on 6.

50. Jackson, *A Place Called Home*, 304. For a thorough indictment of public hous-
    ing projects, see Jane Jacobs, *The Death and Life of Great American Cities*
    (New York: Random House, 1961).

7. THE SOUTH BRONX

1. The 1940, 1950, and 1960 census tract statistics show continued population de-
   clines throughout the borough and regardless of housing quality. U.S. Department of Commerce, Bureau of the Census, *Census Tract Data on Population and Housing, New York City: 1940* (New York: Welfare Council
   Committee on 1940 Census Tract Tabulation for New York City, September
   1942), 5; U.S. Bureau of the Census, *United States Census of the Population:
   1950, New York, New York* (Washington, DC, 1952); U.S. Bureau of the Census, *U.S. Census of Population and Housing: 1960, New York City* (Washington,
   DC, 1962).

2. William G. Conway, "'People Fire' in the Ghetto Ashes," *Saturday Review*, 23
   July 1977, 16.

3. Joel Schwartz, *The New York Approach: Robert Moses, Urban Liberals, and Redevelopment of the Inner City* (Columbus: Ohio University Press, 1993), 89,
   115–17; New York City Housing Authority, *City-Wide Public Housing*, September 30, 1962.

4. Sydney Grusen, "New Faces in the Lower Bronx: Shifting Population Often
   Raises Tense Problems in Housing," *New York Times*, 11 July 1955. Statistics
   are from Ira Rosenwaike, *Population History of New York City* (Syracuse, NY:
   Syracuse University Press, 1972), 133, 139, 141; Bureau of the Census, *U.S. Census of Population: 1950, New York City*; Welfare and Health Council of New
   York City, *Population of Puerto Rican Birth or Parentage, New York City: 1950*
   (New York, 1952); Bureau of the Census, *U.S. Census of Population and Housing: 1960, New York City*; New York City Department of City Planning, 1980
   and 1990 Census Bureau Data, reprinted in *New York Times*, 22 March 1991.

5. Bureau of the Census, *U.S. Census of Population: 1950, New York City*; Welfare
   and Health Council of New York City, *Population of Puerto Rican Birth or
   Parentage, New York City: 1950*; Bureau of the Census, *U.S. Census of Population and Housing: 1960, New York City*; New York Department of City Planning, *1990 Census* (New York, March 25, 1991), Table 2.

6. Anthony Jackson, *A Place Called Home: A History of Low-Cost Housing in
   Manhattan* (Cambridge: MIT Press, 1976), 227–28, 242–46; Joel Schwartz, *The
   New York Approach: Robert Moses, Urban Liberals, and Redevelopment of the
   Inner City* (Columbus: Ohio University Press, 1993), 120–28; Kenneth T. Jack-
   son, *Crabgrass Frontier: The Suburbanization of the United States* (New York:
   Oxford University Press, 1985), 231–45.

7. Jackson, *Crabgrass Frontier*, 196–218; Fred H. Allen, *New York City, Westchester and Nassau Counties in Relation to Real Estate Investment, 1942* (New
   York: Sponsored by The Bank for Savings, Bowery Savings Bank, and Group

Five Mortgage Information Bureau, 1942), 119–20; "Statement of William Reid, Chairman of the New York City Housing Authority, at the Hearing of the Temporary State Commission on Low-Income Housing," New York, 29 Oct. 1963, 15, box 133, folder 1961, Mayor Wagner Papers, NYC Municipal Archives; Sandor Evan Schick, "Neighborhood Change in the Bronx, 1905–1960" (Ph.D. diss., Harvard University, 1982), 110–76. Even Bronx banks, like Dollar Savings, Eastern Savings, and North Side Savings, only issued mortgages for suburban homes. See Jill Jonnes, *South Bronx Rising: The Rise, Fall, and Resurrection of an American City* (New York: Fordham University Press, 2002), 356–62.

8. In 1943, the Bronx Board of Trade lauded plans for public housing in the South Bronx. *New York Times*, 6 June 1943; Charles Abrams, "How to Remedy Our 'Puerto Rican Problem'," *Commentary* (Feb. 1955): 120–27, quote on 123.

9. Twelve public housing projects were completed in black and Spanish Harlem by 1959, six of these before 1955. Moses held as many as 12 city and state offices, often simultaneously. In 1946, Mayor William O'Dwyer appointed Moses New York City Construction Coordinator, making him construction czar of the city. Schwartz, *The New York Approach*, 108, 113–23; Richard Plunz, *A History of Housing in New York City* (New York: Columbia University Press, 1990), 257, 261–74; New York City Housing Authority, *City-Wide Public Housing*, September 30, 1962; Wayne Phillips, "Census Loss Tied to Slum Program," *New York Times*, 6 Sept. 1960.

10. Plunz, *A History of Housing*, 240; New York City Housing Authority, *City-Wide Public Housing*, September 30, 1962. See box 126, folder 1801, Wagner Papers, for letters from neighborhood interests opposing the Castle Hill Houses; and for realtors' early opposition to public housing near Parkchester, see "Public Housing Held Bad for Local Area," *New York Herald Tribune*, 17 March 1951. The one exception to the low-rent South Bronx projects was the St. Mary's Park Houses, which were completed in 1959 for middle-income families. See "Remarks of Mayor Robert F. Wagner at Groundbreaking, St. Mary's Park Houses," 9 May 1956, box 130, folder 1907, Wagner Papers.

11. Schwartz, *The New York Approach*, 131–43, 170–203; Rosalie Genevro, "Site Selection and the New York City Housing Authority, 1934–1939," *Journal of Urban History* 12 (Aug. 1986): 334–52, particularly p. 336 on the high price of slum properties; Richard M. Flanagan, "The Housing Act of 1954: The Sea Change in National Urban Policy," *Urban Affairs Review* 33:2 (Nov. 1997): 265–86.

12. Robert A. Caro, *The Power Broker: Robert Moses and the Fall of New York* (New York: Knopf, 1974), 961–83, 1006–1025. See the exchange between Sophia Y. Jacobs, President, Urban League of Greater New York, and Robert Moses, Chairman, Mayor's Committee on Slum Clearance. Jacobs to Moses, 4 June 1956, and Moses to Jacobs, 8 June 1956, box 138, folder 1999, Wagner Papers; J. Anthony Panuch, *Relocation in New York City: Special Report to*

Mayor Robert F. Wagner, 15 Dec. 1959, box 136, folder 1982, Wagner Papers. Panuch was special advisor to the mayor on housing and urban renewal.

13. C. Wright Mills, Clarence Senior, and Rose Kohn Goldsen, *The Puerto Rican Journey: New York's Newest Migrants* (1950; reprint, New York: Russell & Russell, 1967), 187; Rosenwaike, *Population History of New York City*, 139, 141.

14. The full extent of the city's concern with the Puerto Rican migration can be seen in the Mayor Wagner Papers, especially box 60, folders 693–94; box 132, folders 1953, 1954, and 1958; box 276, folders 3209, 3211–3212, 3214–3218; and box 277, folder 3222; and Mayor's Committee on Unity Papers, box 1615, New York City Municipal Archives.

15. Schwartz, *The New York Approach*, 200; Samuel Lubell, "The Boiling Bronx: Henry Wallace Stronghold," *Saturday Evening Post*, 23 Oct. 1948, 19; Charles Abrams, *Forbidden Neighbors* (New York: Harper & Brothers, 1955), 56–69, 158. Quotes are from Lubell, "The Boiling Bronx." On the link between darker-skinned Puerto Ricans and areas of black settlement see Clara Rodriguez, *Puerto Ricans: Born in the U.S.A.* (Boulder, CO: Westview., 1991), 49–85 and Terry J. Rosenberg, *Residence, Employment and Mobility of Puerto Ricans in New York City* (Chicago: University of Chicago Press, 1974), 66–68.

16. See the following in the Wagner Papers: "Intergroup Relations in New York City: Progress and Problems, A Survey Summary," National Council of Christians and Jews, Manhattan–Westchester Region, February 1954, 7–11, in box 59, folder 685; Reverend Ernest Davies and Gertrude Solomon, The Claremont Area Housing Committee, to Mayor Robert Wagner, 14 April 1954, box 137, folder 1990; New York Commission on Inter-Group Relations, "Memorandum on Tensions in Astoria," box 59, folder 686.

17. Jonnes, *South Bronx Rising*, 99, 205–24; Clara Rodriguez, "Growing up in the Forties and Fifties," in Robert Jensen, project director, *Devastation/Resurrection: The South Bronx* (Bronx, NY: Bronx Museum of the Arts, 1979), 45–50; Samuel Lubell, *The Future of American Politics*, 3rd ed., revised (New York: Harper & Row, 1965), 97. For Puerto Rican life before coming to New York, see Esmeralda Santiago, *When I Was Puerto Rican* (New York: Vintage, 1993); Edwin Rivera, *Family Installments: Memories of Growing up Hispanic* (New York: Penguin, 1983). For a case study of the black migration to the north, see Nicholas Lemann, *The Promised Land: The Great Black Migration and How It Changed America* (New York: Knopf, 1991).

18. Grusen, "New Faces in the Lower Bronx." For examples of that resentment, see Julius Jacobs, *Bronx Cheer: A Memoir* (Monroe, NY: Library Research Associates, 1976); Michael Dorman, *The Making of a Slum* (New York: Delacorte, 1972).

19. New York City's Youth Board was an important part of this endeavor. New York City Youth Board, "Minutes: Committee on Changing Neighborhoods and Shifting Population," 21 Feb. 1956, box 46, folder 561; *Youth Board News*, May 1959, box 156, folder 2162, Wagner Papers.

20. "New York's First Desegregation Project a Success," Office of the Mayor Press

Release, 21 December 1956, box 59, folder 687, Wagner Papers. This release also detailed the committee's activities to promote integration in other parts of the Morrisania neighborhood. Schwartz, *The New York Approach*, 164–69, 202; B. F. McLaurie to Mayor Robert F. Wagner, 17 June 1958, box 132, folder 1953, Wagner Papers.

21. Housed in City Hall and funded by private sources, the Unity Committee was a carryover from the interethnic conflict of the prewar years and the unity campaigns of the war. Office of Mayor LaGuardia, Press Release, 27 Feb. 1944, box 3908, folder 11, LaGuardia Papers; Welfare Council of New York City, *Report of the Committee on Puerto Ricans in New York City*, Feb. 1948; Office of the Mayor, Press Release, 17 Jan. 1956, box 276, folder 3217, Wagner Papers.

22. Ecker quoted in Jackson, *A Place Called Home*, 241–42; Schwartz, *The New York Approach*, 84–107; New York City Commission on Inter-Group Relations, "Research Report on Aspects of Administration and Enforcement of the Fair Housing Practices Law, April 1–September 30, 1958," box 60, folder 694, Wagner Papers.

23. "Melting Pot Politics: Its Practitioners in the East Bronx Work at Their Profession Amidst the Big-City Problems of Racial Tension and Radicalism," *Life*, 27 Oct. 1952, 125–29; Colin L. Powell, *My American Journey* (New York: Random House, 1995), 19, 29; "Text of Wagner Speech," 27 Dec. 1959; box 139, folder 2007, Wagner Papers.

24. See the following sources in the Wagner Papers: New York City Housing Authority, "The First Six Months," 1 Nov. 1958, 12, box 60, folder 695; "Report of Subcommittee on Middle Income Housing," 29 Aug. 1955, quoted from p. a, box 138, folder 1994; "Publicly Aided Housing," April 1961, box 140, folder 2012; New York City Housing Authority, Chairman William Reid, Press Release, 2 Feb. 1959, box 133, folder 1961. Ira Robbins's comments in *New York Times*, 12 Feb. 1961. See also Jackson, *A Place Called Home*, 252–53; Barbara M. Woodfill, *New York City's Mitchell-Lama Progam: Middle-Income Housing* (New York: Rand Institute, June 1971).

25. Plunz, *History of Housing*, 281, 286–87; Jonnes, *South Bronx Rising*, 273–76; Harriet Bailer, Letters to the Editor, *New York Times*, 5 June 1996.

26. City of New York, President of the Borough of the Bronx, "Route Study for Development Plan: Cross-Bronx Thruway," Jan. 1944; James J. Lyons, President of the Borough of the Bronx, "Traffic in the Bronx: Studies and Recommendations for Preventing Congestion—Factors, Objectives, Conclusions," Sept. 1947; Marshall Berman, *All That Is Solid Melts Into Air* (New York: Simon and Schuster, 1982), quote on 282; Caro, *The Power Broker*, 839–43, 850–94; Ray Bromley, "Not So Simple! Caro, Moses, and the Impact of the Cross-Bronx Expressway," *The Bronx County Historical Society Journal* 35 (spring 1998): 5–29; Donald G. Sullivan, "1940–1965, Population Mobility in the South Bronx," in *Devastation/Resurrection*, ed. Jensen, 42.

27. Suzanne Daley, "Lost Neighborhood Found in Memory," *New York Times*, 25 April 1983.

28. Jack Kugelmass, *The Miracle of Intervale Avenue: The Story of a Jewish Congregation in the South Bronx* (New York: Schocken, 1986); Clara Rodriguez, "Growing up in the Forties and Fifties"; Sheila Rule, "Amid Urban Decay, Reflections on Pope's Visit," *New York Times*, 27 Sept. 1979, and "Alexander Avenue, Island in the Bronx," 1 Feb. 1969; Community Council of Greater New York, *Bronx Communities: Population Characteristics and Neighborhood Social Resources* (New York, March 1959), 3–5.

29. Schwartz, *The New York Approach*, chapters 4 to 7; Jackson, *A Place Called Home*, 238–84. The housing and urban renewal folders in the Wagner Papers are filled with references about keeping the middle class in the city.

30. "Bronx Apartment Houses Constructed Prior to and Since 1950 Census," ca. 1955, box 45, folder 555, Wagner Papers; *Real Estate Weekly*, 24 April 1958; Jonnes, *South Bronx Rising*, 128–31.

31. Jonnes, *South Bronx Rising*, 152; Edgar M. Hoover and Raymond Vernon, *Anatomy of a Metropolis:The Changing Distribution of People and Jobs Within the New York Metropolitan Region* (Cambridge: Harvard University Press, 1959), 229–60; Michael N. Danielson and Jameson W. Doig, *New York: The Politics of Urban Regional Development* (Berkeley: University of California Press, 1982), 54–56; Andres Torres, *Between Melting Pot and Mosaic: African Americans and Puerto Ricans in the New York Political Economy* (Philadelphia: Temple University Press, 1995), 9–32; and the following two items in Ronald Takaki, ed., *From Different Shores: Perspectives on Race and Ethnicity in America* (New York: Oxford University Press, 1994): Marta Tienda, "Puerto Ricans and the Underclass Debate," 261–69; Clara E. Rodriguez, "Puerto Ricans and the Political Economy of New York," 118–23.

32. Institute for Urban Studies, Fordham University, *A Profile of the Bronx Economy* (New York, July 1967), 1–47, 113, 179–83, quotes are on ii and 208; Institute for Urban Studies, Fordham University, Office of South Bronx Redevelopment Affairs, *Industrial Activity in the Inner City: A Case Study of The South Bronx* (New York, April 1981).

33. Joseph P. Fried, "Is South Bronx Revival Plan Simply Folly?," *New York Times,* 19 June 1978; Herbert E. Meyer, "How Government Helped Ruin the South Bronx," *Fortune*, Nov. 1975, 144–45; Melissa Epstein, "How Dismantling the Third Avenue El Hurt the South Bronx" (Senior Thesis, Columbia University School of Architecture and Urban Planning, 1998); *New York Affairs* 1:4 (spring 1974): front cover illustration.

34. See the following articles in *New York Times*: John C. Devlin, "Hunts Point Follows the Pattern of Poverty," 23 March 1964, John Kifner, "Giant City Agency to Reorganize Aid to Poor is Urged," 27 June 1966, "Protest on Heatless Homes in Bronx Sent to Mayor," 11 Feb. 1970, "55 in State Senate Ask U.S. Aid to City Slums as Disaster Areas," 18 Feb. 1970; and also Thomas Glynn, "The South Bronx," *Neighborhood,* Aug. 1982, 7–14, 25; Meyer, "How Government Helped Ruin the South Bronx," 140–41. The extreme impoverish-

ment of the South Bronx can be seen in Dennis Smith, *Report from Engine Co. 82* (New York: Saturday Review Press, 1972).

35. Quoted in New York City, Office of the Mayor, *Summary: The South Bronx, A Plan for Revitalization*, Dec. 1977, 2; Michael A. Stegman, *Housing in New York: Study of a City, 1984* (New York: New York City Department of Housing, Preservation and Development, February 1985), 197.

36. For information on gang activity in the Bronx, see Wagner Papers: Office of the Mayor, Press Release, 14 Sept. 1954, box 136, folder 1982; New York City Youth Board, "Juvenile Delinquency in Critical Areas: Rates, Maps, Characteristics, 1957," box 163; New York City Youth Board, "A Realistic Approach to New York City's Teen-Gang Problem," attached to "Memorandum," 23 Aug. 1954, box 45, folder 554; Claudia Zaslavsky, Coordinator, Gun Hill Community Center, to Deputy Mayor Henry Epstein, 29 June 1955, box 46, folder 560; "Youth Board Launches Drive to Reduce Delinquency in the Morrisania–Belmont Section of The Bronx," article published in *Youth Board News*, Feb. 1955, box 46, folder 558; New York City Youth Board, "Interim Report #4: Summer Vigilance and Summer Services for Youth by New York City's Public Agencies," 1 May 1958, box 161, folder 2207. Quoted in Powell, *My American Journey*, 29. For an analysis of New York gangs, see Eric C. Schneider, *Vampires, Dragons, and Egyptian Kings: Youth Gangs in Postwar New York* (Princeton: Princeton University Press, 1999), 1–26, 51–136, 201–16.

37. For the outbreak of crime in the nation, see James Q. Wilson, *Thinking About Crime*, rev. ed. (New York: Basic Books, 1983), 3–30. My concern is not with how best to measure crime but with how it increased dramatically however it was measured.

38. The impact of crime on race relations, political campaigns, and neighborhood life is easily discerned in the *New York Times Index*, 1960 to 1980, under "Crime—New York City." On the link between drugs and crime see the series of articles by Richard Severo in *New York Times*, 23 to 26 Sept. 1969. On the link between minorities and crime see Jim Sleeper, *The Closest of Strangers: Liberalism and the Politics of Race in New York* (New York: Norton, 1990), 104, 133–40; Ronald Barri Flowers, *Minorities and Criminality* (Westport, CN: Greenwood Press, 1988), 57–79. On the link between disorder and crime see Wesley G. Skogan, *Disorder and Decline: Crime and the Spiral of Decay in American Neighborhoods* (Berkeley: University of California Press, 1990).

39. David Burnham, "Bronx Police Aim at Indoor Crime," *New York Times*, 24 Dec. 1969.

40. Jensen, *Devastation/Resurrection*, 54; Ian Fisher, "Pulling Out of Fort Apache, the Bronx," *New York Times*, 23 June 1993; Tom Walker, *Fort Apache: Life and Work in New York City's Most Violent Precinct* (New York: Thomas Crowell, 1976); Smith, *Report from Engine Co. 82*, 11. Smith's firehouse was around the corner from the police precinct.

41. McCandlish Phillips, "Fatal Mugging Stirs Fears in Bronx Neighborhood," *New York Times*, 15 Feb. 1967; Charles G. Bennett, "Councilman Sees 'Terror' in Bronx," *New York Times*, 2 March 1967; Nevard quoted in Homer Bigart, "Two Communities Seek More Police," *New York Times*, 10 March 1967.

42. "40 in Bronx Seek Gun Permits for Protection Against Addicts," *New York Times*, 26 Sept. 1969.

43. Martin Tolchin, "Gangs Spread Terror in the South Bronx," *New York Times*, 16 Jan. 1973, quote on 28.

44. Victor Marrero was director of the Bronx Model Cities program. Marrero quoted in Martin Tolchin, "Rage Permeates All Facets of Life in the South Bronx," *New York Times*, 17 Jan. 1973. See also Gary Hoenig, *Reaper: The Story of a Gang Leader* (New York: Bobbs-Merrill, 1975); Jon Bradshaw, "Savage Skulls," *Esquire*, June 1977, 74–82, 131–44; Jonnes, *South Bronx Rising*, 236–48; Fisher, "Pulling Out of Fort Apache, the Bronx"; Schneider, *Vampires, Dragons, and Egyptian Kings*, 217–45. On gangs in general, see Malcolm W. Klein, *The American Street Gang: Its Nature, Prevalence, and Control* (New York: Oxford University Press, 1995).

45. See the week-long series on city conditions, *New York Times*, 1–8 June 1969. On the welfare movement see Larry R. Jackson and William A. Johnson, *Protest by the Poor: The Welfare Rights Movement in New York City* (Lexington, MA: Lexington Books, 1974), 103–4, 121–22; Carmen Arroya quoted in Jonnes, *South Bronx Rising*, 178–79.

46. On teachers, police, and housing controversies, see the following three articles in Jewel Bellush and Stephen M. David, eds., *Race and Politics in New York City: Five Studies in Policy-Making* (New York: Praeger, 1971): Marilyn Gittell, "Education: The Decentralization–Community Control Controversy"; Edward T. Rogowsky, Louis H. Gold, and David W. Abbott, "Police: The Civilian Review Board Controversy"; Jewel Bellush, "Housing: The Scattered-Site Controversy." On Lincoln Hospital, see two articles in Andres Torres and Jose E. Velasquez, eds., *The Puerto Rican Movement: Voices from the Diaspora* (Philadelphia: Temple University Press, 1998), 155–72, 21–27: Pablo Guzmán, "La Vida Pura: A Lord of the Barrio," 165–66; Iris Morales, "¡Palante, Siempre Palante! The Young Lords," 216.

47. Richard Severo, "Hunts Point: Ruled by Addicts," *New York Times*, 24 Sept. 1969; Dorman, *The Making of a Slum*, 79–105, 119–34; John Sibley, "Bathgate Scene is Different Now," *New York Times*, 1 June 1965; Martin Tolchin, "South Bronx: A Jungle Stalked by Fear, Seized by Rage," *New York Times*, 15 Jan. 1973. Walker, *Fort Apache*, conveys the despair and rage that permeated the Simpson and Fox streets area of the "Old East Bronx."

48. Brant quoted in Jonnes, *South Bronx Rising*, 346. The extent and exact location of population shifts are not revealed by boroughwide census figures or by Community Board District statistics, which the city began compiling in 1970.

49. See three articles in *New York Times*, 15 July 1977: Selwyn Raab, "Ravage Continues Far Into Day, Gunfire and Bottles Beset Police," Robert D. McFadden,

"New York Power Restored Slowly, Looting Widespread," Joseph B. Treaster, "Blackout Arrests Swamp City's Criminal-Justice System"; and two reports in *New York Times*, 17 July 1977: Robert D. McFadden, "Businessmen Angry as Beame Inspects City's Looted Areas," E. J. Dionne Jr., "Owner of a Looted Store in Bronx Exchanges Words With the Mayor." An analysis of the episode is found in Robert Curvin and Bruce Porter, *Blackout Looting! New York City, July 13, 1977* (New York: Gardner Press, 1979).

50. *Community District Needs: The Bronx, Fiscal Year 1990* (City of New York, Department of City Planning), 224.

51. New York City Housing Authority, *Project Data*, 31 Dec. 1977.

52. For Forest Houses see petitions, police department memos, and letters from the police commissioner to the mayor, August to November 1955, box 127, folder 1829, Wagner Papers; for crime statistics in housing projects see Office of the Mayor, Press Release, 30 March 1957, box 60, folder 691, Wagner Papers. See also Schwartz, *The New York Approach*, 289–94; Oscar Newman, *Defensible Space: Crime Prevention Through Urban Design* (New York: Macmillan, 1972); Phillip Thompson, "Public Housing in New York City," in *Housing and Community Development in New York City: Facing the Future*, ed. Michael H. Schill (Albany: State University of New York Press, 1999), 119–42. For an in-depth study of a public housing project, see Sudir Alladi Venkatesh, *American Project: The Rise and Fall of a Modern Ghetto* (Cambridge: Harvard University Press, 2000).

53. New York City Housing Authority, *Project Data*, 31 Dec. 1977.

54. This premise is based on Robert J. Sampson, "The Community," in *Crime*, ed. James Q. Wilson and Joan Petersilia (San Francisco: ICS Press, Institute for Contemporary Studies, 1995), 193–216; Wilson, *Thinking About Crime*, 21–39; Skogan, *Disorder and Decline*, 1–84. See also Rodriguez, *Puerto Ricans: Born in the U.S.A.*, especially chapter 5, "Housing and the South Bronx," 106–19. Quoted in Women's City Club of New York, Inc., *With Love and Affection: A Study of Building Abandonment* (New York, 1977), 3.

55. The literature on building abandonment is vast. My understanding of it is based on George Sternlieb, Robert W. Burchell, James W. Hughes, and Franklin J. James, "Housing Abandonment in the Urban Core," *Journal of the American Institute of Planners* 40:5 (Sept. 1974): 321–32; George Sternlieb and James W. Hughes, *Housing and Economic Reality: New York City, 1976* (New Brunswick: The Center for Urban Policy Research, 1976); Peter Marcuse, *Housing Abandonment: Does Rent Control Make a Difference?* (New York, June 1981); and David Bartelt and Ronald Lawson, "Rent Control and Abandonment in New York City: A Look at the Evidence," in *Critical Perspectives in Housing*, ed. Rachel G. Bratt, Chester Hartman, and Ann Meyerson (Philadelphia: Temple University Press, 1986), 180–83. Nathan Glazer quoted in Glazer, "The South Bronx Story: An Extreme Case of Urban Decline," *Policy Studies Journal* 16 (winter 1987): 271.

56. Statistics from Michael A. Stegman, *The Dynamics of Rental Housing in New*

York City (Piscataway, NJ: Center for Urban Policy Research, 1982), 177–79. Since the number of lost housing units ranged from 57,000 to almost 109,000 because of what was counted, when it was counted, how it was counted, and even whether it was demolished or not, anecdotal descriptions and photographs convey the enormity of the devastion better. See Frank Kristoff, "Housing and People in New York City: A View of the Past, Present, and Future," *City Almanac* 10 (Feb. 1976): 5; and discussion of what was counted in Michael Goodwin, "1980 Census Housing Figures Show 2 New York Cities," *New York Times*, 14 June 1981. For photos of the devastation, see Camilo Jose Vergara, *The New American Ghetto* (New Brunswick: Rutgers University Press, 1995); Mel Rosenthal, *In the South Bronx of America* (Willimantic, CT: Curbstone Press, 2000).

57. See articles in *New York Times*: David K. Shipler, "The Changing City: Housing Paralysis," 5 June 1969; Fried, "Is South Bronx Revival Plan Simply Folly?," 19 June 1978; David W. Dunlap, "Bronx Housing Devastation Found Slowing Substantially," 22 March 1982.

58. Charles Kaiser, "Survival of South Bronx Row Houses Celebrated," *New York Times*, 10 Nov. 1976; "Hanging On: A Landmark Isle," *New York Times*, 20 March 1983; also Landmarks Preservation Commission, *Clay Avenue Historic District Report* (New York, 1994); Lori M. Maida, "Belmont: A Community Fighting to Survive" (Ph.D. diss., Fordham University, 1987). See map showing vacant and devastated housing south of Fordham Road that accompanied Dunlap, "Bronx Housing Devastation Found Slowing Substantially," *New York Times*, 22 March 1982.

59. The period after which the city could take over a tax-delinquent property went from 4 years in 1970 to 1 year in 1977. But by 1968 the city was already the biggest owner of apartment buildings in the city. Women's City Club, *With Love and Affection*, 1–6; Marcuse, *Housing Abandonment*, 40; Sullivan, "The Process of Abandonment," 69–71.

60. Deborah Wallace and Roderick Wallace, *A Plague on Your Houses: How New York Was Burned Down and National Public Health Crumbled* (New York: Verso, 1998), 21–63, quoted from 55; Joseph P. Fried, "Housing Abandonment Spreads in Bronx and Parts of Brooklyn," *New York Times*, 12 April 1976; New York Urban Coalition, *Housing Rehabilitation Task Force* (New York, January 1976), 15.

61. Sternlieb, Burchell, Hughes, and James, "Housing Abandonment in the Urban Core," 324–26; Women's City Club, *With Love and Affection*, 2; Peter Salins, *The Ecology of Housing Destruction: Economic Effects of Public Intervention in the Housing Market* (New York: New York University, 1980), 19–38; Alan S. Oser, "Causes of Abandonment and What to do About Them Despair Housing Officials," *New York Times*, 14 May 1976; Rodriguez, *Puerto Ricans: Born in the U.S.A.*, 110.

62. Severo, "Hunts Point: Ruled by Addicts"; Mel Ziegler, "Biography of an Unwanted Building," *New York*, 24 May 1971, 30–34. Martin quoted in Gelvin

Stevenson, "The Abandonment of Roosevelt Gardens," in *Devastation/Resurrection*, ed. Jensen, 80.

63. Alan S. Oser, "Bronx Fires: Final Stage of a Long Process," *New York Times*, 20 June 1975; David Vidal, "Bronx Fires Leave Trail of Homelessness and Fear," *New York Times*, 23 June 1975. The extremely high interest rates of the late 1970s made low-premium fire insurance policies attractive in the high-risk area of the South Bronx. Insurers reinvested premium deposits for quick profits and reinsured their newly issued policies with Lloyds of London to cover the resulting spate of fire claims. The scheme ended with Lloyds losing millions of dollars and many landlords being indicted for insurance fraud and arson. See Michael Jacobson and Philip Kasinitz, "Burning the Bronx for Profit," *The Nation*, 15 Nov. 1986, 512–15, quote is on 514.

64. Joseph P. Fried, "Vandalized South Bronx Project Gets New Chance," *New York Times*, 6 July 1978; Martin Gottlieb, "The Scrapping of New York," *Daily News*, 5 to 7 Jan. 1981. Reverend Moore quoted in Joseph B. Treaster, "20% Rise in Fires is Adding to Decline of South Bronx," *New York Times*, 18 May 1975.

65. Bernard Weinraub, "Once-Grand Concourse," *New York Times*, 2 Feb. 1965; Steven V. Roberts, "Grand Concourse: Hub of Bronx Is Undergoing Ethnic Changes," *New York Times*, 21 July 1966; Jonnes, *South Bronx Rising*, 268–99, quote is from 273. The first tenants began moving into Co-op City in December 1969. See *New York Times*, 9 Nov. 1969, VIII, 1.

66. West Bronx landlord quoted in Ziegler, "Biography of an Unwanted Building," 32–33; banker quoted in Oser, "Bronx Fires: Final Stage of a Long Process"; Dena Kleiman, "West Tremont Typical of Blight," *New York Times*, 13 April 1978.

67. For the city Youth Services Administration's effort to work with gangs, see Hoenig, *Reaper*, 87–97. See also Miriam Ostow and Charles Brecher, "Work and Welfare," 155–78, in *New York Is Very Much Alive: A Manpower View*, ed. Eli Ginzberg (New York: McGraw-Hill, 1973); Robert Kolodny, *Self-Help in the Inner City: A Study of Lower Income Cooperative Housing Conversion in New York* (New York: United Neighborhood Houses of New York, Inc., September 1973), 118–19; Flora Sellers Davidson, "City Policy and Housing Abandonment: A Case Study of New York City, 1965–1973" (Ph.D. diss., Columbia University, 1979), 221–22; Frank P. Braconi, "In Re *In Rem*: Innovation and Expediency in New York's Housing Policy," in *Housing and Community Development in New York City*, ed. Schill, 96–97.

68. Jonnes, *South Bronx Rising*, 182–98, 256–59; and *New York Times* articles, C. Gerald Fraser, "Bronx Poverty Post Stirs Clash of Negroes and Puerto Ricans," 18 April 1968; David K. Shipler, "Aide Dies in Fight on Poverty Funds," 8 August 1969; Sandra Perlman Schoenberg and Patricia L. Rosenbaum, *Neighborhoods That Work: Sources for Viability in the Inner City* (New Brunswick: Rutgers University Press, 1980), 22–29; R. Allen Hays, *The Federal Government & Urban Housing: Ideology and Change in Public Policy* (Albany: State University of New York Press, 1995), 111–30.

69. Jonnes, *South Bronx Rising*, 311–32; Thomas Glynn, "Charlotte Street, the Bronx," *Neighborhood*, August 1982, 27–29; and Manes quoted in Fried, "Is South Bronx Revival Plan Simply Folly?," *New York Times*, 19 June 1978.

70. Brooks and Merola quoted in Jonnes, *South Bronx Rising*, 252 and 261; *New York Times* articles: "Priest is Ejected After Scolding City Council About Bronx Slum," 18 Feb. 1970; "Councilmen to Tour Hunts Point Homes," 2 March 1970. See also Badillo's views on arson in Wallace and Wallace, *A Plague on Your Houses*, 62.

71. Tolchin, "South Bronx: A Jungle Stalked by Fear, Seized by Rage."

72. Removal of the Third Avenue Elevated Line eliminated downtown transit for 300,000 Bronx residents, most of whom lived in low-rent public housing. Epstein, "How Dismantling the Third Avenue El Hurt the South Bronx," 30–31; three artices in *New York Times*: Joseph P. Fried, "City's Housing Administrator Proposes 'Planned Shrinkage' of Some Slums," 3 Feb. 1976; Francis X. Clines, "Blighted Areas' Use Is Urged by Rohatyn," 16 March 1976; Thomas A. Johnson, "Rohatyn Scored by Congressman," 17 March 1976; Roger Starr, "Making New York Smaller," *New York Times Magazine*, 14 Nov. 1976. The two officials were Roger Starr, head of the city's Housing and Development Administration, and Felix Rohatyn, chairman of the Municipal Assistance Corporation, which was overseeing the city's finances. The link between arson and planned shrinkage is central to Wallace and Wallace, *A Plague on Your Houses*, 21–82. For the cutback on city services, see Peter Marcuse, "Neighborhood Policy and the Distribution of Power: New York City's Community Boards," *Policy Studies Journal* 16:2 (winter 1987): 281–82.

73. Badillo quoted in Johnson, "Rohatyn Scored by Congressmen;" and Father Luce quoted in Glynn, "The South Bronx," 12.

74. On Badillo and Abrams, see Jonnes, *South Bronx Rising*, 267, 354; Wallace and Wallace, *A Plague on Both Your Houses*, 62–63; and two *New York Times* articles: "In Defense of the Bronx," 16 Nov. 1976; Francis X. Clines, "About New York: A 'Hidden' Side of the Bronx," 6 July 1978.

75. Jack Newfield and Wayne Barrett, *City for Sale: Ed Koch and the Betrayal of New York* (New York: Harper & Row, 1988), 444.

76. For crime and the underground economy of the city see Stanley Friedlander and Charles Brecher, "A Comparative View," in *New York Is Very Much Alive*, ed. Ginzberg, 20–41; Jagna Wojcicka Sharf, "The Underground Economy of a Poor Neighborhood," in *Cities of the United States: Studies in Urban Anthropology*, ed. Leith Mullings (New York: Columbia University Press, 1987), 19–50.

77. Jonnes, *South Bronx Rising*, 281–87; Dena Kleiman, "City Urges U.S. to House Aged in Concourse Plaza," *New York Times*, 12 Dec. 1978; Nicholas King, "South Bronx: A Crusade Goes Sour," *National Review*, 20 Feb. 1981, 162–63; Tim Golden, "C'est le Bronx Où Sont les Maisons Abandonées?," *New York Times*, 16 Nov. 1990; Craig Horowitz, "A South Bronx Renaissance," *New York*, 21 Nov. 1994.

78. Rockefeller quoted in Charles J. Orlebeke, *New Life at Ground Zero: New York, Home Ownership, and the Future of American Cities* (Albany, NY: The Rockefeller Institute Press, 1997), 2, italics in the original.

8. THE ROAD BACK

1. Robert Jensen and Cathy A. Alexander, "Resurrection: The People Are Doing It Themselves," in Robert Jensen, project director, *Devastation/Resurrection: The South Bronx* (Bronx, NY: Bronx Museum of the Arts, 1979), 83–112, quote on 83; Terry quoted in Thomas Glynn, "The South Bronx," *Neighborhood,* Aug. 1982, 16; Charles J. Orlebeke, *New Life at Ground Zero: New York, Home Ownership, and the Future of American Cities* (Albany, NY: The Rockefeller Institute Press, 1997), 21.

2. Mary K. Nenno, "Changes and Challanges in Affordable Housing and Urban Development," in *Affordable Housing and Urban Redevelopment in the United States,* ed. Willem Van Vliet (Thousand Oaks, CA: Sage, 1997), 1–21; Kathryn Wylde, "The Contribution of Public-Private Partnerships to New York's Assisted Housing Industry," in *Housing and Community Development in New York City: Facing the Future,* ed.Michael H. Schill (Albany: State University of New York Press, 1999), 73–91; James Barron, "$5 Billion Plan For Apartments Pushed in Bronx," *New York Times,* 28 Feb. 1989.

3. Quoted in Jill Jonnes, *South Bronx Rising: The Rise, Fall, and Resurrection of an American City* (New York: Fordham University Press, 2002), 347–48. See also David Gonzalez, "Bronx Community Groups Find Strength in Unity," *New York Times,* 17 July 1994; Wolfgang Saxon, "Anne Devenney, 79, Bronx Guardian Dies," *New York Times,* 16 Feb. 2000; Jordan Moss, "Fighting Fires With Fire," *City Limits,* April 2000. For an analysis of the efficacy of the NWBCCC, see Joseph Anthony Trumino, "The Northwest Bronx Community and Clergy Coalition: A Neighborhood Organization and Its Membership in Conflict and Struggle" (Ph.D. diss., City University of New York, 1991).

4. Nancy and Frank Potts quoted in Janice Simpson and Derek Reveron, "Own Your Own Apartment House—for the Price of a Second-hand Car," *New York Post,* 1 Aug. 1977; and also Roberta Brandes Gratz, *The Living City: How America's Cities Are Being Revitalized in a Big Way* (New York: Wiley, 1994), 84–85, 103–10. Frank Potts may have been referring to the displacement of blacks from other areas of the city because of urban renewal policies. See Caro, *The Power Broker,* 961–83.

5. Roger M. Williams, "The New Urban Pioneers: Homesteading in the Slums," *Saturday Review,* 23 Jan. 1977, 9; quoted in Thomas Glynn, "Something Good Is Growing in the South Bronx: People's Development Corporation," *Neighborhood,* Dec. 1977, 14; Jensen and Alexander, "Resurrection: The People Are Doing It Themselves," 85–88; Jonnes, *South Bronx Rising,* 303–13, 320–21.

6. John Holtzclaw, "Greening the South Bronx," *Sierra,* July 1979, 30; Glynn, "The South Bronx," 22; Jonnes, *South Bronx Rising,* 326; Amy Waldman, "In

the Rebuilt South Bronx, A Pioneer of Sweat Equity Fights to Keep His Ideals," *New York Times*, 18 Jan. 2000.

7. Jensen and Alexander, "Resurrection: The People Are Doing It Themselves," 84–85; Glynn, "The South Bronx," 18–19; Diane Winston, "Self-Help and the Private Sector: LISC in the South Bronx," Master's Project, Columbia University School of Journalism, 1982, 21–26; Gratz, *The Living City*, 83–132, Velez quoted on 130; Press Release, 24 March 1984, Mayor Edward Koch Papers, New York City Municipal Archives.

8. Jensen and Alexander, "Resurrection: The People Are Doing It Themselves," 94–96; Gigante quoted in Orlebeke, *New Life at Ground Zero*, 173–74.

9. Peter McLaughlin, "Hunts Point Puts Hopes in Building Boom," *New York Daily News*, 7 Aug. 1977; Winston, "Self-Help and the Private Sector," 16–21, Gigante quoted on 19; Dexter Filkins, "In Bronx Revival, Ferrer Is Credited With Only a Supporting Role," *New York Times*, 5 Aug. 2001. The 2,100 figure is from Jill Jonnes, *We're Still Here: The Rise and Fall of the South Bronx* (New York: Atlantic Monthly Press, 1986), 379; this is the older edition of Jonnes, *South Bronx Rising*.

10. Brooks quoted in Glynn, "The South Bronx," 17–18; "Help From the Desperados: For New Hope Plaza, a New Look," *New York Times*, 29 May 1983; Kathleen Teltsch, "Once Desperate, A Bronx Housing Group Earns Praise," *New York Times*, 30 Oct. 1987; Filkins, "In Bronx Revival, Ferrer Is Credited With Only a Supporting Role."

11. Gratz, *The Living City*, 134–35; Winston, "Self-Help and the Private Sector," 5–14; Shawn G. Kennedy, "Landmarking's Double-Edged Sword," *New York Times*, 13 Jan. 1991. By 1990, the Bronx had 52 official landmarks, 5 historic districts, and 94 additional Bronx places proposed. See Gary Hermalyn and Robert Kornfeld, *Landmarks in The Bronx* (Bronx, NY: The Bronx County Historical Society, 1989).

12. United Bronx Parents Records, 1966–1989, Archives of Center for Puerto Rican Studies, Hunter College Library, New York City; John Darnton, "Gigante vs. Velez in Ring of Slum Politics," *New York Times*, 19 Nov. 1973; Robert Halpern, *Rebuilding the Inner City: A History of Neighborhood Initiatives to Address Poverty in the United States* (New York: Columbia University Press, 1995), 106–42; Brooks quoted in Teltsch, "Once Desperate, A Bronx Housing Group Earns Praise."

13. Gratz, *The Living City*, 118; Wylde, "The Contribution of Public-Private Partnerships to New York's Assisted Housing Industry," 79, 84; Orlebeke, *New Life at Ground Zero*, 194–95; Rachel G. Bratt, Avis C. Vidal, Alex Schwartz, Langley C. Keyes, and Jim Stockard, "The Status of Nonprofit-Owned Affordable Housing: Short-Term Successes and Long-Term Challenges," *Journal of the American Planning Association* 64 (winter 1998): 39–51.

14. David Rogers, "Community Control and Decentralization," in *Urban Politics New York Style*, ed. Jewel Bellush and Dick Netzer (Armonk, NY: M.E. Sharpe, 1990), 143–88; and three books by Jonathan Kozol, *Savage Inequalities:*

Children in America's Schools (New York: HarperPerennial, 1992); *Amazing Grace: The Lives of Children and the Conscience of a Nation* (New York: Crown, 1995); *Ordinary Resurrections: Children in the Years of Hope* (New York: Crown, 2000). School Districts 9 and 12 had long histories of corruption and bribery charges. See Ralph Blumenthal and Sam Howe Verhovek, "Patronage and Profit in Schools: A Tale of a Bronx District Board," *New York Times*, 16 Dec. 1988; Joseph Berger, "Fernandez Weighs Action on Bronx District 9," *New York Times*, 28 Jan. 1996.

15. Victor Bach, "The Future of HUD-Subsidized Housing: The New York City Case," in *Housing and Community Development in New York City*, ed. Schill, 143–48; R. Allen Hays, *The Federal Government & Urban Housing: Ideology and Change in Public Policy* (Albany: State University of New York Press, 1995), 101–232. Housing unit statistics are in New York Rent Guidelines Board, *Housing NYC: Rents, Markets and Trends '97* (New York, 1997), 121.

16. Father Giganti quoted in Michael T. Kaufman, "Hunts Point Goal: Preserve Housing," *New York Times*, 27 June 1974; Office of the Mayor, *Summary: The South Bronx, A Plan For Revitalization, December 1977*, 5.

17. Orlebeke, *New Life at Ground Zero*, 180–85; Jonnes, *South Bronx Rising*, 356–75; Maura McDermott, "Change in the Bank," *City Limits*, Sept./Oct. 2000, 11–12.

18. Miller quoted in Thomas Glynn, "Anita Miller: A Warrior for the South Bronx," *Neighborhood*, Aug. 1982, 34–37; Wylde, "The Contribution of Public-Private Partnerships to New York's Assisted Housing Industry," 81–84; Rich Cohen, "The Enterprise Foundation: How a National Intermediary Assists Nonprofit Community Development," in *Housing in America: Mobilizing Bankers, Builders and Communities to Solve the Nation's Affordable Housing Crisis*, ed. Jess Lederman (Chicago: Probus, 1993), 241–54.

19. Thomas Glynn, "Charlotte Street, the Bronx," *Neighborhood*, Aug. 1982, 27–31; Jonnes, *South Bronx Rising*, 377–88; and the following *New York Times* articles: Philip Shenon, "Taste of Suburbia Arrives in the South Bronx," 19 March 1983; "Jimmy Carter Revisits the South Bronx," 23 June 1992; Jim Yardley, "Clinton Praises Bronx Renewal As U.S. Model," 11 Dec. 1997. Logue quoted in Carter Wiseman, "Little House on the Rubble," *New York*, 1 June 1981, 54.

20. Hays, *The Federal Government and Urban Housing*, 233–50; W. Dennis Keating and Janet Smith, "Past Federal Policy for Urban Neighborhoods," in *Revitalizing Urban Neighborhoods*, ed. W. Dennis Keating, Norman Krumholz, and Philip Star (Lawrence: University of Kansas Press, 1996), 55; Felice Michetti, "The New York City Capital Program for Affordable Housing," in *Housing in America*, ed. Lederman, 199–213; Jacobson quoted in William E. Geist, "Residents Give A Bronx Cheer to Decal Plan," *New York Times*, 12 Nov. 1983.

21. Jim Rooney, *Organizing the South Bronx* (Albany: State University of New York Press, 1995), 52–55. The politicians were Democratic Party leaders

Patrick Cunningham and Stanley Friedman, Borough President Stanley Simon, and Congressman Mario Biaggi. Congressman Robert Garcia was also convicted, but was later exonerated by an appellate court. Joseph P. Fried, "After Capital Hill, A Climb Out of a Valley," *New York Times*, 18 Nov. 2001.

22. Alan S. Oser, "Public Housing in Abandoned Buildings," *New York Times*, 4 Oct. 1987; Frederick M. Binder and David M. Reimers, *All the Nations Under Heaven: An Ethnic and Racial History of New York City* (New York: Columbia University Press, 1995), 225–31; Ellen Percy Kraly and Ines Miyares, "Immigration to New York: Policy, Population, and Patterns," in *New Immigrants in New York*, ed. Nancy Foner, rev. and updated ed. (New York: Columbia University Press, 2001), 33–79; Department of City Planning, *Community District Needs, The Bronx, Fiscal Year 2000* (City of New York, 2000), quote on 36; New York City Department of City Planning, *Citywide and Borough Population (1990 & 2000)*, 1–3, http://www.nyc.gov/html/popstart.

23. Koch's plan began with $4.2 billion in 1986 and expanded to $5.1 billion a few years later. The South Bronx received the bulk of the rebuilding efforts. Michetti, "The New York City Capital Program for Affordable Housing"; Alan Finder, "Housing Plan Would Fix Up 5,200 Units," *New York Times*, 24 Dec. 1986; Greg G. Van Ryzin and Andrew Genn, "Neighborhood Change and the City of New York's Ten-Year Housing Plan," *Housing Policy Debate* 10:4 (1999): 799–838. Commissioner Biderman quoted in James Barron, "$5 Billion Plan For Apartments Pushed in Bronx," *New York Times*, 28 Feb. 1989.

24 ."A Success Story in the Bronx," *New York Times*, 2 July 1989. LISC helped turn Low Income Housing Tax Credits into rehab funds and the NWBCCC secured reliable contractors.

25. Orlebeke, *New Life at Ground Zero*, 1–148, quote on 59, italics in the original.

26. Lynda Simmons, "Twenty-Five Years of Community Building in the South Bronx: Phipps Houses in West Farms," in *Affordable Housing and Urban Redevelopment in the United States*, ed. Van Vliet, 73–94; Emily M. Bernstein, "Project Mixes Working Class and Ex-Homeless in Bronx," *New York Times*, 16 Sept. 1994; Alan Finder, "New York Pledge to House Poor Works a Rare, Quiet Revolution," *New York Times*, 30 April 1995.

27. Michetti, "The New York City Capital Program for Affordable Housing," 203; Kathleen McGowan, "Building Blocks," *City Limits*, Jan. 2000, 12–15, 27, quote on 13.

28. Mayor Koch and Father Gigante quoted in Orlebeke, *New Life at Ground Zero*, 59, 174; Michetti, "The New York City Capital Program for Affordable Housing," 209; New York City Housing Partnership, "Developments in the Bronx, 1987–2000," Aug. 2000, statistics supplied to the author.

29. Alan S. Oser, "In Brownsville, Churches Joining to Build Homes," *New York Times*, 1 May 1983; Jim Rooney, *Organizing the South Bronx*, 139–218, quotes from 205, 212.

30. Rooney, *Organizing the South Bronx*, 151–218; Bruce Lambert, "Way Cleared for Long-Delayed Housing," *New York Times*, 14 April 1991; Santiago quoted

in David Gonzalez, "South Bronx: Despite Hype, Hope Builds," *New York Times*, 8 June 1996; Jane H. Lii, "South Bronx Churches Will Expand Afford-able Housing," *New York Times*, 4 Dec. 1997.

31. Mervyn Rothstein, "A Renewal Plan in the Bronx Advances," *New York Times*, 10 July 1994; Rachelle Garbarine, "Neighborhood Rises in the South Bronx," *New York Times*, 25 Dec. 1998; Carl Vogel, "Melrose's Thorny Predicament," *City Limits*, Sept./Oct. 1999, 13–15, 32; "New Homes for South Bronx," *New York Times*, 8 Oct. 2000. Quotes are in Rooney, *Organizing the South Bronx*, 217; and Verena Dobnik, "South Bronx Homes and Gardens are an Urban Phoenix," *Staten Island Advance*, 17 Oct. 1999.

32. Quoted in Rooney, *Organizing the Bronx*, 207, 212.

33. Procida and Ferrer quoted in Craig Horowitz, "A South Bronx Renaissance," *New York*, 21 Nov. 1994, 59. For the city's commitment to housing the poor and homeless from the 1980s on and the city's push to get city housing back to taxpaying status, see Frank P. Braconi, "In Re *In Rem*: Innovation and Ex-pediency in New York's Housing Policy," in *Housing and Community Devel-opment in New York City*, ed. Schill, 96–97.

34. Simmons, "Twenty-Five Years of Community Building in the South Bronx: Phipps Houses in West Farms," 82–83;" "Touch of Art Deco in the Bronx," *New York Times*, 28 Nov. 1999; Matthew Strozier, "How West Farms Was Won," *City Limits*, Sept./Oct. 2000, 18–20, quote on 20; Vivian Gornick, "My Neighborhood, Its Fall and Rise," *New York Times*, 24 June 2001.

35. This assessment is based on *The New York Times*, 1980 to 2001; Bronx Bor-ough President Fernando Ferrer, *Strategic Policy Statements* for 1990, 1994, and 1998; Bronx Borough President Fernando Ferrer, *The 2000 State of the Borough Report*; Lori M. Maida, "Belmont: A Community Fighting to Sur-vive" (Ph.D. diss., Fordham University, 1987); New York City Housing Part-nership, "Developments in the Bronx, 1987–2000."

36. For tenant ownership efforts, see Robert Kolodny, *Self-Help in the Inner City: A Study of Lower Income Cooperative Housing Conversion in New York* (New York: United Neighborhood Houses of New York, Inc., September 1973); An-drew White and Susan Saegert, "Return From Abandonment: The Tenant In-terim Lease Program and the Development of Low-Income Cooperatives in New York City's Most Neglected Neighborhoods," in *Affordable Housing and Urban Redevelopment in the United States*, ed. Van Vliet, 158–80; Sam Howe Verhovek, "On One Women's Grit, A Building Revives," *New York Times*, 22 Aug. 1987; Kathleen McGowan and Philip Shishkin, "The Promised Land," *City Limits*, March 1999. Melendez quoted in Juan Forero, "No Longer A War Zone, Hunts Point Gains Status," *New York Times*, 23 Aug. 2000.

37. Menshel quoted in "Bronx Tale," *New York*, 19–26 Dec. 1994, 84; Carol S. Co-hen and Michael H. Phillips, "Building Community: Principles for Social Work Practice in Housing Settings," *Social Work* 42 (Sept. 1997): 471–81, quote on 471. For other community groups see Patrick Breslin, "On These Sidewalks of New York, the Sun is Shining Again," *Smithsonian Magazine*,

April 1995; Mitchell Sviridoff and William Ryan, "Investing in Community: Lessons and Implications of the Comprehensive Community Revitalization Program," January 1996; both at http://www.cpn.org/cpn/sections/topics/community/stories-studies/south_bronx.html.

38. The Bronx became a finalist in April and one of the winners in June. See Bob Kappstatter in the *New York Daily News*: "Bronx Shines in U.S. Spotlight," 23 April 1997; and "Apple's Best Kept Secret," 11 June 1997. Quotation is from the April article.

39. See F. Romall Smalls, "The Bronx is Named an 'All-America' City," *New York Times*, 20 July 1997; Adam Nossiter, "As a Hospital Is Fixed, A Wound Is Healed," *New York Times*, 8 April 1996. Barbara Stewart, "Making It Work; Where the Ex-Rich Lived," *New York Times*, 14 Sept. 1997; Ferrer quoted in Bob Kappstatter, "This Borough's Pride is Working Out," *New York Daily News*, 23 April 1997.

40 Halpern, *Rebuilding the Inner City*, 204–8; Sviridoff and Ryan, "Investing in Community." For descriptions of all the initiatives, see The Aspen Institute Roundtable on Comprehensive Community-Building Initiatives (CCIs), http://www.commbuild.org; and "Comprehensive Community Revitalization Program," Alliance for Redesigning Government, National Academy of Public Administration, http://www.alliance.napawash.org. Quotes are from The Aspen Institute Roundtable Web site; and Sheila Thomson, "Bronx Profile: Eddie Calderon-Melendez," *New York Newsday*, Bronx Edition, 23 Nov. 1993.

41. Crime statistics are in Alex Schwartz, "New York City and Subsidized Housing: Impacts and Lessons of the City's $5 Billion Capital Budget Housing Plan," *Housing Policy Debate* 10:4 (1999): 864; Citizens Housing and Planning Council, *A Preliminary Assessment of Community Redevelopment in the South Bronx* (New York: Citizens Housing Council, 1998), 18–25.

42. Evelyn Nieves, "Refugee Found Guilty of Killing 87 in Bronx Happy Land Fire," *New York Times*, 20 Aug. 1991; Michael Cooper, "Officers in Bronx Fire 41 Shots, And an Unarmed Man is Killed," *New York Times*, 5 Feb. 1999.

43. Ray Bromley, "Coping and Caring: The Aftermath of the Happy Land Tragedy," Paper presented at the 23rd Annual Meeting of the Urban Affairs Association, Cleveland, Ohio, April 29–May 2, 1992; and the following *New York Times* articles: Juan Forero, "Bronx Ministers Hold Marches to Appeal for Calm on Verdict," 24 Feb. 2000; Juan Forero, "Veteran of Police and Pulpit Helps Soothe Tensions in the Bronx," 14 March 2000; Alan Feuer, "Signs of Hope in the Bronx Neighborhood Where Diallo Died," 16 Feb. 2002. On Albanians youths see Howard Pinderhughes, *Race in the Hood: Conflict & Violence Among Urban Youth* (Minneapolis: University of Minnesota Press, 1997), 41–43, 115–28, 144–48.

44. On mortgage scandals, see Terry Pristin, "City Requests $160 Million to Fix Up Homes in Scandal," *New York Times*, 6 July 2001. On the Beekman Houses, see Pranay Gupte, "Tenants Decry State of 7-Year-Old Housing Project,"

New York Times, 7 May 1978; and three articles in *City Limits*: Kim Nauer, "Anatomy of a Sweetheart Deal," Nov. 1997; Kim Nauer, "Reversal of Fortune," Dec. 1997; Matt Pacenza, "Dream Off?," April 2001. On Banana Kelly, see the three *New York Times* articles by Amy Waldman: "Buildings Savior Now a Troubled Landlord," 27 June 2000; "State Subpoenas Records of Bronx Community Group," 19 Feb. 2001; "A Rebuilder in the Bronx Scales Back," 29 March 2001. Both Banana Kelly and Promesa were dropped from the Surdna Foundation's Community Revitalization Program amid charges of mismanagement of funds.

45. Seth Kugel, "Little Africa Flourishes, FuFu Flour and All," *New York Times*, 17 Feb. 2002; Dennis Conway and Ualthan Bigby, "Where Caribbean Peoples Live in New York City," in *Caribbean Life in New York City*, ed. Constance R. Sutton and Elsa M. Chaney (New York: Center for Migration Studies of New York, 1987), 74–83; Department of City Planning, *Community District Needs, The Bronx, Fiscal Year 2000*; New York City Department of City Planning, *Citywide and Borough Population (1990 & 2000)*, 1–3; "New York City Latino Population: Census 2000," Prof. Cesar Ayala, Lehman College, CUNY, http://www.lehman.cuny.edu/depts/latinampuertorican/latinoweb/Census2000/NYC/main.htm.

46. Wylde, "The Contribution of Public-Private Partnerships to New York's Assisted Housing Industry," 76; *Community District Needs, The Bronx, Fiscal Year 2000*; *Community District Profiles, 2002* (City of New York, Department of City Planning), http://www.nyc.gov; Alessandra Stanley, "Hospital, Family Doctor and Benefactor," *New York Times*, 19 Dec. 1990. For an analysis of African Americans taking public sector jobs, see Roger Waldinger, *Still the Promised City? African-Americans and New Immigrants in Postindustrial New York* (Cambridge: Harvard University Press, 1996).

47. Procida and Morales quoted in Horowitz, "A South Bronx Renaissance," 58; Charlotte Street resident quoted in Barbara Stewart, "Market's Nod To a Rebirth: In South Bronx Enclave, Rising Property Values and Suburban Living," *New York Times*, 2 Nov. 1997.

48. Garcia quoted in Matthew Purdy, "Left to Die, the South Bronx Rises From Decades of Decay," *New York Times*, 13 Nov. 1994; Cruz quoted in Kim Nauer, "Anatomy of a Sweetheart Deal."

49. F. Austin, "Real Estate Development of Bronx County," *North Side News*, Bronx County Progress Section, 17 May 1914, 83.

50. Montgomery Schuyler, "An Oasis in The Bronx." *Architectural Record* 41 (Feb. 1917): 177.

51. Robert Abrams, who later became New York State Attorney General, was describing his roots in the Perham Parkway section of the Bronx. See Clines, "About New York: A 'Hidden' Side of the Bronx," *New York Times*, 6 July 1978.

52. Sydney Gruson, "New Faces in the Lower Bronx: Shifting Population Often Raises Tense Problems in Housing," *New York Times*, 11 July 1955; Samuel

Lubell, "The Boiling Bronx: Henry Wallace Stronghold," *Saturday Evening Post*, 23 Oct. 1948, 66–67.

53. See analysis of rent control and Bronx housing in Sandor E. Schick, "Neighborhood Change in the Bronx, 1905–1960" (Ph.D. diss., Harvard University, 1982), 128–76.

54. Brant quoted in Jonnes, *South Bronx Rising*, 346. Concourse Village was built over the Melrose freight yards.

55. Anthony Downs, *Neighborhoods and Urban Development* (Washington, DC: The Brookings Institution, 1981), 5.

56. Borough President Fernando Ferrer quoted in Frank Lombardi, "Bronx Considers Spruce Up Plans," *New York Daily News*, 10 April 1990; Purdy, "Left to Die, the South Bronx Rises From Decades of Decay."

57. See articles in the *New York Times*: Rachel L. Swarns, "Co-op City Suffers While Its Board Bickers," 29 May 1996; Iver Peterson, "A New Era for the Grand Concourse," 24 Jan. 1988; Alan S. Oser, "Starting the Rehabilitation Journey at Parkchester," 15 April 1999.

58. Bureau of the Census, *2000 Supplementary Survey for New York City Congressional Districts*, http://www.fiscalpolicy.org/CountyData. In 1990 the 16th Congressional District encompassed the original borders of the South Bronx and was then one of the poorest districts in the nation. *Congressional Districts in the 1990s: A Portrait of America* (Washington, D.C.: Congressional Quarterly, 1993).

59. Strozier, "How West Farms Was Won"; and the following three *New York Times* articles: Yardley, "Clinton Praises Bronx Renewal As U.S. Model"; Jim Yardley, "Second Opinion on South Bronx Revival: Where the President Did Not Visit," 13 Dec. 1997; Lee Stuart quoted in Douglas Martin, "A Garden Caught in a Housing Squeeze," 18 May 1998.

60. Emanuel Tobier, "The Bronx in the Twentieth Century: Dynamics of Population And Economic Change," *The Bronx County Historical Society Journal* 25 (fall 1998): 70.

BIBLIOGRAPHY

ARCHIVAL AND MANUSCRIPT SOURCES

Subject and Neighborhood Vertical Files. Bronx County Historical Society.
Community Service Society Records. Columbia University Library.
William R. Grace. Mayor's Papers. New York City Municipal Archives.
Fiorello LaGuardia. Mayor's Papers. New York City Municipal Archives.
Robert Moses. New York City Department of Parks Papers. New York City Municipal Archives.
Mott Papers. Columbia University Library.
William O'Dwyer. Mayor's Papers. New York City Municipal Archives.
Chauncey Smith. Papers. New-York Historical Society.
Mayor's Committee on Unity Papers. New York City Municipal Archives.
Robert F. Wagner. Mayor's Papers. New York City Municipal Archives.
Lillian Wald Collection. Columbia University Library.

NEWSPAPERS AND PERIODICALS

Bronx Home News
City Limits
City Record
Commercial and Financial Chronicle
Daily Up-town News
Harlem (Local) Reporter & Bronx Chronicle
Neighborhood
Newsday
New York Daily News
New York Evening Post
New York Herald
New York Post
The New York Times
New York Tribune
North Side News

Sunday Mercury
Real Estate Record and Builders' Guide
Westchester Gazette
Westchester Herald
Morrisania Gazette
Plain Dealer
Westchester Clarion
Westchester Times

PUBLISHED PRIMARY SOURCES

Auction Pamphlets. Map Room. New York Public Library.

Congressional Quarterly. *Congressional Districts in the 1990s: A Portrait of America.* Washington, D.C.: Congressional Quarterly, 1993.

Consolidated Edison. *Population Growth of New York City by Districts, 1940.* New York: Consolidated Edison, December 1948.

Davenport, John I. *Registry of Voters in the City of New York, by Wards, Assembly and Election Districts.* 2 vols. New York: The City of New York, 1874. Vol. 2.

Frisbee, D. B. and William T. Coles. *Morrisania and Tremont Directory, 1871–72.* Morrisania, NY: Times Print, 1871.

Henry, [John A.], ed. *Henry's Directory of Morrisania and Vicinity for 1853–4.* Morrisania, NY, 1853.

Laidlaw, Walter, ed. *Population of the City of New York, 1890–1930.* New York: Cities Census Committee, 1932.

——. *Statistical Sources for Demographic Studies of Greater New York, 1910.* New York: New York Federation of Churches, 1910.

——. *Statistical Sources for Demographic Studies of Greater New York, 1920.* New York: Cities Census Committee, 1922.

New York City Latino Population: Census 2000. http://www.lehman.cuny.edu/ depts/latinampuertorican/latinoweb/Census2000/NYC/main.htm.

The News, New York Times, Daily Mirror, and Journal-American. *New York City Market Analysis.* New York: News Syndicate Co., New York Times Co., Daily Mirror, and Hearst Consolidated Publications, 1943.

New York Herald. *The New York Market.* New York: New York Herald, 1922.

New York City. Department of City Planning. *1970 New York City Population.* New York, 1971.

——. *1980 New York City Population.* New York, 1981.

——. *1990 Census.* New York, 25 March 1991.

——. *Citywide and Borough Population, 1990 & 2000.*http://www.nyc.gov/ html/dcp/html/popstart.html.

——. *2000 Census Community Districts.* Table PL P–103. "New York City Community Districts, 1990 and 2000." http://www.nyc.gov/html/dcp/html/popstart.html.

New York City Housing Partnership. "Developments in the Bronx, 1987–2000." August 2000.

———. *Revitalizing Neighborhoods Through Affordable Housing and Community Involvement.* New York: New York City Housing Partnership, no date.

———. "Nelson Gardens: 18 Affordable Three-Family Townhouses." New York: New York City Housing Partnership, no date.

———. "Hunts Point Chazen Partnership Homes: New and Affordable Two & Three Family Homes." New York City Housing Partnership, no date.

U.S. Department of Commerce. Bureau of the Census. *Census Tract Data on Population and Housing, New York City: 1940.* New York: Welfare Council Committee on 1940 Census Tract Tabulation for New York City, September 1942.

———. *County & City Data Book, 1994: A Statistical Abstract.* August 1994.

———. *2000 Supplementary Survey for New York City Congressional Districts.* http://www.fiscalpolicy.org/CountyData.

———. *U.S. Census of the Population: 1950, Census Tract Statistics, New York City.* Washington, DC, 1952.

———. *U.S. Census of Population and Housing: 1960 Census Tracts.* Washington, DC: U.S. Government Printing Office, 1962.

———. *U.S. Census of Population and Housing: 1970 Census Tracts.* Washington, DC: U.S. Government Printing Office, 1972.

———. *U.S. Census of Population and Housing, 1980.* Washington, DC: U.S. Government Printing Office, 1983.

Welfare Council of New York City. *Heads of Families by Color and Nativity and Country of Birth of Foreign Born Head, By Health Areas, New York, 1930.* New York: Welfare Council of NYC, 1934.

———. *Homes by Tenure and Value or Monthly Rental: By Health Areas, New York City, 1930.* New York: Welfare Council of NYC, 1933.

———. *Population in Health Areas: New York City, 1930.* New York: Welfare Council of NYC, 1931.

———. Committee on Puerto Ricans in NYC. *Report of the Committee on Puerto Ricans in New York City.* February 1948; reprint, New York: Arno Press, 1975.

Welfare and Health Council of New York City. *Population of Puerto Rican Birth or Parentage, New York City: 1950.* New York, 1952.

MAPS

Beers, F. W. *Atlas of New York and Vicinity, 1868.* New York: F. W. Beers, A. D. Ellis, & G. G. Soule, 1868.

———. *Map of the Town of Morrisania, Westchester Co., N.Y.* New York: Beers, Ellis & Soule, c. 1864.

———. *Map of 23d Ward, New York City, 1876.* New York: J. B. Beers & Co., 1876.

Bromley & Co., G. W. *Atlas of the Entire City of New York, 1879.* New York: Geo. W. Bromley & E. Robinson, 1879.

———. *Atlas of the Borough of The Bronx, 1912.* 2 vols. New York: G. W. Bromley & Co., 1912.

Bromley, George W. and Walter S. Bromley. *Atlas of The City of New York, 23rd &*
24th Wards, 1893. Philadelphia: G. W. Bromley and Co., 1893.

——. *Atlas of The City of New York, 23rd & 24th Wards, 1897.* Philadelphia: G. W.
Bromley and Co., 1897.

——. *Atlas of the City of New York: Borough of the Bronx.* Philadelphia: G. W.
Bromley and Co., 1905.

——. *Atlas of the City of New York: Borough of the Bronx, South of 172nd Street.*
Philadelphia: G. W. Bromley and Co., 1923.

Dripps, M. *Map of the Southern Part of Westchester County, 1853.* New York: M.
Dripps, 1853.

Findley, A[ndrew]. "Map of Central Morrisania, 1 February 1851." Chauncey Smith
Papers. New-York Historical Society.

——. "Map of the Village of Mott Haven in the Manor of Morrisania, Town of
West Farms." Westchester, N.Y., January 1, 1850. Mott Papers. Columbia University Library. New York.

Henwood, R. "Map of the Village of Grove Hill in the Town of West Farms, County of Westchester and State of New York, 1853. 22 July 1853. The property of John
Shaw." Westchester County Map Folder. New-York Historical Society.

Mason, D. V. and G. S. Greene. *Map of the Town of Morrisania.Westchester Coun-*
ty, Made by and under the direction of the undersigned commissioners. January 6,
1871. Westchester Co., NY, 1871.

Potter Bros. *Map of the Northern Portion of the City of New-York, Comprising the*
12th Ward, and the new 23d and 24th Wards (Except that portion lying east of
Broadway and St. Ann's Avenue.) New York: Potter Bros., Brokers, [1873].

Robinson, E. and R. H. Pidgeon. *Robinson's Atlas of the City of New York: Embrac-*
ing all territory within its Corporate Limits. New York: E. Robinson, 1885.

Serrell, H. R. "Map of the Village of Eltona." 6 June 1851. Revised 14 February 1852.
Westchester County Map Folder. New-York Historical Society.

GOVERNMENT RECORDS AND REPORTS

Assessment Roll of the Town of West Farms for the Years 1857. Manuscript. New-
York Historical Society.

New York City. *Public Documents of the City of New York: Annual Reports, 1868.*
New York: New York Printing Co., 1869.

New York City Board of Aldermen. *Documents of the Board of Aldermen, 1874–1879.*
New York, 1875–1980.

——. *Proceedings of the Board of Aldermen of the City of New York, 1874.* New York:
Martin B. Brown, 1879. Vol. 154.

New York City Board of Apportionment. *Minutes of the Board of Apportionment of*
the City and County of New York, 1871–1873. New York: New York Printing Co.,
1871–1873.

New York City Department of Bridges. *Report of the Commissioner of Bridges, 1898,*

to Hon. Robert A. Van Wyck, Mayor of the City of New York. New York: Martin
B. Brown Co., 1899.

New York City. Bronx Borough President. *Annual Reports, 1902–1939*. New York,
1903–1940.

——. Borough President of the Bronx, Fernando Ferrer. *Strategic Policy Statement,
1990*.

——. Borough President of the Bronx, Fernando Ferrer. *Strategic Policy Statement,
1994*.

——. Borough President of the Bronx, Fernando Ferrer. *Strategic Policy Statement,
1998*.

——. Borough President of the Bronx, Fernando Ferrer. *The 2000 State of the Borough Report*.

——. President of the Borough of the Bronx. James J. Lyons. *Route Study for the
Development Plan: Cross-Bronx Thruway*. January 1944.

——. Central Park Commissioners. *Eleventh Annual Report of the Board of Commissioners of the Central Park for the Year Ending December 31, 1867*. New York,
1868.

——. Central Park Commissioners. "Report of the Commissioners of the Central
Park in Compliance with the Provisions of 'An Act for the Improvement of Certain Parts of Westchester County, Harlem River and Spuyten Duyvil Creek,
passed May 11, 1869,' 24 March 1870." In New York State,. *Senate Documents,
1870*. Albany, NY, 1870. Vol. 3. No. 76.

——. Central Park Commissioners. *Twelfth Annual Report of the Board of Commissioners of the Central Park for the Year Ending December 31, 1868*. New York:
Evening Post Steam Presses, 1869.

New York City Board of Estimate and Apportionment. *Minutes of the Board of Estimate and Apportionment of the City and County of New York, 1875–1884*. New
York, 1876–1885.

——. *Proceedings of the Board of Estimate and Apportionment, 1890*. New York,
1891.

New York City. City Planning Commission. *Plan for New York City*. 2 vols. New
York: New York City Planning Commission, 1969. Vol. 2: *The Bronx*.

New York City. Department of City Planning. *Community District Needs, The
Bronx, Fiscal Year 2000*. New York, 2000.

New York City Housing Authority. *Real Property Inventory, City of New York, 1934*.
New York: New York City Housing Authority, 1934.

——. *City-Wide Public Housing*. 30 September 1962.

——. *Project Data*. 31 December 1977.

New York City Landmarks Preservation Commission. "Mott Haven Historic District." No. 1, 29 July 1969/LP–0451. New York: Landmarks Preservation Commission, 1969.

New York City Department of Public Parks. "Abstracts of the Weekly Proceedings
of the Department of Public Parks. 1875–1879." In *City Record*, 1875–1879.

——. *Laws Respecting the Central Park and Other Works Under The Control of the Department of Public Parks.* New York, 1870.

——. *Minutes and Documents of the Board of Commissioners of the Department of Public Parks for the Years 1880–1883.* New York, 1881–1883.

——. *Minutes of Proceedings of the Board of Commissioners of the Department of Public Parks for the Years 1878–1879.* New York, 1879.

——. "Quarterly Reports for the Years 1875–1879." In *City Record,* 1875–1879.

——. "Report of the Board of Commissioners of the Department of Public Parks of the City of New York, in Conformity with an Act of the Legislature, passed April 15, 1871, Relating to Improvements of Portions of the Counties of Westchester and New York, The Improvement of Spuyten Duyvil Creek and the Harlem River, and to Facilities of Communication Between Said Counties." By Henry G. Stebbins. In New York State, *Senate Documents.* Vol. 4. No. 72. Albany, NY: Argus Co., 1872.

——. "Report of the Board of Commissioners of the Department of Public Parks of the City of New York, 15 March 1871." In New York State, *Assembly Documents, 1871.* No. 88.

——. *Third Annual Report of the Board of Commissioners of the Department of Public Parks, 1872–1873.* New York: William C. Bryant & Co., 1875.

——. *Department of Parks Documents.* 2 volumes.

——. *Department of Parks Documents.* "A Communication from Commissioner William R. Martin relative to the plans and improvements of the Fort Washington district, and the 23d and 24th Wards. 19 March 1875." 30 March 1875. No. 65.

——. *Department of Parks Documents.* "A Communication from Commissioner William R. Martin, relative to the prosecution of public improvements in this city. 20 February 1875." 5 March 1875. No. 64.

——. *Department of Parks Documents.* "Communication from the Landscape Architect and the Civil and Topographical Engineer, in relation to the proposed plan for laying out the Central District of the Twenty-third and Twenty-fourth Wards, lying east of Jerome Avenue and west of Third Avenue and the Harlem Railroad. 7 November 1877." By Frederick Law Olmsted and J. J. Robertson Croes. No. 76.

—— *Department of Parks Documents.* "Memorandum prepared by George S. Greene, Engineer, Relating to plans for streets and avenues in the Twenty-fourth Ward, between the Hudson River and the Croton Aqueduct, September 1875." 28 February 1875. No. 74.

——. *Department of Parks Documents.* "I. Preliminary Report of the Landscape and Civil and Topographical Engineer, upon the laying out of the Twenty-third and Twenty-fourth Wards. II. Report of the Landscape Architect and the Civil and Topographical Engineer, Accompanying a plan for laying out that part of all the Twenty-fourth Ward, lying west of the Riverdale Road. 20 December 1876." By Frederick Law Olmsted and J. J. Robertson Croes. No. 72.

——. *Department of Parks Documents.* "A Report from the Topographical Engineer on the drainage of the Twenty-third and Twenty-fourth Wards. 2 March 1881." By E. B. Van Winkle. No. 88.

——. *Department of Parks Documents.* "Report of the Civil and Topographical Engineer and the Landscape Architect, accompanying a plan for local steam transit routes in the Twenty-third and Twenty-fourth Wards, 21 March 1877." By Frederick Law Olmsted and J. J. Robertson Croes. No. 75.

——. *Department of Parks Documents.* "Report of the Civil and Topographical Engineer on the Condition and extent of works now in progress under contracts in the Twenty-third and Twenty-fourth Wards, and as to what action is necessary in regard to the same, 6 January 1874." 8 January 1874. By William H. Grant. No. 56.

——. *Department of Parks Documents.* "Report of the Civil and Topographical Engineer relative to the condition of all works under his direction, 25 June 1873." By William H. Grant. No. 45.

——. *Department of Parks Documents.* "Report of the Civil and Topographical Engineer upon a plan for laying out certain of the principal streets and avenues in the Twenty-third and Twenty-fourth Wards. 20 January 1875." By George S. Greene. No. 62.

——. *Department of Parks Documents.* "Report of the Civil and Topographical Engineer with reference to desirable improvements and additions in the Twenty-third and Twenty-fourth Wards. 16 December 1874." 20 January 1875. By George S. Greene. No. 61.

——. *Department of Parks Documents.* "Report of Commissioner [Henry G.] Stebbins upon the plans for laying out that part of the Twenty-fourth Ward lying west of Riverdale Road. 28 February 1877." No. 74.

——. *Department of Parks Documents.* "Report of Hon. Wm. R. Martin, President, upon the subject of laying-out the Twenty-third and Twenty-fourth Wards. 20 December 1876." No. 73.

——. *Department of Parks Documents.* "Statement presented by Commissioner [William R.] Martin to the Board of Estimate and Apportionment, showing the reasons why the appropriations for this Department for 1876 should not be reduced below amount appropriated for 1875." 20 December 1875. No. 68.

New York City. Office of the Mayor. *Summary: The South Bronx, A Plan for Revitalization.* New York, December 1977.

New York City Rapid Transit Board of Commissioners. *The Minutes of Proceedings of the Board of Commissioners of Rapid Transit, in the City of New York, From July to December 1875.* New York: Martin B. Brown, 1877.

New York City Rapid Transit Commissioners. "Report of the Rapid Transit Commissioners appointed on the sixteenth day of June 1881." In New York City, *Proceedings of the Board of Aldermen, 1881–1882.* Vol. 164, 453–71.

——. "Report of the New Rapid Transit Commissioners for the Annexed District. 8 December 1879." In *New York Times,* 11 December 1879.

——. "Resolutions passed by the Commissioners of Rapid Transit, in session 10 June 1879." In New York City, *Proceedings of the Board of Aldermen, 1879,* 814–45.

New York City Rapid Transit Railroad Commissioners. *Report of the Board of Rapid Transit Railroad Commissioners in and for the City of New York in pur-*

suance of the provisions of section 5 of chapter 4 of the Laws of 1891. 20 October 1891.

New York City Department of Street Improvements of the 23rd and 24th Wards. *Quarterly Reports of the Commissioner, 1891–1897.* New York: Martin B. Brown, 1892–1898.

New York City Youth Board. *Juvenile Delinquency in Critical Areas: Rates, Maps, Characteristics, 1957.*

New York State. "An Act to Incorporate the Hudson and Harlem River Canal Company." In New York State, *Laws of 1863.* Chap. 365.

——. "Annual Report of the State Engineer and Surveyor of the State of New York." In New York State, *Assembly Documents, 1870.* No. 154, 833–37. Albany, NY, 1870.

——. "Annual Report of the Railroad Commission for the Fiscal Year Ending September 30, 1856." In *Accompanying Documents.* New York State Engineer and Surveyor. Albany, NY: C. Van Benthuysen, 1857.

New York State. *Assembly Documents.* Various years.

——. *Census for 1865.* Albany, NY: Charles Van Benthuysen & Sons, 1867.

——. *Census of State of New York for 1875.* Albany, NY, 1877.

——. "Communication from the Secretary of State Showing the Population in Each Election District of the City of New York. 15 February 1876." In New York State, *Assembly Documents, 1876.* No. 55, p. 14. New York, 1876.

——. *Dual System of Rapid Transit for New York City.* New York: Public Service Commission for First District, September 1912.

——. "Exhibits showing the Enumeration of the State by Counties, Cities, Towns and Election Districts for the Year 1892." In New York State, *Senate Documents, 1892.* No. 60. Albany, NY: James B. Lyon, 1892.

——. *Laws of New York State.* Various years.

——. *Manual for the Use of the Legislature of the State of New York, 1906.* New York: Brandow Printing Co., 1906.

——. "Report of the Committee on the Incorporation of Cities and Villages, on the bill entitled 'An Act concerning the public health of the counties of New York, Kings and Richmond and the waters thereof.' 7 February 1861." In New York State, *Assembly Documents, 1861.* Vol. 2. No. 59.

——. "Report of the Commission Appointed in Relation to a Public Park in the Twenty-third and Twenty-fourth Wards of the City of New York, and Portions of Westchester County. 4 April 1882." In New York State, *Assembly Documents, 1882.* No. 67.

——. *Report to the New York Legislature of the Commission to Select and Locate Lands for Public Parks in the Twenty-third and Twenty-fourth Wards of the City of New York, and in the Vicinity Thereof.* New York: Martin B. Brown, 1884.

——. "Report of the Select Committee Appointed to Examine into the Condition of Tenant Houses in New-York and Brooklyn. 9 March 1857." In New York State, *Assembly Documents, 1857.* Vol. 3. No. 205.

——. Report of the Special Committee of the Senate in Relation to the Public Affairs of the Twenty-third and Twenty-fourth Wards of the City of New York. 26 February 1890." In New York State, *Senate Documents, 1890*. No. 36.

——. "Report of the Special Legislative Committee on Building Associations in the City of New-York." In New York State, *Assembly Documents, 1856*. Vol. 3. No. 46, 1–10.

——. "Second Annual Report of the Metropolitan Board of Health of the State of New York, 1867." In New York State, *Assembly Documents, 1868*. Vol. 9. No. 122.

——. *Senate Documents*. Various years.

——. State Board of Housing. *Report of the State Board of Housing on the Standard of Living of 400 Families in a Model Housing Project, The Amalgamated Housing Corporation*. By Asher Achinstein. New York: Burland Printing Co., 1931.

Panuch, J. Anthony. *Relocation in New York City: Special Report to Mayor Robert F. Wagner*. 15 December 1959.

South Bronx Development Organization. *South Bronx Industrial Fair*. New York: City of New York, State of New York, Port Authority of NY and NJ, n.d.

U.S. Department of Housing and Urban Development. *The Dynamics of Neighborhood Change*, by James Mitchel. Office of Policy Development and Research. San Francisco: U.S. Department of Housing and Urban Development, May 1975.

U.S. Works Projects Administration. Historical Records Survey. *Guide to Vital Statistics in the City of New York, Borough of The Bronx, Churches*. New York, 1942.

Westchester County Board of Supervisors. *Reports of the Special Committee on the New Harlem Bridge*. New York: Press of Wynkoop, Hallenbeck & Thomas, 1864.

SECONDARY SOURCES—BOOKS

Alicea, Gil C., with Carmine DeSena. *The Air Down Here: True Tale from a South Bronx Boyhood*. San Francisco: Chronicle, 1995.

Abrams, Charles. *Forbidden Neighbors*. New York: Harper & Brothers, 1955.

Albion, Robert Greenhalgh. *The Rise of New York Port, 1815–1860*. New York: Charles Scribner's Sons, 1939.

Allen, Fred H. *New York City, Westchester and Nassau Counties in Relation to Real Estate Investment, 1942*. New York: Sponsored by The Bank for Savings, Bowery Savings Bank, and Group Five Mortgage Information Bureau, 1942.

American Council of Learned Societies. *Report of Committee on Linguistic and National Stocks in the Population of the United States*, in American Historical Association. *Annual Report, 1931*, vol. 1. Washington, DC: U.S. Government Printing Office, 1932.

Arnold, Bion J. *Reports Upon Interborough Subway: Submitted to the Public Service Commission for the First District of State of N.Y.* New York: Martin B. Brown Press, 1908.

The Aspen Institute. *The Aspen Institute Roundtable on Comprehensive Community-Building Initiatives* (CCIs). http:www.combuild.org.

Baldassare, Mark., ed. *Cities and Urban Living*. New York: Columbia University Press, 1983.

Baldassare, Mark. *Residential Crowding in Urban America*. Berkeley: University of California Press, 1979.

Barry, Colman J. *The Catholic Church and German Americans*. Milwaukee: Bruce Publishing Co., 1953.

Barth, Gunther Paul. *City People: The Rise of Modern City Culture in Nineteenth-Century America*. New York: Oxford University Press, 1980.

Bayor, Ronald H. *Neighbors in Conflict: The Irish, Germans, Jews, and the Italians of New York City, 1929–1941*. Baltimore: Johns Hopkins University Press, 1978.

Bayor, Ronald H., ed. *Neighborhoods in Urban America*. Port Washington, NY: Kennikat Press, 1982.

Beauregard, Robert A. *Voices of Decline: The Postwar Fate of US Cities*. Cambridge, MA: Blackwell, 1988.

Bellush, Jewel and Stephen M. David, eds. *Race and Politics in New York City: Five Studies in Policy-Making*. New York: Praeger, 1971.

Bellush, Jewel and Dick Netzer. *Urban Politics New York Style*. Armonk, NY: M. E. Sharpe, 1990.

Berman, Marshall. *All That Is Solid Melts Into Air*. New York: Simon and Schuster, 1982.

Bishop, J. Leander. *A History of American Manufactures, from 1608 to 1860*. 1868; reprint, New York: Johnson Reprint Corporation, 1967.

Bolton, Reginald Pelham. *Building for Profit: Principles Governing the Economic Improvement of Real Estate*. 3rd ed. New York: De Vinne Press, 1922.

Boorstin, Daniel J. *The Americans: The Democratic Experience*. New York: Random House, 1973.

——. *The Americans: The National Experience*. New York: Random House, 1965.

Bourne, Larry S., ed. *Internal Structure of the City: Readings in Urban Form, Growth, and Policy*. 2nd ed. New York: Oxford University Press, 1982.

Bratt, Rachel G., Chester Hartman, and Ann Meyerson, eds. *Critical Perspectives in Housing*. Philadelphia: Temple University Press, 1986.

Breen, Matthew P. *Thirty Years of New York Politics*. New York: the author, 1899.

Bronx Board of Trade. *The Bronx in the City of New York: A Comprehensive General and Industrial Survey*. Bronx, NY: Bronx Board of Trade, 1931.

——. *"The Nation's Ninth City:" The Bronx, New York's Fastest Growing Borough*. New York: Bronx Board of Trade, 1922.

——. *Yearbook, 1916*. New York: Bronx Board of Trade, 1916.

——. *Yearbook, 1920*. New York: Bronx Board of Trade, 1920.

Bronx Chamber of Commerce. *Yearbook and Business Directory of the Bronx Chamber of Commerce*. Bronx, NY: Bronx Chamber of Commerce, 1929.

Bronx Council of Social Agencies. *A Study of the Lower Bronx*. New York: Bronx Council of Social Agencies, 1939.

Carman, Harry James. *The Street Surface Railway Franchises of New York City*. Columbia University Studies on History, Economics, & Public Law, 88. New York: Columbia University Press, 1919.

Caro, Robert A. *The Power Broker: Robert Moses and the Fall of New York*. New York: Knopf, 1974.

Chamber of Commerce of the State of New York. *Rapid Transit in New York and in Other Great Cities*. New York: Chamber of Commerce of the State of New York, 1906.

Chapin, H[erman] Gerald. *Bronx Borough a Separate County: Address delivered before the North Side Board of Trade, November 25, 1903*. New York: North Side Board of Trade, 1903.

Charyn, Jerome. *Bronx Boy*. New York: St. Martin's Press, 2002.

———. *The Black Swan*. New York: St. Martin's Press, 2000.

———. *The Dark Lady of Belorusse*. New York: St. Martin's Press, 1997.

Chenault, Lawrence R[oyce]. *The Puerto Rican Migrant in New York City*. New York: Columbia University Press, 1938.

Citizens Housing and Planning Council. *A Preliminary Assessment of Community Redevelopment in the South Bronx*. New York: Citizens Housing and Planning Council, 1998.

Comfort, Randall. *History of Bronx Borough, City of New York*. New York: North Side News Press, 1906.

Community Council of Greater New York. *Bronx Communities: Population Characteristics and Neighborhood Social Resources*. New York, March 1959.

Cook, Harry T. *The Borough of The Bronx, 1639–1913: Its Marvelous Development and Historical Surroundings*. New York: the author, 1913.

Cowen, Philip. *Memories of an American Jew*. New York: The International Press, 1932.

Cromley, Elizabeth Collins. *Alone Together: A History of New York's Early Apartments*. Ithaca, NY: Cornell University Press, 1990.

Cumbler, John T. *A Social History of Economic Decline: Business, Politics, and Work in Trenton*. New Brunswick: Rutgers University Press, 1989.

Curry, Daniel. *New York: A Historical Sketch of the Rise and Progress of the Metropolitan City of America by a New Yorker*. New York: Carlton & Phillips, 1853.

Danforth, Brian J. *Mott Haven: Nineteenth-Century Landmark District in The South Bronx*. New York: West Bronx Restoration Committee, Hunter College, 1976.

Danforth, Brian J. and Victor B. Caliandro. *Perception of Housing and Community: Bronx Architecture of the 1920s*. Bronx, NY: West Bronx Restoration Committee, Graduate Program in Urban Planning, Hunter College, CUNY, 1977.

Danielson, Michael and Jameson W. Doig. *New York: The Politics of Urban Regional Development*. Berkeley: University of California Press, 1982.

Davis, Albert E. *The Borough Beautiful: A Bronx Opportunity, being a paper read before the New York Improvement Commission, July 27, 1904*. New York: 1904.

Davis, James Leslie. *The Elevated System and the Growth of Northern Chicago*. Evanston, IL: Department of Geography, Northwestern University, 1965.

D'Erasmo, Rocky. *Fordham Was a Town: A Nostalgic Look Into Fordham's Little Italy During the Twenties and Thirties*. Bronx, NY: the author, 1978.

Derrick, Peter. *Tunneling to the Future: The Story of the Great Subway Expansion That Saved New York.* New York: New York University Press, 2001.

Dolan, Jay P. *The Immigrant Church: New York's Irish and German Catholics, 1815–1865.* Baltimore: Johns Hopkins University Press, 1975.

Dollar Savings Bank. *Golden Anniversary: Commemorating Fifty Years of Progress in the Bronx, 1890–1940.* New York: Dollar Savings Bank of the City of New York, 1940.

Dorman, Michael. *The Making of a Slum.* New York: Delacorte, 1972.

Downs, Anthony. *Neighborhoods and Urban Development.* Washington, DC: The Brookings Institution, 1981.

Ernst, Robert. *Immigrant Life in New York City, 1825–1863.* New York: King's Crown Press, Columbia University, 1949.

Edsall, Thomas H. *History of the Town of Kings Bridge: Now Part of the 24th Ward, New York City.* New York: the author, 1887.

Fein, Albert, ed. *Landscape Into Cityscape: Frederick Law Olmsted's Plans for a Greater New York City.* Ithaca, NY: Cornell University Press, 1967.

Firey, Walter. *Land Use in Central Boston.* Cambridge: Harvard University Press, 1947.

Flanagan, William G. *Contemporary Urban Sociology.* New York: Cambridge University Press, 1993.

Flowers, Ronald Barri. *Minorities and Criminality.* New York: Greenwood Press, 1988.

Foner, Nancy, ed. *New Immigrants in New York.* Rev. and updated ed. New York: Columbia University Press, 2001.

Foord, John. *The Life and Public Services of Andrew Haswell Green.* Garden City, NY: Doubleday, Page & Co., 1913.

French, J[ohn] H[omer]. *Gazetteer of the State of New York.* Empire State Historical Publication Series, no. 72. 1860; reprint, New York: Ira J. Friedman, 1969.

Gamm, Gerald. *Urban Exodus: Why the Jews Left Boston and the Catholics Stayed.* Cambridge: Harvard University Press, 1999.

Ginzberg, Eli. *New York Is Very Much Alive: A Manpower View.* New York: McGraw-Hill, 1973.

Goetze, Rolf. *Understanding Neighborhood Change: The Role of Expectations in Urban Revitalization.* Cambridge, MA: Ballinger, 1979.

Goldman, Albert. *The Bronx of Yesteryear: A Story of Continued Urbanization traced from its Origin to the Splendid Present.* New York, n.d.

Gratz, Roberta Brandes. *The Living City: How America's Cities Are Being Revitalized in a Big Way.* New York: Wiley, 1994.

Grebler, Leo. *Housing Market Behavior in a Declining Area: Long-term Changes in Inventory and Utilization of Housing on New York's Lower East Side.* New York: Columbia University Press, 1952.

Grodinsky, Julius. *Jay Gould: His Business Career, 1867–1892.* Philadelphia: University of Pennsylvania Press, 1957.

Haffen, Louis F. *Address by Louis F. Haffen, President Borough of the Bronx Deliv-*

ered at Complimentary Dinner at the Longwood Club, October 2, 1905*. Bronx, NY, 1905.

———. *Borough of The Bronx: A Record of Unparalleled Progress and Development.* New York, 1909.

Hallman, Howard W. *Neighborhoods: Their Place in Urban Life.* Beverly Hills, CA: Sage, 1984.

Halpern, Robert. *Rebuilding the Inner City: A History of Neighborhood Initiatives to Address Poverty in the United States.* New York: Columbia University Press, 1995.

Harris, Neil. *The Artist in American Society: The Formative Years, 1790–1860.* New York: George Brazilier, 1966.

Harvey, David. *The Urbanization of Capital.* Baltimore: Johns Hopkins University Press, 1985.

Hays, R. Allen. *The Federal Government & Urban Housing: Ideology and Change in Public Policy.* Albany: State University of New York Press, 1995.

Hawkes, McDougall. *The Improvement of the Bronx Waterfront.* New York: North Side Board of Trade, 23 November 1903.

Hermalyn, Gary and Robert Kornfeld. *Landmarks in The Bronx.* Bronx, NY: The Bronx County Historical Society, 1989.

Hestor, Randolph T. *Neighborhood Space.* Stroudsbury, PA: Dowden, Hutchinson, & Ross, 1975.

Hinsdale, E. B. *The New Parks: Opinion of E. B. Hinsdale On the Question Raised as to the Power of the City of New York to Issue Bonds for Improvements by Reason of the Constitutional Amendment.* New York: C. G. Burgoyne, 1884.

Hoenig, Gary. *Reaper: The Story of a Gang Leader.* New York: Bobbs-Merrill, 1975.

Hoover, Edgar M. and Raymond Vernon. *Anatomy of a Metropolis:The Changing Distribution of People and Jobs Within the New York Metropolitan Region.* Cambridge: Harvard University Press, 1959.

Horowitz, C. Morris and Lawrence J. Kaplan. *The Estimated Jewish Population of the New York Area, 1900–1975.* New York: Demographic Study Committee of the Federation of Jewish Philanthropies of New York, 1959.

Hoyt, Homer. *The Structure and Growth of Residential Neighborhoods in American Cities.* Washington, DC: Federal Housing Administration, 1939.

Hylan, John F., Mayor. *Seven Years of Progress: Important Public Improvements and Achievements by the Municipal and Borough Governments of the City of New York, 1918–1925.* Report Submitted to the Board of Aldermen. New York, March 1925.

Immaculate Conception Church. *Diamond Jubilee Souvenir of the Immaculate Conception Church, 1853-May 1928.* Bronx, NY: Immaculate Conception Church, 1928.

Institute for Urban Studies. Fordham University. *A Profile of the Bronx Economy.* New York, July 1967.

———. Office of South Bronx Redevelopment Affairs. *Industrial Activity in the Inner City: A Case Study of The South Bronx.* New York, April 1981.

Jackson, Anthony. *A Place Called Home: A History of Low-Cost Housing in Manhattan.* Cambridge: MIT Press, 1976.

Jackson, Kenneth T. *Crabgrass Frontier: The Suburbanization of the United States.* New York: Oxford University Press, 1985.

Jackson, Larry R. and William A. Johnson. *Protest by the Poor: The Welfare Rights Movement in New York City.* Lexington, MA: Lexington Books, 1974.

Jacobs, Jane. *The Death and Life of Great American Cities.* New York: Random House, 1961.

Jacobs, Julius. *Bronx Cheer: A Memoir.* Monroe, NY: Library Research Associates, 1976.

Jenkins, Stephen. *The Story of The Bronx: From the Purchase Made by the Dutch from the Indians in 1639 to the Present Day.* New York: G. P. Putnam's Sons, 1912.

Jensen, Robert, project director. *Devastation/Resurrection: The South Bronx.* Bronx, NY: Bronx Museum of the Arts, 1979.

Jonnes, Jill. *South Bronx Rising: The Rise, Fall, and Resurrection of an American City.* New York: Fordham University Press, 2002.

Kaganoff, Benzion C. *A Dictionary of Jewish Names and Their History.* New York: Schocken, 1977.

Keating, Dennis W., Norman Krumholz, and Philip Starr. *Revitalizing Urban Neighborhoods.* Lawrence: University of Kansas Press, 1996.

Keller, Suzanne. *The Urban Neighborhood: A Sociological Perspective.* New York: Random House, 1968.

Klein, Malcolm W. *The American Street Gang: Its Nature, Prevalence, and Control.* New York: Oxford University Press, 1995.

Kolodny, Robert. *Self-Help in the Inner City: A Study of Lower Income Cooperative Housing Conversion in New York.* New York: United Neighborhood Houses of New York, Inc., September 1973.

Kozol, Jonathan. *Savage Inequalities: Children in America's Schools.* New York: Crown, 1991.

——. *Amazing Grace: The Lives of Children and the Conscience of a Nation.* New York: Crown, 1995.

——. *Ordinary Resurrections: Children in the Years of Hope.* New York: Crown, 2000.

Kugelmass, Jack. *The Miracle of Intervale Avenue: The Story of a Jewish Congregation in the South Bronx.* New York: Schocken, 1986.

Lawson, Ronald, ed. *The Tenant Movement in New York City, 1904–1984.* New Brunswick: Rutgers University Press, 1986.

Lederman, Jess, ed. *Housing in America: Mobilizing Bankers, Builders and Communities to Solve the Nation's Affordable Housing Crisis.* Chicago: Probus, 1993.

Lemann, Nicholas. *The Promised Land: The Great Black Migration and How It Changed America.* New York: Knopf, 1991.

Leven, Charles L., James T. Little, Hugh O. Nourse, and R. B. Read, eds. *Neighborhood Change: Lessons in the Dynamics of Urban Decay.* New York: Praeger, 1976.

Logan, John R. and Harvey L. Molotch. *Urban Fortunes: The Political Economy of Place.* Berkeley: University of California Press, 1987.

Lubell, Samuel. *The Future of American Politics*. 3rd ed. Rev. New York: Harper & Row, 1965.

Lubove, Roy. *The Progressives and the Slums: Tenement House Reform in New York City, 1890–1917*. Pittsburgh: University of Pittsburgh Press, 1962.

——. *The Urban Community: Housing and Planning in the Progressive Era*. Englewood Cliffs, NJ: Prentice-Hall, 1967.

Ludewig, Chas. H. *A Quiet Holiday in the Bronx*. New York: the author, 1899.

Ludlow, William H. *Population Densities for New York City: A Technical Study of Urban Population Densities in Relation to City Planning*. New York: Citizen's Housing Council of New York, May 1944.

Lyons, James J. *Traffic in The Bronx: Studies and Recommendations For Preventing Congestion—Factors, Objections, Conclusions*. New York: Office of the President of The Borough of The Bronx, September 1947. William O'Dwyer. Mayor's Papers. Oversize Box 5401. New York City Municipal Archives.

McCrosky, T. T. *Residential Area Analysis*. New York: U.S. Works Progress Administration, August 1938.

——. *Zoning for the City of New York*. New York: U.S. Works Progress Administration, Mayor's Committee on City Planning, August 1938.

MacLysaght, Edward. *A Guide to Irish Surnames*. Baltimore, MD: Genealogical Book Company, 1964.

McNamara, John. *History in Asphalt: The Origin of Bronx Street and Place Names, Borough of The Bronx, New York City*. New York: Harbor Hill Books and Bronx County Historical Society, 1978.

McNamara, Kristy Maher and Robert P. McNamara. *The Urban Landscape: Selected Readings*. New York: University Press of America, 1995.

Malone, Dumas, ed. *Dictionary of American Biography*. 23 vols. New York: Charles Scribner's Sons, 1934. Vol 13.

Mandelbaum, Seymour J. *Boss Tweed's New York*. New York: Wiley, 1965.

Marcuse, Peter. *Housing Abandonment: Does Rent Control Make a Difference?* New York, June 1981.

Marsh, Luther R. *The Future of New York: remarks by Luther R. Marsh at the First Panel Sheriff's Dinner, January 14, 1885*. New York: Dempsey & Carroll Print, 1885.

——. *New Parks: Luther R. Marsh's Reply to the Memorial of Mayor Grace Against the New Parks Act*. New York: C. G. Burgoyne, 1885.

——. *The Sinking Fund and the New Parks*. New York, 1885?.

Martin, Edgar W. *The Standard of Living in 1860*. Chicago: University of Chicago Press, 1942.

Martin, John. *Rapid Transit: Its Effect on Rents and Living Conditions And How to Get It*. New York: Committee on Congestion of Population, March 1909.

Michelson, William. *Environmental Choice, Human Behavior, and Residential Satisfaction*. New York: Oxford University Press, 1977.

Mills, C. Wright., Clarence Senior, and Rose Kohn Goldsen. *The Puerto Rican Jour-*

ney: *New York's Newest Migrants*. 1950; reprint, New York: Russell & Russell, 1967.

Moore, Deborah Dash. *At Home in America: Second-Generation New York Jews*. New York: Columbia University Press, 1981.

Morgenthau, Henry. *All in a Lifetime*. In collaboration with French Strother. Garden City, NY: Doubleday, Page & Co., 1922.

Morris, Fordham. *Address delivered at the Banquet in the Pavilion at Oak Point on the Occasion of the Celebration of the Opening of the Harlem Ship Canal. June 17, 1895*. New York: North Side Board of Trade, 1895.

Morris, Lewis G. *Harlem River; Its Use Previous to and Since The Revolutionary War and Suggestions Relative to Present Contemplated Improvement*. New York: J. D. Torrey, 1857.

———. *Peremptory Sale at Auction: Estate of Lewis G. Morris, Monday, March 15, 1869*. Bronx Pamphlets. New York Public Library.

Morris High School. *The Morris Annual, 1905*. Bronx, NY: Morris High School, 1905.

Morrisania Bible Society. *Constitution and By-Laws of the Morrisania Bible Society: Auxiliary to the Westchester County Bible Society, 1860*. Morrisania, NY, 1860.

Morrisania Fire Dept. *Annual Report of the Chief Engineer of the Fire Department of the Town of Morrisania*. Morrisania, NY, 1866.

Mullaly, John. *The New Parks Beyond the Harlem*. New York: *Real Estate Record & Builders' Guide*, 1887.

Mullings, Leith. *Cities of the United States: Studies in Urban Anthropology*. New York: Columbia University Press, 1987.

Municipal Art Society of New York. City Plan Committee. *A Discussion of the Rapid Transit Problem in and about New York*. New York: Municipal Art Society, 1905.

Myers, Gustavus. *The History of Public Franchises in New York City (Boroughs of Manhattan and the Bronx)*. New York: Reform Club, Committee on City Affairs, 1900.

National Council of Christians and Jews. *Intergroup Relations in New York City: Progress and Problems: A Survey Summary*. Manhattan–Westchester Region, February 1954.

Newfield, Jack and Wayne Barrett. *City for Sale: Ed Koch and the Betrayal of New York*. New York: Harper & Row, 1988.

Newman, Oscar. *Defensible Space: Crime Prevention Through Urban Design*. New York: Macmillan, 1972.

[New York Park Association.] *The Demand of the People for MORE PUBLIC PARKS*. New York: Edward F. Weeks, 24 March 1884.

———. *More Public Parks: How New York Compares With Other Cities: Lungs for the Metropolis, The Financial and Sanitary Aspects of the Question*. New York: New Park Association, 1882.

———. *The Park Question*. New York: New York Park Association, n.d.

New York Rent Guidelines Board. *Housing NYC: Rents, Markets, and Trends, '97*. New York, 1997.

New York Urban Coalition. *Housing Rehabilation Task Force*. New York, January 1976.

North Side Association. *Proceedings of the North Side Association of the 23rd and 24th Wards of the City of New York for The Year 1874*. New York: Torrey Brothers, 1875.

——. *Proceedings of the North Side Association of the 23rd and 24th Wards of the City of New York, for the Year 1875*. New York: Press of Bedell & Bro., 1876.

North Side Board of Trade. *Address of Albert E. Davis, president of the North Side Board of Trade, delivered at its Meeting held at 520 Willis Avenue, January 28, 1902*. New York: North Side Board of Trade, 1902.

——. *Address of Albert E. Davis, president of the North Side Board of Trade, delivered at its Meeting Held at 520 Willis Avenue, 27 January 1903*. New York: North Side News Book and Job Print, 1903.

——. *Address of John C. De La Vergne, President of the North Side Board of Trade, delivered at its first meeting held at the Melrose Lyceum, March 6th, 1844*. New York: North Side Board of Trade, 1894.

——. *Address of Olin J. Stephens, president of the North Side Board of Trade of the City of New York, delivered at Meeting Held February 2, 1905*. New York: North Side Board of Trade, 1905.

——. *Address of Olin J. Stephens, president of the North Side Board of Trade of the City of New York, Delivered at its meeting held at Metropolis Theatre Building, 3rd & 142th Street. January 24, 1906*.

——. *Annual Report of the Secretary of the North Side Board of Trade for the Year 1904, Charles E. Reid, Secretary*. New York: North Side Board of Trade, 1904.

——. *The Great North Side or Borough of The Bronx*. New York: North Side Board of Trade, 1897.

——. *The Great North Side: Its Past and Future, Its Advantages as a Commercial and Manufacturing Centre. North Side News. Supplement*. 18 May 1901.

——. *Inaugural Address of the President for the Year 1910, Address of the Retiring President and Annual Reports of the Standing Committees and of the Secretary for the Year 1909 to The North Side Board of Trade in the City of New York*. New York: North Side Board of Trade, 1910.

——. *Inaugural Address of the President for the Year 1911 and Annual Reports of the Standing Committee and of the Secretary for the Year 1910 to The North Side Board of Trade in the City of New York*. New York: North Side Board of Trade, 1911.

——. *Third Annual Report of the Secretary of the North Side Board of Trade of the City of New York. March 6th, 1897*. New York: North Side Board of Trade, 1897.

——. *Tree Planting and Housing Accommodations, Being a Report of the Committee on Literature and Publication to the North Side Board of Trade of the City of New York, 27 September 1905*. New York: Kieling Bros., 1905.

——. *Where New York's Future Lies*. New York: North Side Board of Trade, 1903.

North Side News. Bronx County Progress Section. 17 March 1914.

Olmsted, Frederick, Jr. and Theodora Kimball. *Forty Years of Landscape Architecture*. 2 vols. New York: G. P. Putnam's Sons, Knickerbocker Press, 1928.

Orlebeke, Charles J. *New Life at Ground Zero: New York, Home Ownership, and the Future of American Cities*. Albany, NY: The Rockefeller Institute Press, 1997.

Passonneau, Joseph R. and Richard Saul Wurman. *Urban Atlas: 20 American Cities*. Cambridge: MIT Press, 1966.

Pinderhughes, Howard. *Race in the Hood: Conflict and Violence Among Urban Youth*. Minneapolis: University of Minnesota Press, 1997.

Plan of New York and Its Environs. *Plan of New York and Its Environs: The Meeting of May 10, 1922*. New York: Russell Sage Foundation, 1922.

Plunz, Richard. *A History of Housing in New York City*. New York: Columbia University Press, 1990.

Powell, Colin L. *My American Journey*. New York: Random House, 1995.

Pratt, Edward Ewing. *Industrial Causes of Congestion of Population in New York City*. New York: Columbia University, Longmans, Green & Co., 1911.

Price, Mark. *A History of the Bronx Public Schools (From Consolidation to the Present) 1898–1944*. New York: Board of Education, 1945.

Proshanky, Harold, William H. Ittelson, and Leanne G. Rubin, eds. *Environmental Psychology: Man and His Physical Setting*. New York: Holt, Rinehart and Winston, 1970.

Real Estate Record and Builders' Guide. A History of Real Estate, Building and Architecture in New York City During the Last Quarter of A Century. 1898; reprint, New York: Arno Press, 1967.

Reeves, William Fullerton. *The First Elevated Railroads in Manhattan and the Bronx of the City of New York: The Story of Their Development and Progress*. New York: New-York Historical Society, 1936.

Regional Plan Association, Inc. *The Economic Status of the New York Metropolitan Region in 1944*. New York: Regional Plan Association, 1944.

Reps, John W. *The Making of Urban America: A History of City Planning in the United States*. Princeton: Princeton University Press, 1965.

Richardson, James F. *The New York Police: Colonial Times to 1901*. New York: Oxford University Press, 1971.

Rivera, Edwin. *Family Installments: Memoirs of Growing Up Hispanic*. New York: William Morrow, 1982.

Rodriguez, Clara E. *Puerto Ricans: Born in the U.S.A.* San Francisco: Westview, 1991.

Rooney, Jim. *Organizing the South Bronx*. Albany: State University of New York Press, 1995.

Roper, Laura Wood. *FLO: A Biography of Frederick Law Olmsted*. Baltimore: Johns Hopkins University Press, 1973.

Rosen, Louis. *The South Side: The Racial Transformation of An American Neighborhood*. Chicago: Ivan R. Dee, 1998.

Rosenberg, Terry J. *Residence, Employment and Mobility of Puerto Ricans in New York City*. Chicago: University of Chicago, Department of Geography Research Paper No. 151, 1974.

Rosenthal, Mel. *In the South Bronx of America*. Willimantic, CT: Curbstone Press, 2000.

Rosenwaike, Ira. *Population History of New York City*. Syracuse, NY: Syracuse University Press, 1972.

Rossi, Peter H. *Why Families Move: A Study in the Social Psychology of Urban Residential Mobility*. Glencoe, IL: Free Press, 1955.

Rub, Timothy, ed. *Building a Borough: Architecture and Planning in The Bronx, 1890–1940*. New York: Bronx Museum of the Arts, 1986.

St. Augustine's Church. *Golden Jubilee, 1849–1899. October 8, 1899*. New York: St. Augustine's Church, 1899.

Salins, Peter. *The Ecology of Housing Destruction: Economic Effects of Public Intervention in the Housing Market*. New York: New York University, 1980.

Sanchez-Korrol, Virginia E. *From Colonia to Community: The History of Puerto Ricans in New York City, 1917–1948*. Westport, CT: Greenwood Press, 1983.

Sann, Paul. *Kill the Dutchman! The Story of Dutch Schultz*. New Rochelle, NY: Arlington House, 1971.

Santiago, Esmeralda. *When I Was Puerto Rican*. New York: Vintage, 1993.

Scharf, John Thomas. *History of Westchester County, New York: including Morrisania, Kingsbridge, and West Farms which Have Been Annexed to New York City*. 2 vols. Philadelphia: L. E. Preston & Co., 1886.

Schill, Michael H., ed. *Housing and Community Development in New York City: Facing the Future*. Albany: State University of New York Press, 1999.

Schnieder, Eric C. *Vampires, Dragons, and Egyptian Kings: Youth Gangs in Postwar New York*. Princeton: Princeton University Press, 1999.

Schoenberg, Sandra Perlman and Patricia L. Rosenbaum. *Neighborhoods That Work: Sources for Viability in the Inner City*. New Brunswick: Rutgers University Press, 1980.

Schuyler, David. *The New Urban Landscape: The Redefinition of City Form in Nineteenth-Century America*. Baltimore: Johns Hopkins University Press, 1988.

Schwartz, Joel. *The New York Approach: Robert Moses, Urban Liberals, and Redevelopment of the Inner City*. Columbus: Ohio University Press, 1993.

Sherman, P. Tecumseh. *Inside the Machine: Two Years in the Board of Aldermen, 1898–1899, A Study of the Legislative Features of the City Government of New York City under the Greater New York Charter*. New York: Cooke & Fry, 1901.

Shonnard, Frederick and W. W. Spooner. *History of Westchester County, New York: From the Earliest Settlement to the Year 1900*. New York: New York History Co.; 1900.

Skogan, Wesley G. *Disorder and Decline: Crime and the Spiral of Decay in American Neighborhoods*. Berkeley: University of California Press, 1990.

——, ed. *Reaction to Crime and Violence. The Annals* 539 (May 1995).

Sleeper, Jim. *The Closest of Strangers: Liberalism and the Politics of Race in New York*. New York: Norton, 1990.

Smith, Dennis. *Report from Engine Co. 82*. New York: Saturday Review Press, 1972.

Smith, Neil. *Uneven Development: Nature, Capital, and the Production of Space*. Cambridge, MA: Blackwell, 1991.

Smith, Wallace F. *Filtering and Neighborhood Change*. Research Report No. 24.

Berkeley: Center for Real Estate and Urban Economics: Institute of Urban and Regional Development. University of California, 1964.

Spann, Edward K. *The New Metropolis: New York City, 1840–1857*. New York: Columbia University Press, 1981.

Sparks, Jared. *The Life of Gouverneur Morris with Selections From His Correspondence and Miscellaneous Papers*. 3 vols. Boston, 1832.

Spengler, Edwin Harold. *Land Values in New York in Relation to Transit Facilities*. 1930; reprint, New York: AMS Press, 1968.

Stegman, Michael A. *The Dynamics of Rental Housing in New York City*. Piscataway, NJ: Center for Urban Policy Research, Rutgers University, 1982.

———. *Housing in New York: Study of a City, 1984*. New York: New York City Department of Housing, Preservation and Development, February 1985.

Sterne, Simon. *The Park Act of 1884: Its Dangers and Consequence, An Open Letter To the Citizens of New York*. New York: Committee of Twenty-five Taxpayers, appointed at the Mass Meeting at Chickering Hall, 1885.

Sternlieb, George and James W. Hughes. *Housing and Economic Reality: New York City, 1976*. New Brunswick: The Center for Urban Policy and Research, 1976.

Sugrue, Thomas. *The Origins of the Urban Crisis: Race and Inequality in Postwar Detroit*. Princeton: Princeton University Press, 1996.

Sutton, Constance R. and Elsa M. Chaney. *Caribbean Life in New York City: Sociocultural Dimensions*. New York: Center for Migration Studies of New York, 1987.

Takaki, Ronald, ed. *From Different Shores: Perspectives on Race and Ethnicity in America*. New York: Oxford University Press, 1994.

Taxpayers' Alliance. *The New North End: Bronx Borough*. New York: Diagram Publishing Co., 1910.

Tieck, William A. *Riverdale, Kingsbridge, Spuyten Duyvil: A Historical Epitome of the Northwest Bronx*. Old Tappan, NJ: Fleming H. Revell, 1968.

Torres, Andres. *Between Melting Pot and Mosaic: African Americans and Puerto Ricans in the New York Political Economy*. Philadelphia: Temple University Press, 1995.

Torres, Andres and Jose E. Velazquez, eds. *The Puerto Rican Movement: Voices from the Diaspora*. Philadelphia: Temple University Press, 1998.

Trotsky, Leon. *My Life*. New York: Grosset & Dunlap, 1930.

Ultan, Lloyd. *The Beautiful Bronx (1920–1950)*. New Rochelle, NY: Arlington House, 1979.

Ultan, Lloyd and Gary Hermalyn. *The Bronx in the Innocent Years, 1890–1925*. New York: Harper & Row, 1985.

Van Vliet, William, ed. *Affordable Housing and Urban Redevelopment. Urban Affairs Annual Reviews*. Vol. 4. Thousand Oaks, CA: Sage, 1997.

Venkatesh, Sudir Alladi. *American Project: The Rise and Fall of a Modern Ghetto*. Cambridge: Harvard University Press, 2000.

Vergara, Camilo Jose. *The New American Ghetto*. New Brunswick: Rutgers University Press, 1995.

Wagner, Eliot. *Grand Concourse: A Novel*. New York: Bobbs-Merrill, 1954.

Waldinger, Roger. *Still the Promised City? African-Americans and New Immigrants in Post-Industrial New York*. Cambridge: Harvard University Press, 1996.

Walker, James Blaine. *Fifty Years of Rapid Transit: 1864 to 1917*. 1918; reprint, New York: Arno Press & New York Times, 1970.

Walker, Tom. *Fort Apache: Life and Work in New York City's Most Violent Precinct*. New York: Thomas Crowell, 1976.

Wallace, Deborah and Roderick Wallace. *A Plague on Your Houses: How New York Was Burned Down and National Public Health Crumbled*. New York: Verso, 1998.

Ward, David. *Cities and Immigrants: A Geography of Change in Nineteenth-Century America*. New York: Oxford University Press, 1971.

——. *Poverty, Ethnicity, and the American City, 1940–1925: Changing Conceptions of the Slum and the Ghetto*. New York: Cambridge University Press, 1989.

Ware, Norman. *The Industrial Worker, 1840–1860: The Reaction of American Industrial Society to the Advance of the Industrial Revolution*. 1924; reprint, Chicago: Quadrangle, 1964.

Warner, Sam Bass, Jr. *The Private City: Philadelphia in Three Periods of Its Growth*. Philadelphia: University of Pennsylvania Press, 1968.

——. *Streetcar Suburbs: The Process of Growth in Boston, 1870–1900*. Cambridge: Harvard University Press and MIT Press, 1962.

Wells, James L. *Bronx Real Estate: An Address to the North Side Board of Trade, January 24th, 1909*. New York: North Side Board of Trade, 1909.

——. *The Completion of the Harlem Ship Canal*. New York: North Side Board of Trade, January 1907.

——. *The Growth of The Bronx, New York City, Since Consolidation, January 1, 1898 to January 1, 1906*. New York: The Bronx League, January 10, 1906.

Wells, James L., Louis F. Haffen, and Josiah A. Briggs, eds. *The Bronx and Its People: A History, 1609–1927*. 3 vols. New York: Louis Historical Publishing Co., 1927.

Wenger, Beth S. *New York Jews and the Great Depression: Uncertain Promise*. Syracuse, NY: Syracuse University Press, 1999.

Westchester County Bible Society. *Annual Report, 1864*. White Plains, NY: Westchester County Bible Society, 1864.

Willis, N[athaniel] Parker. *Hurry-Graphs or, Sketches of Society, Taken From Life*. New York: Charles Scribner, 1851.

Wilson, James Q. *Thinking About Crime*. New York: Basic Books, 1975.

Wilson, James Q. and Joan Petersilia, eds. *Crime*. San Francisco: ICS Press, 1995.

Witke, Carl. *We Who Built America: The Saga of the Immigrant*. New York: Prentice-Hall, 1939.

Women's City Club. *With Love and Affection: A Study of Building Abandonment*. New York, 1977.

Woodfill, Barbara M. *New York City's Mitchell-Lama Program: Middle-Income Housing*. New York: Rand Institute, June 1971.

Wright, Gwendolyn. *Building the Dream: A Social History of Housing in America*. New York: Pantheon, 1981.

Zahler, Helene Sara. *Eastern Workingmen and National Land Policy, 1829–1862*. New York: Columbia University Press, 1941.

Zucker, Augustus E. *The Forty-Eighters: Political Refugees of the German Revolution of 1848*. New York: Columbia University Press, 1950.

SECONDARY SOURCES—ARTICLES

Abrams, Charles. "How to Remedy Our 'Puerto Rican Problem'." *Commentary*, February 1955, 120–27.

Alliance for Redesigning Government. "Comprehensive Revitalization Program." National Academy of Public Administration. http://www.alliance.napawash.org.

Austin, F. "Real Estate Development of Bronx County." *North Side News*, Bronx County Progress Section, 17 May 1914.

Bach, Victor. "The Future of HUD-Subsidized Housing: The New York City Case." In *Housing and Community Development in New York City: Facing the Future*, ed. Schill, 143–75.

Bartelt, David and Ronald Lawson. "Rent Control and Abandonment in New York City: A Look at the Evidence." In *Critical Perspectives in Housing*, ed. Bratt, Hartman, and Meyerson, 180–83.

Bayor, Ronald H. "The Neighborhood Invasion Pattern." In *Neighborhoods in Urban America*, ed. Bayor, 86–102.

Beagle, Peter. "Goodby to the Bronx." *Holiday*, December 1964, 96–97, 141–43, 150–51.

Bellush, Jewel. "Housing: The Scattered-Site Controversy." In *Race and Politics in New York City: Five Studies in Policy Making*, ed. Bellush and David, 96–133.

Boynton, E. B. "Confidence in Bronx Real Estate Unshaken." *North Side News*, Bronx County Progress Section, 17 May 1914, 86–87.

Braconi, Frank P. "In Re *In Rem*: Innovation and Expediency in New York's Housing Policy." In *Housing and Community Development in New York City*, ed. Schill, 96–97.

Bradshaw, Jon. "Savage Skulls." *Esquire*, June 1977, 74–82, 131–44.

Bratt, Rachel G., Avis C. Vidal, Alex Schwartz, Langley C. Keyes, and Jim Stockard. "The Status of Nonprofit-Owned Affordable Housing: Short-Term Successed and Long-Term Challenges." *Journal of the American Planning Association* 64 (winter 1998): 39–51.

Breslin, Patrick. "On These Sidewalks of New York, The Sun is Shining Again." *Smithsonian Magazine*, April 1995.

Bromley, Ray. "Not So Simple! Caro, Moses, and the Impact of the Cross-Bronx Expressway." *The Bronx County Historical Society Journal* 35 (spring 1998): 5–29.

"The Bronx Church House." *Architectural Record* 22 (December 1907): 509–10.

"Bronx Tale." *New York*, 19–26 December 1994, 84.

Brown, William R. "Reminiscences of the Central Bronx." *Real Estate Record and Builders' Guide*, 18 November 1911.

Calhoun, Richard B. "New York City Fire Department Reorganization, 1865–1870: A Civil War Legacy." *New York Historical Society Quarterly* 40 (January/April 1976): 7–34.

Cauldwell, William. "Annexation." In North Side Board of Trade, *The Great North Side or Borough of The Bronx*, 19–27. New York: Knickerbocker Press, 1897.

Cohen, Carol S. and Michael H. Phillips. "Building Community: Principles for Social Work Practice in Housing Settings." *Social Work* 42 (September 1997): 471–81.

Cohen, Rich. "The Enterprise Foundation: How a National Intermediary Assists Nonprofit Community Development." In *Housing in America*, ed. Lederman, 241–54.

Conway, Dennis and Ualthan Bigby. "Where Caribbean Peoples Live in New York City." In *Caribbean Life in New York City*, ed. Sutton and Chaney, 74–83.

Conway, William G. "'People Fire' in the Ghetto Ashes." *Saturday Review*, 23 July 1977, 15–16.

Cressey, Paul F. "Population Succession in Chicago, 1898–1930." *American Journal of Sociology* 44 (July 1938).

Davis, Henry K. "History of Bronx County." *North Side News*, Bronx County Progress Section, 17 May 1914.

Dawson, Henry B. "Rambles in Westchester County, New York, A Fragment." In *The Gazette Series*, vol. 5, ed. Henry B. Dawson. Yonkers, NY, 1866.

Dobnik, Verena. "South Bronx Homes and Gardens are an Urban Phoenix." *Staten Island Advance*, 17 October 1999.

"The Evolution of the Tenement House." *Real Estate Record and Builders' Guide*, 28 September 1889.

"The Federal Census of New York." *Federation* 2 (April–June 1902): 18–22.

Firey, Walter. "Sentiment and Symbolism as Ecological Variables." *American Sociological Review* 10 (April 1945): 140–48.

Flagg, Ernest. "The Planning of Apartment Houses and Tenements." *Architectural Review* 10 (1893): 85–90.

Flanagan, Richard M. "The Housing Act of 1954: The Sea Change in National Urban Policy." *Urban Affairs Review* 33:2 (November 1997): 265–86.

Friedlander, Stanley and Charles Brecher. "A Comparative View." *New York is Very Much Alive: A Manpower View*, 220–41. Ed. Eli Ginzberg. New York: McGraw-Hill, 1973.

Genevro, Rosalie. "Site Selection and the New York City Housing Authority, 1934–1939." *Journal of Urban History* 12 (August 1986): 334–52.

Gill, W. W. "Residential Sections." In Taxpayers' Alliance, *The New North End: Bronx Borough*. New York: Diagram Publishing Co., 1910.

Gittell, Marilyn. "Education: The Decentralization–Community Control Controversy." In *Race and Politics in New York City: Five Studies in Policy Making*, ed. Bellush and David., 134–63.

Glazer, Nathan. "The South Bronx Story: An Extreme Case of Urban Decline." *Policy Studies Journal* 16 (winter 1987): 269–76.

Glynn, Thomas. "Anita Miller: A Warrior for the South Bronx." *Neighborhood*, August 1982, 34–37.

——. "Charlotte Street, the Bronx." *Neighborhood*, August 1982, 26–31.

——. "Something Good is Growing in the South Bronx: People's Development Corporation." *Neighborhood*, December 1977, 7–17.

——. "The South Bronx." *Neighborhood*, August 1982, 3–26.

Gottlieb, Martin. "The Scrapping of New York." *New York Daily News*, 5 January 1981.

Green, Joseph Warren, Jr. "New York City's First Railroad, The New York and Harlem, 1832 to 1867." *New York Historical Society Quarterly Bulletin* 9 (January 1926): 107–23.

Guzmán, Pablo. "La Vida Pura: A Lord of the Barrio." In *The Puerto Rican Movement*, ed. Torres and Velasquez, 165–66.

Herter, Peter. "How to Invest in Tenement Property: Where to Build and What to Build." *Real Estate and Builders' Guide*, 5 May 1900.

"Hillside Homes." *American Architect* 148 (May 1979): 17–33.

Holtzclaw, John. "Greening the South Bronx." *Sierra*, July 1979, 30.

Horowitz, Craig. "A South Bronx Renaissance." *New York*, 21 November 1994, 54–59.

Jacobson, Michael and Philip Kasinitz. "Burning The Bronx for Profit." *The Nation*, 15 November 1986, 512–15.

Jensen, Robert and Cathy Alexander. "Resurrection: The People Are Doing It Themselves." In *Devastation/Resurrection*, ed. Jensen, 83–112.

Kaplan, Milton. "Private Enterprise in The Bronx: Rags to Riches on Washington Avenue." *Commentary*, August 1950, 162–66.

Kappstatter, Bob. "Apple's Best Kept Secret," *New York Daily News*, 11 June 1997.

——. "This Borough's Pride is Working Out," *New York Daily News*, 23 April 1997.

——. "Bronx Shines in U.S. Spotlight," *New York Daily News*, 23 April 1997.

Keating, Dennis and Janet Smith. "Past Federal Policy for Urban Neighborhoods." In *Revitalizing Urban Neighborhoods*, ed. Keating, Krumholz, and Starr, 50–57.

Kraly, Ellen Percy and Ines Miyares. "Immigration to New York: Policy, Population, and Patterns." In *New Immigrants in New York*, ed. Foner, 31–79.

Kristoff, Frank. "Housing and People in New York City: A View of the Past, Present, and Future." *City Almanac* 10 (February 1976): 5.

Lake, Eleanor. "Trouble on the Street Corner." *Common Sense*, May 1943, 147–49.

Lawn, Victor H. "House for the Goose, House for the Gander." *The Survey*, 15 December 1926, 371–73.

Lee, Terrence. "Urban Neighborhoods as a Social-Spatial Schema." In *Environmental Psychology: Man and His Physical Setting*, ed. Proshansky, Ittelson, and Rivlin, 349–70.

"List of Churches." *Federation* 2 (December 1902): 59–62.

Lombardi, Frank. "Bronx Considers Spruce-up Plans." *New York Daily News*, 10 April 1990.

Lowry, Ira S. "Filtering and Housing Standards: A Conceptual Analysis." *Land Economics* 36 (November 1960): 362–70.

Lubell, Samuel. "The Boiling Bronx: Henry Wallace Stronghold." *Saturday Evening Post,* 23 October 1948, 18–19, 61–67.

Lubove, Roy. "The Urbanization Process: An Approach to Historical Research." *Journal of the American Institute of Planners* 33 (January 1967): 33–39.

Mack, T. J. "The Bronx Grows, 1894–1939." *Bronxboro,* February–March 1939, 8.

McDermott, Maura. "Change in the Bank," *City Limits,* September/October 2000.

McGowan, Kathleen. "Building Blocks," *City Limits,* January 2000, 12–15, 27.

McGowan, Kathleen and Philip Shishkin. "The Promised Land," *City Limits,* March 1999.

McLaughlin, Peter. "Hunts Point Puts Hopes in Building Boom." *New York Daily News,* 7 August 1977.

Marcuse, Peter. "Neighborhood Policy and the Distribution of Power: New York City's Community Boards." *Policy Studies Journal* 16:2 (winter 1987): 281–82.

"Melting Pot Politics: Its Practitioners in the East Bronx Work at Their Profession Amidst the Big-City Problems of Racial Tension and Radicalism." *Life,* 27 October 1952, 125–29.

Meyer, Herbert E. "How Government Helped Ruin the South Bronx." *Fortune,* November 1975, 140–54.

Michetti, Felice. "The New York City Capital Program for Affordable Housing." In *Housing in America,* ed. Lederman, 199–213.

Morales, Iris. "¡Palante, Siempre Palante! The Young Lords." In *The Puerto Rican Movement: Voices from the Diaspora,* ed. Torres and Velázquez, 210–27.

Moss, Jordan. "Fighting Fires With Fire." *City Limits,* April 2000.

Nauer, Kim. "Anatomy of a Sweetheart Deal." *City Limits,* November 1997.

——. "Reversal of Fortune." *City Limits,* December 1997.

Nenno, Mary K. "Changes and Challenges in Affordable Housing and Urban Redevelopment." In *Affordable Housing and Urban Redevelopment in the United States,* ed. Van Vliet, 1–21.

Ostow, Miriam and Charles Brecher. "Work and Welfare." In *New York Is Very Much Alive: A Manpower View,* ed. Ginzberg, 155–78.

Pacenza, Matt. "Dream Off?" *City Limits,* April 2001.

Plunz, Richard. "Reading Bronx Housing, 1890–1940." In *Building a Borough,* ed. Rub, 30–76.

Prahl, Augustus J. "The Turner." In *The Forty-Eighters,* ed. Zucker, 79–110.

"Public Housing Held Bad for Local Area." *New York Herald Tribune,* 17 March 1951.

Rodriguez, Clara. "Growing Up in the Forties and Fifties." In *Devastation/Resurrection,* ed. Jensen, 45–50.

——. "Puerto Ricans and the Political Economy of New York." In *From Different Shores,* ed. Takaki, 118–23.

Rogers, David. "Community Control and Decentralization." In *Urban Politics: New York Style,* ed. Bellush and Netzer, 143–87.

Rogowsky, Edward T., Louis H. Gold, and David W. Abbott. "Police: The Civilian Review Board Controversy." In *Race and Politics in New York City*, ed. Bellush and David, 59–97.

Rub, Timothy. "The Institutional Presence in The Bronx." In *Building a Borough*, ed. Rub, 78–109.

Sack, Bert. "I Grew Up With The Bronx." *The Bronx County Historical Society Journal* 1 (January 1964): 29–36.

Sampson, Robert J. "The Community." In *Crime*, ed. Wilson and Petersilia, 193–216.

Schuyler, Montgomery. "An Oasis in The Bronx." *Architectural Record* 41 (February 1917): 177–82.

Schwartz, Alex. "New York City and Subsidized Housing: Impacts and Lessons of the City's $5 Billion Capital Budget Housing Plan." *Housing Policy Debate* 10:4 (1999).

Schwartz, Joel. "Morrisania's Volunteer Firemen, 1848–1874: The Limits of Local Institutions in a Metropolitan Age." *New York History* 55 (1974): 159–78.

Shanley, Charles Dawson. "Germany in New York." *Atlantic Monthly*, May 1867, 555–64.

Sharff, Jagna Wojcicka. "The Underground Economy of a Poor Neighborhood." In *Cities of the United States*, ed. Mullings, 19–50.

Simmons, Lynda. "Twenty-five Years of Community Building in the South Bronx: Phipps Houses in West Farms." In *Affordable Housing and Urban Redevelopment in the United States*, ed. Van Vliet, 73–94.

Simpson, Janice and Derek Reveron. "Own Your Own Apartment House, for the the Price of a Second-hand Car." *New York Post*, 1 August 1977.

Starr, Roger. "Making New York Smaller." *New York Times Magazine*, 14 November 1976.

Sternlieb, George, Robert W. Burchell, James W. Hughes, and Franklin J. James. "Housing Abandonment in the Urban Core." *Journal of the American Institute of Planners* 40:5 (September 1974): 321–32.

Stevenson, Gelvin. "The Abandonment of Roosevelt Gardens." In *Devastation/Resurrection*, ed. Jensen, 72–80.

Stokols, D. "A Social Psychological Model of Human Crowding." *Journal of the American Institute of Planners* 38 (1972): 72–84.

Strozier, Matthew. "How West Farms Was Won." *City Limits*, September/October 2000, 18–20.

Sullivan, Donald G. "1940–1965, Population Mobility in the South Bronx." In *Devastation/Resurrection*, ed. Jensen, 37–44.

———. "The Process of Abandonment." In *Devastation/Resurrection*, ed. Jensen, 69–71.

Sviridoff, Mitchell and William Ryan. "Investing in Community: Lessons and Implications of the Comprehensive Community Revitalization Program." January 1996. http://www.cpn.org/cpn/sections/topics/community/stories-studies/south_bronx.html.

Thomson, Sheila. "Bronx Profile: Eddie Calderon-Melendez." *New York Newsday*, 23 November 1993, Bronx Edition.

Thompson, Philip. "Public Housing in New York City." In *Housing and Community Development in New York City*, ed. Schill, 119–42.

Tienda, Marta. "Puerto Ricans and the Underclass Debate." In *From Different Shores*, ed. Takaki, 261–69.

Tobier, Emanuel. "The Bronx in the Twentieth Century: Dynamics of Population and Economic Change." *The Bronx County Historical Society Journal* 25 (fall 1998): 69–102.

Trillin, Calvin. "U.S. Journal: The Bronx, The Coops." *The New Yorker*, 1 August 1977, 49–54.

Ultan, Lloyd. "1776–1940: The Story of The South Bronx." In *Devastation/Resurrection*, ed. Jensen, 14–36.

Van Ryzin, Gregg G. and Andrew Genn. "Neighborhood Change and the City of New York's Ten-Year Housing Plan." *Housing Policy Debate* 10:4 (1999): 799–838.

Veiller, Lawrence. "Two New-Law Flats." *Real Estate Record and Builders' Guide*, 8 February 1902.

Vogel, Carl. "Melrose's Thorny Predicament." *City Limits*, September/October 1999.

Wellman, Barry and Barry Leighton. "Networks, Neighborhoods, and Communities: Approaches to the Study of the Community Question." In *Internal Structure of the City*, ed. Bourne, 245–59.

White, Andrew and Susan Saegert. "Return from Abandonment: The Tenant Interim Lease Program and the Redevelopment of Low Income Cooperatives in New York City's Most Neglected Neighborhoods." In *Affordable Housing and Urban Redevelopment in the United States*, ed. William Van Vliet, 158–228.

Williams, Roger M. "The New Urban Pioneers: Homesteading in the Slums." *Saturday Review*, 23 January 1977.

Wirth, Louis. "Urbanism as a Way of Life." *American Journal of Sociology* 44 (1938): 1–24.

Wiseman, Carter. "Little House on the Rubble." *New York*, 1 June 1981, 54.

Wylde, Kathryn. "The Contribution of Public-Private Partnerships to New York's Assisted Housing Industry." In *Housing and Community Development in New York City*, ed. Schill, 73–91.

Ziegler, Mel. "Biography of an Unwanted Building." *New York*, 24 May 1971.

Zoebelein, George M. "The Bronx: A Struggle for County Government." *Bronx County Historical Society Journal* 1 (January 1964): 3–24.

NEW YORK TIMES ARTICLES

"Alexander Avenue: Island in the South Bronx." 1 February 1969.

Barron, James. "$5 Billion Plan For Apartment Pushed in Bronx." 28 February 1989.

Berger, Joseph. "Fernandez Weighs Action on Bronx District 9." 28 January 1996.

Bennett, Charles G. "Councilman Sees 'Terror' in Bronx." 2 March 1967.

Bennetto, Leslie. "Panel Declares Treatment Plant City Landmark." 9 June 1982.

Bernstein, Emily M. "Project Mixes Working Class and Ex-Homeless in Bronx." 16 September 1994.

Bigart, Homer. "Two Communities Seek More Police." 10 March 1967.

Blumenthal, Ralph and Sam Howe Verhovek. "Patronage and Profit in Schools: A Tale of a Bronx District Board." 16 December 1988.

"Bronx Board Plans Six Year Program." 22 January 1939.

Burnham, David. "Bronx Police Aim At Indoor Crime." 24 December 1969.

Chambers, Bradford. "Boy Gangs of New York: 500 Fighting Units." *New York Times Magazine*, 10 December 1944, 16, 55.

Clines, Frances X. "About New York: A 'Hidden' Side of the Bronx." 6 July 1978.

——. "Blighted Areas' Use Is Urged by Rohatyn." 16 March 1976.

Cooper, Michael. "Officers in Bronx Fire 41 Shots, and an Unarmed Man Is Killed." 5 February 1999.

"Councilman to Tour Hunts Point Homes." 2 March 1970.

Daley, Suzanne. "Lost Neighborhood Found in Memory." 25 April 1983.

Darnton, John. "Gigante vs. Velez in Ring of Slum Politics." 19 November 1973.

Devlin, John C. "Hunts Point Follows the Pattern of Poverty." 23 March 1964.

Dionne Jr., E. J. "Owner of Looted Store in Bronx Exchanges Words With the Mayor." 17 July 1977.

Dunlap, David W. "Bronx Housing Devastation Found Slowly Substantially." 22 March 1982.

Ferretti, Fred. "After 70 Years, South Bronx Is At a Dead End." 21 October 1977.

Feuer, Alan. "Signs of Hope in the Bronx Neighborhood Where Diallo Died." 16 February 2002.

"Few Bronx Slums Merit Clearance." 23 March 1934.

"55 in State Senate Ask U.S. Aid to City Slums as Disaster Areas." 18 February 1970.

Filkins, Dexter. "In Bronx Revival, Ferrer Is Credited With Only a Supporting Role." 5 August 2001.

Finder, Alan. "Housing Plan Would Fix Up 5,200 Units." 24 December 1986.

——. "New York Pledge to House Poor Works a Rare, Quiet Revolution." 30 April 1995.

Fisher, Ian. "Pulling Out of Fort Apache, the Bronx." 23 June 1993.

Forero, Juan. "Bronx Ministers Hold Marches to Appeal for Calm on Verdict." 24 February 2000.

——. "No Longer a War Zone, Hunts Point Gains Status." 23 August 2000.

——. "Veteran of Police and Pulpit Helps Soothe Tensions in the Bronx." 14 March 2000.

"Forty in Bronx Seek Gun Permits for Protection Against Addicts." 26 September 1969.

Fraser, C. Gerald. "Bronx Poverty Post Stirs Clash of Negroes and Puerto Ricans." 18 April 1968.

Fried, Joseph P. "After Capital Hill, A Climb Out of a Valley." 18 November 2001.

——. "City's Housing Administrator Proposes 'Planned Shrinkage' of Some Slums." 3 February 1976.

——. "Housing Abandonment Spreads in Bronx and Parts of Brooklyn." 12 April 1976.

——. "Is South Bronx Revival Plan Simply Folly?" 19 June 1978.

——. "Vandalized South Bronx Project Gets New Chance." 6 July 1978.

Garbarine, Rachelle. "Neighborhood Rises in the South Bronx." 25 December 1998.

Geist, William E. "Residents Give a Bronx Cheer to Decal Plan." 12 November 1983.

Golden, Tim. "C'est le Bronx? Où Sont les Maisons Abandonnées?" 16 November 1990.

Gonzalez, David. "Bronx Community Groups Find Strength in Unity." 17 July 1994.

——. "Despite Hype, Hope Builds." 8 June 1996.

Goodwin, Michael. "1980 Census Housing Figures Show 2 New York Cities." 14 June 1981.

Gornick, Vivian. "My Neighborhood, Its Fall and Rise." 24 June 2001.

Grusen, Sydney. "New Faces in the Lower Bronx: Shifting Population Often Raises Tense Problems in Housing." 11 July 1955.

Gupte, Pranay. "Tenants Decry State of 7-Year-Old Housing Project." 7 May 1978.

"Hanging On: A Landmark Isle." 20 March 1983.

"Help From the Desperados: For New Hope Plaza, a New Look." 29 May 1983.

"In Defense of the Bronx." 16 November 1976.

"Jimmy Carter Revisits the South Bronx." 23 June 1992.

Johnson, Thomas A. "Rohatyn Scored by Congressman." 17 March 1976.

Kaiser, Charles. "Survival of South Bronx Row Houses Celebrated." 10 November 1976.

Kaufman, Michael T. "Hunts Point Goal: Preserve Housing." 27 June 1974.

Kennedy, Shawn G. "Landmarking's Double-Edged Sword." 13 January 1991.

Kifner, John. "Giant City Agency to Reorganize Aid to Poor is Urged." 27 June 1966.

Kleiman, Dena. "City Urges U.S. to House Aged in Concourse Plaza." 12 May 1978.

——. "West Tremont Typical of Blight." 13 April 1978.

Kugel, Seth. "Is Melrose a Melrose By Any Other Name?" 23 June 2003.

——. "Little Africa Flourishes, FuFu Flour and All." 17 February 2002.

Lambert, Bruce. "Way Cleared for Long-Delayed Housing." 14 April 1991.

Lii, Jane H. "South Bronx Churches Will Expand Affordable Housing." 4 December 1997.

McFadden, Robert D. "Businessmen Angry as Beame Inspects City's Looted Areas." 17 July 1977.

——. "New York Power Restored Slowly, Looting Widespread." 15 July 1977.

Martin, Douglas. "A Garden Caught in a Housing Squeeze." 18 May 1998.

Nieves, Evelyn. "Refugee Found Guilty of Killing 87 in Bronx Happy Land Fire." 20 August 1991.

"New Homes for South Bronx." 8 October 2000.

Nossiter, Adam. "As a Hospital is Fixed, A Wound Is Healed." 8 April 1996.

Oser, Alan S. "Bronx Fires: Final Stage of a Long Process." 20 June 1975.

———. "Causes of Abandonment and What to Do About Them Despair Housing Officials." 14 May 1976.

———. "In Brownsville, Churches Joining to Build Homes." 1 May 1983.

———. "Public Housing in Abandoned Buildings." 4 October 1987.

———. "Starting the Rehabilitation Journey At Parkchester." 15 April 1999.

Peterson, Iver. "A New Era for the Grand Concourse." 24 January 1888.

Phillips, McCandlish. "Fatal Mugging Stirs Fears in Bronx Neighborhood." 15 February 1967.

Phillips, Wayne. "Census Loss Tied to Slum Program." 6 September 1960.

"Priest is Ejected After Scolding City Council About Bronx Slums." 18 February 1970.

Pristin, Terry. "City Requests $160 Million to Fix Up Homes in Scandal." 6 July 2001.

"Protest on Heatless Homes in Bronx Sent to Mayor." 11 February 1970.

Purdy, Michael. "Left to Die, the South Bronx Rises From Decades of Decay." 13 November 1994.

Raab, Selwyn. "Ravage Continues Far Into Day, Gunfire and Bottles Beset Police." 15 July 1977.

Roberts, Steven V. "Grand Concourse: Hub of Bronx in Undergoing Ethnic Changes." 21 July 1966.

Rosen, Ira. "The Glory That Was Charlotte Street." *New York Times Magazine*, 7 September 1979, 43–44, 74–75, 106–9.

Rothstein, Mervyn. "A Renewal Plan in the Bronx Advances." 10 July 1994.

Rule, Sheila. "Amid Urban Decay: Reflections on Pope's Visit." 27 September 1979.

Saxon, Wolfgang. "Anne Devenney, 79, Bronx Guardian Dies." 16 February 2000.

Severo, Richard. "Hunts Point: Ruled by Addicts." 24 September 1969.

Shenon, Philip. "Taste of Suburbia Arrives in the South Bronx." 19 March 1983.

Shipler, David K. "The Changing City: Housing Paralysis." 5 June 1969.

———. "Aide Dies in Fight on Poverty Funds." 8 August 1969.

Sibley, John. "Bathgate Scene Is Different Now." 1 June 1965.

"Six Youths Convicted of Rape." 22 May 1943.

Smalls, F. Romall. "The Bronx Is Named an 'All-America' City." 20 July 1997.

Stanley, Alessandra. "Hospital, Family Doctor and Benefactor." 19 December 1990.

Stewart, Barbara. "The Bronx: An All-America City, Thonx." 19 November 1997.

———. "Making It Work: Where the Ex-Rich Lived." 14 September 1997.

———. "Market's Nod to a Rebirth: In South Bronx Enclave, Rising Property Values and Suburban Living." 2 November 1997.

Swarns, Rachael L. "Coop City Suffers While Its Board Bickers." 29 May 1996.

"A Success Story in the Bronx." 2 July 1989.

Teltsch, Kathleen. "Once Desperate, A Bronx Housing Group Earns Praise." 30 October 1987.

Tolchin, Martin. "Gangs Spread Terror in the South Bronx." 16 January 1973.

———. "Rage Permeates All Facets of Life in the South Bronx." 17 January 1973.

——. "South Bronx: A Jungle Stalked By Fear, Seized By Rage." 15 January 1973.

"Touch of Art Deco in the Bronx." 28 November 1999.

Treaster, Joseph B. "Blackout Arrests Swamp City's Criminal Justice System." 15 July 1977.

——. "20% Rise in Fires Is Adding To Decline of South Bronx," 18 May 1975.

"12 Accused of Rape in a Bronx Theatre." 1 April 1942.

"2 Youths Convicted of 'Mugging' Attack." 2 April 1943.

Verhovek, Sam Howe. "On One Woman's Grit, A Building Revives." 22 August 1987.

Vidal, David. "Bronx Fires Leave Trail of Homelessness and Fear." 23 June 1975.

Waldman, Amy. "Buildings Savior Now A Troubled Landlord." 27 June 2000.

——. "In the Rebuilt South Bronx, A Pioneer of Sweat Equity Fights to Keep His Ideals." 18 January 2000.

——. "A Rebuilder in the Bronx Scales Back." 29 March 2001.

——. "State Subpoenas Records of Bronx Community Group." 19 February 2001.

Weinraub, Bernard. "Once-Grand Concourse." 2 February 1965.

Yardley, Jim. "Clinton Praises Bronx Renewal As U.S. Model: Charlotte St., Reborn Sees 3d President." 11 December 1997.

——. "Second Opinion on South Bronx Revival: Where the President Did Not Visit." 13 December 1997.

UNPUBLISHED WORKS

Bromley, Ray. "Coping and Caring: The Aftermath of the Happy Land Tragedy." Paper presented at the 23rd Annual Meeting of the Urban Affairs Association. Cleveland, Ohio, April 29–May 2, 1992.

Golden, Martha. "The Grand Concourse: Tides of Change." Landmarks Scholars Program. New York: NYC Landmarks Preservation Commission, spring 1976.

Handshuh, Pearl, Charlotte L. Simon, and Laura Zelman. "Boulevard Prospect Area, Bronx, New York City: A Survey by Honor Students, Hunter College." Mayor's Committee on Unity. New York, 1945.

Hart, Neil Edward. "The Sidewalks were Red." Florida, 1972. Memoir. Grand Concourse Vertical File. Bronx County Historical Society.

Kempton, Helen P. "A Study of The Bronx." Report. March 1921. Community Service Society Papers. Box 21. File 37–13. Columbia University Library.

Sack, Bert. "Bensonia." In Bert Sack. Miscellaneous Material. Vertical File. New York Public Library.

Wray, Stephen. "Westchester's only Draft Riot." Manuscript. New-York Historical Society.

DISSERTATIONS AND THESES

Brooks, Robert Clarkson. "History of the Street and Rapid Transit Railways of New York City." Ph.D. diss., Cornell University, 1903.

Cortina, Mary. "Neighborhood Change in the Bronx, 1950–1980: A Case Study." Ph.D. diss., Fordham University, 1990.

Davidson, Flora Sellers. "City Policy and Housing Abandonment: A Case Study of New York City, 1965–1973." Ph.D. diss., Columbia University, 1979.

Derrick, Peter E. "The New York City Transit Crisis of 1918–1925." M.A. thesis, Columbia University, 1967.

Devine, Richard. "Institutional Mortgage Investment in an Area of Racial Transition: A Case Study of Bronx County, 1960–1970." Ph.D. diss., New York University, 1974.

Epstein, Melissa. "How Dismantling the Third Avenue El Hurt the South Bronx." Senior thesis, Columbia University School of Architecture and Urban Planning, 1998.

Fein, Albert. "Frederick Law Olmsted: His Development as a Theorist and Designer of the American City." Ph.D. diss., Columbia University, 1969.

Fisher, Irving David. "Frederick Law Olmsted and the Philosophic Background to the City Planning Movement in the United States." Ph.D. diss., Columbia University, 1976.

Giordano, Richard William. "A History of the Morrisania Section of the Bronx in Three Periods: 1875, 1925, 1975." M.A. thesis, Columbia University, 1981.

Kaplan, Barry Jerome. "A Study in the Politics of Metropolitanization: The Greater New York City Charter of 1897." Ph.D. diss., State University of New York at Buffalo, 1975.

Maida, Lori M. "Belmont: A Community Fighting to Survive." Ph.D. diss., Fordham University, 1987.

Mazaraki, George Alexander. "The Public Career of Andrew Haswell Green." Ph.D. diss., New York University, 1966.

Meyer, Katherine Jeannette. "A Study of Tenant Associations in New York City with Particular Reference to The Bronx, 1920–1927." M.A. thesis, Columbia University, 1928.

Muller, Ada H. "A Study of a Bronx Community." M.A. thesis, Columbia University, 1915.

Schick, Sandor E. "Neighborhood Change in the Bronx, 1905–1960." Ph.D. diss., Harvard University, 1982.

Schwartz, Joel. "Community Building on the Bronx Frontier: Morrisania, 1848–1875." Ph.D. diss., University of Chicago, 1972.

Trumino, Joseph Anthony. "The Northwest Bronx Community and Clergy Coalition: A Neighborhood Organization and Its Membership in Conflict and Struggle." Ph.D. diss., City University of New York, 1991.

Winston, Diane. "Bronx Community Groups." Master's Project, Columbia University School of Journalism, 1982.

INDEX

Huckleberry Road, 54; *see also* Union Railway Company

Human Rights, Commission on. *See* Commission on Human Rights

Hunter College, 96

Hunts Point, 7–8, 35, 66, 86, 119, 128

Hunts Point–Crotona Park East, 19, 65–71, 96–97; African Americans, 99; Depression of 1930s, 102; population of, 78, 98, 122; Puerto Ricans, 100

Hunts Point–Longwood section, 84, 137

Hunts Point Multi-Service Center, 133

Hunts Point/Southern Boulevard district, 79

Hunts Point Terminal Produce Market, 118

Hunts Point–West Farms tract, 19, 31, 34–35

Hutchinson River Parkway, 96

Immaculate Conception Roman Catholic Church, 28

Immigrants, 5, 64, 70–71, 76–78, 97, 130, 137, 150

Independent D subway, 57; *see also* Rapid transit; Subways

Industry, 9, 16, 25, 30, 118–19, 135; Mott Haven village, 21; factories, 62–63, 74, 103–104, 149, 179*n*17; Port Morris, 22, 164*n*26

Institutions, 96, 147

Integration efforts, 114–15

Interborough Rapid Transit, 66, 73; *see also* Rapid transit; Subways

Intergroup efforts to lessen ethnic violence, 104–105

Inter-Group Relations. *See* Commission on Inter-Group Relations

Interracial councils. *See* Integration efforts

Intervale Avenue subway station, 68

Irish, 28, 36–38, 40, 64, 70, 77, 96, 98–99, 104–105, 110, 117, 151, 162*n*17,

167*n*66, 168*n*67; Mott Haven, 24–25, 163*n*20

Italians, 64, 70, 76–78, 96–99, 104, 110, 117, 125, 151

Jackson Engine No. 4, 163*n*18

Jacobs, Sophia Y., Urban League president, 113

Jacobson, Robert, director of Bronx office of City Planning Commission, 136

Janes estate, 48

Janes and Kirtland Foundry, 30

Jenkins, Stephen, 89

Jerome Avenue, 18

Jerome Avenue subway, 57; *see also* Rapid transit; Subways

Jews, 64, 70, 76–77, 96, 98–99, 110, 115–17, 126, 151, 183*n*56; anti-Semitism, 104–105; Co-op City, 116; Eastern European, 76; rent strikes, 102; socialist ideals of, 102; Jewish landlords, 102

Johnson, George F., builder, 68

Jones, Colonel John D., 68

Jose de Diego Beekman Houses. *See* Diego Beekman Houses

Juvenile delinquency, 105, 119, 149

Kelly Street, 131, 133

Kempton, Helen, social worker, 87

Kennedy, John F., 1960 presidential candidate, 118, 192*n*2

Kingsbridge, 95, 101, 145

Kingsbridge, town of, 4, 14–15, 17

Kingsbridge Heights, 147

Knoeppel, John H., 171*n*19, 177*n*4

Koch, Mayor Ed, 127, 137–39, 141; capital housing program, 137, 212*n*23

Kozol, Jonathan, 134

Kramer, Sam, city housing official, 141

Labor, U. S. Department of, "Own-

Mount Hope Housing Company, 138, 142–43

Mount Vernon, 102

Mullaly, John, 49–50, 172*n*33, 173*n*34, 173*n*37

Muller, Ada H., 89

Municipal Loan Program, 127

National Civic League, 1, 143

Nehemiah Homes, 140

Neighborhood change, 1, 3, 5–7, 88, 92, 94, 106–107, 149–50, 204*n*48

Neighborhood decay, 2, 106, 110, 124; determined where low income housing would be, 107, 150; government policies against, 127, 148–49

Neighborhood Partners Initiative, 143

Neighborhood Preservation Companies Program. *See* New York State Neighborhood Preservation Companies Program

Neighborhood Preservation Program, 127

Neighborhoods, 2, 6–7, 59–79, 91–92, 94–108, 147; *see also* Ethnic neighborhoods

Neighborhood Strategies Project, 143

Nevard, Deputy Police Commissioner Jacques, 120

New Haven Railroad, 25, 157*n*27

New Tenement House Law of 1901. *See* Tenement House Law of 1901

New Village, 31; *see also* Morrisania

New York Affairs, 119

New York Central Freight Yards, 71

New York City, 4, 14, 99; capital housing program of Mayor Ed Koch, 137, 212*n*23; Charter of Greater New York, 80; charter revision of 1901, 81; city workers, 121; community planning boards (*see* Community District Boards); congestion in, 15, 184*n*2; consolidation of, 4; corruption scandals,

136, 211–12*n*21; crime, 119–21; decentralization of city services, 133–34, 210–11*n*14; disorder, 119–22; draft riots, 22; fair housing laws, 115; fiscal crisis, 121, 128; immigration, 136; population, 14, 15, 45; repossession of tax delinquent buildings, 204*n*59; scandals (*see* corruption scandals); school districts, 134; suburban movement, 15, 83, 148; urban riots, 121; urban services, 15, 41, 121

New York City Department of Parks, 17, 41, 44, 45; Bureau of Design and Superintendence, 42

New York City Housing Authority, 116

New York City Housing Partnership, 135, 138–42

New York Community Trust, 143

New York County, 4

New York Equity Fund, 139

New York Evening Post, 61, 64

New York and Fordham Railway, 52, 53

New York and Harlem Railroad, 11, 20–23, 63, 157*n*27; Port Morris branch, 33

New York Herald, 49

New York Park Association, 49, 172*n*33, 173*n*37

New York State, 138

New York State Committee in Relation to the Public Affairs of the 23rd and 24th Wards, 44

New York State Neighborhood Preservation Companies Program, 134

New York Times, 3, 42, 45, 121, 126

New York University, 94, 127

New York Urban Coalition, 125

New York Yankees, 1, 94, 129

Nonprofit organizations, 139, 141

North Melrose, 26, 29

North New York, 12, 22–23, 25, 53, 63; building boom, 60, 61, 178*n*12

Protestant Americans, 24, 36–38, 167*n*64, 168*n*67
Public housing, 107, 111–13, 122–24, 134, 199*n*9; Castle Hill Housing project, 115; Clasons Point Gardens, 111; Forest Houses, 114, 123; St. Mary's Park Houses, 199*n*10; problems with, 123–24, 148–49
Public improvements, 41–44, 50, 58, 75, 81, 88, 96; *see also* Urban services
Public works during New Deal, 96, 106
Public-Private housing partnerships, 130
Puerto Ricans, 99–100, 105, 109–10, 113–15, 144, 148–49; Committee on Puerto Ricans, 115; discrimination, 118; in the Bronx, 112, 195*n*17; in New York City, 113–14, 194*n*16; in South Bronx, 114–17, 148; unskilled, 118
Purroy, Henry D., 44

Race, 120, 127, 149
Racial change, 1, 109–17, 146
Racial conflict, 120–21, 153*n*3
Railroads, 51, 146
Rapid transit, 45, 51–58, 146, 174*n*43; elevated transit, 44–45, 52, 56, 174*n*45; routes, 51–53, 56–57; Suburban Rapid Transit, 52–54, 59, 186*n*13; *see also* Third Avenue El; Subways; Streetcars
Rapid Transit Act of 1894, 176*n*62
Rapid transit commissions, 52–53, 55
Ray, Thomas, 25
Reagan, President Ronald, 1, 70, 129, 135
Real estate business cycles, 88
Real Estate Record and Builders' Guide, 3, 46, 51, 62, 74, 86
Real estate speculation, 59; *see also* land speculation
Redlining, 111, 126–27, 149, 198–99*n*7
Reform efforts, 167*n*64; Bible crusades, 24; temperance, 21, 24, 32

Rehabilitated housing, 133, 137–39
Relief Cases, 102
Rent control, 111, 125, 148
Rents, 63, 179*n*18, 182*n*35
Rent strikes, 102
Rent supplements. *See* Section 8 federal low-income rent program
Residential mobility, 92–93, 97, 101, 147, 149; *see also* Transiency
Revitalization efforts, 130, 136–38, 150
Revival of the Bronx, 130, 137–42, 150
Revival of housing market, 130
Rider, William, 25
Right-angle streets, 25; *see also* Grid street layout
Risse, Louis A., 45, 172*n*25, 172*n*26
Riverdale, 87, 145, 150–51
Robbins, I. D., 140; *see also* Nehemiah Homes
Robbins, Ira, 116
Rockefeller, David, 129, 138
Rodriguez, Clara, 126
Roeber, John, 28
Rogers estate, 66
Rohatyn, Felix, 208*n*72
Ronner, John H.J., 171*n*19
Rooming houses, 97
Roosevelt, President Franklin Delano, 94, 192*n*2
Root, Elihu, 59
Row houses, 124, 163*n*24
Rueda, Ramon, 131–32

Sartoris, Renee, former Charlotte Street resident, 117
Saville, Rabbi Herman, 102
Scandals, 144; *see also* Corruption scandals
Scandinavians, 70, 99
School districts, 134, 210*n*14
Schultz, Dutch, 19
Schuyler, Montgomery, 147
Schwartz, Joel, 3
Scots, 99

Subways (*continued*)
67; Independent D line, 57; Interborough Rapid Transit, 66, 73; *see
also individual lines*
Surdna Foundation, 143
"Sweat equity," 131, 134; *see also*
Community development corporations; Urban Homesteading
Assistance Board

Tammany Hall, 16, 44
Tax shelters, 132; *see also* Housing
initiatives
Tax subsidies for apartments, 87
Taxpayer groups, 44
Taxpayers' Alliance, 82
Temperance, 21, 24, 32–33
Temple Hand-in-Hand, 64
Tenant activism, 103
Tenant complaints, 87
Tenants, 97, 150, 193*n*10
Tenement House Law of 1901 (New
Law), 68–69, 85, 90, 101, 146
Tenement house reform, 15
Tenements, 72, 74–77, 84–86, 101, 146;
see also Apartments
Terry, Margaret, 130
Tiffany, E. A., 35
Tiffany, Lyman, 66
Third Avenue, 11, 33, 52–53, 59, 96–97,
186*n*13
Third Avenue El, 54, 57, 83, 89, 149,
193*n*9, 197*n*42, 208*n*72; Morrisania,
74; Mott Haven, 60, 178*n*6
Thomas Gardens, 87
Throgs Neck, 150
Tobier, Emanuel, 151
Tolerance committees, 105; *see also*
Intergroup efforts to lessen ethnic
violence
"Towers in the park," 111; *see also*
Public housing
Towns in West Farms and Morrisania,
10

Transiency, 88, 97, 99, 124, 193*n*11; *see
also* Residential mobility
Transit. *See* Rapid Transit
Tremont, 84, 99
Triborough Bridge, 96, 103
Truman, President Harry S, 192*n*2
Tweed, William Marcy, 16
23rd and 24th Wards, 4, 16–17;
dwellings in, 160*n*47
Tyler, President John, 80

Undercliff-Sedgwick Neighborhood
Safety Service Council, 143; *see also*
All-America City Award
Union Avenue, 33
Unionport, 102
Union Railway Company. *See*
Streetcars
United Bronx Parents, 133
University Avenue, 87
University Heights, 95, 102, 147
Upper Morrisania, 74; *see also*
Claremont
Urban decay, 1, 5, 150, 203–204*n*56;
"milk" a building, 125–26, 148–49;
profit from the destruction, 129,
207*n*63; reasons for, 2, 153*n*3; South
Bronx, 1, 5, 106–109, 119–22, 128,
141
Urban development, 1–3, 5–7, 41, 52,
56, 58–59, 150; as a business, 129, 146;
models of, 84, 88
Urban growth. *See* Urban development
Urban Homesteading Assistance Board
(UHAB), 133–34; *see also* Commu-
nity development corporations
Urban Horizons, 143; *see also* Women's
Housing and Economic Develop-
ment Corporation; All-America City
Award
Urbanization. *See* Urban development
Urban League, 113
Urban renewal, 112–13, 117–18, 134,
148–49